"Anyone who wants a comprehensi Eucharistic liturgy and Eucharistic t brilliantly provided in this book. An Catholic university have combined their considerable learning and skills to give us a text that will remain a standard for scholar and student alike for years to come."

> —John F. Baldovin, SJ
> Professor of Historical and Liturgical Theology
> Boston College

"Bradshaw and Johnson provide a much needed summary of contemporary liturgical scholarship on the Eucharist. This will be a convenient and essential classroom textbook."

> —Bryan D. Spinks
> Goddard Professor of Liturgical Studies
> Yale Divinity School

"Can one book give a complete overview of the history and theology of the eucharistic prayer from its origins to its recent manifestations, from East to West, from Catholic to Protestant, Anglican to Orthodox, with generous quotations and insightful analogy, charts and footnotes, and an ability to make you feel at the end that you have really understood more about how Christians offer their most important prayer? Well, yes. It's this one."

> —Paul Turner
> Author of *Glory in the Cross:*
> *Holy Week in the Third Edition*
> *of* The Roman Missal

"In this long-awaited companion to *The Rites of Christian Initiation* (2007), Bradshaw and Johnson draw upon their own extensive research, as well as up-to-date scholarship in several academic fields, in order to unravel and analyze the development of the Eucharist from the early church's meals and emerging rites through to (selected) rites in the twentieth century. Rites, practices, and theologies from the West and East are carefully examined from within their respective social, cultural, and religious contexts. Along with the extensive commentary, the use of liturgical texts, comparative charts, and summaries within each chapter makes this volume an especially valuable resource for student and specialist alike."

> —Karen B. Westerfield Tucker
> Professor of Worship
> Boston University

Paul F. Bradshaw
Maxwell E. Johnson

The
Eucharistic Liturgies

Their Evolution and Interpretation

A PUEBLO BOOK

Liturgical Press   Collegeville, Minnesota
www.litpress.org

A Pueblo Book published by Liturgical Press

Cover design by David Manahan, OSB. Illustration by Frank Kacmarcik, OblSB; background photo courtesy of ThinkStock.

Library of Congress Cataloging-in-Publication Data

Bradshaw, Paul F.
    The Eucharistic liturgies : their evolution and interpretation / Paul F. Bradshaw and Maxwell E. Johnson.
        p. cm.
    "A Pueblo book."
    Includes index.
    ISBN 978-0-8146-6240-3 — ISBN 978-0-8146-6266-3 (e-book)
    1. Lord's Supper (Liturgy)—History.   2. Liturgics—History.   I. Johnson, Maxwell E., 1952-   II. Title.
BV823.B64 2012
264'.36—dc23   2012003776

IN MEMORIAM

This book is dedicated to the memory of
The Rt. Rev. Kenneth W. Stevenson,
our friend and fellow scholar (1949–2011)

Contents

Abbreviations

AAS   *Acta Apostolicae Sedis* (Vatican Polyglot Press, 1909ff.)

AIR   Edward Yarnold, *The Awe-Inspiring Rites of Initiation: The Origins of the R.C.I.A.*, 2nd ed. (Collegeville, MN: Liturgical Press, 1994).

ANF   Ante-Nicene Fathers

BAS   The Anaphoras of St. Basil of Caesarea (various versions: ArmBAS = Armenian Basil; ByzBAS = Byzantine Basil; EgBAS = Egyptian Basil; SyrBAS = Syriac Basil)

CHR   The Anaphora of St. John Chrysostom

ET   English Translation

JAS   The Anaphora of St. James

LCC   Library of Christian Classics (Louisville: Westminster/John Knox Press)

LW   *Luther's Works* (Philadelphia/St. Louis)

NPNF   Nicene and Post-Nicene Fathers

OCA   Orientalia Christiana Analecta (Rome: Pontificio Istituto Orientale)

OCP   *Orientalia Christiana Periodica*

PEER   R. C. D. Jasper and G. J. Cuming, *Prayers of the Eucharist: Early and Reformed*, 3rd ed. (Collegeville, MN: Liturgical Press, Pueblo, 1987).

Acknowledgments

In addition to excerpts from materials copyrighted by Liturgical Press, Collegeville, Minnesota, especially eucharistic prayer texts in English translation from PEER, the authors express gratitude to the following publishers for their generous permission to reproduce copyrighted materials:

Augsburg Fortress Press, Minneapolis, MN, for excerpts from:

Martin Luther, *The Babylonian Captivity of the Church, 1520*, in LW 36: 18, 27; 28; 31–33; 35; 51–52; 127.

The New American Library, Inc., for excerpts from UlrichZwingli, "Action or use of the Lord's Supper, 1525," in Bard Thompson (ed.), *Liturgies of the Western Church* (NewYork: The World Publishing Co., Meridian, 1961), 153–54.

Faith and Order Commission, World Council of Churches, Geneva, Switzerland, for excerpts from *Baptism, Eucharist, and Ministry* (Geneva: World Council of Churches, 1982).

The Very Rev. M. Daniel Findikyan of St. Nersess Armenian Seminary, New Rochelle, NY, for the translation of the Armenian Anaphora of St. Athanasius, which appears in M. Daniel Findikyan (ed.), *The Divine Liturgy of the Armenian Church* (New York: St. Vartan Press, 1999), 28–39.

Excerpts from the English translation of *The Roman Missal* © 2010, International Commission on English in the Liturgy Corporation. All rights reserved.

Oregon Catholic Press, Portland, OR, for the following excerpts from Robert Cabié, *History of the Mass* (Washington, D.C.: The Pastoral Press, 1992):

Amalarius of Metz, *Liber officialis*, III.18, pp. 72–73.
Pope Innocent III, *De sacro alteris mysterio*, liber III, 1–3, p. 82.
Pope Pius V, *Quo primum tempore*, p. 87.

The Society for the Promotion of Christian Knowledge, London, England, for excerpts from Nicholas Cabasilas, *A Commentary on the Divine Liturgy*, trans. J. M. Hussey and P. A. McNulty (London: SPCK, 1960), 26–28.

Excerpts from © 1960 John Calvin, *Institutes of the Christian Religion*, IV, 17 (1559). Trans. Ford Lewis Battles, LCC, XXI, 1364–1404. Used by permission of Westminster John Knox Press. www.wjkbooks.com.

Excerpts from © 1992 Wilhelm Schneemelcher, ed., *New Testament Apocrypha, II: Writings Relating to the Apostles, Apocalypses and Related Subjects*, 359–60, 391–92, 401. Used by permission of Westminster John Knox Press. www.wjkbooks.com.

Excerpts from © 1989 James F. White, *Protestant Worship: Traditions in Transition*, 38, 59, 64, 65–66. Used by permission of Westminster John Knox Press. www.wjkbooks.com.

Where not otherwise acknowledged, translations are the work of the authors.

Introduction

When we told our friend Professor Teresa Berger of the Yale Divinity School and Institute of Sacred Music that we were in the process of coauthoring a book on the Eucharist, she gently teased us, in reference to the rather critical approach both of us take in scholarly method, saying something to the effect of "We need a book that tells us what we *can* say about the Eucharist, not about what we *can't* say." We think it appropriate, therefore, to begin with a disclaimer or two about what we *don't* say or do in this study. That is, this is not a book about Eucharist and justice, Eucharist and inculturation, Eucharist and music, Eucharist and art and architecture, Eucharist and inclusive or exclusive language, Eucharist and gender issues, Eucharist and postmodernism, or any of the possible pairings of the topic of the Eucharist with other pertinent issues. Plenty of excellent studies—books and articles—are available on any and all of those topics.[1] Further, this book is also not about any calls for new liturgical reforms, nor does it offer a critique of the modern liturgical reforms, positive or negative. To borrow a line from our friend, Fr. Robert Taft, SJ, our intent here is to be liturgical "informers," not liturgical "reformers,"[2] though, of course, we expect it will be quite clear as to where we stand on various issues.

---

[1] Cf. Mark Searle, ed., *Liturgy and Social Justice* (Collegeville, MN: Liturgical Press, 1980); Anscar Chupungco, *Liturgical Inculturation: Sacramentals, Religiosity, and Catechesis* (Collegeville, MN: Liturgical Press, Pueblo, 1995); Edward Foley, *From Age to Age: How Christians Have Celebrated the Eucharist*, rev. exp. ed. (Collegeville, MN: Liturgical Press, 2008); Teresa Berger, *Gender Differences and the Making of Liturgical History* (Burlington, VT: Ashgate, 2011); Nathan Mitchell, *Real Presence: The Work of Eucharist*, new and exp. ed. (Chicago; Liturgy Training Publications, 2001); and Nathan Mitchell, *Meeting Mystery: Liturgy, Worship, Sacraments* (Maryknoll, NY: Orbis Books, 2007).

[2] Robert Taft, *A History of the Liturgy of St. John Chrysostom*, vol. 6: *The Communion, Thanksgiving, and Concluding Rites*, Orientalia Christiana Analecta 281 (Rome: Pontificio Istituto Orientale, 2008), 786.

This book, then, is intended to be, primarily, a book of liturgical information; it is *descriptive* and not *prescriptive*. It is, as its title indicates, about the liturgical history and theology of the Eucharist from the time of the New Testament up to and including the liturgical reforms of the modern period in the mid-twentieth and now early twenty-first centuries. Although it is primarily descriptive, this does not mean that we shy away from making historical and theological judgments. *Au contraire*. What it does mean, rather, is that as liturgical historians our task is not to advocate particular liturgical practices based on our historical and theological analyses and conclusions.

In many ways, this volume, as suggested years ago by our now deceased Notre Dame colleague, Professor James F. White (d. 2004), is intended to be a companion to *The Rites of Christian Initiation: Their Evolution and Interpretation*,[3] which, we are pleased to note, has become today a standard textbook on Christian initiation rites in several schools and graduate programs across the United States and elsewhere. We are hoping for the same success with this volume, and introductions to various chapters here are occasionally based on parallel introductions in that book. Like that volume, our study proceeds historically. We move from the origins of the Eucharist (chap. 1) to the second and third centuries (chap. 2), with two chapters (chaps. 3 and 4) on the formative period and great patristic figures (e.g., Basil of Caesarea, John Chrysostom, Ambrose of Milan, and Augustine of Hippo) of the fourth and fifth centuries both in East and West. Unlike most studies of the Eucharist written by Western liturgical scholars, this book provides in chapter 5 an introduction to and developmental summary of the diverse eucharistic liturgies of the Christian East (Armenian, Byzantine, Coptic, East Syrian, Ethiopic, Maronite, and West Syrian) together with attention to their principal eucharistic prayers still in use today, though often edited herein for length. Chapter 6 continues with our treatment of the Western churches in the Middle Ages, including the various Western rites (e.g., Ambrosian, Gallican, and Mozarabic, in addition to the Roman), while chapter 7 is concerned with the Protestant and Catholic Reformations in the sixteenth century and beyond, including the 1570 *Missale Romanum* of Pius V; the various editions of the *Book of Common Prayer* in England; and the various liturgical books of the other Reforming movements, espe-

---

[3] Maxwell E. Johnson, *The Rites of Christian Initiation: Their Evolution and Interpretation*, rev. exp. ed. (Collegeville, MN: Liturgical Press, Pueblo, 2007).

cially Reformed and Lutheran in Germany, Switzerland, and Sweden. Chapter 8 essays the modern period, including the influence of the European Liturgical Movement, the Second Vatican Council and the 1969 *Missale Romanum* of Pope Paul VI, together with the eucharistic developments in other churches, most notably Anglican, Lutheran, Reformed, and Methodist. Each chapter ends not with a written conclusion but with various summary points, which we hope will make this book more user-friendly for teacher and student alike. Similarly, each chapter contains an abundance of liturgical texts for ease of reference, either in our own translations from the original languages or from other standard English translations of those texts.

Apart from chapters 1 and 7, where the materials did not allow us to do so, the other six chapters are all divided into rite(s) and eucharistic theology. And with regard to eucharistic theology we have tended to place most of our emphasis on two topics, namely, eucharistic or real presence, including theories of and approaches to the "consecration" of the bread and wine, and eucharistic sacrifice. While these are surely not the only possible topics in eucharistic theology and practice,[4] they have been the most central and most ecumenically challenging and divisive issues since the sixteenth-century Reformations. And while we do not claim to have solved the challenges posed by either of these topics, we are able to point to wide liturgical and theological convergence on both of them within various churches today. As such, we trust that the reader will find that, although there are some things that *cannot* be said or are no longer held in the light of recent scholarship, there is a great deal we *can* say about the Eucharist.

Finally, a word of thanks is due to the following people who enabled this book to be completed and published: to The Rev. Cody Unterseher, graduate student in liturgical studies at the University of Notre Dame, for his invaluable assistance with hunting down references, his close editorial proofreading of the manuscript, and his help with the index; to members of *Das Institut für Eklektische Liturgiewissenschaft*, namely, The Rev. Stefanos Alexopoulos, priest and professor in Athens, Greece, and The Very Rev. M. Daniel Findikyan, priest, professor, and dean of St. Nersess Armenian Seminary, New Rochelle, New York, and also to Dr. Nicholas Russo, assistant dean for undergraduate studies, the University of Notre Dame, for their assistance with and

---

[4] Cf. Kevin W. Irwin, *Models of the Eucharist* (Mahwah, NJ: Paulist Press, 2005).

critical reading of chapter 5; to Peter Dwyer and Hans Christoffersen of the Liturgical Press, Collegeville, Minnesota, for their willingness to publish this work under the Pueblo imprint; and to Ruth McCurry, commissioning editor of SPCK Books, London, England, for the appearance of this book as the 2012 volume in the Alcuin Club Collections series.

Paul F. Bradshaw and Maxwell E. Johnson

August 15, 2011

The Assumption of the Blessed Virgin Mary
The Dormition of Our Lady, the Most Holy Theotokos
St. Mary the Virgin
Mary, Mother of Our Lord

Chapter 1

Origins

The historical root of the Christian Eucharist has traditionally been sought in the words and actions of Jesus at the Last Supper that he is said to have eaten with his disciples on the night before he died, and that is recorded in varying forms in Matthew 26:20-29; Mark 14:17-25; Luke 22:14-20; and 1 Corinthians 11:23-26. Modern liturgical scholarship concerning eucharistic origins, therefore, at first tended to focus on a literary-critical and traditio-historical analysis of these texts. In the last fifteen to twenty years, however, there has been a growing awareness that study of the Last Supper needs to be set within the broader context of the other meals in which Jesus participated and within the even wider sociological context of the form and dynamics of the Hellenistic group supper and the culture relating to meals in antiquity in general, which is where we begin.

MEAL CUSTOMS IN THE GRECO-ROMAN WORLD

In the ancient world, social life centered around eating and drinking every bit as much as it does for most people today, whether that was, for example, a banquet given at a rich person's house or a regular gathering of associations that were often formed around a trade guild or profession. There has been a good deal of interest in recent years in the way in which the earliest Christian assemblies would have resembled such groups.[1] Despite minor local variations that were due to particular social or ethnic distinctions, formal meals were broadly similar in character throughout that culture, and all would have

---

[1] For associations, see, for example, Philip A. Harland, *Associations, Synagogues, and Congregations* (Minneapolis, MN: Fortress Press, 2003); Richard S. Ascough, *Paul's Macedonian Associations: The Social Context of Philippians and 1 Thessalonians* (Tübingen: Mohr Siebeck, 2003); for meal practices, Matthias Klinghardt, *Gemeinschaftsmahl und Mahlgemeinschaft* (Tübingen: Francke Verlag, 1996); Dennis E. Smith, *From Symposium to Eucharist: The Banquet in the Early Christian World* (Minneapolis, MN: Fortress Press, 2003); Hal Taussig, *In the Beginning Was the Meal: Social Experimentation and Early Christian Identity* (Minneapolis, MN: Fortress Press, 2009).

contained some religious dimension, even if that were not their primary orientation.

Accustomed as we are to visualize the Last Supper through its depiction by Renaissance artists as having the disciples seated at one long table with Jesus in the center, it requires an effort to understand that this was not, in fact, how people in the ancient world dined. Instead, participants would normally have reclined on a number of couches arranged around three sides of the room, with the food presented in common dishes on low tables in front of them, from which they would have helped themselves with their hands. Often diners would share couches, and they would all be ranked according to their social status, with the host at one end and the most important guest immediately to the right and the others in descending social order around the room.[2] Moreover, the wealthy might invite to dinner not only friends of similar social standing but also people of lower status, known as clients, who gave their patron loyal support in any of his ventures and in return received aid and protection of their interests. They would often be seated apart, however, and the food and drink served to them would be of a quite different quality from that being enjoyed by the host and his more privileged guests.[3] Similarly, there were times when these clients would have to make do with a charitable handout of food to take home rather than with a place at table.[4]

Such formal meals thus not only created and strengthened social bonds between the participants but defined boundaries between communities (who was included, who excluded) and relative status within them. Reclining was itself a sign of status, since traditionally it had been the preserve of free citizens, while women, children, and slaves

[2] See further Blake Leyerle, "Meal Customs in the Greco-Roman World," in *Passover and Easter: Origin and History to Modern Times*, ed. Paul F. Bradshaw and Lawrence A. Hoffman (Notre Dame, IN: University of Notre Dame Press, 1999), 29–61; and Jan Michael Joncas, "Tasting the Kingdom of God: The Meal Ministry of Jesus and Its Implications for Contemporary Worship and Life," *Worship* 74 (2000): 329–65.

[3] See John D'Arms, "The Roman *Convivium* and the Idea of Equality," in *Sympotica: A Symposium on the "Symposium,"* ed. Oswin Murray (Oxford: Clarendon Press, 1990), 308–20.

[4] For references to primary sources, see Charles A. Bobertz, "The Role of Patron in the Cena Dominica of Hippolytus' Apostolic Tradition," *Journal of Theological Studies* 44 (1993): 170–84, here at 175–76; Klinghardt, *Gemeinschaftsmahl und Mahlgemeinschaft*, 143–49.

did not usually recline but ate quite separately. In time, however, this rule came to be relaxed and women might recline among the men, although there was still a danger that such women could be viewed as courtesans; on rare occasions slaves might be invited to eat with their masters.[5]

In contrast to modern times where wine is generally served throughout a meal, at these banquets a meal of several courses of food was eaten first, and then hands were washed and the tables removed before the second half of the evening began, the drinking-party or *symposium* (from the Greek word *symposion*, meaning literally "drinking together"). As each bowl of wine was needed, it was prepared by being diluted with something like two to three times its volume of water, and then a libation was offered to a particular deity, accompanied by a short prayer. Such a sharp separation of the two halves of the evening was not always preserved, however: Pliny the Elder reports that the custom of taking an aperitif of wine mixed with water before the meal began had been introduced during the reign of the Roman emperor Tiberias (14–37 CE),[6] and wine drunk unmixed during the meal itself is attested even earlier, in the first century BCE.[7] Nevertheless, occasions like these were—at least ideally—not just drinking parties. They were as much occasions for conversation, philosophical speculation, and the recitation of poetry or mythical stories, as well as for the fostering of relationships.

Naturally, meals among the poor did not follow the pattern of those among the rich. There, bread with salt and water would have formed the staple ingredients, augmented if possible with a little cheese or whatever else they could obtain—perhaps as leftovers from the banquets of the rich.[8] Not having couches, they would sit on the ground or on cushions, a custom still found today in the Middle East.

---

[5] On the role of women, see Kathleen E. Corley, *Private Women, Public Meals: Social Conflict in the Synoptic Tradition* (Peabody, MA: Hendrickson, 1993); Carolyn Osiek, Margaret Y. MacDonald, with Janet H. Tulloch, *A Woman's Place: House Churches in Earliest Christianity* (Minneapolis, MN: Fortress Press, 2006), esp. 144–63. On the position of slaves among early Christians, see Jennifer A. Glancy, *Slavery in Early Christianity* (Minneapolis, MN: Fortress Press, 2006).

[6] Pliny the Elder, *Naturalis historia* 14.28.143.

[7] Diodorus Sicilus, 4.3.

[8] See Andrew B. McGowan, *Ascetic Eucharists* (Oxford: Clarendon Press, 1999), 79, 93.

JEWISH MEAL PRACTICES

Formal meals among Jews in the first century generally would have followed the pattern of those in the prevailing culture. There is, for example, clear evidence both from the Jewish sectarian community at Qumran and also from the Therapeutae residing by Lake Mareotis in Egypt, described—if in a somewhat idealized manner—by Philo, that at their shared meals participants were arranged according to their status within the community:

> They shall eat in common and bless in common and deliberate in common. Wherever there are ten men of the Council of the Community there shall not lack a Priest among them. And they shall all sit before him according to their rank and shall be asked their counsel in all things in that order. And when the table has been prepared for eating, and the new wine for drinking, the Priest shall be the first to stretch out his hand to bless the first-fruits of the bread and new wine. (1QS 6.3-8)[9]

> So then they assemble, white robed and with faces in which cheerfulness is combined with the utmost seriousness but before they recline . . . they take their stand in a regular line in an orderly way. . . . [T]hey pray to God that their feasting may be acceptable. . . . After the prayers, the seniors recline according to the order of their admission, since by senior they do not understand the aged . . . but those who from their earliest years have grown to manhood and spent their prime in pursuing the contemplative branch of philosophy. . . . The feast is shared by women also, most of them aged virgins. . . . The order of reclining is so appointed that the men sit by themselves on the right and the women by themselves on the left. Perhaps it may be thought that couches though not costly still of a softer kind would have been provided. . . . Actually they are plank beds of the common kinds of wood, covered with quite cheap strewings of native papyrus. . . . They do not have slaves to wait upon them as they consider that the ownership of slaves is entirely against nature . . . but the services are rendered by free men who perform their tasks as attendants not under compulsion. . . . No wine is brought during those days but only water. . . . The table too is kept pure from the flesh of animals; the food laid on it is loaves of bread with salt as a seasoning, sometimes also flavoured with hyssop as a relish for the daintier appetites. . . . When the guests have laid themselves down arranged in rows as I have described . . . the

[9] See also 1QSa 2.16–20. ET from Geza Vermes, *The Dead Sea Scrolls in English*, 4th ed. (Sheffield: Sheffield Academic Press, 1995), 77.

President of the company . . . discusses some question arising in the Holy Scriptures or solves one that has been propounded by someone else. . . . When then the President thinks he has discoursed enough . . . then the President rises and sings a hymn composed as an address to God, either a new one of his own composition or an old one by poets of an earlier day. . . . After him all the others take their turn as they are arranged and all in the proper order while all the rest listen in complete silence except when they have to chant the closing lines or refrains, for then they all lift up their voices, men and women alike. When everyone has finished his hymn the young men bring in the tables mentioned a little above on which is set the truly purified meal of leavened bread seasoned with salt mixed with hyssop.[10]

We may also recall the admonition given by Jesus to his followers not to take one of the higher places at table at a marriage feast lest someone more exalted should arrive and displace them (Luke 14:7-9).

Chief among regular Jewish formal meals was the weekly Sabbath supper, eaten on Friday evenings before sunset and the onset of the Sabbath, when the lighting of fires and cooking would be prohibited, resulting in little food, often cold, being eaten during the day itself.[11] According to the Mishnah (the first systematic collection of rabbinic judgments about religious practices made around the end of the second century CE), nothing was to be eaten without God having first been blessed for it, and short blessings to be used for each kind of food are quoted there.[12] It is unlikely, however, that this fully fledged system was already in use in the first century prior to rabbinic attempts to codify Judaism after the destruction of the temple in the year 70, and even later it may not have exercised influence outside rabbinic circles.[13] On the other hand, the custom of saying some sort of blessing

---

[10] Philo, *De vita contemplativa* 66–81; ET from F. H. Colson, *Philo IX*, Loeb Classical Library (London: Heinemann; Cambridge, MA: Harvard University Press, 1941), 153–65. See also Joan E. Taylor, *Jewish Women Philosophers of First-Century Alexandria: Philo's 'Therapeutae' Reconsidered* (Oxford: Oxford University Press, 2003).

[11] See William Horbury, "*Cena Pura* and Lord's Supper," in *The Beginnings of Christianity*, ed. Jack Pastor and Menachem Mor (Jerusalem: Yad Ben-Zvi Press, 2005), 219–65.

[12] Tractate *Berakoth* 6.1–3.

[13] Tzvee Zahavy suggested that the rabbis built upon an older tradition of merely saying blessings over wine and grace at the end of a meal: see *idem*,

of God (in Hebrew *berakah*) over certain items at a meal was certainly known among pious Jews in the first century. The Qumran community, as we have seen, said blessings over bread and new wine together at the very beginning of their communal meals, and Josephus also reports that they said grace both before and after their meals, praising God for bestowing their food upon them.[14]

It is often assumed that at least the substance of what later became the standard Jewish grace at the end of the meal, known as the *Birkat ha-mazon*, was already in use in the first century. Although the full text of this prayer is known from only the ninth century onward, it does have a tripartite structure, and the Mishnah refers to the grace after meals as comprising three blessings without specifying what they were, as if they were well-known to its readers (*Ber.* 6.8). Moreover, the *Book of Jubilees*, usually dated somewhere in the middle of the second century BCE, puts a grace into the mouth of Abraham that displays a very similar tripartite structure: a blessing of God for creation and the gift of food, a thanksgiving for the long life granted to Abraham, and a supplication for God's mercy and peace.[15] Louis Finkelstein's study of the earliest extant texts of the *Birkat ha-mazon* suggests that something like the following came closest to its early Palestinian version:

> Blessed are you, Lord our God, ruler of the universe, who feed the whole world with goodness, with grace, and with mercy. Blessed are you, Lord, who feed all.
> We give thanks to you, Lord our God, that you have caused us to inherit a good and pleasant land, the covenant, the Law, life and food. For all these things we give thanks to you and praise your name for ever and ever. Blessed are you, Lord, for the land and for the food.

"Three Stages in the Development of Early Rabbinic Prayer," in *From Ancient Israel to Modern Judaism*, ed. Jacob Neusner and others, vol. 1, Brown Judaic Studies 159 (Atlanta, GA: Scholars Press, 1989), 233–65, here at 240–41, 252–53, 259–63; reproduced in expanded form in Tzvee Zahavy, *Studies in Jewish Prayer* (Lanham, MD: University Press of America, 1990), 1–44, here at 14–16, 24, 31–34. See also Baruch M. Bokser, "*Ma'al* and Blessings over Food: Rabbinic Transformation of Cultic Terminology and Alternative Modes of Piety," *Journal of Biblical Literature* 100 (1981): 557–74.

[14] Josephus, *Jewish War* 2.8.5.

[15] *Jubilees* 22:6–9; ET from James H. Charlesworth, ed., *The Old Testament Pseudepigrapha* II (Garden City, NY: Doubleday, 1985), 97.

Have mercy, Lord our God, on your people Israel, on your city Jerusalem, on your Temple and your dwelling-place and on Zion your resting-place, and on the great and holy sanctuary over which your name was invoked; and the kingdom of the dynasty of David may you restore to its place in our days, and build Jerusalem soon. Blessed are you, Lord, who build Jerusalem.[16]

Nevertheless, this reconstruction must be treated with considerable caution. A growing number of Jewish scholars have expressed doubts as to whether such prayers would have existed in the first century in the fixed forms in which they are later found.[17] Although the general structure and themes of this prayer may have become widely established at an early point, it is most improbable that it had assumed any defined text or that it was the only form of grace in use at this period. Indeed, the very same passage in the Mishnah that prescribes the tripartite blessing records the existence of one variant—that a single blessing containing the substance of the three could be said—and a fragmentary text of what may be a somewhat different meal-prayer has survived from the third-century synagogue at Dura-Europos in Syria[18] and another in the Qumran literature.[19] These suggest the existence of some diversity of practice prior to the later (relative) success of rabbinic attempts to standardize Jewish liturgy.

Within the cultic system of the Jerusalem temple, many of the offerings that were made were fully consumed by fire. Nevertheless, there also existed there what are known as "communion-sacrifices," in which part of what had been offered was returned to those who had brought it to be eaten by them together, so that in effect they shared a

[16] See Louis Finkelstein, "The Birkat Ha-Mazon," *Jewish Quarterly Review* 19 (1928/29): 211–62.

[17] Among recent contributions, see, for example, Stefan C. Reif, "The Second Temple Period, Qumran Research, and Rabbinic Liturgy: Some Contextual and Linguistic Comparisons," in *Liturgical Perspectives: Prayer and Poetry in Light of the Dead Sea Scrolls*, ed. Esther G. Chazon (Leiden: Brill, 2003), 133–49; and Richard S. Sarason, "Communal Prayer at Qumran and among the Rabbis: Certainties and Uncertainties," in ibid., 151–72.

[18] See Jacob Neusner, *A History of the Jews in Babylonia*, vol. 1 (Leiden: Brill, 1965 = Brown Judaic Studies 62; Chico, CA: Scholars Press, 1984), 161, n. 3.

[19] See Moshe Weinfeld, "Grace after Meals in Qumran," *Journal of Biblical Literature* 111 (1992): 427–40; but cf. Russell C. D. Arnold, *The Social Role of Liturgy in the Religion of the Qumran Community* (Leiden: Brill, 2006), 92–94.

sacred meal with God as a sign of his acceptance of them through the sacrificial act. The most important of these communion-sacrifices was the annual Passover celebration. Although in origin this had been a nomadic spring ritual intended to secure fecundity for the flock, it had become for the Israelite people a remembrance of their deliverance by God from slavery in Egypt. Following the prescriptions in Exodus 12, on the day of the festival (14 Nisan) each family was supposed to take a lamb and offer it for sacrifice in the temple at Jerusalem and then consume it together in a ritual meal that evening. Although it was traditionally assumed that the meal in the first century would have followed substantially the same pattern as we find in later sources, today most Jewish scholars agree that many of the customs described in that literature only came into being after the destruction of the temple. Prior to this, one cannot assume that, besides the lamb, the meal would have included more than the eating of *matzah* (unleavened bread) and bitter herbs and probably also the drinking of wine.[20]

It was just such a Passover meal that the Synoptic Gospels record as having been the Last Supper of Jesus with his disciples, although John's gospel differs in locating the supper on the evening before this annual festival, with the result that in his version Jesus dies on the cross at the same hour as the lambs are being slaughtered in the temple and thus becomes the true Passover lamb "sacrificed for us" (in the words of St. Paul, 1 Cor 5:17), whose bones are therefore not broken (John 19:33; cf. Exod 12:46; Num 9:12).

EARLY CHRISTIAN MEALS: THE PARTICIPANTS

One of the striking features of the recorded actions of Jesus is his apparent disregard for some of the established customs of the pious society of his day with regard to meals. Not only were his disciples criticized for eating with unwashed hands, unlike the Pharisees (Mark 7:1ff.), but Jesus himself was described by his enemies as "a glutton and a drunkard, a friend of tax collectors and sinners" (Matt 11:19; Luke 7:34). That he was willing to accept invitations to eat with those whom the pious would have regarded as beyond the pale is supported by other stories in the gospels (see, for example, Matt 9:10-13; Mark 2:15-17; Luke 5:29-32). In his teaching, Jesus also continued the Jewish tradition of portraying the kingdom of God at the end of time with the image of

---

[20] See Joshua Kulp, "The Origins of the Seder and Haggadah," *Currents in Biblical Research* 4 (2005): 109–34, esp. 112–13 and the scholars cited there.

a great banquet, at which all those who enjoyed God's favor would sit down together and feast in abundance, but again with the novel twist that those regarded as outsiders would be invited while those expecting to have a place there would be denied it (see, for example, Matt 8:11-12; Luke 13:28-29). His feeding miracles functioned as performative versions of this teaching, as symbolic anticipations of the future messianic banquet (Matt 14:13-21; 15:33-39; Mark 6:31-44; 8:1-9; Luke 9:10-17; John 6:5-15), so that those who ate with him then could be assured that they would also feast with him in the age to come. He was thus moving the boundary markers with regard to those whom his contemporaries deemed acceptable to God and challenging the conventional divisions within society. Indeed, modern biblical scholarship on the life and ministry of Jesus, especially that of the late Norman Perrin, asserts that his table companionship with tax collectors and sinners was "the aspect of Jesus' ministry which must have been most meaningful to his followers and most offensive to his critics."[21] As Nathan Mitchell has written:

[Jesus] sat at table not as the charming, congenial, ringleted centerpiece of a Rembrandt painting, but as a vulnerable vagrant willing to share potluck with a household of strangers. Normally, a table's prime function is to establish social ranking and hierarchy (by what one eats, how one eats, with whom one eats). Normally, a meal is about social identification, status, and power. . . . But the very *randomness* of Jesus' table habits challenged this system of social relations modeled on meals and manners. . . . It was not simply that Jesus ate with objectionable persons—outcasts and sinners—but that he ate with anyone, indiscriminately. Hence his reputation: He has no honor! He has no shame! . . . [Such] commensality was "a strategy for building or rebuilding peasant community on radically different principles from those of honor and shame, patronage and clientage." For Jesus, *healing* (the gift he brings to a home) calls forth *hospitality* (those healed offer refreshment, food and drink, a place at table). . . . The table companionship practiced by Jesus thus recreated the world, redrew all of society's maps and flow charts. Instead of symbolizing social rank and order, it blurred the distinctions between hosts and guests, need and plenty. Instead of reinforcing rules of etiquette, it subverted them, making the last first and the first last.[22]

[21] Norman Perrin, *Rediscovering the Teaching of Jesus* (London: SCM Press; New York: Harper & Row, 1967), 102.
[22] Nathan Mitchell, *Eucharist as Sacrament of Initiation*, Forum Essays 2 (Chicago: Liturgy Training Publications, 1994), 89–90; quoting John Dominic

Not all who followed him seem to have understood his message in quite such a radical way, however. This seems to have been a particular problem in the church in Corinth, where Paul criticizes the Christians both because of the existence of divisions within their community and more particularly because at their communal meals some go ahead and eat and drink too much while others go hungry. This failure to recognize the fundamental equality of all and to share what they have with one another leads him to conclude that "when you assemble together, it is not to eat the Lord's supper" (1 Cor 11:20)—a designation for the event not otherwise found in the New Testament and hardly known in other early Christian literature.[23] What is envisaged here is obviously a substantial meal in the home of one of the wealthier church members to which individuals brought their own contributions of food—a custom known in the contemporary culture as the *eranos*[24]—which explains why the host failed to delay the serving of the meal until all were present and what there was to eat could be shared equally between rich and poor. The tradition of participants all bringing bread and wine (and sometimes other foodstuffs) to the celebration was continued in later eucharistic practice for several centuries. Those scholars who persist in seeing the Eucharist, even at this early date, as something distinct from the meal have long disputed whether it took place before or after the supper.[25] But that is to apply an anachronistic matrix to the event: the meal was the Eucharist, or rather in this instance was failing to be the Eucharist because missing from it was the practical expression of love and care for all, and especially the poor, that was meant to be a vital dimension of Christian eating together. A similar failure to live out Jesus' radical message can be seen behind the letter of James, where the author censures the

---

Crossan, *The Historical Jesus: The Life of a Mediterranean Jewish Peasant* (San Francisco: HarperCollins, 1991), 344.

[23] Among its rare occurrences are *Apostolic Tradition* 27.1 and Tertullian, *Ad uxorem* 2.4.

[24] See Peter Lampe, "Das korinthische Herrenmahl im Schnittpunkt hellenistisch-römisher Mahlpraxis und paulinischer Theologia Crucis (1 Kor 11,17-34)," *Zeitschrift für die neutestamentliche Wissenschaft* 82 (1990–91): 183–213; also his English article, "The Eucharist: Identifying with Christ on the Cross," *Interpretation* 48 (1994): 36–49.

[25] See, for example, Joachim Jeremias, *The Eucharistic Words of Jesus* (London: SCM Press; New York: Scribner, 1966), 121; Eduard Schweizer, *The Lord's Supper according to the New Testament* (Philadelphia, PA: Fortress Press, 1967), 5.

recipients for showing partiality to the rich in their midst while despising the poor in their assemblies (Jas 2:1-9).

That provision of sustenance for the poor was meant to be an essential part of the shared life of Christians is also shown by the reference in Acts 6:1-6 to a daily distribution of food to widows outside the context of a communal meal and to the need of appointing certain men to take charge of it so as to reduce the burden on the original twelve,[26] and by later evidence of Christian eucharistic practice, where it continued to be an integral part, as we shall see in the next chapter. It is no wonder, therefore, that some communities used the Greek term *agape*, "love," as the name for their shared eucharistic meals.[27]

In addition to the tendency to cling to conventional views of social status within the Christian assembly, there was another problem with regard to participation that faced many of the earliest communities: should Gentile Christians be permitted to eat together with Jewish Christians? Although the propriety of admitting Gentiles to the church appears to have been agreed to at a quite early stage, this did not apparently convince everyone straightaway that the Jewish prohibition against sharing meals with Gentiles should also be abandoned, as Paul records a dispute at Antioch over this matter (Gal 2:11-14). Although we hear no more about this disagreement, it must eventually have been settled, for we find in later sources that the boundary of participation at table with regard to the pure and impure was no longer between Jew and Gentile but between the baptized and the unbaptized.[28]

[26] See further Reta Halteman Finger, *Of Widows and Meals: Communal Meals in the Book of Acts* (Grand Rapids, MI: Eerdmans, 2007).

[27] Although earlier scholars generally tried to distinguish the *agape* meal from the Eucharist proper, Andrew McGowan has convincingly argued that the two were synonyms for the same event: see *idem*, "Naming the Feast: *Agape* and the Diversity of Early Christian Meals," *Studia Patristica* 30 (1997): 314–18.

[28] See *Didache* 9.5; *Apostolic Tradition* 26.2; 27.1; Justin Martyr, *First Apology* 66.1 (below, pages 15, 18–19, 27–28, 45); also Andrew B. McGowan, "The Meals of Jesus and the Meals of the Church: Eucharistic Origins and Admission to Communion," in *Studia Liturgica Diversa: Essays in Honor of Paul F. Bradshaw*, ed. Maxwell E. Johnson and L. Edward Phillips (Portland, OR: Pastoral Press, 2004), 101–15.

EARLY CHRISTIAN MEALS:
THE BREAKING OF THE BREAD

The phrase "the breaking of the bread" is included in a summary of the features of the life of the earliest Christian community in Jerusalem in Acts 2:42, and this is followed by a similar mention in 2:46: "And day by day continuing in the temple with one accord and breaking bread in their homes, they took their food with gladness and singleness of heart." Later in the book Paul is said to have gathered with the Christian community at Troas on the first day of the week "to break bread" (Acts 20:7, 11), and finally, in Acts 27:33-36, on a sea voyage when the ship's company have not eaten for days, Paul takes bread, gives thanks to God, breaks it, and eats, thus encouraging the rest to eat as well. To these instances should be added Luke 24:30-35, where Jesus is said to have been known to the two disciples at Emmaus "in the breaking of the bread."

These passages have given rise to a longstanding debate between scholars as to the meaning of the phrase. Some have asserted that it was a standard Jewish expression for having a meal while others insist that it referred only to the blessing ritual over bread at the beginning and should not be regarded as shorthand for the whole meal. There has been, therefore, not only a difference of opinion as to whether such occasions would have included wine but also a deep division between those who have thought that a form of eucharistic celebration was intended, separated from ordinary eating, and those who have regarded the references as being simply to normal meals, especially in the light of Acts 27:33-36, where Paul eats on board ship with those who were not members of the Christian community. Judgments on this question largely have been influenced by such considerations as to whether the scholars involved could conceive of a Eucharist without wine and whether they believed that sacrament and substantial meal must have been distinguished from one another at a very early date.[29]

It would seem, however, that once again anachronistic categories are being applied to these texts. Not only is it improbable that the earliest Christians would have been able to recognize any distinction between

---

[29] For examples of contrasting views, see Gregory Dix, *The Shape of the Liturgy* (London: Dacre, 1945), 63n2; Joseph A. Fitzmyer, *The Acts of the Apostles* (New York: Doubleday, 1998), 270–71; Jeremias, *The Eucharistic Words of Jesus*, 120–21 and n. 1; Xavier Léon-Dufour, *Sharing the Eucharistic Bread* (New York: Paulist Press, 1987), 21–28.

a Eucharist and an ordinary meal, but the separation of a bread ritual from a complete meal also seems false in this context. As we have said, among the poor—and the Christian community in Jerusalem is constantly described as having been impoverished—bread would have constituted the main, if not the sole, ingredient of most meals. A Christian meal that consisted principally of bread might well therefore be adequately described by its opening ritual: in this case the breaking of bread really *was* the meal. These communal events would have been intended not only to satisfy the hunger of the participants but no doubt also to remember Jesus, with whom the disciples had regularly shared such meals in his lifetime, and to look forward to their reunion with him when he came again in glory.

The apparent absence of wine from these occasions might have been dictated solely by economic factors, but it could also have been the result of a desire to avoid consuming elements associated with pagan sacrifice: meat and wine. In an important contribution to the question of eucharistic origins, Andrew McGowan has explored the evidence for the existence of a variety of early Christian meal patterns where wine was not used,[30] the roots of which are already attested in the New Testament. In his letter to the Romans, Paul repeats the admonition he had given already in 1 Corinthians 8:10-13, that those who eat meat should be careful that their actions do not cause others to stumble, because the meat would have been from an animal offered in sacrifice to a pagan deity, but here he mentions not only eating meat but also drinking wine as possible causes of such stumbling (Rom 14:13-21). Wine is included because it was socially unthinkable in the ancient world to drink wine without a libation to the gods, at least at a banquet if not more generally. In addition, the counsel in 1 Timothy 5:23 no longer to be a water-drinker but to take some wine "for the sake of your stomach and your frequent ailments" may appear to be merely medical advice, but behind it seems to lie a tradition of abstinence by some believers.[31]

The use of water rather than wine appears to have continued in some Christian traditions for several centuries. McGowan has assembled enough indications of "bread-and-water" Eucharists from second- and third-century sources that it is not easy to dismiss them

[30] McGowan, *Ascetic Eucharists*, passim.
[31] For further exploration of the background of these passages, see ibid., 221–33; and for other possible allusions, 235–38.

as merely the practices of a few deviant groups.[32] Even the vehemence of the attacks by their opponents on these supposed deviants is itself evidence that they were seen as a significant threat. In some cases it is apparently within heretical movements that the practice is located, but in other cases are those who did not belong to such groups. The clearest evidence for an "orthodox" use of water comes from Cyprian, bishop of Carthage in North Africa from 249 to 258. He admits that while "very many bishops . . . keep the pattern of the truth of the gospel and of the tradition of the Lord," there are "some, whether by ignorance or naivety," who offer water and not wine in their eucharistic celebrations (*Ep.* 63.1). This is obviously not some recent aberration from an accepted norm, because he later describes it as "the custom of certain persons who have thought in time past [*in praeteritum*] that water alone should be offered in the cup of the Lord" (63.14), and he argues at length that wine mixed with water is what "the tradition of the Lord" requires.

EARLY CHRISTIAN MEALS: THE *DIDACHE*
Important information about early Christian meal practices comes from a document regarded by most scholars as contemporary with many of the New Testament books, the *Didache* or *Teaching of the Twelve Apostles*.[33] Chapters 9 and 10 give directions about the conduct of a meal:

> 9.1 *Concerning the thanksgiving* [eucharistia], *give thanks thus:*
> 2 *First, concerning the cup:*
> We give thanks to you, our Father, for the holy vine of David your servant,[34] which you have made known to us through Jesus your servant; glory to you for evermore.

[32] Ibid., 143ff. See also Thomas O'Loughlan, "Another Post-Resurrection Meal and Its Implications for the Early Understanding of the Eucharist," in *A Wandering Galilean: Essays in Honour of Seán Freyne*, ed. Zuleika Rodgers et al. (Leiden/Boston: Brill, 2009), 485–503, where he points to a reference in Jerome's *De viris illustribus* to a passage in the *Gospel according to the Hebrews* as embodying another ancient eucharistic tradition in which bread alone seems to have been used.
[33] For the Greek text, see Willy Rordorf and André Tuilier, *La doctrine des douze apôtres*, Sources chrétiennes 248 (Paris: Cerf, 1978; 2nd ed., 1998).
[34] The Greek word *pais*, translated throughout this extract as "servant," can also mean "child."

3   *Concerning the broken bread:*[35]

We give thanks to you, our Father, for the life and knowleᵤ which you have made known to us through Jesus your servant; glory to you for evermore.

4   As this broken bread was scattered upon the mountains and having been gathered together became one, so may your church be gathered together from the ends of the earth into your kingdom; for yours is the glory and the power through Jesus Christ for evermore.

5   *Let no one eat or drink of your Eucharist but those who have been baptized in the name of the Lord. For concerning this also the Lord has said, "Do not give what is holy to the dogs."*

10.1   *After you have had your fill, give thanks thus:*

2   We give thanks to you, holy Father, for your holy name which you have enshrined in our hearts, and for the knowledge and faith and immortality which you have made known to us through Jesus your servant; glory to you for evermore.

3   You, Almighty Master, created all things for the sake of your Name and gave food and drink to humans for enjoyment, that they might give thanks to you; but to us you have granted spiritual food and drink and eternal life through Jesus your servant.

[35] The Greek word *klasma*, "broken bread" or "fragment," may be being used proleptically here, as breaking usually follows rather than precedes the blessing in Jewish practice, but it has been suggested that it is perhaps also influenced by knowledge of a version of the story of the feeding of the five thousand in John 6:1-15, where there is reference in verse 12 to "fragments" being "gathered," which may be intended symbolically of the gathering of Christian disciples "that nothing may be lost"; see C. F. D. Moule, "A Note on *Didache* ix.4," *Journal of Theological Studies* 6 (1955): 240–43; Francis J. Moloney, *The Gospel of John* (Collegeville, MN: Liturgical Press, Michael Glazier, 1998), 198–200. An alternative possibility is that the breaking of the bread may actually have been intended to precede the saying of the prayer here. Although this sequence is not otherwise recorded in early Jewish or Christian sources, it would not be dissimilar from other variations in the order of ritual actions that we encounter in different groups of both Christians and Jews (e.g., bread-cup or cup-bread; the debates in the Mishnah tractate *Berakoth* over the order that certain blessings were to be said), and the Babylonian Talmud records a dispute among third-century rabbis over the possibility of blessing bread that was already broken (*b. Ber.* 39a-b). In addition, we should note that *Didache* 14.1 has the identical order: "break bread and give thanks."

4   Above all we give thanks to you because you are mighty; glory to you for evermore. Amen.

5   Remember, Lord, your church, to deliver it from all evil and to perfect it in your love, and gather it together from the four winds, having been sanctified, into your kingdom which you have prepared for it; for yours is the power and the glory for evermore. Amen.

6   May grace come, and this world pass away. Amen.
Hosanna to the God of David.
If anyone is holy, let him come; if anyone is not, let him repent.
Marana tha.[36] Amen.

7   *But allow the prophets to give thanks as long as they wish.*

Many scholars have tried to interpret these prayers as conscious reworkings of the Jewish *Birkat ha-mazon*, but in the light of modern Jewish scholarship about when that particular prayer crystallized, it is better to understand both texts as parallel outworkings of a common tradition. Because the prayers in the *Didache* do not include the Last Supper narrative or any mention of the death of Jesus or his body and blood but only "spiritual food and drink," and are unlike later eucharistic rites, many earlier scholars denied that what was envisaged here was a Eucharist and offered other explanations for it.[37] More recently, however, there has emerged a growing consensus that it was one of the forms of early Christian meal out of which the later Eucharist developed. A further possibility also has been suggested: that the setting into which the prayers are placed is actually an artificial construct by the redactor of the whole work and that the prayers in chapter 9 and those in chapter 10 (which duplicate one another to a greater extent than one might have expected) were originally different versions of the same tradition of praying before (and not after) the Christian meal, those in chapter 9 representing a more primitive form of the material with the units over cup and bread still being clearly differentiated from one another, while in chapter 10 they have been molded into a more continuous whole.[38]

---

[36] An acclamation in Aramaic meaning "Our Lord, come!" also found in 1 Cor 16:22 and (in Greek) in Rev 22:20.

[37] For details of these, see Paul F. Bradshaw, *Eucharistic Origins* (London: SPCK; New York: Oxford University Press, 2004), 25–30.

[38] Paul F. Bradshaw, "Yet Another Explanation of *Didache* 9–10," *Studia Liturgica* 36 (2006): 124–28; reproduced in abbreviated form in *idem, Reconstructing*

Be that as it may, the principal focus of the meal is on remembrance of and thanksgiving for the revelation brought by Jesus and petition for the final gathering of the church into God's kingdom. It is also to be noted that the texts were not mandatory: those with the gift of prophetic utterance might amplify them as much as they wished (10.7). Although the contents of "the cup" are not specified (as is often the case in early Christian writings), it would appear that in this instance wine is being used, because of the reference in 9.2 to "the holy vine of David." Unlike the standard Greco-Roman *symposium* or the Last Supper narrative, the blessing over the wine is said along with that for the bread at the beginning of the meal and not at the end. This was not necessarily unusual in a Jewish context, however: as we have already noted above, this was also the practice at Qumran, and even the Mishnah itself provides for the possibility of a blessing over wine before a meal, which would then exempt one from the obligation to say a blessing over wine after the meal.[39]

Nor may it have been unusual within Christian meal practice. Indeed, it has been suggested that a cup-and-bread blessing sequence before meals may have been the pattern familiar to Paul. Although he recounts the narrative of the Last Supper in 1 Corinthians 11:23-25, with the cup following the meal, this was not necessarily the order followed by the Corinthian church in their regular meals together. As we have suggested earlier, when Paul cites the narrative, it is not to remind the Corinthians of a ritual pattern that they are neglecting but rather to underscore a meaning of the meal of which they have lost sight. Moreover, earlier in the letter, in his discussion about the question of eating meat sacrificed to idols, Paul appeals to the eucharistic practice of the Corinthians and poses the rhetorical question: "The cup of blessing which we bless, is it not a sharing in the blood of Christ? The bread which we break, is it not a sharing in the body of Christ? Because there is one bread, we who are many are one body, for we all partake of the one bread" (1 Cor 10:16-17). Although nearly all New Testament commentators have traditionally dismissed this apparent inversion from the alleged "normal" order of "bread-cup" as simply a rhetorical device that enables Paul to pick up

---

Early Christian Worship (London: SPCK, 2009; Collegeville, MN: Liturgical Press, Pueblo, 2011), 39–44.

[39] *Ber.* 6.5. See further Andrew B. McGowan, "The Inordinate Cup: Issues of Order in Early Eucharistic Drinking," *Studia Patristica* 35 (2001): 283–91.

the theme of bread directly in the following sentence,[40] Enrico Mazza has forcefully argued that the sequence represents the actual meal practice at Corinth and even that it reflects the use of a threefold pattern of prayer at the meal similar to that found in *Didache* 9: a thanksgiving over the cup, a thanksgiving over the bread, and a prayer for unity linked to the theme of bread, even though the *Didache* is concerned with the eschatological unity of the church and Paul with the unity of the assembly sharing in the eucharistic bread.[41]

Paul is not the only possible additional witness to a Christian meal pattern that placed the blessing over cup and bread together at the beginning. In addition to a quotation by Irenaeus (bishop of Lyons in the last quarter of the second century) of a passage from the fragmentary works of Papias (an early second-century bishop of Hierapolis in Asia Minor) that might be an allusion to the practice of the blessing over the cup preceding that over the bread, to which McGowan has drawn attention,[42] there are also signs of something similar behind the apparently very early directions for the conduct of Christian meals preserved in a somewhat later church order known as the *Apostolic Tradition*. Because we are largely dependent on a late Ethiopic translation made via Coptic and Arabic intermediaries for this part of the text, which has attracted accretions and become confused, its original form cannot be reconstructed with great certainty; it seems, though, to have read something like this:

> He is to give thanks [for] the cup and he is to give some of the fragments to all the faithful. And as those believers who are there are eating the supper, they are to take a little bread from the bishop's hand before they break their own bread. . . . It is proper that everyone, before they taste and drink anything, take the cup and give thanks over it and drink and eat because they are pure. But to the catechumens let

---

[40] See, for example, Hans Conzelmann, *I Corinthians* (Philadelphia, PA: Fortress Press, 1975), 171–72; Schweizer, *The Lord's Supper according to the New Testament*, 4.

[41] Enrico Mazza, *The Origins of the Eucharistic Prayer* (Collegeville, MN: Liturgical Press, Pueblo, 1995), 66–97.

[42] Andrew B. McGowan, "'First regarding the cup . . .': Papias and the Diversity of Early Eucharistic Practice," *Journal of Theological Studies* 46 (1995): 551–55.

exorcised bread be given and let them each offer a cup. Let a catechu-
men not sit at the Lord's supper.[43]

Although in this form the material appears somewhat contradictory
and may be a fusion of two traditions, so that it is not clear whether
the participants share a common cup or say blessings individually,
it would seem that the blessing over the cup came at the beginning
of the meal before the blessing over the bread, just as in the *Didache*.
Likewise, unbaptized catechumens might still be present and fed with
bread that had been exorcized (instead of that over which thanks had
been given) and allowed their own drinking vessels instead of the
common cup, just as the unbaptized in *Didache* were not permitted to
share the same food at the same table because they were not yet pure.
It is much later before we have evidence of them being prohibited
from attending the rite altogether and being dismissed from the assembly before the eucharistic action began. Other parts of the text give
instructions about suppers being given for the benefit of the poor and
about donations of food being presented to them to take home (28.3,
30A), customs which we have earlier noted were prevalent in the surrounding culture and a particular feature of early Christian life, and
like the Jewish Therapeutae, those at a supper are to listen in silence to
the discourse of the president (28.4).

EARLY CHRISTIAN MEALS: THE LAST SUPPER
The pioneers of modern liturgical scholarship in the eighteenth and
nineteenth centuries generally presumed that Jesus would have left
precise instructions to his disciples as to what they were to say and do
when they continued the practice established by him at the Last Supper, and so by comparing ancient liturgies with one another it ought
to be possible to discover from what was common to them all the core
elements that went back to apostolic times. This was never an easy

[43] *Apostolic Tradition* 29C [=25].15–27.1, reconstructed. Although traditionally
attributed to a Hippolytus of Rome in the third century, an increasing number
of scholars now recognize this church order to be a composite work containing
material from different places and time periods in the first few centuries. For
a discussion of its character and the full range of textual witnesses and further
comments on the passage, see Paul F. Bradshaw, Maxwell E. Johnson, and L.
Edward Phillips, *The Apostolic Tradition: A Commentary* (Minneapolis, MN:
Fortress Press, 2002), esp. 141–45, 156–60.

task, because these ancient rites varied so much from one another, and it became increasingly difficult to maintain the thesis as more evidence for early eucharistic practices emerged in the late nineteenth and early twentieth centuries. It began to seem as if there had never been a single apostolic archetype from which later eucharistic rites, and especially their prayers, had descended. Some scholars dealt with this difficulty by admitting that there might have been two or more distinct traditions, others by denying that some primitive texts, especially the *Didache*, were genuine eucharistic rites at all, and others by a combination of both lines of argument.

It was the Anglican Benedictine scholar Gregory Dix who—in his fat volume *The Shape of the Liturgy*, first published in 1945—enabled the traditional theory of a single origin for all later mainstream eucharistic practice to survive, albeit in a modified form. He argued that what went back to the Last Supper was not a form of prayer as such but a pattern of ritual action that was faithfully followed by subsequent generations of Christians:

> The New Testament accounts of that supper as they stand in the received text present us with what may be called a "seven-action scheme" of the rite then inaugurated. Our Lord (1) took bread; (2) "gave thanks" over it; (3) broke it; (4) distributed it, saying certain words. Later He (5) took a cup; (6) "gave thanks" over that; (7) handed it to His disciples, saying certain words. . . . With absolute unanimity the liturgical tradition reproduces these seven actions as four: (1) The offertory; bread and wine are "taken" and placed on the table together. (2) The prayer; the president gives thanks to God over bread and wine together. (3) The fraction; the bread is broken. (4) The communion; the bread and wine are distributed together.
>
> In that form and in that order these four actions constituted the absolutely invariable nucleus of every eucharistic rite known to us throughout antiquity from the Euphrates to Gaul.[44]

Today, Dix's theory would be challenged by a good number of scholars, not only for tying the origin of the Eucharist too closely to the Last Supper—a view he shared with almost every earlier liturgical historian—but also because it simply is not the case that all early eucharistic meals followed either a sevenfold or a fourfold shape, a view that can be sustained only by refusing to accept any testimony

[44] Dix, *The Shape of the Liturgy*, 48.

to the contrary.[45] As we have seen, for a proper understandii roots of Christian eucharistic practice, the Last Supper need: within the broader context both of the conventional meal pa the culture of the time and also of the other meals that Jesus first followers seem to have shared, including of his miracul◡◡ ◟◟◟ung of large crowds. It is also important to note that, like the *Didache*, by no means all of the other early references to Christian meals link them to his sayings about bread and cup being his body (or flesh) and blood, and that even of those that do so, most make no explicit reference to the occasion of the Last Supper and view the eucharistic elements as life-giving and spiritually nourishing rather than in sacrificial terms, as we shall see in more detail in the next chapter. Indeed, the Fourth Gospel itself locates Jesus' saying about bread being his flesh in connection with one of the miraculous feedings and not in connection with the Last Supper or his death, and so speaks of it primarily in terms of life and nourishment: "the bread of God is that which comes down from heaven, and gives life to the world. . . . I am the bread of life; whoever comes to me shall not hunger, and whoever believes in me shall never thirst. . . . I am the living bread that came down from heaven; if any eat of this bread, they will live for ever" (John 6:33, 35, 51).[46] It looks, therefore, as though the association with the Last Supper that is made by Paul and the writers of the Synoptic Gospels did not become widely established for some time. This in turn helps explain why many Christian meals bore no resemblance to the pattern of the Last Supper and were weekly rather than annual events with their celebration unrelated to the day of the week on which that supper was said to have occurred.

Even in the Synoptic accounts of the Last Supper there are signs that the sayings over bread and cup have been grafted onto an earlier version of the narrative of a final Passover meal of which they formed no part and which had previously centered on a conversation about

[45] See, for example, Bryan D. Spinks, "Mis-shapen: Gregory Dix and the Four-Action Shape of the Liturgy," *Lutheran Quarterly* 4 (1990): 161–77.

[46] Many scholars judge the material that follows this extract, which refers also to the blood of Christ, to be a later interpolation. For a summary of the debate, see Francis J. Moloney, *The Johannine Son of Man*, 2nd ed. (Rome: Libreria Ateneo Salesiano, 1978), 93ff.; and also Margaret Daly-Denton, "Water in the Eucharistic Cup: A Feature of the Eucharist in Johannine Trajectories through Early Christianity," *Irish Theological Quarterly* 72 (2007): 356–70.

betrayal and the eschatological saying, "I shall not drink of the fruit of the vine." Clues that the words over bread and cup may be an insertion are provided in Mark 14 by the repetition of "as they were eating" (vv. 18 and 22) and also of the cup being drunk before the interpretative words about it are said (subsequently amended in Matthew's version from the narrative statement, "they all drank of it," to the command, "Drink of it, all of you"; Matt 26:27). If the interpretative sayings are bracketed, as here, a perfectly intelligible narrative is left:

> [17]And when it was evening, he came with the twelve. [18]And as they were at table eating, Jesus said, "Truly, I say to you, one of you will betray me, one who is eating with me." [19]They began to be sorrowful, and to say to him one after another, "Is it I?" [20]He said to them, "It is one of the twelve, one who is dipping bread in the same dish with me. [21]For the Son of man goes as it is written of him, but woe to that man by whom the Son of man is betrayed! It would have been better for that man if he had not been born." [[22]And as they were eating, he took bread, and blessed, and broke it, and gave it to them, and said, "Take; this is my body."] [23]And he took a cup, and when he had given thanks he gave it to them, and they all drank of it. [24]And he said to them, "[This is my blood of the covenant, which is poured out for many.] [25]Truly, I say to you, I shall not drink again of the fruit of the vine until that day when I drink it new in the kingdom of God."

Something similar also seems to have been the case in the independent account of the Passover meal in Luke 22, which, though the order is different, follows a similar line in focusing on the eschatological theme and the conversation about betrayal. Here matters are more complicated, however, because there exist both shorter and longer manuscript traditions of the text,[47] the longer being indicated here by the use of italics:

> [14]And when the hour came, he sat at table, and the apostles with him. [15]And he said to them, "I have earnestly desired to eat this Passover with you before I suffer; [16]for I tell you I shall not eat it until it is fulfilled in the kingdom of God." [17]And he took a cup, and when he had given thanks he said, "Take this, and divide it among yourselves; [18]for I tell you that from now on I shall not drink of the fruit of the vine until the kingdom of God comes." [[19]And he took bread, and when he

---

[47] For details, see Jeremias, *The Eucharistic Words of Jesus*, 139–52.

had given thanks he broke it and gave it to them, saying, "This is body *which is given for you. Do this in remembrance of me.* [20]*And like* *the cup after supper, saying, "This cup which is poured out for you is t* *new covenant in my blood."*] [21]But behold the hand of him who betrays me is with me on the table. For the Son of man goes as it has been determined; but woe to that man by whom he is betrayed." [22]And they began to question one another, which of them it was that would do this.

Doubts may be cast on the longer version having been part of the earliest form of the text not only because two cups are then mentioned, one before and one after supper (vv. 17 and 20), but also because there is the apparently contradictory situation of Jesus declaring in verse 18 that he will no longer drink of the fruit of the vine and then in verse 20 of his doing so. But if the shorter version is the original one and the longer an expansion by a later hand, as seems more likely,[48] it is easy to see how the Evangelist, having subsequently read Mark's gospel, might have thought it necessary to add to his account the saying about the bread but not the cup, either because he already had a reference to a cup or more probably because he was himself familiar with a Christian meal tradition that involved only "the breaking of the bread," as witnessed by his use of this expression throughout Luke and Acts.

Thus, the Last Supper version of the eucharistic sayings of Jesus may not have been as dominant in first-century Christianity as the existence of four accounts of it in the New Testament books may tempt us to suppose. Paul in 1 Corinthians 11 may even have been the originator of the tradition of associating Jesus' sayings about the bread and cup being his body and blood with the Last Supper and consequently giving them a sacrificial interpretation, which was later taken up in Mark's gospel and through that in Matthew and Luke. He is certainly the first witness we have to the idea that the Christian meal is therefore a commemoration of Christ's *passio*: "as often as you eat this bread and drink the cup, you proclaim the Lord's death until he comes" (1 Cor 11:26). All this, Paul claims, is something that he "received from the Lord" (1 Cor 11:23), but it is also part of his wider understanding of the Christian meal as, in some sense, constituting a communion-sacrifice:

[48] See Bart D. Ehrman, *The Orthodox Corruption of Scripture* (New York: Oxford University Press, 1993), 197–209.

The cup of blessing which we bless, is it not a sharing in the blood of Christ? The bread which we break, is it not a sharing in the body of Christ? Because there is one bread, we who are many are one body, for we all partake of the one bread. Consider Israel according to the flesh: are not those who eat the sacrifices sharing in the altar? . . . You cannot drink the cup of the Lord and the cup of demons. You cannot partake of the table of the Lord and the table of demons. (1 Cor 10:16-18, 21)

Although, as we shall see, the concept of sacrifice came to play an increasingly significant part in the interpretation of the Eucharist among Christians, this particular Old Testament model soon faded away, with the result that in later centuries the need to receive communion ceased to be thought as an essential part of the rite.

SUMMARY
1. Modern scholarship is changing the way we understand the origins of the Eucharist in context of the meal customs of the ancient world.
2. Jewish and early Christian meal practices would, broadly speaking, have followed those of the surrounding Greco-Roman culture.
3. The earliest meals shared among Christians appear to have taken varying forms rather than following a single standard pattern, in part depending on whether they were hosted within a rich person's house or comprised solely a gathering of impoverished believers.
4. The presence or absence of wine at these meals might have been merely the result of economic circumstances but might also have been a conscientious decision based on the connection of both meat and wine to pagan cults.
5. There are no grounds for distinguishing a sacramental Eucharist from other sorts of Christian meals in the earliest period: *agape* and Eucharist are synonyms at this time, and it was only much later that meal and Eucharist became separated from one another.
6. The association of the bread that was eaten with the body of Christ (and in some cases the cup with his blood) seems at first not to have been made in every early Christian community.
7. The association of Christian meals with the Last Supper and the sacrificial interpretation arising from that (perhaps stemming from Paul in 1 Corinthians 10–11) was not one that was taken up very widely until the New Testament books began to be recognized as Scripture in the third century.

Chapter 2

The Second and Third Centuries

FROM MEAL TO RITE

We do not know exactly when the full meals described in the previous chapter were abandoned by Christians (or, in the case of those consisting principally or exclusively of bread, were reduced in quantity to purely symbolic amounts) to produce the kind of eucharistic rite with which later generations were familiar. Some scholars have imagined that it must have happened very early, during the first century, but there is no evidence for this. It is possible that the development may be first attested in a letter written by Pliny the Younger to the Roman emperor Trajan around 112 when he was governor of the province of Bithynia in Asia Minor, which describes the practices reported to him by former Christians whom he has interrogated there:

> They had met regularly before dawn on a fixed day to chant verses alternately among themselves in honour of Christ as if to a god, and also to bind themselves by oath, not for any criminal purpose, but to abstain from theft, robbery and adultery, to commit no breach of trust and not to deny a deposit when called upon to restore it. After this ceremony it had been their custom to disperse and reassemble later to take food of an ordinary, harmless kind; but they had in fact given up this practice since my edict, issued on your instructions, which banned all political societies.[1]

We need to bear in mind, however, that this evidence is secondhand and not necessarily correctly understood by Pliny in every respect. In

---

[1] Pliny, *Ep.* 10.96; ET from Pliny, *Letters*, trans. Betty Radice, Loeb Classical Library 59 (Cambridge, MA: Harvard University Press, 1969), 288–89. The emphasis put by the Christians on the food being of an ordinary and harmless kind was no doubt intended to counter common accusations from their pagan contemporaries that they indulged in cannibalism and other deviant activities; see Andrew B. McGowan, "Eating People: Accusations of Cannibalism against Christians in the Second Century," *Journal of Early Christian Studies* 2 (1994): 413–42.

any case, it relates only to one part of the ancient world and not more generally to the Roman Empire. Ignatius of Antioch, also writing early in the second century to the Christians in the city of Smyrna, further west in Asia Minor, seems to treat the terms Eucharist and *agape* as synonyms for the same event, which implies the retention of the meal at least in Antioch if not at Smyrna itself:

> Let no one do anything connected with the church without the bishop. Let that be deemed a valid Eucharist, which is [administered] either by the bishop, or by one to whom he has entrusted it. Wherever the bishop shall appear, there let the people be; just as, wherever Jesus Christ is, there is the catholic church. It is not lawful without the bishop either to baptize or to hold an *agape*; but whatever he shall approve, that is also pleasing to God, so that everything that you do may be secure and valid. (*Smyrnaeans* 8)

Many have concluded that the "fixed day" to which Pliny referred must have been Sunday, but it seems more likely that Saturday was meant, with a morning assembly that paralleled that of the Jewish synagogue on the Sabbath and a meal in the evening. Because Jews counted each new day as beginning in the evening and not the morning, however, that Saturday evening meal would have been reckoned by the Christians as occurring on Sunday, or "the Lord's day" as they were beginning to call it by this time.

The first extensive description of Christian eucharistic practice that we have comes from Justin Martyr, writing in Rome in the middle of the second century. He deals with it twice, first in the context of the baptism of new converts and again in relation to the regular weekly custom:

> After washing the one who has believed and assented, we lead him to those called "brethren" where they are assembled, to make common prayers fervently for ourselves and for the one who has been illuminated and for all others everywhere, that, having learned the truth, we may be deemed worthy to be found both good citizens through deeds and guardians of the commandments, so that we may be saved with eternal salvation. Having ended the prayers, we greet one another with a kiss.[2] Then are brought to the president of the brothers bread

---

[2] Although the kiss is mentioned by Justin only in connection with the baptismal Eucharist, it is described as the conclusion of normal congregational

26

and a cup of water and of wine-mixed-with-water, and he, having taken, sends up praise and glory to the Father of all through the name of the Son and of the Holy Spirit, and makes thanksgiving at length for [our] having been deemed worthy of these things from him. When he has finished the prayer and the thanksgiving, all the people present assent, saying, "Amen." Amen means in the Hebrew tongue "So be it." And when the president has given thanks and all the people have assented, those called by us "deacons" give to each one of those present to share of the bread and wine and water over which thanks have been given, and they take [them] to those not present. (*First Apology* 65)

And afterward we continually remind one another of these things. Those who have provide for all those in need; and we are always together with one another. And for all the things with which we are supplied we bless the Maker of all through his Son Jesus Christ and through the Holy Spirit. And on the day called "of the Sun" an assembly is held in one place of all living in town or country, and the memoirs of the apostles or the writings of the prophets are read for as long as time allows. Then, when the reader has finished, the president in a discourse makes an admonition and exhortation for the imitation of these good things. Then we all stand up together and send up prayers; and as we said before, when we have finished the prayer, bread and wine and water are brought, and the president likewise sends up prayers and thanksgivings according to his ability, and the people assent, saying the Amen; and the distribution and participation by everyone in those things over which thanks have been given takes place; and they are sent to those not present through the deacons. And those who have the means and so desire give what they wish, each according to his own choice; and what is collected is deposited with the president. And he provides for both orphans and widows, and those in need through sickness or through other cause, and those who are in prison, and strangers sojourning, and, in a word, he becomes a protector for all those who are in want. And we all make an assembly together on Sunday, because it is

---

prayer in several other sources from the end of the second century onward (Tertullian calls it "the seal of prayer": *De oratione* 18) and as a regular part of the eucharistic liturgy. In Greco-Roman culture, social convention usually restricted kissing to very close friends or members of one's own family; hence, for Christians to kiss one another when they were not so related was a powerful countercultural symbol, indicating that they regarded their fellow believers as their brothers and sisters and the church as their true family. See further Michael Philip Penn, *Kissing Christians: Ritual and Community in the Late Ancient Church* (Philadelphia: University of Pennsylvania Press, 2005).

the first day, on which God, having transformed the darkness and matter, made the world; and Jesus Christ our Savior rose from the dead the same day; for they crucified him the day before Saturday; and the day after Saturday, which is Sunday, appearing to his apostles and disciples, he taught these things which we have also presented to you for consideration. (*First Apology* 67)

Although it has commonly been assumed that Justin is speaking here of a rite separated from a meal and held on a Sunday morning, it is important to note that he does not explicitly say this: it could have been held on a Saturday evening (even if Justin calls it Sunday), and the bread, wine,[3] and water could have been in sufficient quantities to constitute a filling meal, as could the leftovers that were taken to those unable to be present, especially as financial provision for those in need is mentioned in immediate juxtaposition to the reference to that act. The readings, sermon, and prayers that are described as preceding the eucharistic action have also been thought to derive from the Jewish synagogue assemblies on Sabbath mornings but now transferred to Sunday mornings and prefixed to the remnant of the original Christian meal practice. Yet it needs to be remembered that evening meals themselves could be accompanied by readings, discourse, hymns, and prayers, as we saw in the preceding chapter.[4]

Primarily on the basis of Justin's description, as well as taking into account the meal contexts of Jesus' postresurrection appearances in the gospels (especially the Emmaus event in Luke 24), Gordon Lathrop has deduced what might be called an ecumenical, transcultural, and possibly even "apostolic" authoritative *ordo* for Christian worship. He writes:

> These are the essentials of Christian worship. A community *gathers in prayer* around the scriptures *read* and *proclaimed*. This community of the word then tastes the meaning of that word by keeping the meal of

---

[3] It is possible that the references to wine in Justin's account are a later interpolation and that the meal consisted only of bread and water. See further McGowan, *Ascetic Eucharists*, 151–55.

[4] In addition to the practice of the Therapeutae described in some detail there, we may add what is mentioned in the church order known as the *Apostolic Tradition*, where in chapter 28 the bishop is to give a discourse at the Christian supper. On the nature of this document, see above, page 19, n. 43.

Christ, *giving thanks* over bread and cup and *eating* and *drinking*. ⹁ this word-table community, the body of Christ, which gathers ot᷄ people to its number, continually *teaching* both itself and these n comers the mercy and mystery of God and *washing* them in the ⸗ of that God. All of these essential things urge the community toward the world—toward prayer for the world, sharing with the hungry of the world, caring for the world, giving witness to the world. . . . Around these central things, which will be most evident in Sunday and festival worship, other gatherings of Christians may also take place.[5]

Along with the fact that Lathrop's suggestion of an *ordo* may be a little over-systematized to fit the full facts of history, it must be stated that there is probably no such thing as a pure *ordo* existing anywhere in some idealized form apart from its very concrete, cultural, ecclesial, and linguistic ritual expressions.[6] That is, the deducing of an *ordo*, in large part, is a logical construct, an abstraction made on the basis of very minimal descriptions of the patterns of Christian liturgy in the early period.

Even Justin Martyr is not necessarily giving an *ordo* for Christian liturgy for all times and all places but a brief outline for the Roman emperor Antoninus Pius, of what—perhaps—*one* Christian community at Rome was doing in its baptismal and Sunday worship in the middle of the second century. Although the order described by Justin was destined to become the standard pattern of eucharistic rites more or less everywhere from the fourth century onward—with readings, sermon, and prayers ending with the exchange of a kiss and followed by the presentation of the eucharistic elements to the president, his thanksgiving[7] over them, and the consumption of them by everyone— it would be dangerous to jump to the conclusion that this uniformity

[5] Gordon Lathrop, *What Are the Essentials of Christian Worship?* (Minneapolis, MN: Augsburg Fortress Press, 1994), 22. See also *idem, Holy Things: A Liturgical Theology* (Minneapolis, MN: Fortress Press, 1993).

[6] See John Baldovin, "The Church in Christ, Christ in the Church," in *The Many Presences of Christ*, ed. T. Fitzgerald and D. Lysik (Chicago: Liturgy Training Publications, 1999), 25–27.

[7] Because Justin speaks of the president extemporizing "prayers and thanksgivings" in the plural in his description of the Sunday practice, some have concluded that separate prayers over bread and cup were still being said at this time (as apparently also was the case in the assembly described in the

of practice had already been achieved at this early date, especially as there exists some evidence to the contrary. For, whether or not the full meal had been abandoned by Justin's community in Rome, it seems that fifty years later in North Africa at least some Christian groups were maintaining an evening supper in which discourse and hymns followed rather than preceded the meal, even if that were now alongside a further morning distribution of bread (and wine?). Tertullian, writing just before the end of the second century and defending the propriety of the activities of Christians against the charges of scandalous behavior that were being brought against them by pagans, offers an indication of what went on in their gatherings:

> We gather in an assembly and congregation, so that we may surround God with prayers, as if with united force. This violence is pleasing to God. We also pray for the emperors, for their ministers and authorities, for the state of the age, for the peace of the world, for the delay of the end. We meet for the recollection of our sacred writings, in case any aspect of the present times serves either to forewarn or to remind. Certainly, we nourish our faith with the sacred words, we arouse our hope, we strengthen our trust; and at the same time by inculcating the precepts we confirm good habits. In the same place also there are exhortations, chastisements, and sacred censures. For with great gravity one is judged, as is fitting among those certain that they are in the sight of God; and the greatest anticipation of the future judgment occurs when any one has sinned to such an extent as to be excluded from participation in prayer, the assembly, and all sacred intercourse. Approved elders preside over us, having attained that honor not by purchase, but by testimony, for none of the things of God is bought with money. Although there is a treasure-chest, it is not filled with purchase-money, as of a religion that was bought. Once a month or whenever they desire, everyone puts in a small donation, but only if they wish and only if they are able; for no one is compelled, but contributes voluntarily. These are, as it were, the deposits of piety. For they are not spent from there on banquets and drinking parties and eating-houses, but on feeding and burying the poor, on boys and girls destitute of means and parents, and on the elderly now confined to the house, likewise the shipwrecked; and any in the mines, on the islands, or in prisons, who have become the foster-children of their confession, provided that it is for belonging to the cause of God. (*Apologeticum* 39)

Didascalia: see below, page 35), rather than a single, continuous eucharistic prayer as found in later centuries.

It is impossible to tell from this whether what is being described is a gathering for a meal or merely a service of the word on its own, which we learn did exist in Tertullian's church from a passage in another of his works.[8] Later in the same chapter of the *Apologeticum*, however, he is clearly talking about a Christian supper when he says:

> Our supper reveals its meaning by the name that it is called among the Greeks, affection [*agape*]. Whatever it costs, our expenditure is gain in the name of piety, since with that feast we assist any in need; not as among you parasites, who strive for the glory of serving their licentiousness while filling their bellies amid outrageous behavior; but as with God, there is a great respect for the lowly. If the reason for our feast is honorable, consider the rest of its ordering: as it is an act of religious duty, it permits no vileness or immodesty; no one reclines before prayer to God is first tasted; as much is eaten as satisfies those who are hungry, as much is drunk as is appropriate for the chaste. They are satisfied with that, as those who remember that even during the night they have to worship God; they converse as those who know that the Lord is listening. After the washing of hands and [the bringing in of] lights, each one is invited into the midst to sing to God, as they are able, either from the holy scriptures or of their own composition: this proves how little is drunk. Prayer similarly concludes the feast. We depart from it, not as troops of mischief-doers nor bands of vagabonds, nor for outbursts of licentiousness, but [to have] the same care of our modesty and chastity as those who had gathered not so much for a banquet as for instruction.

Because Tertullian uses the term *agape* to denote the event, scholars have traditionally concluded that this was a supper separated from the Eucharist proper. But this is not necessarily so. Like many other writers of the period, he uses the word "Eucharist" to refer to the consecrated bread itself rather than the rite, and the synonyms that he does employ for the rite seem more apposite to an evening meal than to some other kind of occasion ("the Lord's supper," *De spectaculis* 13; "the Lord's banquet," *Ad uxorem* 2.4; "God's banquet," *Ad uxorem* 2.8). Moreover, the gathering involves prayer at the beginning and the end, moderate eating and drinking, the singing of religious songs, and concern for those in need—all characteristics of earlier Christian

---

[8] *De cultu feminarum* 2.11, where he states that "either the sacrifice is offered or the word of God is dispensed."

eucharistic meals—and is even described by Tertullian as "an act of religious duty" (*officio religionis*). Thus, on the basis of this, Andrew McGowan has claimed that an evening meal was still the normal eucharistic practice in North Africa at this time.[9]

On the other hand, in a work written about ten to fifteen years later, Tertullian states that "we take also in gatherings before daybreak and from the hand of none but the presidents the sacrament of the Eucharist, which was commanded by the Lord both [to be] at meal-times and [to be taken] by all" (*De corona* 3). Does this not demonstrate that the celebration of the Eucharist had been transferred from the evening supper to the early morning? The practice cannot have been recent innovation, as it forms part of a list of customs that Tertullian says arise from tradition rather than Scripture. McGowan, however, suggests that this sentence is referring instead to the act of receiving communion from elements consecrated at a preceding evening meal. We know from another passage in Tertullian's works that the faithful might take the consecrated bread home and consume it there, because he warns that this practice may be a problem for a woman married to an unbeliever: "Will not your husband know what you secretly taste before [taking] any food? And if he knows [it is] bread, does he not believe it to be that which it is said [to be]? And will any [husband], not knowing the reason for these things, simply endure them, without complaint, without suspicion of [whether it is] bread or poison?" (*Ad uxorem* 2.5). What is being referred to in the earlier passage, however, is clearly something different from this domestic custom, as it is said to be received "at the hand of . . . the presidents." It may be a congregational version of such domestic communion, held on what were known as "station days"—the regular Wednesday and Friday fast days each week. Tertullian again offers evidence for some sort of eucharistic gatherings on these days in his treatise on prayer when he attempts to counter what was apparently a widespread objection to participation in these assemblies, raised on the grounds that reception of the eucharistic bread would break the fast. Tertullian proposes the solution that people should attend the gathering but reserve the sacrament for later consumption, thus fulfilling both aspects of the day— worship and fasting:

[9] See Andrew B. McGowan, "Rethinking Agape and Eucharist in Early North African Christianity," *Studia Liturgica* 34 (2004): 165–76.

> Similarly also on station days, many do not think that they should
> attend the sacrificial prayers, because the station would be undone by
> receiving the Lord's body. Does then the Eucharist destroy a service
> devoted to God or bind it more to God? Surely your station will be
> more solemn if you have also stood at God's altar? If the Lord's body is
> received and reserved, each point is secured, both the participation in
> the sacrifice and the discharge of the duty. (*De oratione* 19)

Although the language used here might suggest that a complete
eucharistic celebration was taking place, McGowan believes that the
words and phrases are quite consistent with Tertullian's language about
prayer in general and that therefore this need not indicate a full eucharistic rite but rather the distribution of consecrated bread at the conclusion of a morning gathering for prayer or for a service of the word. If he
is correct, then it was possible for the reception of communion to take
place not only at home by those who had been present at the Eucharist
as well as by those prevented from being there but also at additional
communal gatherings held in the mornings as well as at the evening
suppers, so important was the act of frequent participation in Christ's
body thought to be. Thus, what we have here appears to be a transi-
tional stage: the traditional supper is still preserved, but a newer custom
of receiving communion divorced from the supper has emerged in addition to it, apparently based on the earlier practice of distributing leftover
food from an evening meal to the needy on the following morning.

Whatever may have been the situation in North Africa in Tertullian's time, however, it appears that by the middle of the third century
a complete eucharistic rite was certainly being celebrated in the morning there. In the year 253 Cyprian, bishop of Carthage, wrote a letter
to a certain Caecilius, bishop of Biltha, contending strongly against
the use of water alone in the cup; in the course of this lengthy treatise
he also reveals other aspects of contemporary eucharistic practice and
theology. One of the major planks of his argument for the use of wine
mixed with water was that Christians must follow in their celebration
exactly what Christ did at the Last Supper. He had then, however, to
deal with the difficulty that Christ's Supper took place in the evening,
but the custom with which he was apparently familiar was of a morning celebration. He did so by claiming that Christ's action signified the
end of the old age, whereas Christians celebrate the dawn of the new:

> But still it was not in the morning, but after supper that the Lord of-
> fered the mixed cup. Ought we therefore to celebrate the Lord's

[supper] after supper, that we may thus offer the mixed cup by repeating the Lord's [supper]? It was fitting for Christ to offer about the
evening of the day, so that the very hour of sacrifice might show the
setting and evening of the world, as it is written in Exodus, "And all
the people of the synagogue of the children of Israel shall kill it in the
evening" [Exod 12:6]; and again in the Psalms, "the lifting up of my
hands [as] an evening sacrifice" [Ps 141:2]. But we celebrate the resurrection of the Lord in the morning. (*Ep.* 63.16.2–4)

On the other hand, Andrew McGowan has argued that the transition from evening to morning celebration was, in fact, only then taking
place in other parts of the local province and so was still the subject
of some debate. For Cyprian had just said in his letter, "Does any one
perhaps flatter himself with the thought that even if in the morning
water alone is seen to be offered, yet when we come to supper, we
offer the mixed cup? But when we dine, we cannot call the people
together to our banquet so that we may celebrate the truth of the sacrament with all the brotherhood present" (*Ep.* 63.16.1). McGowan understands this to mean that Cyprian's opponents are saying that while
they drink water at their morning assembly, they do use the mixed cup
of wine at their evening supper, to which Cyprian responds that the
evening gathering is unsuitable because it is not possible to assemble
the whole Christian community in one place for a supper.[10]
  From this, McGowan concludes that while Cyprian's own church
in Carthage seems to have moved decisively to morning eucharistic
celebrations some considerable time earlier because of the problem of
catering for very large numbers, other congregations in smaller towns
around were still continuing to have something quite similar to what
we appear to encounter in Tertullian some fifty years before, both an
evening supper and a morning distribution of communion on another
day. The sole difference seems to be that the people addressed here by
Cyprian are distributing only water and not wine with the bread at
these morning assemblies, which may by now have become full eucharistic celebrations, even though the evening suppers also continued
alongside them. Their justification—or rationalization—for this particular mixed practice is also revealed by Cyprian in the letter: they appear to be afraid that the smell of wine on their breath in the morning
might give them away as being Christians during the persecution that

---

[10] Ibid., 172–75.

the church was currently undergoing. Cyprian's response was characteristically robust: "How can we shed our blood for Christ, who blush to drink the blood of Christ?" (*Ep.* 63.15).

We know less about what was going on in other parts of the world at this time. Only very meager information can be gleaned about eucharistic practice from the works of the theologian Origen (ca. 185–ca. 254), who taught in both Alexandria and Caesarea.[11] And while the *Didascalia*, a Syrian church order usually dated to the first half of the third century but which may in fact contain material from the late first to the fourth century,[12] has much to say about how the various groups of people that comprise the Christian assembly (laymen; single, married, and widowed women; deacons; and presbyters) should be segregated in their seating, it reveals nothing about the elements that make up the rite or their order. It does, however, state that a visiting bishop should be invited to sit with the bishop who presides, to preach, and to pray over the bread and cup. He is expected to decline the last invitation, but then the local bishop should "at least let him speak over the cup" (*Didascalia* 2.58)—which apparently implies that in this stratum of the material there were still separate prayers over bread and cup rather than a single prayer over both and that perhaps the prayer over the cup came first.

A little more light may be shed on Syrian practices by the third-century apocryphal *Acts of Thomas*, in spite of the critical problems and difficulties of interpretation presented by this work.[13] Scattered throughout its narrative are several brief descriptions of eucharistic celebrations by the Apostle, nearly all of which conclude the initiation of new converts and which may well be indications of the kinds of practices that actually existed in East Syria, from where it seems to

<hr />

[11] See Harald Buchinger, "Early Eucharist in Transition? A Fresh Look at Origen," in *Jewish and Christian Liturgy and Worship: New Insights into Its History and Interaction*, ed. Albert Gerhards and Clemens Leonhard (Leiden: Brill, 2007), 207–27.

[12] See Alistair Stewart-Sykes, *The Didascalia Apostolorum: An English Version with Introduction and Annotation* (Turnhout, Belgium: Brepols, 2009).

[13] For editions of the text and a brief discussion of some of the problems associated with it, see Paul F. Bradshaw, *The Search for the Origins of Christian Worship*, 2nd ed. (London: SPCK; New York: Oxford University Press, 2002), 107. ET from Wilhelm Schneemelcher, ed., *New Testament Apocrypha II*, 2nd ed. (Cambridge: James Clarke; Louisville, KY: Westminster John Knox Press, 1992), 322–411.

have originated. Bread alone is mentioned in most cases (chaps. 27, 29, 49–50, 133), with a cup of water being specified in addition only in chapter 121—the two being called "the body of Christ and the cup of the Son of God"—and a cup with indeterminate contents in chapter 158, where the two are described as the "body which was crucified for us" and "the blood which was poured out for our salvation." Three of the descriptions include words that were said as the elements were distributed: "This Eucharist shall be to you for compassion and mercy, and not for judgment and requital" (29); "Let this be to thee for forgiveness of sins and eternal transgressions" (50); "Let this Eucharist be to you for salvation and joy and health for your souls" (158); and three have prayers of invocation (see below). Although in some cases early morning is indicated as the hour of celebration, this does not preclude it having been thought of as a filling meal, especially as a period of fasting normally preceded the rite of initiation in early Christianity. Whatever we make of these various references to eucharistic practice in the third century, eventually the separation of the Eucharist from a full meal became universal, except for celebrations conducted at the graves of deceased Christians, to which we shall return toward the end of the chapter, where substantial eating and drinking appears to have continued to accompany the rite.

POSSIBLE EARLY EUCHARISTIC PRAYERS

While no texts of eucharistic prayers that were actually used—apart from *Didache* 9–10—can be dated with any confidence prior to the middle of the fourth century (chiefly because the dominant tradition seems to have been at first to extemporize the prayers and later to transmit them orally), the prayers included in some of the apocryphal scriptures may not be very different from those that were used in certain circles, even though these are literary works rather than liturgical texts as such. The *Acts of John*, usually dated in the late second or early third century, and commonly thought to have originated in Syria, contains two different prayers supposedly spoken by the apostle John, each at a Eucharist involving bread alone:

We glorify thy name that converteth us from error and pitiless deceit; we glorify thee who hast shown before our eyes what we have seen; we testify to thy goodness, in various ways appearing; we praise thy gracious name, O Lord, [which] has convicted those that are convicted by thee; we thank thee, Lord Jesus Christ, that we confide in [. . .], which is unchanging; we thank thee who hadst need [. . .] of [our] nature that is being saved; we thank thee that hast given us this unwavering [faith] that thou alone art [God] both now and for ever; we thy servants, that are assembled and gathered with [good] cause, give thanks to thee, O holy one.

What praise or what offering or what thanksgiving shall we name as we break this bread, but thee alone, Jesu. We glorify thy name of Father which was spoken by thee; we glorify thy name of Son which was spoken by thee. We glorify thine entering of the door; we glorify thy Resurrection that is shown us through thee; we glorify thy Way; we glorify thy Seed, the Word, Grace, Faith, the Salt, the inexpressible Pearl, the Treasure, the Plough; the Net, the Greatness, the Diadem, him that for our sakes was called the Son of Man, the truth, repose, knowledge, power, commandment, confidence, liberty and refuge in thee. For thou alone, O Lord, are the root of immortality and the fount of incorruption and the seat of the aeons, who art called all these things on our account, that calling on thee through them we may know thy greatness, which at the present is invisible to us, but visible only to the pure as it is portrayed in thy man only.[14]

Some of the themes—praise of the divine name, the gift of revelation and knowledge, and (in the first) reference to the gathering of the church—are reminiscent of elements in the prayers in *Didache* 9–10, although it is important to note that the structure of the prayers is quite different. They are composed exclusively of praise and do not contain any petitionary elements; they are not made up of a small number of clearly distinguishable units, each with its own doxological conclusion, but rather of a quite lengthy series of short, parallel acclamations; they appear to be addressed to Christ rather than the Father; and they make no reference to food (or drink), except in the introduction to the second prayer, but focus on more abstract gifts and appear to allude to Christ's salvific acts—perhaps to the incarnation in the first and more clearly to the resurrection in the second. This suggests a quite different cultural milieu for their origin than that of the *Didache* texts.

The prayers related to the Eucharist that are contained in the *Acts of Thomas* are quite different again. All of them are invocations rather than thanksgivings, a trend that we shall note later in this chapter seems already to have been familiar to Irenaeus in the late second

[14] *Acts of John* 85, 109; ET from Schneemelcher, ed., *New Testament Apocrypha II*, 200–202.

In one case (49–50) the apostle invokes both Jesus and the
rit with a number of different images. He begins: "Jesus, who
 us worthy to partake of the Eucharist of thy holy body and
blood,[15] behold we make bold to approach thy Eucharist, and to call
upon thy holy name; come thou and have fellowship with us!" And he
continues:

> [Come gift of the Most High;] Come, perfect compassion; Come fellow-
> ship of the male; [Come, Holy Spirit;] Come, thou that dost know the
> mysteries of the Chosen; Come, thou that hast part in all the combats
> of the noble Athlete; [Come, treasure of glory; Come, darling of the
> compassion of the Most High;] Come, silence that dost reveal the great
> deeds of the whole greatness; Come, thou that dost show forth the
> hidden things and make the ineffable manifest; Holy Dove that bearest
> the twin young; Come, hidden Mother; Come, thou that art manifest in
> thy deeds and dost furnish joy and rest for all that are joined with thee;
> Come and partake with us in this Eucharist which we celebrate in thy
> name, and in this love-feast [*agape*] in which we are gathered together
> at thy call.

In a second instance (133) he is said to bless the bread with these
words: "[Bread] of life, those who eat of which remain incorruptible;
bread which fills hungry souls with its blessing—thou art the one
[thought worthy] to receive a gift, that thou mayest become for us forgiveness of sins, and they who eat it become immortal. We name over
thee the name of the mother of the ineffable mystery of the hidden
dominions and powers, we name [over thee the name of Jesus]." Before the bread is then distributed, a further petition is made: "Let the
power of blessing come and [settle upon the bread], that all the souls
which partake of it may be washed of their sins!" And at a Eucharist at
which both bread and cup are used, the prayer begins: "Thy holy body
which was crucified for us we eat, and thy blood which was poured
out for us for salvation we drink. Let thy body, then, become for us
salvation, and thy blood for remission of sins" (158).[16]
Where did prayers of this type originate? Such direct invocations
for the deity to be present are not characteristic of Jewish prayers from
this period nor of Greco-Roman prayers, although it has been sug-

[15] This, even though only bread is mentioned as having been used.
[16] ET from Schneemelcher, ed., *New Testament Apocrypha II*, 359–60, 391–92,
401.

38

gested that their roots might lie in the magic spells of the ancient Mediterranean world.[17] The most likely antecedent for an early Christian use of direct invocation seems to be the eschatological entreaty for the return of the risen Lord, "Our Lord, come!" found in Aramaic (*marana tha*) in 1 Corinthians 16:22 and *Didache* 10.6 and in Greek in Revelation 22:20. As the expectation of an imminent Parousia began to decline, it would not have been unnatural for the invocation to have been interpreted instead as a call for Christ to be present within the act of worship and so subsequently to constitute the sole content of the prayer in these Syrian examples here. That the appeal could be to the Spirit as well as, or instead of, Christ should not surprise us, since clear differentiation of roles had not yet been reached in the evolving doctrine of the triune God. Later still, short invocations of this kind also begin to be inserted into other eucharistic prayers, as we shall see in the fourth-century examples in this and the next chapter.

Apart from these instances in early apocryphal literature, there are several later eucharistic texts that seem to scholars to be amplified versions of prayers that may have their origin in the third century, or even earlier. By stripping off what appear to be subsequent accretions and developments, it may be possible to glimpse what their older core might have been like. All of them commence with a dialogue between the presiding minister and the congregation, along the lines of "Lift up your hearts," "We lift them up to the Lord," etc., which we know was already in use in the third century.[18] One of these prayers is the Anaphora of Addai and Mari. Although all the extant manuscripts of this prayer are of a late date, the comparative geographical and ecclesiastical isolation of East Syria from which it comes and its strongly Semitic character have encouraged scholars to believe that parts of it may be very ancient. Unlike other early extant eucharistic prayers, it appears to have been composed in Syriac rather than Greek. What follows is a tentative attempt to reconstruct a possible very early form of this prayer, before other elements were added and inserted. Among those later elements were a *Sanctus* unit and an invocation of the Holy Spirit on the bread and wine, but apparently not a narrative of institution,

---

[17] See Caroline Johnson, "Ritual Epicleses in the Greek *Acts of Thomas*," in *The Apocryphal Acts of the Apostles: Harvard Divinity School Studies*, ed. François Bovon, Ann Graham Brock, and Christopher R. Matthews (Cambridge, MA: Harvard University Center for the Study of World Religions, 1999), 171–204.

[18] Cyprian, *De dominica oratione* 31.

Institution

even though we find that being added to most other prayers from the fourth century onward. Its tripartite structure of two units expressing praise and a third of petition is reminiscent of the pattern of the prayers in *Didache* 9–10, although the petition seems primarily for God to remember Christians who have died rather than for the ingathering of the church into the kingdom—something perhaps stemming originally from the use of the prayer at anniversaries of the departed, a practice to which we shall return toward the end of this chapter. It is possible, however, that additional petitions for the living may also have been part of this primitive stratum.

> Glory to you, the adorable and glorious Name, who created the world in his grace and its inhabitants in his compassion, and redeemed humankind in his mercy, and has wrought great grace towards mortals.
>
> We, Lord, your sinful servants, give you thanks because you have brought about in us your grace that cannot be repaid; you put on our humanity to give us life through your divinity; you lifted up our low state and raised our fall; you restored our immortality; you forgave our debts, you justified our sinfulness, you enlightened our understanding, you vanquished our enemies and made triumphant our lowliness. For all your graces towards us, we send up to you glory and honor, now and for ever and ever.
>
> Lord, in your abundant mercies make a gracious remembrance of all the upright and just fathers, of the prophets, apostles, martyrs and confessors. . . .
>
> And for your wonderful plan for us, we, redeemed by your blood, give you thanks with open mouth in your church, now and for ever and ever.[19]

Another prayer that was traditionally thought to date from the third century in its final form is that in the church order known as the *Apostolic Tradition*. Although there is now a growing consensus among scholars that it did not attain this form until the fourth century, it is also recognized that some of the language in it is more consistent with a second-century date and that therefore its core is probably much earlier than its final redaction. Because its construction and contents

[19] ET adapted from Sarhad Jammo, "The Anaphora of the Apostles Addai and Mari: A Study of Structure and Background," OCP 68 (2002): 5–35, although not accepting his reconstruction in all respects. For earlier studies of the prayer and discussion of its development, see Bradshaw, *Eucharistic Origins*, 128–31.

40

resemble later eucharistic prayers belonging to the West Syrian region, it seems very likely that this prayer either originated there or at least underwent development there.[20] Unlike the Anaphora of Addai and Mari, it appears to have had a basic bipartite structure, with a continuous narrative of the work of Christ in the first part and a petition for the unity of the communicants in the second, between which the statement concerning the offering of the bread and cup was probably an early addition. In the following translation, parts that are thought to be later than the rest are shown in italics. As can be seen, these include the narrative of institution and an invocation of the Holy Spirit on the church's offering but in this case not a *Sanctus* unit.

We render thanks to you, God, through your beloved servant Jesus Christ, whom in the last times you sent to us as savior and redeemer and angel of your will, who is your inseparable word, through whom you made all things and it was well pleasing to you, [whom] you sent from heaven into the virgin's womb, and who conceived in the womb was incarnate and manifested as your Son, *born from the Holy Spirit and the virgin*; who fulfilling your will and gaining for you a holy people stretched out [his] hands when he was suffering, that he might release from suffering those who believed in you; who *when he* was *being* handed over to voluntary suffering, that he might destroy death and break the bonds of the devil, and tread down hell and illuminate the righteous, and fix a limit and manifest the resurrection, *taking bread [and] giving thanks to you, he said: "Take, eat, this is my body that will be broken for you." Likewise also the cup, saying, "This is my blood that is shed for you. When you do this, you do my remembrance." Remembering therefore his death and resurrection*, we offer to you the bread and cup, giving thanks to you because you have held us worthy to stand before you and minister to you. And we ask that *you would send your Holy Spirit in the oblation of [your] holy church, [that]* gathering [them] into one you will give to all who partake of the holy things [to partake] in the fullness of the Holy Spirit, for the strengthening of faith in truth, that we may praise and glorify you through your servant Jesus Christ, through whom [be] glory and honor to you, *Father and Son with the Holy Spirit*, in your holy church, both now and to the ages of ages. Amen.[21]

[20] See Matthieu Smyth, "The Anaphora of the So-Called *Apostolic Tradition* and the Roman Eucharistic Prayer," in *Issues in Eucharistic Praying*, ed. Maxwell E. Johnson (Collegeville, MN: Liturgical Press, Pueblo, 2011), 71–97.

[21] For further discussion of its contents, see Bradshaw, Johnson, and Phillips, *The Apostolic Tradition*, 37–48.

Another prayer that has similar shape and language and so may well have originated in the same region, though apparently coming under Egyptian influence later as it was expanded, is that contained in the Barcelona Papyrus, dating from around the middle of the fourth century. Once again, what we believe to be later additions—the *Sanctus* unit, the invocation of the Holy Spirit, and the narrative of institution—are indicated by the use of italics:

It is fitting and right to praise you, to bless you, to hymn you, to give you thanks, O Master, God Pantocrator of our Lord Jesus Christ, who created all things from nonexistence into being, all heaven and the earth, the sea and all that is in them, through your beloved servant Jesus Christ, our Lord, through whom you have called us from darkness into light, from ignorance to knowledge of the glory of his name, from decay of death into incorruption, into life eternal; *who sits on the chariot, cherubim and seraphim before it; beside whom stand thousands of thousands and myriads of myriads of angels, archangels, thrones and dominions, hymning and glorifying, with whom we are also hymning, saying: Holy, holy, holy, Lord of Sabaoth, heaven and earth are full of your glory, in which you have glorified us through your Only-Begotten, the firstborn of every creature, Jesus Christ our Lord,* who sits on the right hand of your greatness in heaven, who is coming to judge the living and the dead, through whom we offer you these your creatures, the bread and the cup: *we ask and beseech you to send on them your Holy and comforter Spirit from heaven to represent them materially and to make the bread the Body of Christ and the cup the Blood of Christ of the New Covenant, as he himself, when he was about to hand [himself over], having taken bread and given thanks, broke it and gave it to his disciples, saying: "Take, eat, this is my body"; likewise after supper, having taken a cup, having given thanks, he gave it to them, saying: "Take, drink the blood which is shed for many for remission of sins." And we also do the same in your remembrance, like those—whenever we meet together, we make the remembrance of you, of the holy mystery of our Teacher and King and Savior Jesus Christ.* Even so we pray to you, Master, that in blessing you will bless and in sanctifying, sanctify . . . for all communicating from them for undivided faith, for communication of incorruption, for communion of the Holy Spirit, for perfection of belief and truth, for fulfillment of all your will, so that in this and again we will glorify Your all-revered and all-holy name, through Your sanctified servant, our Lord Jesus Christ, through whom glory [be] to You, power unto the undefiled ages of ages. Amen.[22]

[22] ET adapted from Michael Zheltov, "The Anaphora and the Thanksgiving Prayer from the Barcelona Papyrus: An Underestimated Testimony to the

There is also a manuscript catalogued as Strasbourg Papyrus 254, which dates from the fourth or fifth century and by verbal parallels reveals itself to be an early version of the Anaphora of St. Mark and so having originated in Egypt but which appears so primitive in its form that many scholars believe it to have come into being considerably earlier. Because it is in such a fragmentary condition, some others have argued that it does not constitute a complete prayer but only part of a much longer one that may already have included elements usually otherwise thought to be fourth-century additions. Once again, however, in its present state it has a simple bipartite form, intersected by a statement of offering that draws on Malachi 1:11, but unlike the other examples we have examined, the first part is concerned exclusively with the theme of creation and the second with wide-ranging intercessions rather than prayer for the church or the communicants. Nowhere, except perhaps in the statement of offering, are there any eucharistic allusions, prompting the possibility that the original core was for more general use and only later adapted for the Eucharist by the insertion of the central section.

. . . to bless [you] . . . [night] and day . . . [you who made] heaven [and] all that is in [it, the earth and what is on earth,] seas and rivers and [all that is] in [them]; [you] who made humanity [according to your] own image and likeness. You made everything through your wisdom, the light [of?] your true Son, our Lord and Saviour Jesus Christ.

Giving thanks through him to you with him and the Holy Spirit, we offer the reasonable sacrifice and this bloodless service, which all the nations offer you, "from sunrise to sunset," from south to north, [for] your "name is great among all the nations, and in every place incense is offered to your holy name and a pure sacrifice."

Through this sacrifice and offering we pray and beseech you, remember your holy and only Catholic Church, all your peoples and all your flocks. Provide the peace which is from heaven in all our hearts, and grant us also the peace of this life. The . . . of the land peaceful things towards us, and towards your [holy] name, the prefect of the province, the army, the princes, councils . . . [*About one-third of a page is lacking here, and what survives is in places too fragmentary to be restored.*]

Anaphoral History in the Fourth Century," *Vigiliae Christianae* 62 (2008): 467–504. For further discussion of the contents of the prayer, see Paul F. Bradshaw, "The Barcelona Papyrus and the Development of Early Eucharistic Prayers," in *Issues in Eucharistic Praying*, ed. Johnson, 129–38.

[for seedtime and] harvest . . . preserve, for the poor of [your] people, for all of us who call upon [your] name, for all who hope in you. Give rest to the souls of those who have fallen asleep; remember those of whom we make mention today, both those whose names we say [and] whose we do not say . . . [Remember] our orthodox fathers and bishops everywhere; and grant us to have a part and lot with the fair . . . of your holy prophets, apostles, and martyrs. Receive(?) [through] their entreaties [these prayers]; grant them through our Lord, through whom be glory to you to the ages of ages.[23]

These are not the only eucharistic prayers in existence that may have developed out of simpler versions from this earlier period—that in the Sacramentary of Sarapion and the Syriac Anaphora of the Twelve Apostles may be mentioned in particular[24]—but the above are sufficient to show that there was no standardized pattern in these early centuries. Prayers might be bipartite or tripartite; might focus on creation or redemption, or both; might pray exclusively for those participating in communion or intercede more widely.

EUCHARISTIC PRESENCE

The sayings of Jesus recorded in New Testament writings that refer to bread and wine as being his body (or flesh) and blood were recalled by a number of second-century Christian writers. Thus Ignatius of Antioch, in a letter to Christians in Philadelphia, in which he is urging them to form a single assembly and not be divided in rival factions, says, "Take care, therefore, to have one Eucharist, for there is one flesh of our Lord Jesus Christ and one cup for union in his blood; one altar, as [there is] one bishop, with the presbytery and deacons, my fellow-servants; so that whatever you do, you do according to God" (*Philadelphians* 4). It is interesting to note that he uses the word "flesh" also found in John's gospel, rather than the word "body," used in the

[23] ET adapted from PEER, 53–54.
[24] See Maxwell E. Johnson, *The Prayers of Sarapion of Thmuis: A Literary, Liturgical, and Theological Analysis*, OCA 249 (Rome: Pontifico Istituto Orientale, 1995), 255–59, 271–76; John R. K. Fenwick, *"The Missing Oblation": The Contents of the Early Antiochene Anaphora*, Grove Liturgical Study 59 (Nottingham: Grove Books, 1989); Robert F. Taft, "The Authenticity of the Chrysostom Anaphora Revisited: Determining the Authorship of Liturgical Texts by Computer," OCP 56 (1990): 5–51 = *idem, Liturgy in Byzantium and Beyond* (Brookfield, VT: Ashgate Variorum, 1995), iii.

44

New Testament accounts of the Last Supper, suggesting that he may not have had them in mind here. In another appeal for unity in his letter to Christians in Ephesus, he calls upon them to break "one and the same bread, which is the medicine of immortality, and the antidote to prevent us from dying, but that we should live for ever in Jesus Christ" (*Ephesians* 20), and in his letter to Christians at Smyrna, he criticizes some who refuse to join in the Eucharist and prayers with the rest because they apparently have a docetic Christology and so "they do not confess the Eucharist to be the flesh of our Savior Jesus Christ, which suffered for our sins, which the Father by his goodness raised up" (*Smyrnaeans* 7). Because in his writings he seems to use the term Eucharist to denote the rite as a whole, he may not be saying in these quotations that what is consumed *are* the flesh and blood of Jesus Christ, but he obviously sees a close association between the two.[25]

For Justin Martyr in the middle of the second century, however, Eucharist has become the name given to the elements themselves:

> of which it is permitted for no one to partake unless he believes our teaching to be true, and has been washed with the washing for forgiveness of sins and regeneration, and so lives as Christ handed down. For not as common bread or common drink do we receive these things; but just as our Savior Jesus Christ, being incarnate through [the] word of God, took both flesh and blood for our salvation, so too we have been taught that the food over which thanks have been given through [a] word of prayer which is from him, from which our blood and flesh are fed by transformation, is both the flesh and blood of that incarnate Jesus. (*First Apology* 66.2)

Here, Justin not only identifies the eucharistic bread and cup with the flesh and blood of Christ but also offers an explanation as to how they become so: it is the result of thanks being given over them (literally, their being "eucharistized") "through [a] word of prayer which is from him." Unfortunately, this phrase has proved difficult to translate. Does it mean "a word of prayer that follows the pattern of Jesus' praying" or "a prayer, the form of words of which come from Jesus [i.e., his words over bread and cup]," or even "through the prayer of the Word [i.e., Jesus] which comes from him [i.e., God]"? Or is it just an elision of the expression found in 1 Timothy 4:5, "every creature of God is

---

[25] See further Frederick C. Klawiter, "The Eucharist and Sacramental Realism in the Thought of St. Ignatius of Antioch," *Studia Liturgica* 37 (2007): 129–63.

nothing is to be refused if it is received with thanksgiving;
ctified by the word of God and prayer"? There seems to be
ıs.[26]

... gh so far, like Ignatius, Justin has been using "flesh" rather than "body," he immediately goes on to quote a version of the Last Supper sayings of Jesus and uses the word "body," thus revealing that he is familiar with that tradition too: "For the apostles in the memoirs composed by them, which are called gospels, have handed down what was commanded them: that Jesus having taken bread, having given thanks, said, 'Do this in my remembrance; this is my body'; and similarly having taken the cup and having given thanks, said, 'This is my blood'; and gave to them alone."[27]

He shows no awareness of the context in which these sayings are found in the New Testament writings, however, and so the "body and blood" language is no more directly linked with the passion and death of Christ than is the "flesh and blood" language: it is seemingly not Christ's dead body, his sacrificed body, that is in mind but his incarnate body, his living body; the bread and cup become the flesh and blood of the incarnate Jesus in order to feed and transform the flesh and blood of believers. His life enables their new life. While it is true, as we shall see later in this chapter, that Christ's suffering is one of the things in remembrance of which Justin believes the eucharistic sacrifice is to be offered, no greater emphasis seems to be placed on that than on thanksgiving for creation or Christ's incarnation.

Later in the second century, Irenaeus consistently uses the language of "body" rather than "flesh" with reference to the bread and, like Justin, sees the eucharistic body and blood of Jesus primarily in terms of nourishment for human flesh and so giving it the hope of resurrection to eternal life rather than as that which was sacrificed for human salvation. In opposition to Gnostics, who denied that Jesus had a human body and so was unable to give eternal life to human flesh, he stressed that what was offered came from the created order:

Then, again, how can they say that the flesh goes to corruption and does not partake of life, when it is nourished by the Lord's body and blood? Therefore, let them either change their opinion or refrain from

---

[26] See further Bradshaw, *Eucharistic Origins*, 91–93.

[27] Justin Martyr, *First Apology* 66.3. See further Bradshaw, *Eucharistic Origins*, 15–16.

46

understanding that would have fueled need to be at table

offering the things just mentioned. But our opinion agrees with the Eucharist, and the Eucharist in turn confirms our opinion. For we offer to God those things which belong to God, proclaiming fittingly the communion and unity of the flesh and the spirit. For as the bread, which is produced from the earth, when it receives the invocation of God is no longer common bread, but the Eucharist, consisting of two realities, the earthly and the heavenly; so also our bodies, when they receive the Eucharist, are no longer corruptible, but have the hope of resurrection.[28]

Although in two passages Irenaeus, like Justin, does employ the expression "eucharistized" (*Adversus haereses* 1.13.2; 4.18.4) with reference to eucharistic consecration and in another passage appears to associate the act of thanksgiving with sanctification ("we make offering to God, not as though to one who stands in need of it, but giving thanks for God's gift and sanctifying what has been created"),[29] yet his preference seems to be to introduce a different Greek word into the vocabulary associated with this idea—*epiklesis*, "invocation," as in the above quotation. In a later passage in the same work, he says, "When, therefore, both the cup that has been mixed and the bread that has been made receive the word of God and become the Eucharist of Christ's body and blood, from which the substance of our flesh is increased and made consistent, how can they deny that flesh is capable of receiving the gift of God which is eternal life, [since] it is nourished by Christ's body and blood, and is his member?"[30]

Although these passages do not necessarily mean that Irenaeus was already familiar with an explicit liturgical formula invoking the Word (*Logos*) within the eucharistic prayer itself,[31] yet they do lay the groundwork for the sort of invocations we saw in the third-century *Acts of Thomas* earlier in this chapter and for the epicleses we encounter in fourth-century eucharistic prayers. In any case, the subsequent trend was for Christian authors to refer to the prayer as a whole as an *epiklesis*, certainly implying that the primary understanding of its function had shifted from praise to petition.

[28] Irenaeus, *Adversus haereses* 4.18.5; ET from David N. Power, *Irenaeus of Lyons on Baptism and Eucharist*, Alcuin/GROW Joint Liturgical Study 18 (Nottingham: Grove Books, 1991), 21.

[29] Irenaeus, *Adversus haereses* 4.18.6; ibid., 21.

[30] Irenaeus, *Adversus haereses* 5.2.3; ibid., 23.

[31] See S. Agrelo, "Epiclesis y eucaristía en S. Ireneo," *Ecclesia Orans* 3 (1986): 7–27.

At the end of the second century, Tertullian speaks in similar realistic terms of the eucharistic elements as do the earlier writers, declaring that the bread is the Lord's body (e.g., *De oratione* 19; *De idolatria* 7) and that human flesh feeds on the body and blood of Christ in order that the soul may be fattened on God (*De resurrectione carnis* 8.3). On the other hand, in his controversy with Marcion, where he is concerned to argue the reality of Christ's incarnate body against his opponent's docetism, he instead makes use of the noun *figura*, "figure," and its related verb *figurare* in relation to body and blood in two passages. First, in seeking to expound the meaning of the Septuagint text of Jeremiah 11:19, "Come, let us cast wood on his bread," he says that bread here signifies body. "For thus did God also in your own Gospel[32] reveal it, calling bread his body, so that thereby you may understand that he has given to bread the figure of his body, whose body the prophet formerly represented [*figuravit*] as bread, while the Lord himself would subsequently interpret this mystery [*sacramentum*]" (*Adversus Marcionem* 3.19.3–4). He returns to this same supposed prophecy of the passion later in the work:

> Having taken bread and given it to the disciples, he made it his body by saying, "This is my body," that is, the figure of my body. A figure, however, there could not have been, unless there were a real body. An empty thing, or phantom, is incapable of a figure. On the other hand, if he pretended the bread was his body, because he lacked a real body, he must therefore have handed over bread for us. It would support Marcion's docetism [*vanitatem*] for bread to have been crucified! But why would he call his body bread, and not rather a melon, which Marcion must have had in place of a heart? He did not understand how ancient was this figure of the body of Christ, who said through Jeremiah: "They have plotted against me, saying, Come, let us cast wood on his bread," meaning the cross on his body. And thus the illuminator of the ancient [prophecies] declared plainly what he had then wished the bread to mean when he called the bread his body. Similarly, when mentioning the cup and making the covenant to be sealed by his blood, he confirms the reality of his body. For blood can belong to no body except one of flesh. For if an unfleshly kind of body were set before us, unless it were fleshly, it would certainly not have blood. Thus, proof of the body depends on the evidence of the flesh, proof of the flesh on the evidence of the blood. (*Adversus Marcionem* 4.40.3–4)

[32] I.e., Luke, the only gospel accepted by the Marcionites.

He then goes on to quote the use of wine as a figure for blood in Isaiah 63 and in Genesis 49:11 and concludes, "Thus he has now also consecrated his blood in the wine who then represented the wine as [literally: in] the blood."

Taking these passages together, the meaning of *figura* for Tertullian in this context is clear. Just as bread and wine in the Old Testament texts are seen as prophetic prefigurations of the body and blood of Christ, so too were the bread and wine that Jesus took at the Last Supper. It is important to note, however, that Tertullian is here speaking about the Last Supper, and he does not say that the bread and wine of the Christian Eucharist are also to be understood in terms of *figura*. Whatever may have been the usage of the word by later writers,[33] such a conclusion does not necessarily follow, any more than Tertullian's apparent belief that it was the words of Jesus that made the bread his body at the Last Supper ("he made it his body by saying, 'This is my body'") mean that he also believed that it was necessary for these words to be recited in the Christian Eucharist in order to consecrate the bread.

On the other hand, two other points should also be noted about the passage quoted above. First, unlike earlier Christian writers, Tertullian does make an explicit link between Jesus' words over bread and cup and the passion, and especially connects the cup with "the covenant to be sealed by his blood." He thus implies that the New Testament narratives are at last beginning to shape eucharistic theology. Second, he uses the language of "consecrate" in relation to the wine, not only here ("he has now also consecrated his blood in the wine"), but also in *De anima* 17.13 ("wine which he consecrated in memory of his blood"). He gives no clearer indication as to what he meant by this word, however, nor—unlike his predecessors Justin and Irenaeus—how he thought the consecration was effected, although the *De anima* quotation would seem to imply that he recognized some sort of distinction existing between the blood of Christ shed on the cross and what was consecrated in the cup. To this passage we may add *Adversus Marcionem* 1.14, where Tertullian uses the word *repraesentat* when speaking of the relationship between the eucharistic bread and Christ's body. On the basis of his use of this verb and its associated noun *repraesentatio*

---

[33] For that usage, see Victor Saxer, "Figura corporis et sanguinis Domini: une formule eucharistique des premiers siècles chez Tertullien, Hippolyte et Ambroise," *Rivista di archeologia cristiana* 47 (1971): 65–89.

in other contexts,[34] "manifests" might be a better translation here than "represents." It is impossible, however, to expound his theology of eucharistic presence any further than this.

The third-century Syrian *Didascalia* also understands the consecration of the bread and wine to result from an invocation, but in this case of the Holy Spirit rather than the Logos: "prayer is also heard through the Holy Spirit, and the Eucharist is accepted and sanctified through the Holy Spirit. . . . Offer an acceptable Eucharist, the likeness of the body of the kingdom of Christ . . . pure bread that is made with fire and sanctified by means of invocations."[35] On the other hand, the theologian Origen simply says that consecration is effected through prayer, but offers no explanation of the nature of the prayer: "we, giving thanks to the Creator of all, also eat the bread that is presented with thanksgiving and prayer over what is given; and it becomes through prayer a holy body and sanctifies those who partake of it with pure intention" (*Contra Celsum* 8.33). Similarly, in his commentary on Matthew's gospel written in 249, he echoes 1 Timothy 4:5 when he speaks of the eucharistic bread being sanctified by the word of God and prayer (*Commentarium in Matthaeum* 11.14). He is also much more cautious than other early Christian writers with regard to realistic language about the bread and cup being the body and blood of the Lord: "God the Word was not saying that the visible bread which he was holding in his hands was his body, but rather the word, in whose mystery the bread was to be broken. He was not saying that the visible drink was his blood, but the word, in whose mystery the drink was to be poured out. For what else could the body and blood of God the Word be except the word which nourishes and the word which 'makes glad the heart' [Psalm 103:15]?"[36]

EUCHARISTIC SACRIFICE

We mentioned in the first chapter St. Paul's interpretation of the Christian meal in terms of the image of a communion-sacrifice. While

---

[34] See the examples cited in Dix, *The Shape of the Liturgy*, 255–56.

[35] *Didascalia* 6.21–22; ET from Michael Vasey and Sebastian Brock, *The Liturgical Portions of the Didascalia*, Grove Liturgical Study 29 (Nottingham: Grove Books, 1982), 32–33.

[36] Origen, *Commentarium in Matthaeum* 85; ET from Daniel J. Sheerin, *The Eucharist*, Message of the Fathers of the Church 7 (Wilmington, DE: Michael Glazier, 1986), 188.

this particular understanding was not taken up by subsequen
tian theologians, the idea of the Eucharist as being in some ser
sacrifice certainly was. The propriety of animal offerings had a
risen within both Judaism and Greek religion before the emerg,
Christianity, and the Jewish sect known as Essenes had already developed the idea that praise and prayer, the "fruit of the lips" (Prov 18:20;
Hos 14:2), could constitute an acceptable temporary substitute for the
temple cult, from which they had separated themselves, believing it
to have become totally corrupt. It is not surprising, therefore, to find
the notion emerging among early Christians that praise and prayer
had permanently replaced the sacrifices in the Jewish temple. Thus,
the letter to the Hebrews could say, "through him [Jesus], therefore, let
us continually offer to God a sacrifice of praise, that is, the fruit of lips
that confess his name" (13:15); Justin Martyr could insist that "prayers
and thanksgivings that are made by those who are worthy are the only
perfect and pleasing sacrifices to God" (*Dialogue with Trypho* 117.2);
and Tertullian, that prayer is "the spiritual victim which has abolished
the former sacrifices" (*De oratione* 28).

Naturally, the thanksgiving prayers of the Eucharist formed a principal expression of this sacrificial praise by Christians, and hence it
is only to be expected that that rite should be referred to in sacrificial
terms. *Didache* 14 appears to be the earliest explicit example of this:
"Having assembled together on the Lord's day of the Lord, break
bread and give thanks, having first confessed your faults, so that your
sacrifice may be pure. Let no one having a dispute with his neighbor
assemble with you until they are reconciled, that your sacrifice may
not be defiled. For this is what was spoken by the Lord, 'In every place
and time offer me a pure sacrifice; for I am a great king, says the Lord,
and my name is wonderful among the nations.'"

The second sentence echoes Matthew 5:23-24: "If, therefore, you are
offering your gift at the altar and there remember that your brother
has something against you, leave your gift there before the altar and
first go and be reconciled with your brother and then come and offer
your gift." This sentiment is combined with the quotation of Malachi
1:11, 14 in order to argue that moral purity is required of those who
participate in the sacrificial act. The quotation of Malachi 1:11 was
taken up in later Christian writings as part of their polemic against
the Jews, arguing that Christian worship was that which was offered
in every place by the Gentiles and so regarded as pure by God and

not the worship that was offered in one place, the temple.[37] They also argued that it was "pure" because it did not involve the shedding of blood—it was instead "a bloodless sacrifice and spiritual worship."[38]

Although at first the Eucharist seems to have been understood as being just one expression of the wider offering of prayer by Christians, it soon attracted to itself a more specific sacrificial interpretation. As we have seen, Justin Martyr asserted that "prayers and thanksgivings made by those who are worthy are the only perfect and pleasing sacrifices to God," but he did go on to say that "Christians have undertaken to make these alone, and in the remembrance [consisting] of their solid and liquid food, in which the suffering that the Son of God underwent for them is remembered" (*Dialogue with Trypho* 117.3). While Justin here understands the Christian sacrifice to be offered in remembrance of Christ's suffering, in an earlier passage, commenting on Isaiah 33:16 ("bread shall be given to him, and his water shall be sure"), he includes remembrance of Christ's incarnation along with his passion; indeed, he seems to give it equal if not greater prominence than the passion. This prophecy, he says, refers "to the bread which our Christ commanded us to offer in remembrance of his being made flesh for the sake of those believing in him, for whom also he suffered; and to the cup which he commanded us to offer in remembrance of his blood, giving thanks."[39]

Elsewhere in the same work he interpreted the offering of the bread of the Eucharist as being the fulfillment of the thank-offering prescribed in the Old Testament for those cured of leprosy (Lev 14:10) and thus still as a part of the offering of thanksgiving:

> The offering of fine flour . . . which was commanded to be offered on behalf of those purified from leprosy, was a type of the bread of

---

[37] See, for example, Justin Martyr, *Dialogue with Trypho* 28.5; 116.3; 117.1, 3.

[38] Athenagoras, *Plea for the Christians* 13. See further Kenneth W. Stevenson, "'The Unbloody Sacrifice': The Origins and Development of a Description of the Eucharist," in *Fountain of Life*, ed. Gerard Austin (Washington, DC: Pastoral Press, 1991), 103–30.

[39] Justin Martyr, *Dialogue with Trypho* 70.4. The verb translated here twice as "offer" is *poiein*, meaning literally "to do," but it can have cultic overtones, as in "do this in remembrance of me," and in the light of the next passage to be quoted (41.3), where the more common verb for offer, *prospherein*, as well as the noun *thusia*, "sacrifice," are used, this seems to be what is intended here.

52

the Eucharist, which our Lord Jesus Christ commanded [us] to do, in remembrance of the suffering which he underwent on behalf of those who are being purified in soul from every wickedness, so that we may at the same time give thanks to God for having created the world with everything in it for the sake of human beings, and for having delivered us from the evil in which we existed, having completely overthrown principalities and powers through him who suffered according to his will. Hence, God is speaking about the sacrifices then offered by you, as I said before, through Malachi, one of the twelve [prophets]: "I have no pleasure in you, says the Lord; and I will not accept your sacrifices at your hands: for, from the rising of the sun to its going down, my name has been glorified among the nations, and in every place incense is offered to my name, and a pure offering; for my name is great among the nations, says the Lord; but you profane it" [Mal 1:10-12]. He is then speaking of us, the nations who in every place offer sacrifices to him, that is, the bread of the Eucharist, and likewise the cup of the Eucharist, stating both that we glorify his name and that you profane [it]. (*Dialogue with Trypho* 41.1–3)

Like Justin, Irenaeus too speaks of the bread and cup as being offered to God and once again chooses a thank-offering, in this case offering of firstfruits (see, for example, Deut 26), as the Old Testament archetype for it:

The Lord gave directions to his disciples to offer first-fruits to God from God's own creatures, not as though God stood in need of them, but that they themselves may be neither unfruitful nor ungrateful. Thus, he took the bread, which comes from creation, and he gave thanks, saying, "This is my body." He did likewise with the cup, which is part of the creation to which we ourselves belong, declaring it to be his blood, and [so] he taught the new offering of the new covenant. This is the offering which the church received from the apostles, and which it offers throughout the whole world, to God who provides us with nourishment, the first-fruits of divine gifts in this new covenant.

Of this offering, among the prophets, Malachi had spoken beforehand in these terms: "I have no pleasure in you, says the Lord almighty, and I will not accept sacrifice from your hands. For from the rising of the sun even to its setting my name is glorified among the nations, and in every place incense is offered to my name, and a pure sacrifice; for my name is great among the nations, says the Lord almighty" [Mal 1:10-11]. By these words, he shows in the plainest manner that the former people [the Jews] shall cease to make offering to God, but that in every place sacrifice shall be offered to God, one that is pure, and that God's name is glorified among the nations.[40]

Even though the older notion of the offering of praise continued to persist alongside it into the fourth century, it appears to have been out of interpretations like these that the bread and cup came more generally to be thought of as the "oblation"—the substance of the eucharistic sacrifice—from the third century onward and, as we have seen, for some eucharistic prayers to incorporate a statement that these were being offered. This idea would no doubt have been encouraged by the fact that the participants continued to bring these gifts with them from home to present, just as they had previously brought food and drink to contribute to the supper.[41]

The understanding of the Eucharist as a sacrifice also had two other consequences. The first was an increased tendency to view martyrdom through eucharistic images. Although the description of a martyr's death as "drinking the cup" is already found in some New Testament texts (Matt 20:22-23; 26:39, 42; and parallels; John 18:11), the imagery was extensively developed in later writings. Thus, Ignatius of Antioch describes his impending death in terms of a desire to be "poured out to God, while an altar is still ready." He is "God's wheat, and I am ground by the teeth of wild beasts that I may be found pure bread of Christ."[42] Similar expressions are found in other sources, among them the *Martyrdom of Polycarp* and the *Passion of Saints Perpetua and Felicity*.[43] Robin Darling Young has commented that martyrdom thus "functioned as a public liturgical sacrifice in which the word of Jesus and his kingdom was confessed and acted out, and an offering made that repeated his own. If the Eucharist of the early Christians was a kind of substitute sacrifice, then the martyrs' was an imitative one."[44] This

---

[40] Irenaeus, *Adversus haereses* 4.17.5; ET from Power, *Irenaeus of Lyons on Baptism and Eucharist*, 15–16.

[41] For examples, see *Didascalia* 2.58; *Apostolic Tradition* 4.2; 20.10; Cyprian, *De opere et eleemosynis* 15.

[42] *Romans* 2.2; 4.1.

[43] See Paul F. Bradshaw and Maxwell E. Johnson, *The Origins of Feasts, Fasts, and Seasons in Early Christianity*, Alcuin Club Collections 86 (London: SPCK; Collegeville, MN: Liturgical Press, 2011), 173–81.

[44] Robin Darling Young, *In Procession before the World: Martyrdom as Public Liturgy in Early Christianity*, The Père Marquette Lecture in Theology, 2001 (Milwaukee, WI: Marquette University Press, 2001), 11.

emphasis is borne out in a special way in the *Martyrdom of Polycarp*, where we encounter the martyr himself being said to pray a eucharistic-type prayer in which he offers *himself*, rather than the bread and cup, in sacrifice as the eucharistic oblation:

> They did not nail him [Polycarp], but tied him. He, with his hands placed behind him and tied like a noble ram [taken] from a great flock for sacrifice, prepared as a burnt offering acceptable to God, looked up to heaven and said:
>
> "Lord God Almighty, Father of your beloved and blessed servant Jesus Christ, through whom we have received the knowledge of you, the God of angels and powers and all creation and of the whole race of the righteous who live before you: I bless you, because you have deemed me worthy of this day and this hour, to receive a part in the number of the martyrs, in the cup of Christ, for resurrection to eternal life of soul and body in the incorruption of the Holy Spirit; among whom may I be accepted before you this day as a rich and acceptable sacrifice, just as you have prepared and revealed beforehand and fulfilled, O ever truthful God. For this and for all things I praise you, I bless you, I glorify you through the eternal and heavenly high priest, Jesus Christ, your beloved servant, through whom be glory to you with him and the Holy Spirit both now and to the ages to come. Amen."[45]

Scholars have often pointed to this prayer as an example of an essentially bipartite anaphoral-type prayer, consisting of praise and supplication with concluding doxology, that a mid-second-century bishop might use to preside at the celebration of the Eucharist, with the exception, of course, that rather than the bread and cup of the Eucharist being offered, it is the martyr himself who becomes the "rich and acceptable sacrifice."[46] Candida Moss has recently challenged the

---

[45] *Martyrdom of Polycarp* 14.
[46] David Tripp argues that Polycarp's prayer was an example of second-century eucharistic praying from Western Anatolia that may well have been related to an early version of the eucharistic prayer in *Apostolic Tradition* 4; see David Tripp, "The Prayer of St. Polycarp and the Development of Anaphoral Prayer," *Ephemerides Liturgicae* 104 (1990): 97–132, here at 104; also Albertus G. A. Horsting, "Transfiguration of Flesh: Literary and Theological Connections Between Martyrdom Accounts and Eucharistic Prayers," in *Issues in Eucharistic Praying*, ed. Johnson, 307–26; and Maxwell E. Johnson, "Sharing 'The Cup of Christ': The Cessation of Martyrdom and Anaphoral Development," in *Acts*

conventional view that the *Martyrdom* was composed immediately after Polycarp's death in the middle of the second century and argued that its sophisticated and nuanced view of martyrdom, as well as the fact that it appears to have had no literary impact before the second half of the third century, makes it difficult to date earlier than that century.[47] And indeed, the style of prayer does seem more in line with eucharistic prayers of the later period, even if it has incorporated within it some more archaic words and phrases.

The second consequence was that the eucharistic sacrifice came to be offered not just for the benefit of the gathered congregation but also in intercession for those who had died. The roots of this lie in the practice in the surrounding culture of families assembling at the graves of their deceased relatives on certain days following the death and on its anniversary thereafter. They would bring food and eat, drink, sing, and dance there, sharing the meal with the departed symbolically, and the drink quite literally, by pouring libations through a hole or tube into the tomb.[48] Not only would Christian families have done the same, but the burial places of martyrs attracted much larger crowds of believers. In both cases this eucharistic meal was understood as a sacrificial offering for the benefit of those who had died. Thus Tertullian states that "we make offerings for the departed, for their birthdays on the anniversary,"[49] and the *Didascalia* instructs its readers to come together "both in your congregations and in your cemeteries and on the departures of those who are fallen asleep . . . and without doubting

---

of the Third International Congress of the Society of Oriental Liturgy, Volos, Greece, 26–30 May 2010, ed. Basilius J. Groen and Steven Hawkes Teeples, Eastern Christian Studies (Leuven, 2012).

[47] Candida Moss, "On the Dating of Polycarp: Rethinking the Place of the *Martyrdom of Polycarp* in the History of Christianity," *Early Christianity* 4 (2010): 1–37.

[48] See Ramsay McMullen, *The Second Church: Popular Christianity A.D. 200–400* (Atlanta, GA: Society of Biblical Literature, 2009), 24–25, 77.

[49] Tertullian, *De corona* 3. See also Tertullian, *De monogamia* 10. The term "birthday" (in Latin, *natale*) was commonly used by early Christians to denote the day of a believer's death, and especially that of the martyrs, as being their birth into eternal life. But cf. Eoin de Bhaldraithe, "*Oblationes pro defunctis, pro nataliciis annua die facimus*: What did Tertullian mean?," *Studia Patristica* 20 (1989): 346–51, who argued that the oblation was only prepared on the anniversary and not actually offered until the following Sunday.

you should pray and offer for those who are fallen asleep."[50] Cyprian too speaks of the Eucharist being offered for the repose of the departed (*Ep.* 1.2) and on the anniversaries of the deaths of martyrs and confessors under persecution (*Ep.* 12.2; 39.3). Although such gatherings came to form the central act of piety of many Christians, behavior at them often attracted disapproval. Tertullian censured those who participated in them for taking food to present to themselves rather than to the departed and for returning home drunk (*De testimonio animae* 4), and similar criticisms continued in the fourth century from ecclesiastical authorities unable to abolish or even control the activities at them, and especially the dancing with its obvious sexual overtones.[51]

It was Cyprian, however, who developed the idea of eucharistic sacrifice beyond any of his predecessors. In the letter to Caecilius, bishop of Biltha, that we quoted earlier in this chapter, Cyprian, like Justin and Irenaeus before him, asserted that what was offered was the bread and cup (*Ep.* 63.2, 9, and passim), and he was explicit that this was done in remembrance of Christ, *in commemorationem eius* (*Ep.* 63.2 and 14), "in remembrance of the Lord and of his passion" (*Ep.* 63.17). But he went further than this and described the act as being "the sacrament of our Lord's passion and of our redemption" (*Ep.* 63.14) and even said that "we make mention of his passion in all sacrifices, for the Lord's passion is the sacrifice that we offer" (*Ep.* 63.17). This language arose out of the same principle of the necessity of imitating Christ that Cyprian had used to argue against the use of water alone in the Eucharist: "Hence it appears that the blood of Christ is not offered if wine is absent from the cup, nor the Lord's sacrifice celebrated with a legitimate consecration unless our oblation and sacrifice correspond to the passion" (*Ep.* 63.9). In the Eucharist, it is not only Christ's action at the Supper but also his sacrifice of himself on the cross that must be imitated: "For if Jesus Christ, our Lord and God, is himself the high priest of God the Father and first offered himself as a sacrifice to the Father, and commanded this to be done in his remembrance, then that priest truly functions in the place of Christ who imitates what Christ did and then offers a true and full sacrifice in the church to God the Father, if he thus proceeds to offer according to what he sees Christ himself to have offered" (*Ep.* 63.14).

---

[50] *Didascalia* 6.22; ET from Vasey and Brock, *The Liturgical Portions of the Didascalia*, 33.

[51] McMullen, *The Second Church*, 29, 60–62.

Cyprian does not speak of the offering as being the corporate action of the priestly people of God, as earlier writers had done, but rather of the bishop functioning as a priest on behalf of the people, the Latin term *sacerdos* being used primarily to denote the episcopal office and only secondarily the presbyteral office, a development also found in some other third-century sources.[52] But Cyprian is the first to take this idea further and view the bishop as acting "in the place of Christ" (*vice Christi*). Scholars are divided over precisely what he meant. Some would interpret Cyprian as saying that in the Eucharist the priest offers the same sacrifice that Christ offered on the cross, i.e., that he "offers Christ," while others do not think that the image should be taken quite so literally, that it means something like, "just as Christ offered himself as a sacrifice, so too does the priest offer the Church's sacrifice in memory of him."[53] If that is so, then Cyprian's remarks that "the Lord's passion is the sacrifice which we offer" and "the blood of Christ . . . is offered" should be understood in the light of that. But whatever Cyprian may have meant, his language certainly paved the way for a closer association between Christ's sacrifice and the eucharistic offering that we find among fourth-century theologians.

SUMMARY

1. The transition from full meal to symbolic rite appears to have been gradual, taking place before the middle of the second century in some places, after the middle of the third century in others, and probably chiefly related to the relative size of a congregation.

2. The use of separate prayers over bread and cup was gradually replaced by a single prayer, at first still largely extemporized, with the primary emphasis shifting from the thanksgiving aspect of it to its character as invocation, *epiklesis*.

---

[52] See Cyprian, *Ep.* 1.1 and *Ep.* 61.3, where presbyters are said to participate in the episcopal priesthood; and also *Didascalia* 2.26, where the bishop is called a "high-priest"; Origen, *De oratione* 28, where the bishop is designated as a priest, and his *Homilia in Exodum* 11.6 and *Homilia in Leviticum* 6.6, where presbyters are described as exercising an inferior form of priesthood.

[53] See further John D. Laurance, *Priest as Type of Christ: The Leader of the Eucharist in Salvation History according to Cyprian of Carthage* (New York: Lang, 1984).

3. Highly realistic language tended to be used to identify the bread and cup as the body and blood of Christ, although some writers display an element of caution in this regard.
4. Praise and prayer were understood as the primary sacrifice that was offered in the Eucharist, although the bread and cup themselves also came to be associated with that offering.
5. The Eucharist might be offered not just for the benefit of the communicants but also for the benefit of Christians who had died, and especially the martyrs, at their place of burial.
6. Cyprian took sacrificial language further and spoke of "the Lord's passion" as being the sacrifice that was offered and of that action being performed by the clergy on behalf of the people.

Chapter 3

The Fourth and Fifth Centuries
Historical Context and Rites

The fourth-century imperial acceptance of Christianity brought about significant and long-lasting changes in the way that the Eucharist was celebrated. Though these changes have at times been exaggerated, we can discern some major shifts that are attributable to what may be called either—or both—the Constantinian "revolution" or "evolution."[1] First, Christians were no longer subject to persecution, but were now followers of a legitimate, respectable, and favored religion, a *cultus publicus* that sought the divine favor in order to secure the well-being of the state. So it needed to have more of the appearance of other contemporary religions—temples, altars, a visible priesthood, and so on—and its worship therefore took on more of the features of the worship of other religions. Its number of adherents grew, and so it occupied larger and grander buildings than before (i.e., basilicas). As John Baldovin has noted, the use of basilicas was particularly important, for their adaptation and use "signified the move of Christian worship into public space. The basic basilican form was that of a public meeting place—as imperial court, court of justice, or assembly hall, etc. It was transformed on a longitudinal axis to meet the requirements of Christian processions, many of which began in outdoor spaces."[2] And James White adds that, with the termination of the basilica in its semicircular apse,

> the bishop simply took the place of the judge on the throne in the apse, flanked by presbyters. In front of him stood the altar table, first wood, later stone. Eventually low screens railed in a space in front of it for the

[1] See Paul Bradshaw, *The Search for the Origins of Christian Worship*, 2nd ed. (London: SPCK; New York: Oxford University Press, 2002), 211ff.
[2] John Baldovin, "Christian Worship to the Eve of the Reformation," in *The Making of Jewish and Christian Worship*, ed. Paul F. Bradshaw and Lawrence A. Hoffman (Notre Dame, IN: University of Notre Dame Press, 1991), 156–83, here at 165.

61

singers, and an ambo (pulpit) accommodated readings; the rest was open congregational space where the people stood, usually divided by sexes. For well over a thousand years the posture of worship was standing.[3]

And with regard to this, preaching was done from the *cathedra* or "chair" until the locus shifted to the ambo (pulpit), a shift credited to John Chrysostom as being the first to preach from the ambo rather than the chair.[4]

Closely related to these architectural shifts, worship became more formal in style and incorporated rituals and symbols from the civic world around to suit this new setting. Hence, there is a rapid growth in ceremonial in this period; many aspects of the imperial court were adopted, with incense, processional lights, and ceremonial fans becoming common. The result of all this, at least in the major cities, says Baldovin, "was what Aidan Kavanagh has called 'liturgy on the town,' the use of public streets and places as well as shrines and basilicas for an open manifestation of Christianity as now the dominant religious force in the society. Similarly, different churches and shrines were increasingly employed for liturgy on different feast days and fast days creating systems that have been called 'stational liturgy.'"[5]

In his short book on the history of monasticism, David Knowles succinctly describes this period of history:

> The conversion of Constantine [brings about] the swift transformation of the Church from a persecuted and fervent sect into a ruling and rapidly increasing body, favoured and directed by the emperor, membership of which was a material advantage. In the sequel, the standards of life and the level of austerity were lowered and the Christian Church became what it has in large measure remained ever since, a large body in which a few are exceptionally devout, while many are sincere believers without any pretension to fervour, and a sizeable number, perhaps even a majority, are either on their way to losing the faith, or retain it in spite of a life which neither obeys in all respects the

---

[3] James White, *A Brief History of Christian Worship* (Nashville, TN: Abingdon Press, 1993), 72.

[4] See ibid., 69.

[5] John Baldovin, "Christian Worship to the Eve of the Reformation," 165. See also *idem, The Urban Character of Christian Worship*, OCA 228 (Rome: Pontificio Istituto Orientale, 1987).

commands of Christ nor shares in the devotional and sacramental life of the Church with regularity.[6]

Hence, because many of the new converts were by no means as well instructed in the Christian faith or as deeply committed as most of its former adherents had been, a second characteristic of this period is the behavior of Christians at worship. And that behavior during church services often left much to be desired. Although, like most preachers, John Chrysostom (ca. 347–407 CE) may have been inclined to exaggerate the extent of their irreverent conduct, there was surely some basis in reality when he accused members of the congregation in Constantinople of roaming around during the services (*In Matt. hom.* 19.7–9); of either ignoring the preacher (ibid., 32/33.6) or pushing and shoving to get nearer to hear him (*In Joh. hom.* 3.1),[7] when not bored or downright exasperated with him (*De sacerdotio* 5.8); of talking, especially during readings,[8] and of leaving before the liturgy was over.[9] The women caused distractions by the way they decked themselves in finery, makeup, and jewelry (*In Matt. hom.* 73/74.3); young people spent their time laughing, joking, and talking (*In Act. hom.* 24.4); and the behavior between the sexes was apparently so bad that Chrysostom claimed that a wall was needed to keep men and women apart (*In Matt. hom.* 73/74.3).[10] All of these factors had a profound effect on the form and nature of the eucharistic celebration in church, although the apparently common practice of also celebrating the Eucharist in private homes was perhaps a residual memory of its former domestic setting.[11]

[6] David Knowles, *Christian Monasticism* (New York: McGraw-Hill, 1969), 12.

[7] See also Sozomen, *Hist. eccl.* 8.5.2; Socrates, *Hist. eccl.* 6.5.5.

[8] Origen had earlier made the same complaint: *In Gen. hom.* 10.1; *In Exod. hom.* 12.2.

[9] This problem was evident also in Antioch; see Chrysostom, *De baptismo Christi* 4.1.

[10] We owe all these references to Robert F. Taft, "'Eastern Presuppositions' and Western Liturgical Renewal," *Antiphon* 5 (2000): 10–22, here at 14.

[11] For the evidence for domestic eucharistic celebrations at this time, see Robert F. Taft, "The Frequency of the Eucharist Throughout History," *Can We Always Celebrate the Eucharist?*, *Concilium* 152, ed. Mary Collins and David Power (Edinburgh/New York, 1982): 13–24, esp. 14 = Robert F. Taft, *Beyond East and West: Problems in Liturgical Understanding* (Washington, DC: Pastoral Press, 1984), 61–80 = *Between Memory and Hope: Readings on the Liturgical Year,*

characteristic, closely related to the second, is that the eu-
iturgy was required increasingly to supply an element of
‒to try to communicate the true meaning of what was going
un and to impress upon the worshipers the majesty and transcendence
of God, the divinity of Christ, and the sense of awe that was the appropriate response in his presence in the eucharistic mystery, as well
as the sort of conduct that was called for in their daily lives. But there
are also signs of other attempts to instill in the congregation the right
attitude of mind. These notes were struck in preaching and teaching about the Eucharist as well as in the liturgical rites themselves.
Thus, Chrysostom in his homilies repeatedly speaks of the "dreadful
sacrifice," of the "fearful moment" when the mysteries are accomplished, and of the "terrible and awesome table" that should only be
approached with fear and trembling.[12] But the language of liturgical
prayer also took on a more exalted tone, apparently with a similar
intent. Although it is difficult to be sure of the exact age of this part of
the text, the opening address of the Egyptian version of the eucharistic
prayer of St. Basil (hereafter, EgBAS), for example, emphasizes the
majesty and transcendence of God:

> It is fitting and right, fitting and right, truly it is fitting and right, I AM,
> truly Lord God, existing before the ages, reigning until the ages; you
> dwell on high and regard what is low; you made heaven and earth and
> the sea and all that is in them. Father of our Lord and God and Savior
> Jesus Christ, through whom you made all things visible and invis-
> ible, you sit on the throne of your glory; you are adored by every holy
> power.[13]

---

ed. Maxwell E. Johnson (Collegeville, MN: Liturgical Press, Pueblo, 2000),
77–96; and Stefanos Alexopoulos, *Presanctified Liturgy in the Byzantine Rite:
A Comparative Analysis of Its Origins, Evolution, and Structural Components*,
Liturgia Condenda 21 (Leuven: Peeters, 2009), 8–33. For a more general survey
of fourth-century liturgical developments, see Bradshaw, *The Search for the Origins of Christian Worship*, chap. 10.

[12] See Edmund Bishop, "Fear and Awe Attaching to the Eucharistic Service," in *The Liturgical Homilies of Narsai*, ed. R. H. Connolly (Cambridge 1909
= Nendeln, Liechtenstein 1967), 92–97; J. G. Davies, "The Introduction of the
Numinous into the Liturgy: An Historical Note," *Studia Liturgica* 8 (1971/72):
216–23; Josef Jungmann, *The Place of Christ in Liturgical Prayer* (London, 1965;
reprinted Collegeville, MN: Liturgical Press, 1989), 245–55.

[13] ET from PEER, 70.

In sharp contrast to this exaltation of the divine, the prayer goes on to describe the earthly worshipers as "sinners and unworthy and wretched."

As another illustration of the use of liturgical action as a means of fostering the appropriate attitude of mind at this period, we may cite the detailed instructions given in the *Mystagogical Catecheses* concerning the reverential gestures to be used by the newly baptized when receiving communion:

> Therefore, when you approach, do not come with arms extended or with fingers spread, but making the left (hand) a throne for the right, as if it is about to welcome a king; and cupping the palm, receive Christ's body, responding *Amen*. Then having carefully sanctified the eyes with a touch of the holy body, consume, taking heed not to drop not any of it. . . . Then after partaking of Christ's body, come also to the cup of the blood, not stretching out the hands but bowing and saying *Amen* in the manner of worship and reverence, sanctify yourself also by partaking of Christ's blood. And while the moisture is still on the lips, touching it with your hands, sanctify both the eyes and forehead and the other organs of sense. (*Mystagogical Catechesis* 5.21–22)

Similar directions were also given by Theodore of Mopsuestia: "You should come up in great fear and with much love because of the greatness of the gift—fear because of its great dignity, love because of its grace. . . . When you have received the body in your hands, you adore it. . . . With a great and sincere love you place it on your eyes, kiss it and address to it your prayers as to Christ our Lord."[14] We can see from this that the eucharistic elements were not only to be treated with great reverence when they were consumed but also regarded as objects of power that could be used to confer blessing on a person's body merely by external contact. This is obviously a further development of the belief, which we first encounter in some third-century sources, that the elements possessed apotropaic powers for those who consumed them. In a similar vein, in the sermon at the funeral of his brother Satyrus, Ambrose of Milan (ca. 339–97 CE) relates how Satyrus once wrapped up the eucharistic bread in a cloth and fastened it round his neck for protection before casting himself into the sea when the ship on which he was traveling was wrecked, and so came safely to land (*De exitu fratris* 1.43).

---

[14] *Baptismal Homily* 5.28; ET from AIR, 242.

Fourth, the sense of their unworthiness that was thus instilled in worshipers led to the practice by many of non-communicating attendance at the Eucharist for considerable periods of time. This was made worse by fourth-century preachers warning their congregations against coming to communion while still leading sinful lives, as part of their efforts to urge them to attain high levels of Christian conduct. John Chrysostom again was particularly vigilant in this regard, frequently emphasizing the sincerity and purity of soul necessary to approach the Lord's Supper and even advising those who were guilty of sin to leave the service before the eucharistic action itself began (see, e.g., *In Eph. hom.* 3.4). Unfortunately, however, this strategy produced an unforeseen result. The aim of preaching such as this was, of course, not to discourage the reception of communion but rather to motivate worshipers toward the amendment of their lives. But, as so often happens, the outcome was exactly the opposite. Many people preferred to give up the reception of communion rather than reform their behavior. Contrary to Chrysostom's advice, many people apparently stayed until the time for communion and then left the church. Indeed, the ecclesiastical authorities were eventually forced to accept this practice, and in the end they began to make provision in the rites at the time of the communion for a formal blessing and dismissal of non-communicants in order to encourage a more orderly departure. Theodore of Mopsuestia appears to be the first to refer to such a blessing.[15]

This development also had a significant effect on people's understanding of the Eucharist. It made it possible for them to think of the rite as complete and effective *without* the need for them to receive communion and thus helped to further the idea that liturgy was something that the clergy did on their behalf, which ultimately did not even require their presence. The more professionalized clergy of this period increasingly dominated public worship, and the people were content to let them do it, the pure acting for the impure, the experts for the ignorant. Even John Chrysostom's very assertion that there were some moments when there was no distinction at all between the roles of priest and people in the Eucharist is itself a tacit admission that there were other times when there most definitely was a difference:

---

[15] *Baptismal Homily* 5.22; ET from AIR, 238. For later developments, see Robert F. Taft, "The Inclination Prayer before Communion in the Byzantine Liturgy of St John Chrysostom: A Study in Comparative Liturgy," *Ecclesia Orans* 3 (1986): 29–60.

But there are times when the priest does not differ from those over whom he presides, such as when the awesome mysteries are to be received. . . . And in the prayers also one may see the people contributing much. . . . Again in the most awesome mysteries themselves the priest prays for the people and the people pray for the priest, for the "with your spirit" is nothing else but this. The [prayer] of thanksgiving again is common, for he does not give thanks alone, but the whole people also [do]. (*In 2 Cor. hom.* 18.3)

Fifth, for those who now began to receive communion only infrequently during the year and for the rest of the time attended without communicating, the Eucharist had not only ceased to be a communal action but was no longer even viewed as food to be eaten. Instead, it became principally an object of devotion, to be gazed on from afar. It is not surprising, therefore, that liturgical commentators in this period began to interpret the rite in terms of a drama that unfolded before the eyes of the spectators—what Alexander Schmemann called the development of a "mysteriological piety" divorced increasingly from true liturgical symbolism and tending toward making Christianity a "Mystery Religion."[16]

The earliest instance of this known to us occurs in the baptismal homilies of Theodore of Mopsuestia. He envisages the whole eucharistic liturgy, from the presentation of the bread and wine to the reception of communion, as a ritual allegory re-enacting the events of Jesus' passion, death, burial, and resurrection. This leads him to reinterpret various liturgical actions as representing elements and moments in that story. So, for example, the bringing up of the bread and wine by the deacons is no longer seen as symbolizing their offering by the people but as Christ being led to his passion, and the deacons spreading cloths on the altar "remind us of winding-sheets."[17] For Theodore, the climax of the rite obviously occurs at the invocation of the Holy Spirit during the eucharistic prayer, since "this is the moment appointed for Christ our Lord to rise from the dead and pour out his grace upon us all." The bread and wine, which until now have symbolized the dead body of Jesus, become his risen body.[18] Finally, the breaking of the bread that follows the prayer is seen as symbolizing Christ's sharing of

[16] Alexander Schmemann, *Introduction to Liturgical Theology* (London: Faith Press, 1966), 81–86.

[17] *Baptismal Homily* 4.25–26; ET from AIR, 216–17.

[18] *Baptismal Homily* 5.11–12; ET from AIR, 233–34.

himself in his various resurrection appearances so that everyone was able to come to him, just as the communicants are now able to do.[19]

Although by the end of the fourth century considerable numbers of people were apparently no longer receiving communion every week, there still must have been those who were doing so, and even some—though we do not know how many—who were continuing to take the sacrament home for daily consumption. As we have seen with Tertullian in North Africa, this had been the custom in the third century, and there is evidence for its survival until the seventh century among some laity and even later in monastic circles.[20] Indeed, Jerome (ca. 347–419 CE) complains about Roman Christians who, debarred from receiving communion in church, persisted in receiving the sacrament at home (*Ep.* 49.15).

In spite of the decline in communicants, however, regular eucharistic celebrations were growing more frequent during this period. We have already seen from our limited third-century sources that, in addition to the weekly Sunday celebration, the Eucharist might take place at funerals and on the anniversaries of death, especially those of martyrs, and in North Africa perhaps even on a daily basis during the time of persecution. Although by the end of the fourth century both Alexandria and Rome were apparently still adhering to Sunday as the only regular day of the week for the Eucharist, this was not the case elsewhere. In northern Syria, Asia Minor, Constantinople, and monastic traditions in Egypt, Saturday as well as Sunday regularly seems to have included a celebration of the Eucharist.[21] We have suggested elsewhere[22] that in parts of the world where Christianity retained a

---

[19] *Baptismal Homily* 5.17–18; ET from AIR, 236–37.

[20] See W. A. Freestone, *The Sacrament Reserved: A Survey of the Practice of Reserving the Eucharist, with Special Reference to the Communion of the Sick, During the First Twelve Centuries,* Alcuin Club Collections 21 (London: Mowbray, 1917), 40–44; Otto Nussbaum, *Die Aufbewahrung der Eucharistie* (Bonn 1979), 266–74; Robert F. Taft, "Home Communion in the Late Antique East," in *Ars Liturgiae: Worship, Aesthetics and Praxis: Essays in Honor of Nathan D. Mitchell,* ed. Clare Johnson (Chicago: LTP, 2003), 1–26; and Alexopoulos, *Presanctified Liturgy in the Byzantine Rite,* 8–33.

[21] For references, see Taft, "The Frequency of the Eucharist Throughout History," 14–15.

[22] See Paul F. Bradshaw and Maxwell E. Johnson, *The Origins of Feasts, Fasts, and Seasons in Early Christianity,* Alcuin Club Collections 86 (London: SPCK; Collegeville, MN: Liturgical Press, Pueblo, 2011), 3–24.

strongly Semitic character, respect for the Sabbath may have been obtained from early times, and possibly even a continuing assembly on that day for a service of the word after the Eucharist had been transferred to Sunday. Although we have no direct evidence of this practice, it seems a more likely explanation as the basis for the development of a full eucharistic rite on that day than that there was a sudden resurgence of a "Judaizing" tendency in the fourth century.[23] On the other hand, testimony from some other places speaks of eucharistic celebrations on Wednesdays, Fridays, and Sundays, while at Antioch it was on Friday, Saturday, and Sunday that the Eucharist was held, and seemingly on Wednesday, Friday, Saturday, and Sunday in Jerusalem, at least outside Lent (provided that our sources always mean a full celebration of the Eucharist on all those days and not just the distribution of communion on some of them). By the end of the century, even a daily Eucharist may have been known in some churches in the West.[24] The traditional fast days of Wednesday and Friday may seem an odd choice as the first to accommodate a full eucharistic celebration, but we need to remember that Tertullian appears to refer to the regular distribution of communion on those days, and if that were a more widespread custom, then its transformation into a complete eucharistic rite may be more readily understandable. That some churches appear to have reverted during Lent to a distribution of communion alone on those days may be an indication that such a service was once the norm throughout the year.[25]

---

[23] Tertullian provides evidence that as early as the beginning of the third century some Christians in North Africa were marking the Sabbath with the same respect as Sunday, by standing for prayer and refraining from keeping any fast on that day, and there is abundant testimony for the existence of services of the word on Saturdays in the fourth century. Willy Rordorf, *Sunday* (London; SCM Press; Philadelphia, PA: Westminster Press, 1968), 142–53, gives further details of all this, but is convinced that it must be a revival rather than a continuation of ancient practice.

[24] See Daniel Callam, "The Frequency of Mass in the Latin Church ca. 400," *Theological Studies* 45 (1984): 613–50.

[25] See, for example, Egeria, *Peregrinatio* 27.6; ET in John Wilkinson, *Egeria's Travels*, 3rd ed. (Oxford: Oxbow, Aris & Phillips, 1999), 129. The Council of Laodicea (380 CE) prohibited the celebration of the Eucharist in Lent except on Saturdays and Sundays (canon 49), and also the feasts of martyrs, except on those same days (canon 51).

Sixth, as we shall examine in detail below, certainly a very significant development in this period was the increasing standardization of written texts of the anaphora, a process closely related to the need for liturgical texts to express orthodox teaching against trinitarian and christological heresy and (undoubtedly) to the increasing lack of proficient and prayerful extemporizers. Explicit evidence for this exists in various North African conciliar decrees, such as canon 23 of the Third Council of Carthage (397) and those attributed to the Council of Milevis I (402) or Milevis II (416), though probably from another Council of Carthage in 407:

> *Canon 23 of the Third Council of Carthage (397)*
> In prayers let no one name (address) the Father instead of the Son, or the Son instead of the Father. And when one stands at the altar let prayer be always directed to the Father. If anyone copies out prayers for himself from elsewhere, these should not be used unless he has first discussed them with more learned brethren.[26]

> *Council of Milevis I (402) or Milevis II (416)*
> It was also resolved that prayers and orations [*preces vel orationes*] or mass [*seu missae*] which have been approved in council whether prefaces or commendations [*sive praefationes sive commendationes*] or blessings [*seu manus impositions*] should be used by all. In church any others at all should not be said except those that have been drawn up or approved in synod by the more prudent, lest perhaps something against faith be composed either through ignorance or through insufficient care.[27]

THE RITES

Nowhere, in the words of John Baldovin, did the post-Constantinian transformation of the scale of worship have a greater impact than on the Eucharist.[28] The liturgical outline provided by Justin Martyr's *First Apology* 65–66 (described in the previous chapter) becomes now the dominant skeleton or pattern for the eucharistic liturgy across a

---

[26] ET from Allan Bouley, *From Freedom to Formula: The Evolution of the Eucharistic Prayer from Oral Improvisation to Written Texts* (Washington, DC: Catholic University of America Press, 1981), 162.

[27] ET from ibid., 163–64.

[28] Baldovin, "Christian Worship to the Eve of the Reformation," 165.

wide range of diverse traditions in East and West. In this so-called classic period, we also find the development of the gradual growth of various influential liturgical centers—the traditional patriarchates of Rome, Alexandria, Antioch, Constantinople, and, at least in honor, Jerusalem—which consolidated local practices and led to the creation of what we still call "rites," those distinct ecclesial ways of being Christian,[29] of living out one's ecclesial identity through distinct forms of liturgy, canon law, and spirituality in particular cultural contexts. It is here where Gordon Lathrop's concept of an *ordo*, or common pattern or liturgical core, now seems to be on target and begins to provide, in the words of James White, "the finest available description of classical Christian worship,"[30] since it is now so clearly discernable within a wide range of liturgical traditions. It must be noted, however, that this shape, which by the end of the fourth century became dominant in relationship to the multiple liturgical shapes or patterns in earlier centuries, was not necessarily the dominant pattern or *ordo* before this time, when a greater variety and plurality likely existed.

The shift from domestic to public space, signified by the adaptation of existing and imperial funding of new basilicas and shrines, made possible the accommodation of large crowds within Christian liturgical assemblies. So also the rites themselves expanded precisely at those points where greater order in the assembly was needed—largely moments of processional movement—with the result that diaconal directions (e.g., "let us stand," "let us kneel," etc.), litanies, psalmody, chants, and prayers became regular elements. Robert Taft has referred to these places in the eucharistic liturgy as "soft spots,"[31] which tend to attract various elements to themselves over time. That is, what liturgical scholars refer to as a "liturgical unit," consisting of a procession covered by a chant and concluded by a collect and closely associated

---

[29] Aidan Kavanagh, *On Liturgical Theology* (New York: Pueblo, 1984), 100.

[30] James White, "How Do We Know It Is Us?," in *Liturgy and the Moral Self: Humanity at Full Stretch Before God*, ed. E. Byron Anderson and Bruce Morrill (Collegeville, MN: Liturgical Press, Pueblo, 1998), 57. On Lathrop's notion of *ordo*, see above, 28–29.

[31] Robert Taft, "The Structural Analysis of Liturgical Units: An Essay in Methodology," in *idem, Beyond East and West: Problems in Liturgical Understanding*, 2nd rev. and enlarged ed. (Rome: Pontificio Istituto Orientale, 1997), 187–202; and *idem*, "How Liturgies Grow: The Evolution of the Byzantine Divine Liturgy," in ibid., 203–38.

with the entrance of clergy and community at the beginning of the liturgy, at the presentation or transfer of the eucharistic gifts to the altar, and at the distribution of communion, now became regular components of the eucharistic liturgy, giving rise to various *introits* or "entrance hymns;" opening collects (prayers); "offertory" or "great entrance" chants and "prayers over the gifts" at the preparation or transfer of the eucharistic offerings; and various chants and prayers related to before, during, and after the reception of communion. In time, and in both East and West, these "soft spots" attracted even more elements, often making the earlier "liturgical units" themselves and occasionally even the underlying *ordo* of the whole, difficult to uncover or discern.

It is, of course, here at these "soft spots," where somewhat later elements such as the *Kyrie eleison* and *Gloria in excelsis* (Rome) or various antiphons such as *Hō Monogenēs* or the *Trisagion* (East) became attached to the "entrance" or opening rites and elements such as the Our Father, the *Agnus Dei*, and the invitation, "Holy things for the holy," to the reception of communion.

1. Liturgy of the Word

The pattern of worship preceding the eucharistic action that was described by Justin Martyr—a service of readings, preaching, and intercessory prayer concluded with the exchange of a kiss—had apparently become of the standard practice of all major centers of Christianity by the middle of the fourth century, if not long before, yet the details of it are still relatively sparse in the contemporary sources. There are no orders of service as such, except for that in *Apostolic Constitutions* 8, and to some extent, prayers 19–30 in the Prayers of Sarapion of Thmuis.[32] We need to be cautious, therefore, about how much the uncorroborated testimony of that material really reflects the authentic practice of even one locale, let alone about applying it more broadly to Christianity in general during this period.[33] Sources do become more plentiful from the fifth century onward, but since the fourth century was a time of rapid liturgical change and development, it would be dangerous

---

[32] Maxwell Johnson, *The Prayers of Sarapion of Thmuis: A Literary, Liturgical, and Theological Analysis*, OCA 249 (Rome: Pontificio Istituto Orientale, 1995), 70–81, 169–98. See also *idem, Liturgy in Early Christian Egypt*, Alcuin/GROW Joint Liturgical Study 33 (Cambridge: Grove Books, 1995), 17–34.

[33] See Bradshaw, *The Search for the Origins of Christian Worship*, 93–97.

to read back that evidence uncritically into the previous century. We are chiefly confined, therefore, to mere passing allusions in various sources for the reconstruction of what went on in this part of the eucharistic rite in the second half of the fourth century. (For the first half of the century, sources are virtually nonexistent.) John Chrysostom is a particularly valuable witness in this regard.[34]

It seems that there was an opening greeting by the bishop, or by a presbyter presiding in his place, with a response from the congregation, before the scriptural readings began, a practice echoed in the West by Augustine.[35] The number of readings seems to have varied from place to place. At Antioch, for example, the Liturgy of the Word included Old Testament readings (often two), a reading from the New Testament epistles, and then the gospel reading. Testimony from elsewhere indicates that there might have been only one reading prior to the gospel, usually from the New Testament, and some sources also speak of a responsorial psalm being sung between the readings.[36]

It is important to note, however, that in this period we do have the early development of various lectionaries, namely, the fifth-century *Armenian*[37] and *Georgian Lectionaries*[38] generally viewed as reflecting the liturgical practice of Jerusalem in the late fourth century, as well as

---

[34] See F. E. Brightman, *Liturgies Eastern and Western* (Oxford: Clarendon Press, 1896), appendix C, 470ff., for the arrangement of the order of service drawn up on the basis of Chrysostom's references; also Reiner Kaczynski, *Das Wort Gottes in Liturgie und Alltag der Gemeinden des Johannes Chrysostomos* (Freiburg 1974); F. van de Paverd, *Zur Geschichte der Messliturgie in Antiocheia und Konstantinopel gegen Ende des vierten Jahrhunderts. Analyse der Quellen bei Johannes Chrysostomos*, OCA 187 (Rome: Pontificio Istituto Orientale, 1970).

[35] See N. M. Denis-Boulet, "Introductory Rites of the Mass," in *The Church at Prayer*, vol. 2: *The Eucharist* (first series), ed. A. G. Martimort et al. (New York: Herder and Herder, 1973), 83.

[36] On the origin of this psalm in the Eucharist, see James W. McKinnon, "The Fourth-Century Origin of the Gradual," *Early Music History* 7 (1987): 91–106 = idem, *The Temple, the Church Fathers and Early Western Chant* (Aldershot: Ashgate, 1998), ix.

[37] Charles Athanase Renoux, trans. and ed., *Le codex arménien Jérusalem 121, II. Édition comparee du texte et de deux autres manuscrits*, Patrologia Orientalis 36.2 (Turnhout: Brepols, 1971).

[38] M. Tarchnischvili, *Le Grand Lectionnaire de l'Église de Jérusalem (Ve–VIIIe siècles)*, CSCO 189, 205 (Louvain, 1959–60).

fifth-century Coptic[39] and Syriac[40] sources. Further, scholars have tried to uncover the lectionary used by Augustine[41] in North African Hippo by analyzing his numerous extant homilies, a process recently undertaken in attempting to discern the lectionary of John Chrysostom used at Antioch and Constantinople by our doctoral student, Gary Phillip Razcka. Beyond Augustine, as well as some evidence provided in the homilies of Pope Leo the Great, our lectionary sources for Western rites tend to come from the early to later medieval period. Nevertheless, Gallican[42] (French and German) and Spanish[43] lectionary sources document the practice of three readings (Old Testament, New Testament, and gospel), while at Rome, only two became the norm (generally New Testament and gospel).

After the biblical readings came the homily, or even homilies, as there is evidence that at least in the East several presbyters might preach alongside the bishop at the same liturgy.[44] After this, there was a substantial series of intercessions, eventually in a litanic form with the assembly responding *Kyrie eleison* (Lord, have mercy) to the various diaconal petitions. Their form appears to have differed from place to place, consisting in some communities (e.g., Rome) of diaconal biddings followed by silent prayer culminating in various collects[45] or, as noted above, consisting elsewhere of litanies. Documents (e.g., *Apostolic Constitutions* 8 and the *Peregrinatio* or "travel diary" of the fourth-century pilgrim to the Holy Land, Egeria) also show that various categories of non-communicating people—e.g., catechumens, *photizomenoi*, energoumens (the possessed), and penitents preparing

---

[39] See Mario Geymonat, "Un antico lezionario della chiesa di Alessanria," in *Laurea Corona: Studies in Honour of Edward Coleiro*, ed. Anthony Bonanno et al. (Amsterdam: B.R. Grüner, 1987), 186–96.

[40] F. C. Burkett, "The Early Syriac Lectionary System," *Proceedings of the British Academy* 10 (1921–23): 301–39.

[41] G. G. Willis, *St. Augustine's Lectionary*, Alcuin Club Collections 44 (London: SPCK, 1962).

[42] P. Salmon, *Le lectionnaire de Luxeuil*, 2 vols., Collectanea biblica Latina 7 and 9 (Rome, 1944–53).

[43] J. Pérez de Urbel and A. González y Ruís-Zorrilla, *Liber commicus*, 2 vols., Monumenta Hispaniae Sacra, ser. Liturg. 2–3 (Madrid, 1940–55).

[44] See, for example, Egeria, *Peregrinatio* 25.1; 26.1; 27.6–7; 42.1; 43.2; van de Paverd, *Zur Geschichte der Messliturgie*, 131.

[45] See John Baldovin, "*Kyrie eleison* and the Entrance Rite of the Roman Eucharist," *Worship* 60 (2006): 334–47.

74

for reconciliation—were regularly dismissed from the assembly with rites that included handlaying and prayer before the general intercessions of the faithful and the Eucharist proper began. The dismissals (*missa*) of these various groups, in fact, are often seen as the reason why in the West the term *Missa* or Mass comes to be used for the eucharistic liturgy itself.[46] That is, the eucharistic portion proper of the rite began after the *missa* of these groups and before the final *missa* of the faithful after communion, eventually giving rise to the first part of the liturgy being termed in some traditions the *Mass of the Catechumens* and the second the *Mass of the Faithful*. Following the intercessory prayers of the faithful, the Liturgy of the Word concluded with the exchange of the kiss of peace.

2. Liturgy of the Eucharist: Eucharistic Prayers

If there is a relative paucity of written eucharistic prayer texts from the first three centuries, the fourth century provides an abundance of sources. Indeed, this is the period of construction for the great classic eucharistic anaphoras that still continue to be used in the various rites of East and West today. In Egypt, for example—a liturgical tradition particularly rich in the number of extant anaphoral texts and fragments— we note, in addition to the *Strasbourg Papyrus* (discussed in the previous chapter), the Deir Balizeh Papyrus; the Louvain Coptic Papyrus and its Barcelona fragment;[47] the Prosphora of Sarapion of Thmuis;[48] the Coptic Anaphora of St. Mark,[49] called "St. Cyril" after Cyril of Alexandria, the earlier version of what will become Greek St. Mark;[50] and the fourth-century anaphora referred to as Egyptian St. Basil.[51] In Syria, divided now into West and East, a number of differing anaphoras also became

---

[46] See See N. M. Denis-Boulet, "Terms Designating the Mass," in *The Church at Prayer*, vol. 2: *The Eucharist*, ed. Martimort et al., 1–5.

[47] For translations of these Egyptian texts, see PEER, 79–81. On the Barcelona papyrus see Michael Zheltov, "The Anaphora and the Thanksgiving Prayer from the Barcelona Papyrus: An Underestimated Testimony to the Anaphoral History in the Fourth Century," *Vigiliae Christianae* 62 (2008): 467–504; and Paul Bradshaw, "The Barcelona Papyrus and the Development of Early Eucharistic Prayers," in *Issues in Eucharistic Praying in East and West*, ed. Maxwell E. Johnson, 129–38.

[48] Johnson, *The Prayers of Sarapion of Thmuis*, 46–51, 199–277.

[49] Brightman, *Liturgies Eastern and Western*, 164–82.

[50] PEER, 59–66.

[51] Ibid., 67–73.

characteristic. For the liturgical traditions of West Syria, the anaphora in book 8 of the *Apostolic Constitutions*, the Anaphora of the Twelve Apostles, the anaphora underlying the catechetical homilies of Theodore of Mopsuestia, the Anaphora of St. John Chrysostom, and various other versions of St. Basil (Byzantine, Armenian, and Syriac) all represent a specific pattern of eucharistic praying.[52] As we saw in the previous chapter, the anaphora in chapter 4 of the so-called *Apostolic Tradition* belongs more to this type of anaphoral construction than to a Roman pattern. While the later Jerusalem liturgy would employ an anaphora of similar type and structure called "St. James," it is difficult to know (as we shall see below) where to locate the earlier anaphora described by Cyril (John) of Jerusalem in his *Mystagogical Catechesis* 5. For East Syria, of course, we encounter again the famous anaphora known as Addai and Mari, with its rather unique features and still used today by the Ancient Church of the East, a prayer closely related to the Anaphora of St. Peter (called *Sharar*, after its first word in Syriac) used today by the Maronite Rite. Table 3.1 shows the unique structure of these anaphoras within these various ritual families of the Christian East.

Our anaphoral sources for the West in this time period are very few. If the eucharistic prayer from chapter 4 of the so-called *Apostolic Tradition* is more correctly viewed as Antiochene or West Syrian, rather than the traditional view that it is Roman, our sources for Western eucharistic praying are Ambrose of Milan's *De Sacramentis*,[53] wherein he quotes from an anaphora closely resembling what we know as the later Roman *canon missae*, as well as various fragments appearing to be part of that Roman *canon* tradition.[54] At the same time, while we have no specific eucharistic texts from the Gallican or Spanish liturgical traditions in this time period, later documents indicate that the overall anaphoral structure in those rites is more akin to the West Syrian or Antiochene pattern noted above, with the notable exception that, apart from the *Sanctus* and Narrative of Institution, every eucharistic prayer is composed of interchangeable, and hence variable, sections.

---

[52] ET for these texts, with only ByzBAS, in ibid., 100–134.
[53] See PEER, 143–46.
[54] Ibid., 155–58.

Table 3.1

Anaphoral Structure (East)		
Antiochene/West Syrian	*East Syrian*	*Alexandrian*
Preface	Preface	Preface
Sanctus/Benedictus	*Sanctus/Benedictus*	Offering-Intercessions
Post-*Sanctus*	Post-*Sanctus*	*Sanctus* (no *Benedictus*)
Institution Narrative	Institution Narrative[55]	Epiclesis I (*Fill . . .*)
Anamnesis	Anamnesis	Institution Narrative
(*For . . .*)	Intercessions	Anamnesis
Epiclesis	Epiclesis	Epiclesis II
Intercessions	Doxology	Doxology
Doxology		
Early Eastern Anaphoras according to Types		
Apostolic Tradition	Addai and Mari	Strasbourg Papyrus
St. Basil (all versions)	St. Peter (*Sharar*)	Louvain Coptic
St. James		Papyrus
Cyril of Jerusalem (?)		John Rylands Papyrus
Apostolic Constitutions,		Deir Balizeh Papyrus
book 8		Saraphion of Thmuis
Twelve Apostles		St. Mark (Greek and
St. John Chrysostom		Coptic)

3. The Eucharistic Liturgy: Communion and Other Rites

The *Mystagogical Catecheses* (5.11–20) describe the recitation of the Lord's Prayer immediately after the eucharistic prayer, followed by an invitation to communion, "Holy things for the holy," with the congregational response, "One is holy, one Lord, Jesus Christ," and then the singing of Psalm 34:8, "Taste and see that the Lord is good," by a cantor before communion was received. There was also a prayer of thanksgiving after communion (*Mystagogical Catecheses* 5.22). These elements are paralleled in some of the other sources. Although Theodore of Mopsuestia does not mention the Lord's Prayer, Ambrose in

---

[55] The earliest text of Addai and Mari, most scholars would claim today, did not have an institution narrative. See above, pages 39–40.

the West alludes to it (*De Sacramentis* 5.24), but while neither Cyril nor Ambrose make reference to the breaking of the bread, Theodore does, as well as describing a commixture of the bread and wine (*Baptismal Homily* 5.15–20), an invitation to communion similar to that found in the *Mystagogical Catecheses*, and a prayer of thanksgiving after communion (*Baptismal Homily* 5.22–23, 29). Theodore is also familiar with several namings of individuals within the rite: in addition to the reading of the names "of the living and the dead who have died believing in Christ" between the washing of hands and the beginning of the eucharistic prayer,[56] and also apparently another commemoration of the living and departed toward the end of the prayer itself (as in the Strasbourg Papyrus and the Prayers of Sarapion), there is a further prayer after the commixture for those who had brought the bread and wine (*Baptismal Homily* 5.21). Chrysostom appears to refer to the breaking of bread, the Lord's Prayer, and invitation to communion as having been elements of the pre-communion rite at Antioch.[57] Both Theodore and Ambrose in the West indicate that the words used at the administration of communion were "The body of Christ," with the communicant's response being "Amen" (*Baptismal Homily* 5.28; *De Sacramentis* 4.25), and Theodore implies that the equivalent phrase for the cup was "The blood of Christ."

DEVELOPMENT OF THE EUCHARISTIC PRAYERS

It is beyond the scope of this study to provide an in-depth treatment of the origins and development of all of the eucharistic prayers from Christian antiquity, especially because so many other detailed resources exist already on this subject and because space here is limited.[58] Nevertheless, it is important to offer a summary of this development in light of the most recent scholarship with, at least, texts of some of the major eucharistic prayers provided. We begin with the Eastern sources and in Jerusalem.

---

[56] *Baptismal Homily* 4.43; ET in AIR, 236 (2nd ed., 224). For the later history of these diptychs (as they were called), see Robert F. Taft, *The Diptychs*, OCA 238 (Rome: Pontificio Istituto Orientale, 1991).

[57] See F. Van de Paverd, "Anaphoral Intercessions, Epiclesis and Communion Rites in John Chrysostom," OCP 49 (1983): 303–39.

[58] See Enrico Mazza, *The Origins of the Eucharistic Prayer* (Collegeville, MN: Liturgical Press, Pueblo, 1995); Paul F. Bradshaw, ed., *Essays in Early Eastern Eucharistic Prayers* (Collegeville, MN: Liturgical Press, Pueblo, 1997); and Johnson, ed., *Issues in Eucharistic Praying*.

1. Eastern Christian Anaphoras

The *Mystagogical Catecheses* attributed to Cyril of Jerusalem, or to his successor, John,[59] provide a good indication of the contents of the eucharistic prayer—but, unfortunately, not the text—in use in that city in the second half of the fourth century. After referring to the washing of the clergy's hands, the exchange of the kiss of peace, and the opening dialogue of the prayer, the author describes its contents as follows:

> After this we recall heaven and earth and sea, sun and moon, stars and all creation—both rational and irrational, both visible and invisible—angels, archangels, virtues, dominions, principalities, powers, thrones, the cherubim of many faces, in effect saying the words of David: "Magnify the Lord with me" [Ps 34:3]. We recall also the seraphim, whom Isaiah in the Holy Spirit saw encircling God's throne and with two wings covering the face and with two their feet and with two flying and saying: "Holy, holy, holy, Lord of Hosts" [Isa 6:3]. For we utter this confession of God handed down to us from the seraphim for this reason, so that we may become partakers of the hymn with the heavenly hosts.
>
> Next, having sanctified ourselves with these spiritual hymns, we call on the merciful God to send the Holy Spirit on those things that are being presented, so that he may make the bread Christ's body and the wine Christ's blood; for clearly whatever the Holy Spirit touches is sanctified and transformed.
>
> Next, after the spiritual sacrifice, the bloodless worship, has been completed, we beseech God over that sacrifice of propitiation for peace among the churches, for the right order of the world, for kings, for soldiers and allies, for those in sickness, for the afflicted, and in short we all pray and offer this sacrifice for all needing help.
>
> Next, we recall also those who have died, first patriarchs, prophets, apostles, martyrs, so that God may receive our petition through their prayers and representations. Next, (we pray) also for the holy fathers and bishops who have already died and in short for all among us who

[59] On authorship of the *Mystagogical Catecheses* see Alexis James Doval, *Cyril of Jerusalem, Mystagogue: The Authorship of the Mystagogic Catecheses*, Patristic Monograph Series 17 (Washington, DC: Catholic University of America Press, 2001); Juliette Day, *The Baptismal Liturgy of Jerusalem: Fourth- and Fifth-Century Evidence from Palestine, Syria and Egypt*, Liturgy, Worship and Society (Aldershot and Burlington, VT: Ashgate, 2007); and Maxwell E. Johnson, "Christian Initiation in Fourth-Century Jerusalem and Recent Developments in the Study of the Sources," *Ecclesia Orans* 26 (2009): 143–61.

have already died, believing that it will be the greatest help to the souls for whom the petition is offered (if it is done) while the holy and most awesome sacrifice is being presented. (*Mystagogical Catechesis* 5.6–9)

Because this is a commentary on the prayer and not a liturgical text as such, we must be careful not to assume that it quotes the prayer precisely and completely in every respect. Nevertheless, it is clear that the prayer has the same general shape as the Strasbourg Papyrus: praise for creation followed by wide-ranging intercessions. It may even have included a similar expression of offering in the middle, as the author uses the phrase "the spiritual sacrifice, the bloodless worship" at the point in the prayer where almost the same language occurs in the Strasbourg prayer. It does, however, include features that were not part of that earlier text—the pre-*Sanctus* reference to the praise of heaven, the *Sanctus*, and an epiclesis. These elements are also found in the Prosphora, or prayer of offering, of Sarapion of Thmuis, where we judge them to be insertions into an earlier nucleus that was also similar in shape to the Strasbourg Papyrus.[60]

Prosphora of Bishop Sarapion of Thmuis (c. 350)

It is right and just to praise, to hymn, to glorify you, the uncreated Father of the only-begotten Jesus Christ. We praise you, uncreated God, incomprehensible, inexpressible, inconceivable to every created substance. We praise you who are known by the only-begotten Son, who through him was spoken and interpreted and made known to created nature. We praise you who know the Son and who reveal to the saints the glories concerning him; you who are known by your begotten Word and known and interpreted to the saints. We praise you, invisible Father, provider of immortality. You are the source of life, the source of light, the source of all grace and truth. Lover of humanity and lover of the poor, you are reconciled to all and draw all to yourself through the coming of your beloved Son.

We pray, make us living people. Give us spirit of light, in order that we may know you the true (God) and Jesus Christ whom you sent. Give us holy Spirit, in order that we may be able to proclaim and describe your inexpressible mysteries. Let the Lord Jesus speak in us and let holy Spirit hymn you through us.

---

[60] See Johnson, *The Prayers of Sarapion of Thmuis*, 46–51, 255–59.

For you are above all rule and authority and power and dominion and every name being named, not only in this age but also in the coming one. Beside you stand a thousand thousands and a myriad myriads of angels, archangels, thrones, dominions, principalities, and powers. Beside you stand the two most-honored six-winged seraphim. With two wings they cover the face, and with two the feet, and with two they fly; sanctifying. With them receive also our sanctification as we say: Holy, holy, holy Lord of Sabaoth; heaven and earth are full of your glory.

Full is heaven and full also is the earth of your majestic glory, Lord of powers. Fill also this sacrifice with your power and with your participation. For to you we offered this living sacrifice, the unbloody offering. To you we offered this bread, the likeness [*homoioma*] of the body of the only-begotten. This bread is the likeness [*homoioma*] of the holy body.

For the Lord Jesus Christ, in the night when he was handed over, took bread, broke it, and gave it to his disciples saying: Take and eat, this is my body which is broken for you for the forgiveness of sins. Therefore we also offered the bread making the likeness [*homoioma*] of the death.

And we implore you through this sacrifice, God of truth; be reconciled to us all and be merciful. And as this bread was scattered over the mountains and, when it was gathered together, became one, so also gather your holy church out of every nation and every region and every city and village and house, and make one living catholic church.

And we also offered the cup, the likeness [*homoioma*] of the blood. For the Lord Jesus Christ, taking a cup after supper, said to the disciples: take, drink, this is the new covenant, which is my blood poured out for you for the forgiveness of sins. Therefore, we also offered the cup presenting the likeness [*homoioma*] of blood.

God of truth, let your holy Word come upon this bread in order that the bread may become body of the Word, and upon this cup in order that the cup may become blood of truth. And make all those who partake to receive a medicine of life for the healing of every illness, and for the strengthening of every advancement and virtue, not for condemnation, God of truth, not for testing and reproach.

For we called upon you, the uncreated, through the only-begotten in holy Spirit. Let this people receive mercy. Let them be made worthy of advancement. Let angels be present with them for abolishing evil and for establishing the church. And we call out also for all who have fallen asleep, for whom also the memorial [*anamnesis*] is made. *After the Announcement of the Names:* Sanctify these souls for you know them all. Sanctify all who have fallen asleep in the Lord. Number them with all your holy powers, and give them a place and mansion in your kingdom.

And receive also the thanksgiving [*eucharistia*] of the people and bless those who offer their offerings and thanksgivings. Give to this entire people health, wholeness, cheerfulness, and every advancement of soul and body.

Through your only-begotten Jesus Christ in holy Spirit. As it was and is and will be to generations of generations and to all the ages of ages. Amen.

In spite of the unique emphases in Sarapion's prayer, especially the epiclesis of the *Logos*, rather than of the Holy Spirit, on the eucharistic gifts, it looks as though all three prayers—*Mystagogical Catechesis 5*, Strasbourg, and Sarapion—share a common (Egyptian) tradition.

It has been claimed that the prayer underlying the baptismal homilies of Theodore of Mopsuestia[61] is also similar to that in the *Mystagogical Catecheses*, although again, as all that we have is a commentary rather than a liturgical text as such, it is difficult to be sure what the prayer itself might have or have not contained. In particular, the commentary seems to imply that very little preceded the *Sanctus* itself but that a recounting of the saving acts of Christ might have followed it; which, if true, would distinguish it from the prayer described in the *Mystagogical Catecheses*.

Whatever the case may be with Theodore, certainly the late fourth- to mid-fifth-century anaphora known as "St. Cyril" (the earlier Coptic version of Mark)[62] shows some clear parallels, again, not only with the *Mystagogical Catecheses* but with Strasbourg and Sarapion. The following presents not the full text of Coptic Mark but only those parallel sections, including, however, the customary Egyptian linkage of the institution narrative by means of the Greek *hoti* ("for" or "because") as in Sarapion; the offering verb in the present tense in the preface ("we offer") but in the aorist within the anamnesis (we "offered" or "have set before you"); and a second epiclesis, more directly consecratory in nature than the first:

Within the Preface

You have made all things through your wisdom, your true light your only begotten Son, our Lord and our God and our Savior and the king

[61] See PEER, 135–37.
[62] See Geoffrey Cuming, *The Liturgy of St. Mark Edited from the Manuscripts with a Commentary*, OCA 234 (Rome: Pontificio Istituto Orientale, 1990).

of us all, Jesus Christ, through whom we give thanks, we offer unto you with him and the Holy Spirit, the holy consubstantial undivided Trinity, this reasonable sacrifice and this unbloody service which all nations offer unto you from the rising of the sun unto the going down of the same and from the north to the south; for your name is great, O Lord, among all the Gentiles and in every place incense is offered unto your holy name and a purified sacrifice.

(Introduction to the Intercessions within the Preface)

And over this sacrifice and this offering we pray and beseech your goodness, O Lover of humanity: Remember, O Lord, the peace of your one only holy catholic and apostolic church. . . .

(Introduction to the Sanctus and the Sanctus)

For you are God who are above every principality and every power and every virtue and every dominion and every name that is named not only in this world but also in that which is to come: for before you stand the thousand thousands and the ten thousand times ten thousand of the angels and archangels serving you: for before you stand your two living creatures exceedingly honorable, the six-winged and many-eyed, seraphim and cherubim, with two wings covering their face, by reason of thy Godhead which none can gaze upon nor comprehend, and with two covering their feet, with two also flying, for at all times all things hallow you. But with them that hallow you, receive our hallowing, O Lord, at our hands also, praising you with them and saying:

(*the people*): Holy, holy, holy, Lord Sabaoth: full are the heaven and the earth of your holy glory. . . .

Epiclesis I

Truly heaven and earth are full of your holy glory, through your only-begotten Son, our Lord and our God and our Savior and the king of us all, Jesus Christ. Fill also this our sacrifice, O Lord, with the blessing that is from you, through the descent upon it of your Holy Spirit; and in blessing bless, and in purifying purify, these your precious gifts *which have been set before your face, this bread and this cup.*

Narrative of Institution and Anamnesis

For your only begotten Son, our Lord and our God and our Savior and the king of us all, Jesus Christ, in the same night in which he gave himself up to undergo the passion in behalf of our sins and the death which he accepted, of his own will, himself to undergo in behalf of us all, took bread upon his holy spotless and undefiled and blessed and life-giving hands. . . . For as often as you shall eat of this Bread and drink of this Cup you show my death, you confess my resurrection, you make my memorial until I come.

(*the people*): Your death, O Lord we acclaim and your holy resurrection and ascension we confess.

Now also, O God the Father almighty, showing the death of your only begotten Son, our Lord and our God and our Savior and the king of us all, Jesus Christ, confessing his holy resurrection and his ascension into the heavens and his session at your right hand, O Father; looking for his second advent, coming from the heavens, fearful and glorious at the end of this world, wherein he will come to judge the world in righteousness to render to everyone according to their works, whether it be good or bad: Before your holy glory we have set your own gift of your own, O our holy Father.

(*the people*): We praise you, we bless you, we give thanks to you, Lord and we ask you our God.

Epiclesis II

Have mercy upon us, O God the Father almighty, and send down from your holy height and from heaven your dwelling place and from your infinite bosom, from the throne of the kingdom of your glory, him, the Paraclete, your Holy Spirit, who is hypostatic, the indivisible, the unchangeable; who is the Lord, the giver of life, who spoke in the law and the prophets and the apostles; who is everywhere, who fills all places and no place contains him: and of his own will after your good pleasure, working sanctification on those in whom he delights, not ministerially: simple in his nature, manifold in his operation, the fountain of the graces of God, who is of one substance with you, who proceeds from you, the sharer of the throne of the kingdom of your glory with your only begotten Son, our Lord and our God and our Savior and the king of us all, Jesus Christ: send him down upon us your servants and upon these your precious gifts *which have been set before You*, upon this bread and upon this cup that they may be hallowed and changed and that he may make this bread the holy body of Christ, and this cup also his precious blood of the New Testament even of our Lord and our God and our Savior and the king of us all Jesus Christ.[63]

---

[63] ET adapted from Brightman, *Liturgies Eastern and Western*, 164–80; emphasis added.

Another anaphora long associated with the Egyptian liturgical tradition, and that has enjoyed a resurgence of interest in contemporary liturgical renewal, is the Coptic version of the Anaphora of St. Basil, known as EgBAS. The earliest witness to this text exists only in an incomplete manuscript, lacking the first third of the prayer and dating from somewhere between 600 and 800, but until recently has commonly been regarded as the oldest extant form of the prayer and as perhaps belonging to the first half of the fourth century.[64] It has been thought that it may have been the native Cappadocian eucharistic prayer brought by Basil when he visited Egypt ca. 357 CE and subsequently amplified by the saint himself into the longer form underlying the Armenian, Byzantine, and Syriac versions. Recent study by Gabriele Winkler, however, has cast considerable doubt on this hitherto widely accepted thesis by pointing to elements in the Armenian versions that may witness to a Syriac recension older than that of the Egyptian versions, suggesting, possibly, even a Syrian original.[65] The general shape of the prayer, though not its precise content, has in part the appearance of being a hybrid between the prayer in the *Apostolic Tradition*, the Strasbourg Papyrus, and the Prosphora of Sarapion—though we are *not* suggesting that its historical origin actually lies in such a combination. Its brief pre-*Sanctus* material has some limited parallels with the equivalent part of Sarapion's prayer; after the *Sanctus* it recounts the saving works of Christ before moving into an institution narrative connected by the use of "for" or "because," an anamnesis/offering formula in the aorist tense—the "famous aorist,"

---

[64] Edition in J. Doresse and E. Lanne, eds., *Un témoin archaïque de la liturgie copte de S. Basile* (Louvain: 1960); ET in PEER, 67–73.

[65] Gabriele Winkler, *Die Basilius-Anaphora: Edition der beiden armenischen Redaktionen und der relevanten Fragmente, Übersetzung und Zusammenschau aller Versionen im Licht der orientalischen Überlieferungen,* Anaphorae Orientales 2 (Rome: Pontificio Istituto Orientale, 2005). See also *idem*, "Zur Erforschung orientalischer Anaphoren in liturgievergleichender Sicht II: Das Formelgut der Oratio post Sanctus und Anamnese sowie Interzessionen und die Taufbekenntnisse," in *Comparative Liturgy Fifty Years after Anton Baumstark (1872–1948)*, ed. Robert F. Taft and Gabriele Winkler, OCA 265 (Rome: Pontificio Istituto Orientale, 2001), 407–93. For the state of the question on this prayer see Annie Vorhees McGowan, "The Basilian Anaphorae: Rethinking the Question," in *Issues in Eucharistic Praying*, ed. Johnson, 219–62.

in the words of Alphonse Raes[66] ("We also, remembering . . . have set forth before you your own from your own, this bread and this cup")— and then an epiclesis and prayer for the communicants, this pattern resembling that of the *Apostolic Tradition*, but it follows this with intercession for the living as well as the departed, thus being more like the Strasbourg Papyrus here than like Sarapion.

Nevertheless, while such "Egyptianisms" do appear in this anaphora, the overall structure of the prayer, as noted in table 3.1 above, connects it most closely with what has been classified as the West Syrian or Antiochene anaphoral pattern. Indeed, a characteristic of this pattern is that it takes its cue from the "holy" of the *Sanctus* itself and so begins its post-*Sanctus* by continuing to proclaim God's holiness, rather than the "full-fill" connection of the first epiclesis to the *Sanctus* in the Alexandrian pattern.

Coptic Anaphora of St. Basil (EgBAS)

The bishop: The Lord be with you all.
People: And with your spirit.
Bishop: Let us lift up our hearts.
People: We have them with the Lord.
Bishop: Let us give thanks to the Lord.
People: It is fitting and right.
Bishop: It is fitting and right, fitting and right, truly it is fitting and right, I AM, truly Lord God, existing before the ages, reigning until the ages; you dwell on high and regard what is low; you made heaven and earth and the sea and all that is in them. Father of our Lord and God and Savior Jesus Christ, through whom you made all things visible and invisible, you sit on the throne of your glory; you are adored by every holy power. Around you stand angels and archangels, principalities and powers, thrones, dominions, and virtues; around you stand the cherubim with many eyes and the seraphim with six wings, forever singing the hymn of glory and saying:

People: Holy, holy, holy Lord (etc.)

Bishop: Holy, holy, holy you are indeed, Lord our God. You formed us and placed us in the paradise of pleasure; and when we had transgressed your commandment through the deceit of the serpent, and

---

[66] For this and other "Egyptianisms," see A. Raes, "Un nouveau document de la Liturgie de S. Basile," OCP 26 (1960): 401–10.

had fallen from eternal life, and had been banished from the paradise of pleasure, you did not cast us off for ever, but continually made promises to us through your holy prophets; and in these last days you manifested to us who sat in darkness and the shadow of death your only-begotten Son, our Lord and God and Savior, Jesus Christ. He was made flesh of the Holy Spirit and of the holy Virgin Mary, and became man; he showed us the ways of salvation, granted us to be reborn from above by water and the Spirit, and made us a people for [his] own possession, sanctifying us by his Holy Spirit. He loved his own who were in the world, and gave himself for our salvation to death who reigned over us and held us down because of our sins.

. . . by his blood. [The earliest Coptic text begins here.] From the cross he descended into hell and rose from the dead and the third day, he ascended into heaven and sat at the right hand of the Father; he appointed a day on which to judge the world with justice and render to each according to his works.

And he left us this great mystery of godliness: for when he was about to hand himself over to death for the life of the world, he took bread, blessed, sanctified, broke, and gave it to his holy disciples and apostles, saying, "Take and eat from this, all of you; this is my body, which is given for you and for many for forgiveness of your sins. Do this for my remembrance."

Likewise also the cup after supper: he mixed wine and water, blessed, sanctified, gave thanks, and again gave it to them, saying, "Take and drink from it, all of you; this is my blood which shall be shed for you and for many for the forgiveness of your sins. Do this for my remembrance. For as often as you eat this bread and drink this cup, you proclaim my death until I come."

We therefore, remembering his holy sufferings, and his resurrection from the dead, and his ascension into heaven, and his session at the right hand of the Father, and his glorious and fearful coming to us (again), have set forth before you your own from your own gifts, this bread and cup. And we, sinners and unworthy and wretched, pray you, our God, in adoration that in the good pleasure of your goodness your Holy Spirit may descend upon us and upon these gifts that have been set before you, and may sanctify and make them holy of holies.

Make us all worthy to partake of your holy things for sanctification of soul and body, that we may become one body and one spirit, and may have our portion with all the saints who have been pleasing to you from eternity.

Remember, Lord, also your one, holy, catholic, and apostolic Church; give it peace, for you purchased it with the precious blood of Christ; and (remember) all the orthodox bishops in it.

Remember first of all your servant Archbishop Benjamin and his colleague in the ministry holy Bishop Colluthus, and all who with him dispense the word of truth; grant them to feed the holy churches, your orthodox flocks, in peace.

Remember, Lord, the priests and all the deacons who assist, all those in virginity and chastity, and all your faithful people; and have mercy on them all.

Remember, Lord, also this place, and those who live in it in the faith of God.

Remember, Lord, also mildness of climate and the fruits of the earth.

Remember, Lord, those who offer these gifts to you, and those for whom they offered them; and grant them all a heavenly reward.

Since, Master, it is a command of your only-begotten Son that we should share in the commemoration of your saints, vouchsafe to remember, Lord, those of our fathers who have been pleasing to you from eternity: patriarchs, prophets, apostles, martyrs, confessors, preachers, evangelists, and all the righteous perfected in faith; especially at all times the holy and glorious Mary, Mother of God; and by her prayers have mercy on us all, and save us through your holy name which has been invoked upon us.

Remember likewise all those of the priesthood who have already died, and all those of lay rank; and grant them rest in the bosom of Abraham, Isaac, and Jacob, in green pastures, by waters of comfort, in a place whence grief, sorrow, and sighing have fled away.

(*to the deacon:*) Read the names. (*The deacon reads the diptychs.*)

Bishop: Give them rest in your presence; preserve in your faith us who live here, guide us to your kingdom, and grant us your peace at all times; through Jesus Christ and the Holy Spirit.

The Father in the Son, the Son in the Father with the Holy Spirit, in your holy, one, catholic, and apostolic Church.[67]

---

[67] ET adapted from PEER, 67–73.

The most widely used form of the Anaphora of St. Basil, known as Byzantine Basil (hereafter, ByzBAS), has been commonly viewed as the editorial work of Basil of Caesarea himself, especially in relationship to the expanded and explicit trinitarian theology associated with his other writings within the context of the *Pneumatomachian* controversy of the late fourth century, most notably his treatise *On the Holy Spirit*.[68] In relationship to EgBAS, ByzBAS also contains the "Egyptianisms" of both the use of "for" or "because" (the Greek *hoti*) to connect the narrative of institution to the anaphora, and the use of the aorist ("And having set forth the likeness [*antitypos*] of the holy body and blood of your Christ"[69]) in relationship to offering. We note also in comparison with EgBAS a move in the epiclesis of the Holy Spirit toward a more explicitly consecratory focus, asking that the Holy Spirit "come upon us and upon these gifts set forth, and bless them and sanctify and *make* this bread the precious body of our Lord and God and Savior Jesus Christ. Amen. And this cup the precious blood of our Lord and God and Savior Jesus Christ." As we shall see below in chapter 5, ByzBAS was the primary eucharistic anaphora in use at Constantinople until the Anaphora of St. John Chrysostom (hereafter, CHR) eventually took precedence over it, especially outside the season of Lent.

Byzantine Anaphora of St. Basil (ByzBAS)

Priest: The grace of our Lord Jesus Christ and the love of the God and Father, and the communion of the Holy Spirit be with you all.
People: And with your spirit.
Priest: Let us lift up our hearts.
People: We have them with the Lord.
Priest: Let us give thanks to the Lord.
People: It is fitting and right [to worship the Father, the Son, and the Holy Spirit, the consubstantial and undivided Trinity].

And the priest begins the holy anaphora:
I AM, Master, Lord God, Father almighty, reverend, it is truly fitting and right and befitting the magnificence of your holiness to praise

---

[68] On this, see the summary of scholarship provided by D. Richard Stuckwisch, "The Basilian Anaphoras," in *Essays on Early Eastern Eucharistic Prayers*, ed. Bradshaw, 109–30, here at 122–30.
[69] See the parallel here to Sarapion's eucharistic use of *homoioma* above, page 81.

you, to hymn you, to bless you, to worship you, to give you thanks, to glorify you, the only truly existing God, and to offer to you with a contrite heart and a humble spirit this our reasonable service. For it is you who granted us the knowledge of your truth; and who is sufficient to declare your powers, to make all your praises to be heard, or to declare all your wonders at all times? [Master], Master of all, Lord of heaven and earth and all Creation, visible and invisible, you sit on the throne of glory and behold the depths, without beginning, invisible, incomprehensible, infinite, unchangeable, the Father of our Lord Jesus Christ the Great God and savior of our hope, who is the image of your goodness, the identical seal, manifesting you the Father in himself, living Word, true God, before all ages wisdom, life, sanctification, power, the true Light by whom the Holy Spirit was revealed, the spirit of truth, the grace of sonship, the pledge of the inheritance to come, the first fruits of eternal good things, lifegiving power, the fountain of sanctification, by whose enabling the whole rational and spiritual Creation does your service and renders you the unending doxology; for all things are your servants. For angels, archangels, thrones, dominions, principalities, powers, virtues, and the cherubim with many eyes praise you, the seraphim stand around you, each having six wings, and with two covering their own faces, and with two their feet, and with two flying, and crying one to the other with unwearying mouths and never-silent doxologies, (*aloud*) singing the triumphal hymn, crying aloud and saying:

People: Holy, [holy, holy, Lord of Sabaoth; heaven and earth are full of your glory. Hosanna in the highest. Blessed is he who comes in the name of the Lord. Hosanna in the highest.]

The priest says privately: With these blessed powers, Master, lover of men, we sinners also cry and say: you are truly holy and all-holy, and there is no measure of the magnificence of your holiness, and you are holy in all your works, for in righteousness and true judgment you brought all things upon us. For you took dust from the earth and formed man; you honored him with your image, O God and set him in the paradise of pleasure, and promised him immortality of life and enjoyment of eternal good things in keeping your commandments. But when he had disobeyed you, the true God who created him, and had been led astray by the deceit of the serpent, and had been subjected to death by his own transgressions, you, O God, expelled him in your righteous judgment from paradise into this world, and turned him back to the earth from which he was taken, dispensing to him the salvation by rebirth which is in your Christ. For you did not turn away finally from your creature, O good one, nor forget the works of your hands, but you visited him in many ways through the bowels of your mercy. You sent forth prophets; you performed works of power through your saints who were pleasing to you in every generation; you spoke to us through the mouths of your servants the prophets, foretelling to us the salvation that should come; you gave the Law for our help; you set angels as guards over us.

But when the fullness of time had come, you spoke to us in your Son himself, through whom also you made the ages, who, being the reflection of your glory and the impress of your substance, and bearing all things by the word of his power, thought it not robbery to be equal with you, the God and Father, but he who was God before the ages was seen on earth and lived among men; he was made flesh from a holy virgin and humbled himself, taking the form of a slave; he was conformed to the body of our humiliation that he might conform us to the image of his glory. For since through man sin had entered into the world, and through sin death, your only-begotten Son, who is in your bosom, O God and Father, being born of a woman, the Holy Mother of God and ever-Virgin Mary, born under the law, was pleased to condemn sin in his flesh, that those who died in Adam should be made alive in him, your Christ. And having become a citizen of this world, he gave us commandments of salvation, turned us away from the error of the idols, and brought us to the knowledge of you, the true God and Father; he gained us for himself, a peculiar people, a royal priesthood, a holy nation; and when he had cleansed us with water and sanctified us by the Holy Spirit, he gave himself as a ransom to death, by which we were held, having been sold under sin. By means of the cross he descended into hell, that he might fill all things with himself, and loosed the pains of death; he rose again on the third day, making a way to resurrection from the dead for all flesh, because it was not possible for the prince of life to be conquered by corruption, and became the first fruits of those who had fallen asleep, the first-born from the dead, so that he might be first in all ways among all things. And ascending into the heavens, he sat down at the right hand of the majesty in the highest, and will also come to reward each man according to his works. And he left us memorials of his saving passion, these things which we have set forth according to his commandments.

For when he was about to go out to his voluntary and laudable and life-giving death, in the night in which he gave himself up for the life of the world, he took bread in his holy and undefiled hands and showed it to you, the God and Father, gave thanks, blessed, sanctified, and broke it, and gave it to his holy disciples and apostles, saying, "Take, eat; this is my body, which is broken for you for the forgiveness of sins."

People: Amen.

Likewise also he took the cup of the fruit of the vine and mixed it, gave thanks, blessed, sanctified, and gave it to his holy disciples and apostles, saying, "Drink from this, all of you; this is my blood, which is shed for you and for many for the forgiveness of sins. [*People*: Amen.] Do this for my remembrance. For as often as you eat this bread and drink this cup, you proclaim my death, you confess my resurrection."

Therefore, Master, we also, remembering his saving Passion, his life-giving cross, his three-day burial, his resurrection from the dead, his ascension into heaven, his session at your right hand, God and Father, and his glorious and fearful second coming; (*aloud*) offer[-ing] you your own from your own, in all and through all,

People: we hymn you, [we bless you, we give you thanks, O Lord, and pray to you, our God.]

Therefore, Master all-Holy, we also, your sinful and unworthy servants, who have been held worthy to minister at your holy altar, not for our righteousness, for we have done nothing good upon earth, but for your mercies and compassions which you have poured out richly upon us, with confidence approach your holy altar. And having set forth the likeness of the holy body and blood of your Christ, we pray and beseech you, O holy of holies, in the good pleasure of your bounty, that your [all-]Holy Spirit may come upon us and upon these gifts set forth, and bless them and sanctify and show (*he signs the holy gifts with the cross three times, saying:*) this bread the precious body of our Lord and God and Savior Jesus Christ. Amen. And this cup the precious blood of our Lord and God and Savior Jesus Christ, [Amen.] which is shed for the life of the world [and salvation]. Amen. (*thrice*)

Unite with one another all of us who partake of the one bread and the cup into fellowship with the one Holy Spirit; and make none of us to partake of the holy body and blood of your Christ for judgment or for condemnation, but that we may find mercy and grace with all the saints who have been well-pleasing to you from of old, forefathers, Fathers, patriarchs, prophets, apostles, preachers, evangelists, martyrs, confessors, teachers, and every righteous spirit perfected in faith; (*aloud*) especially our all-holy, immaculate highly blessed [glorious] Lady, Mother of God and ever-Virgin Mary; (*while the diptychs are read by the deacon, the priest says the prayer:*) Saint John the [prophet,] forerunner and Baptist, [the holy and honored apostles,] this saint *N.* whose memorial we are keeping, and all your saints: at their entreaties, visit us, O God.

And remember all those who have fallen asleep in hope of resurrection to eternal life, and grant them rest where the light of your countenance looks upon them.

Again we pray you, Lord, remember your holy, catholic, and apostolic Church from one end of the world to the other, and grant it the peace which you purchased by the precious blood of your Christ, and [e]stablish this holy house until the consummation of the age, and grant it peace.

Remember, Lord, those who presented these gifts, and those for whom, and through whom, and on account of whom they presented them.

Remember, Lord, those who bring forth fruit and do good work in your holy churches and remember the poor. Reward them with rich and heavenly gifts. Grant them heavenly things for earthly, eternal things for temporal, incorruptible things for corruptible.

[The Intercessions continue.]

Concluding Doxology

. . . and grant us with one mouth and one heart to glorify and hymn your all-honorable and magnificent name, the Father and the Son and the Holy Spirit, now [and always and to the ages of ages.]

People: Amen.[70]

As noted above, ByzBAS constitutes one of the two major eucharistic prayers of what will come to be called the Byzantine Liturgy or Byzantine Rite in Constantinople, the other being, of course, CHR. CHR, however, appears itself to have a predecessor or common ancestor in another earlier Antiochene anaphora known as the Anaphora of the Twelve Apostles. Although the Greek version of Twelve Apostles is no longer extant, both John Fenwick[71] and Robert Taft[72] have

---

[70] ET from PEER, 116–23.

[71] J. R. K. Fenwick, *The Anaphoras of St Basil and St James: An Investigation into their Common Origin*, OCA 240 (Rome: Pontificio Istituo Orientale, 1992).

[72] Robert Taft, "St. John Chrysostom and the Byzantine Anaphora that Bears His Name," in *Essays on Early Eastern Eucharistic Prayers*, ed. Bradshaw, 195–226; and *idem*, "The Authenticity of the Chrysostom Anaphora Revisited: Determining the Authorship of Liturgical Texts by Computer," OCP 56 (1990): 5–51.

convincingly argued it was originally used at Antioch and lies behind both the Syriac version of that prayer, but conflated there with elements from the Syriac version of the Anaphora of St. James (of Jerusalem origin),[73] and also CHR, but conflated with elements from ByzBAS by John Chrysostom himself, ca. 398. From a comparison of parallel material, it appears that the original Anaphora of the Twelve Apostles began with a relatively short thanksgiving for creation and redemption, which (without the obvious trinitarian additions) has a very ancient appearance.[74] To this the *Sanctus*, institution narrative, and anamnesis unit seem to have been attached somewhat crudely. These elements are followed not by an offering section, as in most other prayers of this period, but by what appears to be a reprise of the thanksgiving from the opening section, leading into an epiclesis of the Holy Spirit. What is fascinating about this lack of offering or sacrifice language in the anamnesis of the prayer—the "missing oblation"—is the parallel Fenwick sees here with what he terms the "ancient heart of the Antiochene anamnesis"[75] in the anaphora of book 8 of the *Apostolic Constitutions*, which reads, "Remembering therefore what he endured for us, we give you thanks, almighty God, not as we ought but as we are able."[76] Hence, not *offering* but *thanksgiving* itself seems to be the

---

[73] On the Anaphora of St. James, see below, pages 161–66.

[74] The possibility that this unit constituted the totality of the original prayer has been suggested by a number of scholars, beginning with H. Engberding, "Die syrische Anaphora der zwölf Apostel und ihre Paralleltexte einander gegenüber gestellt und mit neuen Untersuchungen zur Urgeschichte der Chrysostomliturgie begleitet," *Oriens Christianus* 34 (1938): 213–47, here at 239–41. For a more recent assessment see G. J. Cuming, "Four Very Early Anaphoras," *Worship* 58 (1984): 168–72.

[75] J. R. K. Fenwick, *The Missing Oblation: The Contents of the Early Antiochene Anaphora*, Alcuin/GROW Joint Liturgical Study 11 (Cambridge: Grove Books, 1989), 24–25.

[76] ET from PEER, 110. Because this phrase appears before the narrative of institution in the anaphora of book 8 of the *Apostolic Constitutions*, and because a more complete anamnesis occurs after that narrative, based, in part at least, on the anaphora in chapter 4 of the so-called *Apostolic Tradition*, this phrase is sometimes referred to as the "false anamnesis." The more complete or "true" anamnesis reads: "Remembering then his Passion and death and resurrection from the dead, his return to heaven and his future second coming, in which he comes with glory and power to judge the living and the dead, and to reward each according to his works, we offer you, King and God, according to his

key anamnetic emphasis early in this tradition. Whether or not intercessions formed part of the original form is unclear.

Anaphora of the Twelve Apostles

Priest: The love of God the Father [and the grace of the only-begotten Son and our Lord and Great God and Savior Jesus Christ, and the fellowship of the Holy Spirit be with you all.]
People: And with [your spirit.]
Priest: Up with [your hearts.]
People: We have them with the Lord.
Priest: Let us give thanks to the Lord.
People: It is fitting and right

Priest: It is fitting and right that we should adore you and glorify you, who are truly God, and your only-begotten Son and the Holy Spirit. For you brought us out of non-existence into existence; and when we had fallen, you recalled us, and did not cease to work until you brought us up to heaven and granted us the kingdom that is to come. For all these things we give thanks to you and to your only-begotten Son and to the Holy Spirit. For around you stand the cherubim with four faces and the seraphim with six wings with all the heavenly powers, glorifying with never-silent mouths and voices the praise of your majesty, proclaiming, crying, and saying,

People: Holy, holy, holy . . .

Priest (bowing): Holy you are and all-holy, and your only-begotten Son, and the Holy Spirit. Holy are you and all-holy, and magnificent is your glory, for you so loved the world that you gave your only-begotten Son for it, that all who believe in him may not perish but have eternal life.

---

commandment, this bread and this cup, giving you thanks through him that you have deemed us worthy to stand before you and to serve you as priests" (PEER, 110). Fenwick suggests further that Twelve Apostles itself lay behind the eucharistic prayer in *Apostolic Constitutions* 8. He was reticent with regard to what additional source or sources might have been used in this last case, but Raphael Graves has since examined the prayer and concluded that, while there is evidence of some use of the Anaphora of St. Basil, the principal parallels lie with the compiler's own work elsewhere in the *Apostolic Constitutions* rather than with any other known prayer. See Raphael Graves, "The Anaphora of the Eighth Book of the Apostolic Constitutions," in *Essays on Early Eastern Eucharistic Prayers*, ed. Bradshaw, 173–94.

(*aloud*) When he had come and fulfilled all the dispensation which is for us, on the night in which he was betrayed, he took bread in his holy hands, and after he had raised them to heaven, he blessed, sanctified, broke, and gave it to his disciples the Apostles, saying, "Take, eat from it, all of you; this is my body, which is broken for you and for many, and is given for forgiveness of sins and for eternal life."

Likewise the cup also after supper, mixing wine and water; he gave thanks, blessed, sanctified, and after he had tasted it, gave it to his disciples the Apostles, saying, "Take, drink from it, all of you; this is the blood of the new covenant, which is shed for you and for many, and is given for forgiveness of sins and for eternal life. Do this for my remembrance. For as often as you eat this bread and drink this cup, you will proclaim my death and confess my resurrection, until I come."

People: Your death, Lord, [we commemorate, your resurrection we confess, and your second coming we await. We seek from you mercy and pardon, and we pray for forgiveness of sins. May your mercy be on us all.]

Priest: While therefore we remember, Lord, your saving command and all your dispensation which was for us, your cross, your resurrection from the dead on the third day, your ascension into heaven and your session at the right hand of the Father, and your glorious second coming, in which you will come in glory to judge the living and the dead, and to repay all men according to their works in your love for man—for your Church and your flock we beseech you, saying through you and with you to the Father, "have mercy on me,"

People: Have mercy [on us, O God, almighty Father, have mercy on us]—

Priest: we also, Lord, give thanks and confess you on behalf of all men for all things.

People: We praise you, [we bless you, we give thanks to you, Lord, and we ask you, our God, "be gracious, for you are good, and have mercy on us"].

Deacon: [Stand and pray] in silence and awe. [Pray, "peace be with us and tranquility with us all."]

Priest: We ask you therefore, almighty Lord and God of the holy powers, falling on our faces before you, that you send your Holy Spirit upon these offerings set before you, (*aloud*) and show this bread to be the venerated body of our Lord Jesus Christ, and this cup the blood of our Lord Jesus Christ, that they may be to all who partake of them for life and resurrection, for forgiveness of sins, and health of soul and body, and enlightenment of mind, and defense before the dread judgment-seat of your Christ; and let no one of your people perish, Lord, but make us all worthy that, serving without disturbance and ministering before you at all times of our life, we may enjoy your heavenly and immortal and life-giving mysteries, through your grace and mercy and love for man, now [and to the ages of ages].

People: Amen.

Priest (bowing): We therefore offer to you, almighty Lord, this reasonable sacrifice for all men, for your catholic Church, for the bishops in it who rightly divide the word of truth, for my insignificance, and for the priests and deacons, for the orthodox of every land, for all your faithful people, for the safekeeping of your flock, for this holy church, for every town and district of the faithful, for good weather and the fruits of the earth, for faithful brethren who are in misery, for those who offered these offerings, for all who are named in your holy churches: grant help to them all; and for our fathers and brothers who have died before us in the true faith: set them in divine glory on the day of judgment, not entering into judgment with them, for in your sight no man living is innocent.

(aloud) For there is one who was seen on earth without sin, your only-begotten Son our Lord Jesus Christ, who is the great propitiation of our race, through whom we hope to find mercy and forgiveness of sins; on account of whom to them also . . .

People: Remit, forgive [Lord, our offences which we have committed willingly, unwillingly, wittingly or unwittingly].

Priest: Especially therefore let us make the memorial of the holy Mother of God and ever-Virgin Mary, the divine Apostles, the holy prophets, the martyrs glorious in victory, and all your saints who have pleased you, by whose prayers and supplications may we be preserved from evil, and may mercy be upon us in either world; that in this also, as in all things your blessed name may be greatly glorified with (the name) of Jesus Christ and your Holy Spirit.

People: As it was [in the beginning, so now and for ever. Amen].[77]

Whether the anaphora brought by John Chrysostom to Constantinople was the Greek version of Twelve Apostles or its own earlier

[77] ET from PEER, 124–28.

parent text, there is no question that CHR represents the further re-dacting or reworking of such an Antiochene anaphoral source, turning it into the most well-known and most frequently used eucharistic prayer in the Eastern Christian world. Chrysostom's own hand is seen precisely in the strong anti-Arian (anti-Anomoean) characteristics of the trinitarian theology and Christology throughout the prayer. Robert Taft's own assessment of its overall symmetry and theological characteristics bear repeating here:

> The extreme simplicity of the Eucharistic theology expressed in CHR betrays its antiquity. Like A[postolic] T[radition] 4, its Trinitarian structure closely resembles that of the Apostles' Creed. . . . [I]ts structure is "undifferentiated," mingling praise and thanks, remembrance and oblation, throughout, and the same may be said for its theology: the flow and context of the prayer provide no ammunition for theological polemics. After thanking and praising God for creation and salvation and everything that was done for us . . . , we turn to praise again in the Sanctus. . . . In the postsanctus . . . we commemorate again the Christ-economy . . . , especially the Last Supper. . . . In the anamnesis we recall once more what was done for us and the command to repeat it . . . , and then proceed to obey this command, offering the oblation to God . . . and giving praise and thanks again. . . . Finally, we express the offering a second time . . . , asking the Father to send his Spirit on the offered gifts to fructify them unto salvation for those who receive them worthily. . . . The entire anaphora is just that, an "anaphora" or sacrifice of praise and thanks, and attempts to divide it into discrete theological "moments" and exploit them for special dogmatic concerns has no hermeneutic legitimacy. In a word, CHR provides a superb example of the sane, balanced Eucharistic theology of the undivided church of the first millennium.[78]

Anaphora of St. John Chrysostom (CHR)

The priest: The grace of our Lord Jesus Christ, and the love of the God and Father, and the fellowship of the Holy Spirit be with you all.
People: And with your spirit.
Priest: Let us lift up our hearts.
People: We have them with the Lord.
Priest: Let us give thanks to the Lord.

---

[78] Taft, "St. John Chrysostom and the Byzantine Anaphora that Bears His Name," in *Essays in Early Eastern Eucharistic Prayers*, ed. Bradshaw, 225–26.

People: It is fitting and right [to worship the Father, the Son, and the Holy Spirit, the consubstantial and undivided Trinity].

The priest begins the holy anaphora:
It is fitting and right to hymn you, [to bless you, to praise you,] to give you thanks, to worship you in all places of your dominion. For you are God, ineffable, inconceivable, invisible, incomprehensible, existing always and in the same way, you and your only-begotten Son and Your Holy Spirit. You brought us out of non-existence into existence; and when we had fallen, you raised us up again, and did not cease to do everything until you had brought us up to heaven, and granted us the kingdom that is to come. For all these things we give thanks to you and to your only-begotten Son and to your Holy Spirit, for all that we know and do not know, your seen and unseen benefits that have come upon us.

We give you thanks also for this ministry; vouchsafe to receive it from our hands, even though thousands of archangels and ten thousands of angels stand before you, cherubim and seraphim, with six wings and many eyes, flying on high, (*aloud*) singing the triumphal hymn [proclaiming, crying, and saying]:

People: Holy, [holy, holy, Lord of Sabaoth; heaven and earth are full of your glory. Hosanna in the highest. Blessed is he who comes in the name of the Lord. Hosanna in the highest].

The priest, privately:
With these powers, Master, lover of man, we also cry and say: holy are you and all-holy, and your only-begotten Son, and your Holy Spirit; holy are you and all-holy and magnificent is your glory; for you so loved the world that you gave your only-begotten Son that all who believe in him may not perish, but have eternal life.

When he had come and fulfilled all the dispensation for us, on the night in which he handed himself over, he took bread in his holy and undefiled and blameless hands, gave thanks, blessed, broke, and gave it to his holy disciples and apostles, saying, (*aloud*) "Take, eat; this is my body, which is [broken] for you [for forgiveness of sins." *People:* Amen]. (*privately*) Likewise the cup also after supper, saying, (*aloud*) "Drink from this, all of you; this is my blood of the new covenant, which is shed for you and for many for the forgiveness of sins."

People: Amen.

The priest, privately:
We therefore, remembering this saving commandment and all the things that were done for us: the cross, the tomb, the resurrection on

the third day, the ascension into heaven, the session at the right hand, the second and glorious coming again; (*aloud*) offering you your own from your own, in all and for all,

People: we hymn you, [we bless you, we give you thanks, Lord, and pray to you, our God].

The priest says privately:
We offer you also this reasonable and bloodless service, and we pray and beseech and entreat you, send down your Holy Spirit on us and on these gifts set forth; and make this bread the precious body of your Christ, [changing it by your Holy Spirit,] Amen; and that which is in this cup the precious blood of your Christ, changing it by your Holy Spirit, Amen; so that they may become to those who partake for vigilance of soul, for fellowship with the Holy Spirit, for the fullness of the kingdom (of heaven), for boldness toward you, not for judgment or condemnation.

We offer you this reasonable service also for those who rest in faith, [forefathers,] Fathers, patriarchs, prophets, apostles, preachers, evangelists, martyrs, confessors, ascetics, and all the righteous [spirits] perfected in faith; (*aloud*) especially our all-holy, immaculate, highly glorious, Blessed Lady, Mother of God and ever-Virgin Mary; [*diptychs of the dead;*] Saint John the [prophet,] forerunner, and Baptist, and the holy, [glorious,] and honored Apostles; and this saint whose memorial we are keeping; and all your saints: at their entreaties, look on us, O God.

And remember all those who have fallen asleep in hope of resurrection to eternal life, [*he remembers them by name*] and grant them rest where the light of your own countenance looks upon them.

Again we beseech you, remember, Lord, all the orthodox episcopate who rightly divide the word of your truth, all the priesthood, the diaconate in Christ, and every order of the clergy.

We offer you this reasonable service also for the (whole) world, for the holy, catholic, and apostolic Church, for those who live in a chaste and reverend state, [for those in mountains and in dens and in caves of the earth,] for the most faithful Emperor, the Christ-loving Empress, and all their court and army: grant them, Lord, a peaceful reign, that in their peace we may live a quiet and peaceful life in all godliness and honesty.

Remember, Lord, the city in which we dwell, and all cities and lands, and all who dwell in them in faith.

(aloud) Above all, remember, Lord, our Archbishop N.

[*Diptychs of the living.*]

Remember, Lord, those at sea, travellers, the sick, those in adversity, prisoners, and their salvation.

Remember, Lord, those who bring forth fruit and do good works in your holy churches and remember the poor; and send out your mercies upon us all, *(aloud)* and grant us with one mouth and one heart to glorify and hymn your all-honorable and magnificent name, the Father, the Son, and the Holy Spirit, [now and always and to the ages of ages].

People: Amen.[79]

2. Western Christian Anaphoras

Anaphoral sources for the Western rites, as noted above, are very sparse for this period of history. There is some evidence to suggest, along with the North African conciliar documents noted at the beginning of this chapter, that there were various *libelli missarum* ("Mass booklets") in circulation in North Africa, and certainly there were written anaphoral texts in Spain and Gaul, at least by the second half of the fifth century.[80] And as we saw in the previous chapter, until recently the anaphora of chapter 4 of the so-called *Apostolic Tradition* has been viewed by scholars as being *the* earliest extant *Western*, and specifically *Roman*, eucharistic prayer, dating from the beginning of the third century. With the exception of Alistair Stewart-Sykes,[81] however, the emerging scholarly consensus is that this prayer in the form it exists in the fifth-century Verona Latin palimpsest is no later than the mid-fourth century, though it certainly has an earlier core,[82] and thanks especially to the work of Matthieu Smyth, it is now increasingly being viewed as West Syrian or Antiochene in structure and not Roman.[83]

---

[79] ET from PEER, 131–34.

[80] On this see Bouley, *From Freedom to Formula*, 165–87.

[81] Alistair Stewart-Sykes, *Hippolytus: On the Apostolic Tradition* (Crestwood, NY: St. Vladimir's Seminary Press, 2001).

[82] For the text see above, chapter 2, page 41, and see Bradshaw, Johnson, Phillips, *The Apostolic Tradition*, 37ff.

[83] Matthieu Smyth, "The Anaphora of the So-Called 'Apostolic Tradition' and the Roman Eucharistic Prayer," in *Issues in Eucharistic Praying*, ed. Johnson, 71–98.

Not only does this prayer exist in other Eastern sources, such as the Ethiopian translation of the *Apostolic Tradition*, as well as forming the core of the later Ethiopian Anaphora of the Apostles, and appearing as the eucharistic prayer of the *Testamentum Domini*, but apart from the Verona Latin text, it *never* appears in any Western liturgical document. Its influence is also to be discerned in the anaphora of book 8 of the late fourth-century (ca. 381) Antiochene church order, *The Apostolic Constitutions*. In analyzing the multiple sources behind this very lengthy eucharistic prayer, Raphael Graves[84] notes the following literary connections with the *Apostolic Tradition* anaphora:

The Preface

. . . the angel of your great purpose. . . . . For you, eternal God, made all things through him. . . .

The Post-Sanctus

. . . he fulfilled your will . . .
. . . that he might free from suffering . . . and break the bonds of the devil . . .

The Anamnesis

Remembering then his . . . death and resurrection . . . we offer you . . . this bread and this cup, giving you thanks through him that you have deemed us worthy to stand before you and to serve you as priests.

The Epiclesis

And to send down your Holy Spirit upon this sacrifice . . . that those who partake of it may be strengthened to piety. . . .

If, then, the anaphora in chapter 4 of the so-called *Apostolic Tradition* can no longer be viewed with certainty as a Western eucharistic text, it means that our primary witness to a written eucharistic anaphora in the West is the mystagogical lecture *De Sacramentis* (ca. 390) of Ambrose of Milan, together with some other fragments from diverse sources and locales.

---

[84] Raphael Graves, "The Anaphora of the Eighth Book of the Apostolic Constitution," in *Essays in Early Eastern Eucharistic Prayers*, ed. Bradshaw, 178–79.

4.14. Perhaps you will say, "My bread is common (bread)." But that bread is bread before the words of the sacraments; when consecration has been applied, from (being) bread it becomes the flesh of Christ. So let us explain how that which is bread can be the body of Christ. And by what words and by whose sayings does consecration take place? The Lord Jesus. For all the other things which are said in the earlier parts are said by the bishop: praise is offered to God; prayer is made for the people, for kings, for others; when the time comes for the venerated sacrament to be accomplished, the bishop no longer uses his own words, but uses the words of Christ. So the word of Christ accomplishes this sacrament. . . .

21. Do you wish to know how consecration is done with heavenly words? Hear what the words are. The bishop says:

Make for us this offering approved, reasonable, acceptable, because it is the figure of the body and blood of our Lord Jesus Christ; who, the day before he suffered, took bread in his holy hands, looked up to heaven to you, holy Father, almighty, eternal God, gave thanks, blessed, and broke it, and handed it when broken to his apostles and disciples, saying, "Take and eat from this, all of you; for this is my body, which will be broken for many."

22. Notice this. *Likewise after supper, the day before he suffered, he took the cup, looked up to heaven to you, holy Father, almighty, eternal God, gave thanks, blessed, and handed it to his apostles and disciples, saying, "Take and drink from this, all of you; for this is my blood."*

See, all those words up to *"Take,"* whether the body or the blood, are the evangelist's; then they are Christ's words, *"Take and drink from this, all of you; for this is my blood."*

23. Notice these points. He says, *"Who, the day before He suffered, took bread in his holy hands."* Before it is consecrated, it is bread; but when the words of Christ are added, it is the body of Christ. Then hear his words: *"Take and eat from this, all of you; for this is my body."* And before the words of Christ, the cup is full of wine and water; when the words of Christ have been employed, the blood is created which redeems his people. So you see in what ways the word of Christ has power to change everything. Our Lord Jesus himself therefore bore witness that we should receive his body and blood. Ought we to doubt his faith and witness? . . .

25. So you do not say *"Amen"* to no purpose: you confess in spirit that you are receiving the body of Christ. When you seek it, the bishop says to you, *"The body of Christ,"* and you say, *"Amen,"* which means *"It is*

true." What your tongue confesses, let your feelings retain, so that you may know that this is a sacrament whose likeness has come first.

26. Next, you must learn how great a sacrament it is. See what he says: *"As often as you do this, so often you will make remembrance of me until I come again."*

27. And the bishop says:

Therefore, remembering his most glorious Passion and resurrection from the dead, and ascension into heaven, we offer to you this spotless victim, reasonable victim, bloodless victim, this holy bread and this cup of eternal life; and we pray and beseech you to receive this offering on your altar on high by the hands of your angels, as you vouchsafed to receive the gifts of your righteous servant Abel, and the sacrifice of our patriarch Abraham, and that which the high priest Melchizedek offered to you.

5.18. Now what is left but the (Lord's) Prayer? . . .

6.24. . . . What follows? Hear what the bishop says:

Through our Lord Jesus Christ, in whom and with whom honor, praise, glory, magnificence, and power are yours, with the Holy Spirit, from the ages, and now, and always, and to all the ages of ages. Amen.[85]

Of particular importance here is that Ambrose quotes prayer texts closely parallel to what we will come to know as the Roman *canon missae*, the eucharistic prayer that will eventually remain the single anaphora of the Roman Rite until the liturgical reforms of the Second Vatican Council. *De Sacramentis* 4.21–23, 27, and 6.24 are clearly parallel to—but are not identical with—what are called, from the first Latin words of each section of the *canon*, the *Quam oblationem* and *Qui pridie*, the *Unde et memores*, the *Supra quae*, the *Supplices te*, and the concluding doxology. There are, however, two significant differences, together with the fact that these paragraphs are, in general, much less developed than their parallel sections in the Canon. First, the final text of the Roman *canon missae* in its *Quam oblationem* will say: "Vouchsafe, we beseech you, O God, to make this offering wholly blessed, approved, ratified, reasonable, and acceptable; *that it may become to us the body and blood of your dearly beloved Son Jesus Christ our Lord.*"[86] This petition for consecration,

---

[85] ET from PEER, 144–46.
[86] ET from ibid., 145.

in the position of the Alexandrian post-*Sanctus* epiclesis 1, where it is not consecratory, is different in Ambrose, where he quotes the text as: "Make for us this offering approved, reasonable, acceptable, *because it is the figure of the body and blood of our Lord Jesus Christ*." But the following words from 4.23 seem to be an interpretation more consistent with the later Roman Canon than with the prayer Ambrose knew:

23. Notice these points. He says, "*Who, the day before He suffered, took bread in his holy hands.*" Before it is consecrated, it is bread; but when the words of Christ are added, it is the body of Christ. Then hear his words: "*Take and eat from this, all of you; for this is my body.*" And before the words of Christ, the cup is full of wine and water; when the words of Christ have been employed, the blood is created which redeems his people. So you see in what ways the word of Christ has power to change everything. Our Lord Jesus himself therefore bore witness that we should receive his body and blood. Ought we to doubt his faith and witness?

In other words, Ambrose's interpretation of the narrative of institution being somehow "consecratory" is not really born out by the text that he cites! Rather, the eucharistic prayer he knows does not support a theology of consecration by the narrative of institution but, in fact, already uses "sacramental" language in describing the bread and wine as the *figura* (figure) of the body and blood of Christ *before* that narrative is recited.[87] Indeed, the thought of the anaphora here seems to be, "God, bless our offering, *because* this *offering* is already the *figura* of the body and blood of Christ." Here, there are parallels with the Prosphora of Sarapion (*homoioma*) and the various anaphoras of St. Basil (*antitypos*), and not surprisingly, scholars have often sought a close relationship between the Roman Canon and Egyptian liturgical sources.[88] Indeed, if the narrative of institution (*Qui pridie*) in Ambrose's prayer would have been connected to the preceding by the use of "for" or "because," that Egyptian connection would have been

[87] Recall the use of this word to refer to the Eucharist in Tertullian, above, 48–50. On the use of this in Ambrose, see R. Gregoire, "Il sangue eucaristico nei testi eucologici di Serapione di Thmuis," in *Sangue e antroplogia nella liturgia*, ed. F. Valtioni (Rome, 1984), 1281–86; and Enrico Mazza, *The Eucharistic Prayers of the Roman Rite* (New York: Pueblo, 1986), 70–71.

[88] See, most recently, Walter Ray, "Rome and Alexandria: Two Cities, One Anaphoral Tradition," in *Issues in Eucharistic Praying*, ed. Johnson, 99–128.

stronger here still. More important, however, is the fact that in contrast to most Eastern sources, Ambrose understands this "consecration" to be effected not by an invocation of the Holy Spirit but by the recitation of the words of Christ, an understanding that will come to influence Western eucharistic liturgical practice and theology in profound ways.

The second distinction from the later Roman Canon to be noted here is that in Ambrose's equivalent to the Canon's *Supplices te*, we have a reference to "angels" in the plural ("we pray and beseech you to receive this offering on your altar on high by the hands of your *angels*"), while the Roman Canon refers to an "angel" in the singular ("bid these things be borne by the hands of your *angel* to your altar on high"). Scholars have long debated over this distinction and whether or not the "angel" is a christological reference, as in the anaphora of the *Apostolic Tradition* and the anaphora in book 8 of the *Apostolic Constitutions*, or whether Ambrose's "angels" are meant to be the Son and the Holy Spirit.[89] Enrico Mazza is probably correct in concluding that the "angel" or "angels" are references precisely to an angelic ministry, "a heavenly liturgy . . . that is performed by the angels around an altar,"[90] although he too notes that the christological and trinitarian questions must remain open.

Elsewhere, Mazza has noted correctly that the closest parallels to Ambrose's combination of the Canon's *Supra quae* and *Supplices te* are to be located in the Alexandrian tradition, most notably in the anaphoras of St. Mark, both Coptic and Greek versions, where the following appears in the preface intercessions:

> The sacrifices, oblations, and thank offerings of those who offer honor and glory to your holy name, receive them upon your *reasonable altar in heaven* for a sweet-smelling savor, into your vastness in heaven, through the ministry of *your holy angels and archangels*: as *you accepted the gifts of righteous Abel and the sacrifice of our father Abraham* and the two mites of the widow, so also accept the thank offerings of your servants, those of the great and of the small, the hidden and the open, of those who have offered to you these gifts this day.[91]

---

[89] See B. Botte, "L'ange du sacrifice et l'epiclèse de la messe romaine au moyen âge," *Revue de théologie ancienne et médiévale* 1 (1929): 285–308.

[90] Mazza, *The Eucharistic Prayers of the Roman Rite*, 82.

[91] ET adapted from Brightman, *Liturgies Eastern and Western*, 170–71, here from Coptic Mark (Cyril).

Again, therefore, a close anaphoral connection is made between the Egyptian and Roman traditions, and, in fact, that connection is closest in Ambrose over and against later versions of the Roman Canon itself. Nevertheless, as Mazza states:

> One sees very clearly how very strong is the affinity between the Alexandrian text and the Roman tradition, notwithstanding that the Alexandrian text is more developed than that of the *De Sacramentis*. . . . Consequently, we can say that the two prayers belong to the development of the same tradition. That is, we are considering the same prayer in two different moments of its history and as it developed in two different directions, one Roman and the other Alexandrian. This statement is reinforced by the fact that all the elements that these texts have in common belong only to these two anaphoric traditions and to no other. What is held in common by the Alexandrian and Roman liturgies is unique to them.[92]

Scholars, such as M. Righetti and Cyprian Vagaggini, have taken Ambrose's text and added it to other texts and fragments from various sources, some contemporary with Ambrose from north Italy in the fourth century and others from Mozarabic (Spanish) liturgical sources, and have constructed the following tentative *canon missae*[93] for the Roman tradition in the fourth and fifth centuries:

Preface and Te igitur

It is fitting and right, it is just and right, that we should give you thanks for all things, O Lord, holy Father, almighty eternal God, for you deigned in the incomparable splendor of your goodness that light should shine in our darkness, by sending us Jesus Christ as savior of our souls. For our salvation he humbled himself and subjected himself even unto death that, when we had been restored to that immortality which Adam lost, he might make us heirs and sons to himself.

Neither can we be sufficient to give thanks to your great generosity for this loving kindness with any praises; but we ask (you) of your great and merciful goodness to hold accepted this sacrifice which we offer to you, standing before the face of your divine goodness; through Jesus Christ our Lord and God, [through whom we pray and beseech . . .

---

[92] Mazza, *The Origins of the Eucharistic Prayer*, 272; see also 269–72.
[93] ET from PEER, 156–57.

Te igitur, Memento Domine, *and* Quam oblationem

Through him we pray and beseech] you, almighty Father, vouchsafe to accept and bless these offerings and these unblemished sacrifices; above all, those which we offer to you for your holy Catholic Church: vouchsafe to grant it peace, spread through the whole world in your peace.

Remember, Lord, also, we pray, your servants who in honor of your Saints NN. pay their vows to the living and true God, for the forgiveness of all their sins. [Vouchsafe to make their offering blessed, ratified, and reasonable; it is the image and likeness of the body and blood of Jesus Christ, your Son and our Redeemer.

Quam oblationem, Qui pridie, Unde et Memores, Supplices te, *and* Supra quae *(from* **De Sacramentis)**

Make for us this offering approved, reasonable, acceptable, because it is the figure of the body and blood of our Lord Jesus Christ;] who, the day before he suffered, took bread in his holy hands, looked up to heaven to you, holy Father, almighty, eternal God, gave thanks, blessed, and broke it, and handed it when broken to his apostles and disciples, saying, "Take and eat from this, all of you; for this is my body, which will be broken for many." Likewise after supper, the day before he suffered, he took the cup, looked up to heaven to you, holy Father, almighty, eternal God, gave thanks, blessed, and handed it to his apostles and disciples, saying, "Take and drink from this, all of you; for this is my blood."

Therefore, remembering his most glorious Passion and resurrection from the dead, and ascension into heaven, we offer to you this spotless victim, reasonable victim, bloodless victim, this holy bread and this cup of eternal life; [and we pray and beseech you to receive this offering on your altar on high by the hands of your angels, as you vouchsafed to receive the gifts of your righteous servant Abel, and the sacrifice of our patriarch Abraham, and that which the high priest Melchizedek offered to you.

Supra quae *and* Epiclesis

We beseech and entreat you to accept and bless this offering also, as you accepted the gifts of your righteous servant Abel, and the sacrifice of the patriarch Abraham our father, and that which your high priest Melchizedek offered to you.] Let your blessing, I pray, descend here invisibly, as once it used to descend on the victims of the Fathers. Let a sweet-smelling savor ascend to the sight of your divine majesty by the hands of your angel. And let your Holy Spirit be borne down upon those solemn things, to sanctify both the offerings and the prayers alike of the people who stand here and offer, that all we who taste of this body may receive healing for our souls.

Doxology (from **De Sacramentis***)*

Through our Lord Jesus Christ, in whom and with whom honor, praise, glory, magnificence, and power are yours, with the Holy Spirit, from the ages, and now, and always, and to all the ages of ages. Amen.

This reconstruction is and must remain hypothetical, especially because the explicit epiclesis of the Holy Spirit, supplied in this case from a Mozarabic *"post-pridie,"* that is, a prayer after the narrative of institution, has no liturgical parallel in *Roman* liturgical sources whatsoever. It is true that in the *Liber pontificalis* Pope Gelasius I (ca. 492–96) is credited with saying that "the heavenly Spirit . . . is invoked for the consecration of the divine mystery,"[94] but there are no extant Roman liturgical texts to back up this assertion. With regard, then, to the existence of the Roman *canon missae* in the fourth and fifth centuries, the most that can be said is that it was assuming its fixed form in the time of Ambrose of Milan and was quite probably put into its essential form and structure somewhat earlier, that is, during the pontificate of Damasus (366–84). And while various Roman bishops (e.g., Innocent I in the early fifth century and Vigilius in the mid-sixth century) refer to this fixed prayer as a *prex canonica*, it does not reach its final form until the pontificate of Pope Gregory the Great (590–604).[95]

SUMMARY

1. Within the changed ecclesial-cultural-social context of the fourth and fifth centuries, the eucharistic liturgies of both East and West begin to assume the liturgical shape and contents of what will become the various and distinct eucharistic rites associated primarily with the patriarchal sees.
2. The eucharistic liturgies themselves begin to take on various dramatic, architectural, and ritual elements from the surrounding culture as well as catechetical and didactic elements in order that

---

[94] *Liber pontificalis* I.
[95] On the early development of the Roman canon, in addition to Mazza referred to above, see especially Bouley, *From Freedom to Formula*, 206–15. On the further development of this prayer into its final form within the early Middle Ages, see below, pages 205–9.

the liturgies themselves might make up for inadequate or incomplete catechesis.

3. If frequency of eucharistic celebration increases, frequency in the reception of communion decreases in light of the developments noted in 2 above.

4. The anaphoras or eucharistic prayers now assume fixed written forms, shapes, and contents, many of which are still in use within the various liturgical rites today.

Chapter 4

The Fourth and Fifth Centuries
Questions in Anaphoral Development
and Eucharistic Theology

In relationship to the early anaphoras studied in chapter 2, three elements in particular stand out in almost all of the fourth- and fifth-century prayers presented in the previous chapter: (1) the incorporation of the *Sanctus* from Isaiah 6 and, outside Egypt, of an accompanying *Benedictus*; (2) an epiclesis of either the *Logos* (Sarapion) or the Holy Spirit upon the eucharistic gifts, in many cases explicitly requesting their "consecration" and change; and (3) the entrance of the dominical narrative of institution from the biblical Last Supper accounts into the anaphora. Each of these requires discussion, since each of these is an issue of scholarly debate. Further, since these particular elements, together with the various eucharistic rites themselves we have seen developing in these centuries, are related directly to the theological interpretation of the Eucharist, the second half of this chapter is devoted explicitly to those theological issues.

QUESTIONS IN ANAPHORAL DEVELOPMENT

1. Sanctus

The question of the entrance of the *Sanctus* of Isaiah 6:3 into the anaphora—the when and the where—has long been an issue in eucharistic praying, an "unresolved puzzle," in the words of Enrico Mazza.[1] Until recently, there were two primary theories on how this took place.[2] The first, the "Egyptian theory," advanced and popularized by Gregory

---

[1] Enrico Mazza, *The Origins of the Eucharistic Prayer* (Collegeville, MN: Liturgical Press, Pueblo, 1995), 202.

[2] For a more detailed overview see Maxwell E. Johnson, "The Origins of the Anaphoral use of the Sanctus and Epiclesis Revisited: The Contribution of Gabriele Winkler and its Implications," in *Crossroad of Cultures: Studies in Liturgy and Patristics in Honor of Gabriele Winkler*, ed. H-J. Feulner, E. Velkovska, and R. Taft, OCA 260 (Rome: Pontificio Istituto Orientale, 2000), 405–42.

Dix,[3] held that the origins of the anaphoral use of the *Sanctus* were to be found in Alexandria, where it existed by the middle of the third century, a location and date witnessed to, presumably, in Origen of Alexandria's *De principiis* 1 and 4. As nuanced further by Georg Kretschmar,[4] namely, that an anaphoral use of the *Sanctus* did not yet exist in Origen's day but that Origen's *theology* strongly influenced its shape when it *was* adopted for anaphoral use later in the third century, this "Egyptian theory" has had a strong and long-lasting effect on liturgical scholarship. The second theory, the so-called climax theory, advocated by E. C. Ratcliff in an important 1950 essay,[5] argued that the anaphoral *Sanctus* went back to the very origins of Christian eucharistic praying itself and that it originally functioned as the *conclusion* of an anaphoral pattern that consisted only of a lengthy thanksgiving for creation and redemption followed by a thanksgiving for the admission of earthly worshipers into that of the angels of heaven. In part, Ratcliff's argument was based on the line *adstare coram te et tibi ministrare*, "to stand before you and minister to you," in the anaphora of *Apostolic Tradition* 4, which he interpreted as a remnant of an introduction to the *Sanctus* that had once followed at this point. Scholars today tend not to accept Ratcliff's climax theory, although the Egyptian theory still has some rather strong support.

In a highly important two-part article in 1991 and 1992, Robert Taft advances a strong defense of the Egyptian theory for the interpolation of the *Sanctus* into the anaphora.[6] He argues that the Egyptian form of the *Sanctus*, without *Benedictus*, as witnessed to, for example, by Greek St. Mark—and attached to an immediately following epiclesis connecting "heaven and earth are full of your holy glory" to the invocation "fill, O God, this sacrifice also with the blessing from you through the descent of your [all-]holy Spirit"[7]—to be the more primitive form since it appeared to be integral to the structure of the Egyptian anaphora overall. Similarly, along with Kretschmar, he dates its interpolation

[3] Gregory Dix, "Primitive Consecration Prayers," *Theology* 37 (1938): 261–83.

[4] Georg Kretschmar, *Studien zum frühchristlichen Trinitätstheologie* (Tübingen, 1956), 164.

[5] E. C. Ratcliff, "The Sanctus and the Pattern of the Early Anaphora," *Journal of Ecclesiastical History* 1 (1950): 29–36, 125–34.

[6] Robert Taft, "The Interpolation of the Sanctus into the Anaphora: When and Where? A Review of the Dossier," Part 1, OCP 57 (1991): 281–308; Part 2, OCP 58 (1992): 531–52.

[7] See PEER, 64.

into the anaphora to the second half of the third century, in a form highly influenced by Origen of Alexandria's theology of the biblical *Sanctus* of Isaiah 6. Origen writes in *De principiis*:

> My Hebrew teacher also used to teach as follows, that since the beginning or the end of all things could not be comprehended by any except our Lord Jesus Christ and the Holy Spirit, this was the reason why Isaiah spoke of there being in the vision that appeared to him two seraphim only, who with two wings cover the face of God, with two cover his feet, and with two fly, crying one to another and saying, "Holy, holy, holy is the Lord of hosts; the whole earth is full of thy glory" [Isa 6:2-3]. For because the two seraphim alone have their wings over the face of God and over his feet, we may venture to declare that neither the armies of the holy angels nor the holy thrones, nor the dominions, nor principalities, nor powers can wholly know the beginnings of all things and the ends of the universe. (*De principiis* 4.3, 14)[8]

For Taft, as for Dix, the place to see this interpolation of the *Sanctus* into the anaphora most clearly in its Origenist interpretation is in the Prosphora of Sarapion of Thmuis, where the introduction to the *Sanctus* through the post-*Sanctus* epiclesis reads:

> For you are above all rule and authority and power and dominion and every name which is named, not only in this age but also in the coming one. Beside you stand a thousand thousands and a myriad myriads of angels, archangels, thrones, dominions, principalities and powers.
>
> Beside you stand the two most-honored six-winged seraphim. With two wings they cover the face, and with two the feet, and with two they fly, sanctifying. With them receive also our sanctification as we say:
>
> Holy, holy, holy Lord of Sabaoth;
> heaven and earth are full of your glory.
>
> Full is heaven and full also is the earth of your majestic glory, Lord of powers. Fill also this sacrifice with your power and with your participation. For to you we offered this living sacrifice, the unbloody offering.[9]

---

[8] ET from G. W. Butterworth, *Origen on First Principles* (London: Peter Smith, 1936), 311.

[9] Maxwell E. Johnson, *The Prayers of Sarapion of Thmuis: A Literary, Liturgical, and Theological Analysis*, OCA 249 (Rome: Pontificio Istituto Orientale, 1995), 47.

Taft concludes, then, by claiming that the *idea* of interpolating the *Sanctus* into the anaphora came from Egypt, while the *form* the *Sanctus* took in other traditions, like that of Syria with the added *Benedictus*, came from Christianized versions of Jewish synagogue prayer.

At the same time that Taft was preparing his essay on the topic, Bryan Spinks' important study, *The Sanctus in the Eucharistic Prayer*, appeared.[10] Therein, Spinks rejects both of the standard theories of Ratcliff and Dix, claiming that the origins of the anaphoral use of the *Sanctus* were more likely Syrian than Egyptian and its use was probably derived—directly or even indirectly—from synagogue liturgy (Jewish or Christianized), Jewish mysticism (*merkavah*), or simply from biblical language itself, taking different forms in different places. Diametrically opposed to the work of Taft, Spinks argues that the earliest anaphoral use of the *Sanctus* is in the Anaphora of Addai and Mari, already in the third century. And against what would be one of Taft's primary arguments, as well as against both Dix and Kretschmar, Spinks claims that there is "little justification for seeing the theology of Origen" behind Sarapion's text at all.[11] According to Spinks, the reference to "the two most-honored six-winged seraphim" in the Prosphora of Sarapion merely reflects an Alexandrian identification of the two living creatures in the Septuagint version of Habakkuk 3:2, with the seraphim of Isaiah 6:3 being an identification known by both Clement of Alexandria (*Stromateis* 7:12)[12] and Athanasius (*In illud omnia mihi tradita sunt* 6).[13] Consequently, Spinks claims that:

> This link, together with the strange petition which introduces the pericope, might suggest to the speculative mind Origen's theology equating seraphim with the Son and Spirit. However, the text does not actually make this equation and is perfectly consistent with the understanding found in Clement and Athanasius that the two living creatures were the seraphim. The thought of the Thmuis eucharistic prayer seems to be: "Christ and the Holy Spirit speak in us, so that we, like the living creatures [seraphim] who stand beside you, may praise you with the Holy, holy, holy."[14]

[10] Bryan Spinks, *The Sanctus in the Eucharistic Prayer* (Cambridge: Cambridge University Press, 1991).

[11] Ibid., 87.

[12] For ET see ANF 2, 546.

[13] For ET see NPNF 2:4, 90.

[14] Spinks, *Sanctus*, 89.

A few years after publication of that study, however, Spinks nuanced this position, saying that the Dix-Kretschmar approach, as embraced and furthered by Taft, is "suggestive and plausible," and claiming that Sarapion's petition (i.e., "let the Lord Jesus speak in us and let holy Spirit also hymn you through us") is to be "interpreted more naturally as simply reflecting the indwelling of the Son and Spirit. . . . We cannot join the heavenly worship unless Christ and the Holy Spirit make their dwelling in us."[15] It should be noted that Sarapion quite clearly does say, in fact, that *it is the Son and Spirit themselves* who worship God by speaking and hymning *through us*. Thus, the "heavenly worship" to which the liturgical assembly is joined in participation appears to be precisely that which is offered eternally to the Father by the Son and Holy Spirit.[16]

Gabriele Winkler has taken a different methodological approach to our question, and she has done this in two phases. First, of her many significant contributions to the study of early Christian liturgy, one major emphasis has been her thorough and detailed analysis of the Syrian *Acts of the Apostles* and the attention she has drawn to their often-overlooked importance and role within liturgical development in general. As we noted in the previous chapter with regard especially to the epiclesis, in three key articles[17] she turns precisely to these important sources within their overall Christian initiation context, where she argues that both the *Sanctus* and epiclesis emerged in early Syria as portions of the prayers for the consecration of the prebaptismal oil and water. With particular attention to the initiation materials appearing in the *Acts of John*, she notes that the *Sanctus*, addressed only to God the Father, appears in a close relationship to the prebaptismal oil

[15] Bryan Spinks, "The Integrity of the Anaphora of Sarapion of Thmuis and Liturgical Methodology," *Journal of Theological Studies* 49 (1998): 141.

[16] See Maxwell E. Johnson, "The Baptismal Rite and Anaphora in the Prayers of Sarapion of Thmuis: An Assessment of a Recent 'Judicious Reassessment,'" *Worship* 73 (March 1999): 140–68.

[17] Gabriele Winkler, "Nochmals zu den Anfängen der Epiklese und des Sanctus im Eucharistischen Hochgebet," *Theologisches Quartalschrift* 74, no. 3 (1994): 214–31; *idem*, "Further Observations in Connection with the Early Form of the Epiklesis," *Le Sacrement de l'Initiation: Origines et Prospectives, Patrimoine Syriaque Actes du colloque III* (Antelias, Lebanon, 1996), 66–80; and *idem*, "Weitere Beobachtungen zur frühen Epiklese (den Doxologien und dem Sanctus), Über die Bedeutung der Apokryphen für die Erforschung der Entwicklung der Riten," *Oriens Christianus* 80 (1996): 177–200.

of anointing. This, according to Winkler, was the distinctive ritual high-point of Christian initiation in the early Syrian tradition.[18] In the *Acts of John* the *Sanctus* is connected further to the appearance of fire, an element that "goes back to a very ancient strand of the tradition," found in other early Syrian sources, in which fire appeared in the Jordan itself at the baptism of Jesus. Indeed, it is this connection between the appearance of fire, Jesus' own baptism, and Christian baptism as assimilation to Jesus' own baptism that may have suggested the inclusion of the *Sanctus* here in the first place. Furthermore, two other elements are of particular significance. First, it is important to note that the text of the *Sanctus* in the relevant passages from the *Acts of John* does not contain any form of the *Benedictus*, a fact that, according to Winkler, demonstrates that the *Benedictus* was also not a part of the *Sanctus* in the early Syrian tradition. Second, and most important, Winkler underscores the overall initiation context of the *Sanctus* in the early Syrian tradition and suggests that it is from here that it would pass eventually into anaphoral usage.

While the connection between the *Sanctus* and the prebaptismal anointing for Syria is indicated only within the *Acts of John*, an overall initiation context for the *Sanctus* is suggested in other Eastern sources as well. As Winkler notes, not only does the *Sanctus* continue to be present in the East Syrian baptismal rite for the consecration of oil, the West Syrian baptismal rite at the consecration of the baptismal water, the Maronite rite for the consecration of the waters at Epiphany, and the East Syrian Night Office (*Leyla*) for Epiphany,[19] all of which tie the use of the *Sanctus* to the celebration of Jesus' own baptism—his pneumatic birth and assimilation of "Adam"—in the Jordan, but early Eastern sources elsewhere also make a similar connection between the *Sanctus* and Christian initiation. In the homilies of Asterios Sophistes of Cappadocia, for example, it is precisely within the context of the Easter Vigil that reference is made to both neophytes and all the assembly

---

[18] Winkler, "Nochmals zu den Anfängen," 223. Here she refers also to her essay, "Die Licht-Erscheinung bei der Taufe Jesu und der Ursprung des Epiphaniefestes" = ET as "The Appearance of the Light at the Baptism of Jesus and the Origins of Epiphany: An Investigation of Greek, Syriac, Armenian, and Latin Sources," trans. David Maxwell, in *Between Memory and Hope: Readings on the Liturgical Year*, ed. Maxwell E. Johnson (Collegeville, MN: Liturgical Press, Pueblo, 2000), 291–348.

[19] For texts and references see Winkler, "Nochmals zu den Anfängen," 225–29.

singing the *Sanctus* in the anaphora (now, though, in its "later" form with the *Benedictus*). While a similar reference occurs in Gregory of Nyssa, Winkler draws special attention to *Mystagogical Catechesis* 5.6 of Cyril (John) of Jerusalem, where the *Sanctus*, without *Benedictus*, is directed to God the Father (as in the *Acts of John*) and where it has entered the anaphora itself at the conclusion of the initiation rites. According to her, the very fourth-century change in the meaning of the prebaptismal anointing from pneumatic assimilation to Christ to an exorcistic purification in preparation for the gift of the Holy Spirit by the water bath and subsequent *postbaptismal* anointing suggests that this may have caused the *Sanctus* to be shifted from its prebaptismal location to the eucharistic liturgy, the culminating rite of initiation. Such an "original baptismal context" for the anaphoral use of the *Sanctus* in Syria, Cappadocia, and Syro-Palestine is paralleled in the West as well. Indeed, it is *because* the Eucharist itself is an integral part of the overall complex of Christian initiation rites that such a connection between the anaphora and initiation rites can be suggested in the first place.

Second, since the publication of those essays, Winkler's long-awaited, monumental monograph *Das Sanctus* has appeared.[20] Herein, she moves the question beyond the context of Christian initiation in the early Syrian tradition and out of the Syrian *Acts* into Old Testament Pseudepigraphal and other Jewish and Jewish-Christian sources from which the anaphoral *Sanctus* may have been derived in the first place, a research direction taken earlier by Spinks in the first three chapters of his already mentioned study, although Winkler makes use of additional sources. While, according to her, Syria remains the place of origin for the anaphoral use of the *Sanctus*, comparative support is sought within other geographical and ecclesial locales, most notably that of Ethiopia, which, according to her, deserves much greater attention than past scholarship has normally given it.

What we find compelling about Winkler's approach is that it provides the beginning of a *theological* answer to the question of why the *Sanctus* appears in a eucharistic context. That is, as we have seen, the *Sanctus* is sung at the consecration of the prebaptismal oil because the prebaptismal anointing, according to her, was the very highpoint of the ritual. Indeed, it is the very place where the glory and presence, the *Shekinah*, of God is revealed. Note the following from the *Acts of John*:

---

[20] Gabriele Winkler, *Das Sanctus. Über den Ursprung und die Anfänge des Sanctus und sein Fortwirken*, OCA 267 (Rome 2002).

2:9–12: And straightaway fire blazed forth over the oil and the oil did not take fire, for two angels had their wings spread over the oil and were crying: *"Holy, holy, holy, Lord Almighty"* [Isa 6:3].

4:6–10: And in that hour fire blazed forth over the oil, and the wings of the angels were spread over the oil, and the whole assemblage was crying out, men and women and children, *"Holy, holy, holy, Lord Almighty of whose praises heaven and earth are full"* [Isa 6:3].[21]

Thus, Winkler has identified early evidence for the emergence of the *Sanctus* not in a context that today we might call "non-sacramental worship" (such as synagogue prayer, Jewish mysticism, etc.) but in the *very heart* of liturgical worship, the moment of divine revelation in the sacramental event. From this initiatory context, it would be but a small and logical step to the Eucharist. In the conclusion to his own study, Bryan Spinks himself similarly suggests the theological *aptness* of the *Sanctus* in the anaphora:

> Although it is quite possible, and in some cases perhaps desirable, to compile Eucharistic prayers *without* the sanctus, there is every reason to expect that this ancient chant will continue to be utilised in some form in the Eucharistic prayer—not because of tradition, but because it is *appropriate*. For, in Christian theology, the glory of God was revealed in Christ whose love and grace is revealed in the Eucharistic feast. In Christ the space of heaven and the region of the earth are united. In the Eucharist the worshipper enters heaven through Christ, and is represented by our true High Priest. Here time and eternity intersect and become one, and this world and the world to come elide.[22]

We suggest, then, that it is only when the Eucharist itself becomes conceived of as *the* primary location and manifestation of the presence of Christ, the very dwelling of the *Shekinah* here and now, that the *Sanctus* enters into eucharistic praying as the most "appropriate" christological hymn—with or without *Benedictus*—to acclaim and glorify that presence. And when it does, is the language used not so much that of synagogue *berakoth* or domestic worship—Christianized or not—but of the closest biblical parallel, God's self-revelation to Isaiah in the temple, the experience of which still can only be called *mysterium tremendum*

---

[21] ET from W. Wright, *Apocryphal Acts of the Apostles*, vol. 2 (London, 1871), as cited by Winkler, "Nochmals zu den Anfängen," 221–22.

[22] Spinks, *Sanctus*, 206; emphasis added.

et fascinans. Indeed, it is the language of, at least, the heavenly temple, where Christ continually pleads his once-for-all sacrifice (Heb 9:12) and the four living creatures of Revelation 4:8 continually sing the *Sanctus*. In fact, as the great hymn *On Faith* I.73, 1 of St. Ephrem the Syrian (d. 373) demonstrates, it is not just the *Sanctus* but the very contents of Isaiah's encounter with God in Isaiah 6:2-3 that become interpreted in a eucharistic manner, a manner that still governs one understanding of Holy Communion in the Christian East today:

On Faith I.73, 1:

In your Bread there is hidden the Spirit who is not consumed,
in your Wine there dwells the fire that is not drunk;
the Spirit is in your Bread, the Fire in your Wine,
a manifest wonder, which our lips have received.

When the Lord came down to earth to mortal men
he created them again in a new creation, like angels,
mingling Fire and Spirit within them,
so that in a hidden manner they might be of Fire and Spirit.

The Seraph could not touch the fire's coals with his fingers,
But just brought it close to Isaiah's mouth;
The Seraph did not hold it, Isaiah did not consume it,
But us our Lord has allowed to do both.

To the angels who are spiritual Abraham brought
food for the body, and they ate. The new miracle
is that our mighty Lord has given to bodily man
Fire and Spirit to eat and drink.

Fire descended in wrath and consumed sinners,
The Fire of mercy descended and dwelt in the bread.
Instead of that fire which consumed mankind,
You have consumed Fire in the Bread and you come to life.

Fire descended and consumed Elijah's sacrifice,
the Fire of mercies has become a living sacrifice for us:
Fire consumed the oblation,
And we Lord, have consumed your Fire in your oblation.[23]

---

[23] ET from S. Brock, *The Holy Spirit in the Syrian Baptismal Tradition* (New York: John XXIII Center, 1979), 12–13.

And, Cyril (John) of Jerusalem offers his own rationale for the singing of the *Sanctus*: "The reason why we sing this hymn of praise which has been handed down to us from the seraphim is that we may share with the supernatural armies in their hymnody."[24]

With the possible exception of the Anaphora of Addai and Mari, which *may* or *may not* have included the *Sanctus* originally, prior to the written anaphoras and other documents of the fourth century (e.g., the *Te Deum* and the *Acts of John*) our evidence for some kind of possible Christian liturgical—but non-eucharistic—usage of the *Sanctus* is limited indeed. Within extant Christian literature, along with Revelation 4:8, it appears only in 1 Clement 34:5-8; *The Passion of Sts. Perpetua and Fecility* 12.2, narrating their entrance into heaven; and Tertullian's *De oratione* 3.3, the liturgical context of which, if any, is difficult to determine. Hence, whatever the case may have been in the third century, it is only in the fourth century that we know with certainty the presence of the *Sanctus* within the anaphora. Indeed, in that context, the addition of the *Sanctus* to the Church's public eucharistic liturgy could do nothing other than underscore strongly and most appropriately that "awesome" rite now taking place on the altar. And when the *Sanctus* entered the anaphora sometime in the fourth century, it took different forms depending on locale and tradition. In Egypt, it reflected, without *Benedictus*, the Origenist theological interpretation given by Origen himself and exemplified in the Prosphora of Sarapion of Thmuis. In Syro-Palestine, as recorded in Cyril (John) of Jerusalem, it appears to have been similar. In Syria, the form it took was probably related, directly or indirectly, to Jewish synagogue usage or even to Christianized synagogue usage. And in Ethiopia, according to Winkler, it came from Ethiopic Enoch 39, which has itself an original Syrian provenance.[25]

Robert Taft has criticized the theory that the *Sanctus* could have originated in different ways and different places unrelated to each other, saying that "the suggestion that the Sanctus could have landed independently, in both Egypt and elsewhere, in basically the same place in the same shape of the anaphora, between the praise and in-

[24] ET from PEER, 85.
[25] See Gabriele Winkler, "A New Witness to the Missing Institution Narrative," in *Studia Liturgica Diversa: Essays in Honor of Paul F. Bradshaw*, ed. Maxwell E. Johnson and L. Edward Phillips (Portland, OR: Pastoral Press, 2004), 117–28, esp. 121–28.

stitution account, cannot be taken seriously."[26] Hence, since someone had to be first, we continue to find it highly suggestive that the earliest fourth-century anaphoras we possess having the *Sanctus* are Egyptian, namely, the Prosphora of Sarapion of Thmuis from the mid-fourth century, and, if Michael Zheltov's recent dating of the Barcelona Papyrus is accepted,[27] the *early* fourth century. But wherever it first entered eucharistic praying, certainly it is the overall changed ecclesial, social, and cultural context of the fourth century that encouraged its wider dissemination and use throughout the churches of the Christian East, and from the East, undoubtedly, eventually to the West.

2. Epiclesis

The earlier development of what is called the epiclesis, the invocation of the *Logos* and/or Holy Spirit in the anaphora, was discussed in Chapter 2 above.[28] While, as we have seen, those earliest invocations of the *Logos* or the Spirit may simply have asked for the Divine Presence upon the assembly, the prayers we studied in the preceding chapter link the invocation more directly with the eucharistic elements. Thus, the first, and probably earlier, of the two epicleses in Sarapion's Prosphora prays, "Fill also this sacrifice with your power and your participation," probably meaning by the word "sacrifice" the bread and wine. Some texts use rather imprecise verbs like "bless" and "sanctify," as in Addai and Mari: "may your Holy Spirit, Lord, come and rest on this offering of your servants, and bless and sanctify it." ByzBAS, however, in requesting God to send the Spirit on both the assembled community and the eucharistic elements, introduces the verb "show": "And we, sinners and unworthy and wretched, pray you, our God, in adoration that in the good pleasure of your goodness your Holy Spirit may descend upon us and upon these gifts that have been set before you, and may sanctify them and *show* them as holy of holies," a parallel to which is found in

---

[26] Taft, "Interpolation," Part 2, 116.

[27] Michael Zheltov, "The Anaphora and the Thanksgiving Prayer from the Barcelona Papyrus: An Underestimated Testimony to the Anaphoral History in the Fourth Century," *Vigiliae Christianae* 62 (2008): 467–504, here at 495–96.

[28] See above, 38–44. Also especially see the works by Gabriele Winkler listed in note 17 above, 115; and Maxwell E. Johnson, "The Origins of the Anaphoral Use of the Sanctus and Epiclesis Revisited: The Contribution of Gabriele Winkler and its Implications," in *Crossroad of Cultures*, ed. Feulner et al., 405–42.

Twelve Apostles. Similarly, Theodore of Mopsuestia explains that the bishop entreats God "that the Holy Spirit may come and that grace may descend from on high on to the bread and wine that have been offered, so showing us that the memorial of immortality is truly the body and blood of our Lord."[29] Of course, whether in this case the final clause was actually in the prayer or was just Theodore's own interpretation of a far less precise invocation we cannot say. But these two examples reflect a shift toward what has been called an "epiphany" understanding of eucharistic consecration, in which the Spirit is invoked on the gifts in order that the presence of Christ may be revealed in them.

Other fourth-century sources use epicletic language that suggests instead the idea of a change or conversion in the elements of bread and wine, rather than a revealing of what was hidden. The second epiclesis in Sarapion's prayer, for example, asks, "Let your holy Word, God of truth, come upon this bread, that the bread may become body of the Word, and upon this cup, that the cup may become blood of truth." The *Mystagogical Catecheses*, as we saw above, imply that the eucharistic prayer asked God "to send the Holy Spirit on those things that are being presented, so that he may make the bread Christ's body and the wine Christ's blood" (5.7), although this is rather highly developed language for a prayer that otherwise has a quite primitive appearance.

One must be rather cautious, however, in attributing too great an epicletic precision to the above noted distinctions between an "epiphany" understanding versus a more change-oriented understanding of the eucharistic gifts. As Taft has noted:

> Any prayer for the power of God to come upon something in order that it be unto salvation for those who partake of it, or participate in it as God intended, necessarily implies that God do something by his coming to make that object salvific; . . . one should not therefore infer that a more primitive, less explicit epicletic prayer is not, in fact, implicitly consecratory since considerations of this kind reveal more about the structure of a text than its theology.[30]

Along with Taft's caveat, then, we suggest that a better way to conceive of this development in the fourth and fifth centuries is simply to observe

---

[29] *Baptismal Homily* 5.12; ET from AIR, 233.
[30] Robert Taft, "From Logos to Spirit: On the Early History of the Epiclesis," in *Gratias Agamus: Studien zum eucharistischen Hochgebet. Für Balthasar Fischer,* ed. A. Heinz and H. Rennings (Freiburg: Herder, 1992), 493.

that anaphoral epicleses move from implicit to more explicit formulations. We would suggest further that such explicit development has as much to do with the overall context of trinitarian and christological issues in the late fourth century, especially the specific development of an orthodox theology of the Holy Spirit, as it does with liturgical development. That is, it is only natural that fourth-century disputes over the relationship between the Holy Spirit to the Father and the Son between the "Semi-Arians" (*tropikoi* and Pneumatomachians) and orthodox defenders would lead to an increased emphasis on a more explicit role of the Holy Spirit in doctrine and liturgy. In fact, an emphasis on the divinity of the Holy Spirit in this period is argued by great theologians, such as Athanasius of Alexandria[31] and the Cappadocian Fathers,[32] on the basis of the "divine works" that the Spirit does. And in Basil of Caesarea in particular that emphasis leads in the liturgy to what might be called the leveling out of the doxology, that is, the shift from "Glory *to* the Father, *through* the Son, *in* the Holy Spirit" (interpreted in a Semi-Arian manner) to the orthodox formulations of "Glory to . . . with . . . with," and, finally, the coequal "Glory to the Father, to the Son, and to the Holy Spirit." At the Council of Constantinople (381 CE) this emphasis on the divine gifts and activity of the Holy Spirit leads to the phrase, "We believe in the Holy Spirit, the Lord and giver of life, who proceeds from the Father. With the Father and the Son he is worshipped and glorified" being inserted into the text of the Niceano-Constantinopolitan Creed.

3. Institution Narrative

It has become almost a consensus in contemporary scholarship that the narrative of institution did not enter eucharistic praying until the fourth century. In his well-known article on the 2001 agreement on the Eucharist between the Catholic Church and the Assyrian Church of the East, centered on the anaphora of Addai and Mari, Robert Taft, in agreement with an overall fourth-century date for the inclusion of the institution narrative,[33] draws attention to the wide range of extant early

---

[31] See C. R. B. Shapland, trans., *The Letters of Athanasius Concerning the Holy Spirit* (London: Epworth Press, 1951).

[32] See D. Anderson, ed., *St. Basil the Great on the Holy Spirit* (Crestwood, NY; St. Vladimir's Seminary Press, 1980).

[33] Robert Taft, "Mass without Consecration? The Historic Agreement on the Eucharist between the Catholic Church and the Assyrian Church of the East Promulgated 26 October 2001," *Worship* 77 (2003): 482–509, here at 490–93.

eucharistic prayers without the presence of that narrative: namely, *Didache* 9–10, *Apostolic Constitutions* 7, the Strasbourg Papyrus, the Acts of Thomas, the Ethiopian Anaphora of the Apostles (thanks to Gabriele Winkler),[34] and the prayer of the *Martyrdom of Polycarp*.

One of the great insights of Cesare Giraudo[35] is that eucharistic prayers tend to have an overall bipartite structure consisting of "anamnetic" (memorial) and "epicletic" (supplication) sections, into which the narrative of institution is placed. In the Alexandrian and Roman/Ambrosian pattern that narrative occurs within the epicletic section, that is, as part of the supplication for "consecration," while in the West Syrian/Antiochene and East Syrian anaphoras the narrative appears as part of the eucharistic memorial itself, as part of the very contents for which thanksgiving is offered. Together with the fact that Giraudo tends to fit all anaphoras into his overall bipartite structure, however, we also find his explanation for how that narrative came to be interpolated into those anaphoral patterns difficult to accept uncritically. That is, Giraudo refers to the narrative of institution as an "embolism," which gets attached to earlier eucharistic prayers where allusions to biblical texts already appear, a common enough pattern in a variety of biblical prayer texts in general. So, for example, in his *First Apology* 66.1, Justin Martyr is supposedly alluding to the narrative of institution in his reference to the ambiguous "by a word of prayer which is from him," and similar references can be found in Addai and Mari ("have received through the tradition the form that is from you") and in book 7 of the *Apostolic Constitutions* ("we perform these symbols; for he commanded us to proclaim his death").[36] But even if it could be proven that this is *how* in some prayers it may have happened, the catalyst for the interpolation of the narrative, *why* it gets inserted, is not thereby determined.

Another example of how the interpolation may have occurred is the structural location of that narrative within the Prosphora of Sarapion of Thmuis in relationship to the texts of *Didache* 9–10 and their revision by the compiler of *Apostolic Constitutions* 7. As table 4.1 demonstrates, the structure of "cup words—*Didache* 9.4—bread words" has become

---

[34] See Gabriele Winkler, "A New Witness to the Missing Institution Narrative," 117–28.

[35] Cesare Giraudo, *Eucaristia per la Chiesa: Prospettive teologiche sull'eucaristica a partire dala "lex orandi,"* Aloisiana 22 (Rome, 1989).

[36] ET from PEER, 102.

in *Apostolic Constitutions* 7 revised structurally to be "bread words—*Didache* 9.4—cup words," a structure reflected also in the fourth-century Cappadocian document, *De Virginitate*.[37] This, of course, is exactly the structure we see in Sarapion, where the bread and cup words, divided by *Didache* 9.4, now precisely constitute the narrative of institution. Enrico Mazza has identified both this section of Sarapion's eucharistic prayer and also the material in *Apostolic Constitutions* 7 as reflecting what he calls "the ancient and paleoanaphoric structure of the Eucharistic celebration."[38] Hence, Sarapion's Prosphora may well be an early indication of how that narrative came to be attached in certain contexts.[39] But, again if this is explains the how, it does not help much with the why.

Table 4.1

APOSTOLIC CONSTITUTIONS 7.25–26	SARAPION, Prayer 1	DE VIRGINITATE 12–13
Always be thankful, as faithful and honest servants, and concerning the eucharist saying thus:		*And when you sit down at table and come to break the bread, having signed yourself three times, say thus, giving thanks:*
We give thanks to you, our Father, for that life which you have made known to us through Jesus your child, through whom you made all things and care for the whole world; whom you sent to become human for our salvation; whom	To you we offered this bread, the likeness of the body of the only-begotten. This bread is the likeness of the holy body, because the Lord Jesus Christ, in the night when he was betrayed, took bread and broke (it) and gave (it) to his disciples, saying, "Take and eat; this is	**We give thanks to you, our Father, for your holy resurrection. For through your servant Jesus Christ you have made it known to us.**

Table 4.1 continued on next page.

---

[37] Greek text in E. F. von der Goltz, ed., *De virginitate. Eine echte Schrift des Athanasius* (Leipzig, 1905), 46–47. For ET, see Teresa M. Shaw, "Peudo-Athanasius, Discourse on Salvation to a Virgin," in *Religions of Late Antiquity in Practice*, ed. Richard Valantasis (Princeton, NJ: Princeton University Press, 2000), 82–99.

[38] Mazza, *The Origins of the Eucharistic Prayer*, 228.

[39] Johnson, *The Prayers of Sarapion of Thmuis*, 226.

APOSTOLIC CONSTITUTIONS 7.25–26—(Cont'd)	SARAPION, Prayer 1—(Cont'd)	DE VIRGINITATE 12–13—(Cont'd)
you permitted to suffer and to die; whom you raised up, and were pleased to glorify and set down on your right hand; by whom you promised us the resurrection of the dead.	my body which is broken for you for forgiveness of sins." Therefore we also offered the bread making the likeness of the death, and we beseech through this sacrifice, be reconciled to us all and be merciful, God of truth.	
Do you, almighty Lord, everlasting God, **as this was scattered, and having been gathered together became one bread, so gather together your church from the ends of the earth into your kingdom.**	And **as this bread was scattered upon the mountains and having been gathered together became into one, so gather together your holy church** out of every people and every land and every city and street and house, and make one living catholic church. And we also offered the cup, the likeness of the blood, because the Lord Jesus Christ, having taken a cup after the supper, said to his disciples, "Take, drink; this is the new covenant, which is my blood poured out for you for forgiveness of sins." Therefore we also offered the cup, presenting the likeness of blood.	And **as this bread** which (is) on this table was scattered and **being gathered together became one, so may your church be gathered together from the ends of the earth into your kingdom;** for yours is the power and the glory, to the ages of ages. Amen.
We also give thanks, our Father, for the precious blood of Jesus Christ poured out for us and his precious body, of which we celebrate this antitype, as he commanded us, "to proclaim his death." For through him glory (be) to you for evermore. Amen.		
Let none of the uninitiated eat of these things, but only those baptized in the death of the Lord. . . . After the participation, give thanks thus:		*After the service of the ninth (hour), eat your food, having given thanks to God over your table thus:*
We give thanks to you, the God and Father of Jesus our Saviour, for your holy name, which you have enshrined in		Blessed be God, who has nourished me from my youth, who gives food to all flesh. Fill my

us; and for the knowl-
edge and faith and love
and immortality which
you have given us
through Jesus your child.
You, Almighty Lord, the
God of the universe, who
created the world and
everything in it through
him, have planted a
law in our souls, and
prepared in advance
things for the participa-
tion of humans. God of
our holy and blameless
fathers, Abraham and
Isaac and Jacob, your
faithful servants, mighty
God, faithful and true
and without deceit in
promises, who sent on
earth Jesus your Christ
to live with humans as
human, being God the
Word and human, to
take away error by the
roots, even now, through
him, remember this your
holy church, which you
have purchased with
the precious blood of
your Christ, and deliver
it from all evil and per-
fect it in your love and
your truth, and gather
us all together into your
kingdom which you
have prepared for it.
Maranatha. Hosanna to
the Son of David. Blessed
(be) the one coming in
(the) name of (the) Lord,
God (the) Lord, mani-
fested to us in flesh. If
anyone (is) holy, let him
come near; but if anyone
is not, let him become
(so) by repentance.

*Allow also your presbyters
to give thanks.*

heart with joy and glad-
ness that always having
a sufficiency in all things,
we may abound to every
good work in Christ
Jesus our Lord, with
whom to you (is) glory,
honour, power, with the
Holy Spirit to the ages of
ages. Amen.

In the overall historical context discussed at the beginning of the previous chapter, we noted that certain elements were added to the anaphora for *catechetical* reasons as the liturgy itself became increasingly catechetical and didactic. The narrative of institution may well have been one of these elements. If so, then the insertion of the institution narrative into the prayer was parenthetical and made for catechetical purposes, to offer an elucidation of the liturgical action being celebrated. Its migration into the prayer can be explained as a consequence of the breakdown of the catechetical system in the fourth century: those who had been baptized seemed not to have absorbed fully what Christianity was all about and what conduct was expected of them at eucharistic assemblies, and hence the liturgy needed to become itself a catechetical tool, part of which involved the regular repetition of the narrative within the rite, with anamnetic intent.

It is possible, however, that an additional catechetical reason for the interpolation of the narrative of institution into anaphoras had to do with the cessation of martyrdom. That is, to take a parallel from the development of the rites of Christian initiation, Gordon Jeanes,[40] followed by Alistair Campbell,[41] has argued that one of the reasons why Romans 6 baptismal theology came to the fore precisely in this period of history was because of the cessation of martyrdom that necessitated and allowed the wider application of death imagery to baptism in general. Something similar, we think, can be said with regard to the question of the narrative. That is, to paraphrase Campbell, in the age of the martyrs, Christians hardly needed reminding that sharing in "the cup of Christ," the supreme Martyr himself, brought precisely the possibility of sharing in the number of the martyrs, just as their baptism also implied. But in a later age it becomes necessary to underscore that the Eucharist is not simply Christ's body and blood for viaticum or nourishment, life, and immortality but Christ's body and blood as *sacrificed*, as given and shed in his own martyrdom on the cross for the life of the world, an emphasis that the narrative of institution makes clear in a

---

[40] Gordon Jeanes, "Baptism Portrayed as Martyrdom in the Early Church," *Studia Liturgica* 23 (1993): 158–76.

[41] Alistair Campbell, "Dying with Christ: The Origin of a Metaphor?," in *Baptism, the New Testament and the Church: Historical and Contemporary Studies in Honour of R. E. O. White*, ed. Stanley E. Porter and Anthony R. Cross, Journal for the Study of the New Testament Supplement Series 171 (Sheffield: Sheffield Academic Press, 1999), 292–93.

way that nothing else could.[42] And if in an earlier time it was martyr-dom itself that was the public and dramatic ritual of sacrifice and the Eucharist was private and hidden,[43] that becomes now no longer the case, and the Eucharist itself, "the bloodless service upon that sacrifice of propitiation," in the words of Cyril (John) of Jerusalem,[44] becomes *the* public cult and dramatic sacrifice of Christians. And what better way to strongly emphasize and make clear this connection than to have the very words of Christ within the central prayer of the Eucharist itself?[45]

EUCHARISTIC THEOLOGY

Inseparable from our analysis above of elements such as the *Sanctus*, epiclesis, and narrative of institution, as well as the development of the eucharistic prayers themselves, is the eucharistic theology developing in East and West during this time period.

1. Sacrifice

The eucharistic prayers in use in this period have continued to artic-ulate the same concepts of eucharistic sacrifice that are found in earlier centuries—that the offering was one either of praise and thanksgiv-ing or of the bread and cup. As Kenneth Stevenson has shown in his work *Eucharist and Offering*, the metaphor of eucharistic sacrifice has several possible referents and can point at one and the same time to

[42] On sacrifice in Christian antiquity the standard works are those of Robert Daly, *Christian Sacrifice: The Judaeo-Christian Background before Origen*, Studies in Christian Antiquity, vol. 18 (Washington, DC: Catholic University of America Press, 1978); and more recently, *idem*, *Sacrifice Unveiled: The True Meaning of Christian Sacrifice* (London/New York: Continuum, 2009).

[43] See above, 54–56. See also Maxwell E. Johnson, "Sharing 'The Cup of Christ': The Cessation of Martyrdom and Anaphoral Development," in *Acts of the Third International Congress of the Society of Oriental Liturgy, Volos, Greece, 26–30 May 2010*, ed. Basilius J. Groen and Steven Hawkes Teeples, Eastern Christian Studies (Leuven, forthcoming).

[44] *Mystagogical Catecheses* 4.8.

[45] Closely related, of course, would be the celebration of the Eucharist either in the martyrium over the grave of the martyrs or in local diocesan basilicas and cathedrals with the relics of martyrs installed under or within the altars. On this, see Peter Brown, *The Cult of the Saints: Its Rise and Function in Latin Christianity* (Chicago: University of Chicago Press, 1981), 23–49. For a more detailed discussion, see Johnson, "Sharing 'The Cup of Christ.'"

the self-offering of the community, to the gifts (bread and cup) that are offered, and to the entire eucharistic action itself, as that which is offered in thanksgiving for God's gift of salvation.[46] Like the Strasbourg Papyrus, those anaphoras that seem to have concentrated their praise on creation and lacked an institution narrative (*Mystagogical Catecheses*, Theodore of Mopsuestia?) do not even link this offering explicitly with the remembrance of Christ's own sacrifice, but others, such as BAS, do so, and this is a trend that is taken up by all later prayers. In contrast to these texts themselves, however, contemporary commentary on the rites tended to present a rather more advanced theology of sacrifice. Whatever Cyprian may have meant in the third century by his statements that "that priest truly functions in the place of Christ who imitates what Christ did and then offers a true and full sacrifice in the church to God the Father" and "the Lord's passion is the sacrifice that we offer,"[47] some fourth-century Christian writers unquestionably do use language that identifies the church's sacrificial act very closely indeed with the sacrifice of Christ. Thus, for example, *Mystagogical Catechesis* 5.10 asserts that "we offer Christ slain for our sins," and Gregory Nazianzus (ca. 329–90) says that "you sacrifice the Master's body and blood with bloodless knife" (*Ep.* 171). John Chrysostom, on the other hand, struggled in one of his homilies between this way of speaking and the conviction that there was only one sacrifice of Christ, even though there were many celebrations of the Eucharist:

> Do we not offer every day? We do offer indeed, but making a remembrance of his death, and this [remembrance] is one and not many. How [is it] one and not many? Because it was offered once, just as that in the holy of holies. This is a figure [*typos*] of that [sacrifice] and the same as that. For we always offer the same, not one sheep now and tomorrow another, but always the same, so that the sacrifice is one. And yet by this reasoning, since the offering is made in many places, are there many Christs? By no means, but Christ is one everywhere, being complete here and complete there, one body. As therefore, though offered in many places, he is one body and not many bodies, so also [there is] one sacrifice. He is our high priest, who offered the sacrifice that cleanses us. That we offer now also, which was then offered, which cannot be exhausted. This is done is remembrance of what was then done. For, "Do this," he said, "in remembrance of me." It is not another

[46] Kenneth Stevenson, *Eucharist and Offering* (New York: Pueblo, 1986), 3–4.
[47] *Ep.* 63.14, 17.

sacrifice, as the high priest then, but always the same that we do, or rather we perform a remembrance of a sacrifice. (*In Heb. hom.* 17.3)

Because the author of the *Mystagogical Catecheses* says that they believe "that it will be the greatest help to the souls for whom the petition is offered (if it is done) while the holy and most awesome sacrifice is being presented" (5.9), this has often been understood as a reliable explanation as to why eucharistic prayers came to include a wide range of objects of intercession rather than just petition for the communicants: the idea of the Eucharist as a sacrifice must have led to the idea that it could be offered for others, which in turn led to the introduction of intercessions into the eucharistic prayer. The true process of development, however, was quite possibly the other way around, that it was the adoption for eucharistic use of prayers like the Strasbourg Papyrus, already containing a substantial block of intercessory material, that then gave rise to the idea of the Eucharist as a propitiatory sacrifice in the fourth century and encouraged the introduction of intercessions into eucharistic prayers that had previously lacked them.[48]

Whatever the reason for this development might be, it is, again, important not to expect a theological precision that does not exist or an answer to questions that later ages, especially the polemical context of the sixteenth-century Reformation, were asking. Rather, one can say little more for this period than that what is "offered" *in* the Eucharist "is what the New Testament has Jesus order us to offer: the memorial of his own self offering,"[49] that is, the liturgical *doing* of the Eucharist in obedience to his command. Nevertheless, it is equally important to underscore that there is no question but that the Eucharist was widely understood theologically as the Church's "sacrifice" and, as such, the burden of proof to the contrary has always been (and remains) on those who wish somehow to deny this interpretation and who seek to avoid using sacrificial terminology altogether in their eucharistic practice and theology. For even the

---

[48] On the question of intercessions in the anaphora, including the Diptychs, those petitions offered for various bishops and others with whom the local Church is in communion, see the definitive study of Robert Taft, *A History of the Liturgy of St. John Chrysostom, Vol. IV: The Diptychs*, OCA 238 (Rome: Pontificio Istituto Orientale, 1991).

[49] Taft, "Anaphoral Offering," 45.

sacrificial offering language of the Roman *canon missae* keeps as its primary sense that the Eucharist is a *sacrificium laudis*, a sacrifice of praise.

What must not be neglected in all of this is the whole ecclesiological connection to the eucharistic sacrifice that we see in the West, especially in Augustine toward the end of this period. In his *Confessions* and in his famous *On the City of God* (ca. 420), Augustine underscores the eucharistic connection between Christ and his Body, the Church:

> The whole redeemed City itself, that is, the congregation and society of the saints, is offered as a universal sacrifice to God by the High Priest, who offered even himself in suffering for us "in the form of a servant" [Phil 2:7], that we might be the body of so great a head. For this "form of a servant" did he offer, and in this he was offered: for in this he is mediator and priest and sacrifice. And so . . . the Apostle exhorted us to present our bodies as a living sacrifice, holy, pleasing to God, our reasonable service, and to be not conformed to this world but reformed in the newness of our mind, to prove what is the will of God, that which is good and well-pleasing and complete [Rom 12:1-2], the whole sacrifice that we ourselves are. . . .

> This is the sacrifice of Christians: the "many are one body in Christ" [1 Cor 10:17]. This also the Church celebrates in the Sacrament of the altar, familiar to the faithful, where it is shown to her that in this thing that she offers, she herself is offered. (*De Civitate Dei*, 10.6)

> Thus he is priest, himself offering, and himself also that which is offered. Of this thing he willed the sacrifice of Church to be the daily Sacrament; and the Church, since she is the body the head himself, learns to offer herself through him. (*De Civitate Dei*, 10.21)[50]

Such an ecclesiological connection, as we shall see in the next section, is inseparable from Augustine's theology of Christ's eucharistic presence.

2. Real Presence and Communion

As we have seen, the realistic language about the bread and cup being the body and blood of Christ that was used by earlier Christian

---

[50] ET adapted from Darwell Stone, *A History of the Doctrine of the Holy Eucharist* (London: Longmans, Green and Co., 1909), 1:123–24.

writers is also continued in the fourth and fifth centuries, and within the anaphoras themselves, either by means of explicit epicleses (East) or the recital of the narrative of institution (West), we now see petitions that the bread and wine might become the body and blood of Christ. Apart from citations of the words of Jesus at the Last Supper in the institution narratives that are now appearing in prayers, the Prosphora of Sarapion is the only one of the earliest group of prayers that we can be sure did incorporate such realistic language in describing the eucharistic food and drink, although "body of the Word . . . cup of truth" falls short of the stark realism of theological commentators of the period. Alongside this usage, however, there are signs of a desire to find expressions that recognize a more subtle relationship between the eucharistic elements and Christ himself, and words like "figure," "sign," "symbol," "type," and "antitype" make an appearance, and, for that matter, Sarapion's text *does* use the equivalent terminology of *homoioma*, "likeness," to relate the bread and wine to the body and blood of Christ. Similarly, while the *Mystagogical Catecheses* can affirm quite unequivocally, "Do not, therefore, regard the bread and the wine as mere elements, for they are (the) body and blood of Christ according to the master's own declaration" (4.6), it can also state that "the body has been given to you in the form [*typos*] of bread, and the blood has been given to you in the form [*typos*] of wine" (4.3), and that communicants are "to taste not bread and wine but the sign [*antitypon*] of Christ's body and blood" (5.20). At the same time, Ambrose of Milan, as we have seen, testifies that the eucharistic prayer of his church spoke of the elements as being "the figure [*figura*] of the body and blood of our Lord Jesus Christ" (*De Sacramentis* 4.21). We should not make too much of these differences in language, however. In the ancient world a sign or symbol was not thought of as being something quite different from the reality it represented but, on the contrary, was understood as participating in some way in that reality itself.

Western scholars, sometimes fuelled by later confessional positions, have often tried to distinguish between what they have seen to be a more "realist" position in Ambrose of Milan and a more "symbolic" approach in Augustine to the question of the eucharistic presence of Christ and to what is received in communion. Texts like the following from Augustine's treatises and homilies are taken as supportive of that so-called symbolic approach:

He explains how what he speaks of happens, and the meaning of eating his body and drinking his blood: "One that eats my flesh and drinks my blood abides in me, and I in him" [John 6:56]. This, then, is to eat that food and to drink that drink: to abide in Christ, and to have him abiding in oneself. And in this way, one who does not abide in Christ, and in whom Christ does not abide, without doubt neither eats his flesh nor drinks his blood, but rather eats and drinks the Sacrament of so great a thing to that one's own judgment. (*Tractatus in Ioh. Evang.*, 26)[51]

If you wish to understand the body of Christ, hear the Apostle speaking to the faithful: "Now you are the body and members of Christ" [1 Cor 12:27]. If you then are the body and members of Christ, it is your mystery laid on the table of the Lord, your mystery that you receive. To that which you are you answer, "Amen," and in answering you agree. For you hear the words, "The body of Christ," and you answer, "Amen." So be a member of the body of Christ, so that the "Amen" may be true. What, then, is the bread? Let us assert nothing of our own here; let us listen to the reiterated teaching of the Apostle, who when he spoke of this Sacrament said, "We who are many are one bread, one body" [1 Cor 10:17]: understand this and rejoice in unity, truth, goodness, love. "One bread." What is that one bread? "Many are one body." Remember that the bread is not made from one grain but from many. When you were exorcised [before baptism], you were, so to speak, ground; when you were baptized, you were, so to speak, sprinkled. When you received the fire of the Holy Spirit, you were, so to speak, cooked. Be what you see, and receive what you are. . . . Many grapes hang on the cluster, but the juice of the grapes is gathered together in unity. So also the Lord Christ signified us, wished us to belong to him, consecrated on his table the mystery of our peace and unity. (*Sermo* 272)[52]

Recently, however, Joseph Wawrykow has challenged this traditional approach to Augustine, arguing convincingly that such a dichotomy between so-called realist and symbolic approaches does not really exist and that what is actually at stake is but a difference in emphasis. That is:

Augustine's presentation of Eucharist is framed by his understanding of Church as the body of Christ. Christ is the Head of this body; those

---

[51] ET adapted from ibid., 1:93–94.
[52] ET adapted from ibid., 1:95–96.

who are joined to him by faith and charity, having received from Him the Holy Spirit, are His members. In discussing Eucharist, Augustine, first of all, plays up its sign-quality. A sign is a thing that points to another thing (*res*). It signifies that thing, but is not that thing. In the case of the Eucharist, the material elements, the bread and wine point to the *res* that is the power of the sacrament. Taking his cue from 1 Corinthians 10:17, a favorite verse that appears repeatedly throughout his writings, Augustine states that the *res* that is signified by the bread is the Church, the body of Christ, in its fundamental unity, which is grounded in charity. The Eucharist is the sacrament of unity and charity. Just as bread is made out of many grains, so the Church, the body of Christ, is made out of many people who are joined to their Head by their charity. Augustine continues the thought when he turns to reception of the Eucharist. . . . This sacrament testifies to the charity that binds the members to the Head, and reception of the sacrament proclaims that unity, founded in charity. This informs Augustine's account of worthy and unworthy reception of the sacrament, a distinction, he reminds us, that is based on 1 Corinthians 11:28-29. Who eats worthily? A person who is truly a member of the body of Christ. In that eating, that person proclaims his membership in Christ. And, since there is a power to the sacrament, one established by Christ's promise, those who are truly members of Christ and who in their reception are proclaiming that membership in an exercise of their charity, their love of God in Christ, will grow in grace, grow in charity, receiving anew and in heightened form the Holy Spirit who binds Christians to their Head. In that case, the eating that is sacramental will also be spiritual.[53]

What we see in Augustine, therefore, is a concern again for the ecclesiological implications of the Eucharist, what later scholastic theology will call the *res tantum*, signifying the ultimate union between Christ and the Church by the Eucharist. Augustine's concern, hammered out in the context of the Donatist controversy, is not Ambrose's concern, but it is not a contradiction of Ambrose either.

SUMMARY

1. Together with the development of the various anaphoras, specific elements such as the *Sanctus*, explicit epicleses invoking the *Logos* or the Holy Spirit upon the eucharistic gifts, and/or the narrative

---

[53] Joseph Wawrykow, "The Heritage of the Late Empire: Influential Theology," in *A Companion to the Eucharist in the Middle Ages*, ed. Ian Levy, Gary Macy, and Kristen Van Ausdall (Leiden: Brill, 2012), 74–75.

of institution from the New Testament Last Supper accounts come to be interpolated into those anaphoras.

2. Sacrificial language continues to develop and becomes increasingly referred, especially in commentaries on the Eucharist, to the passion of Christ, developing the approach of Cyprian seen in the third century.

3. The realistic language of Christ's body and blood becomes stronger in this time period with either the epiclesis (East) or narrative of institution (West) seen increasingly as "consecratory" in function, in order to "make" the bread and wine the body and blood of Christ, though the language remains at the level of "figure," "sign," "symbol," "type," "antitype" or *homoioma*.

Chapter 5

The Christian East

There are seven distinct living liturgical traditions in the Christian East, the eucharistic liturgies of which each deserve their own chapter.[1] Those living liturgical traditions are the Armenian, Byzantine, Coptic, Ethiopic, East Syrian, West Syrian or Antiochene, and Maronite Rites, all of which exist as both Orthodox and Eastern Catholic Churches, with the exception of the Maronites who have always been in union with Rome. Apart from the Armenian, Coptic, Ethiopic, and Maronite Rites or "families," which are distinct Orthodox or Eastern Catholic Churches, several different churches belong to the Byzantine, East Syrian, and West Syrian "families" or rites. The Byzantine Rite, known to us in its earliest form from the early eighth-century *Barberini*

---

[1] This first section follows closely and builds on the opening pages of chapter 7 from Maxwell E. Johnson, *The Rites of Christian Initiation: Their Evolution and Interpretation*, rev. exp. ed. (Collegeville, MN: Liturgical Press, Pueblo, 2007), 269–75, and is based, in part, on the essay by Ephrem Carr, "Liturgical Families in the East," in *Handbook for Liturgical Studies*, vol. 1: *Introduction to the Liturgy*, ed. Anscar J. Chupungco (Collegeville, MN: Liturgical Press, Pueblo, 1997), 11–24. See also Bryan D. Spinks, "Eastern Christian Liturgical Traditions: Oriental Orthodox," in *The Blackwell Companion to Eastern Christianity*, ed. Ken Parry (Oxford: Wiley-Blackwell, 2007), 339–67; Gregory Woolfenden, "Eastern Christian Liturgical Traditions: Eastern Orthodox," in ibid., 319–38; Christine Chaillot, "The Ancient Oriental Churches," in *The Oxford History of Christian Worship*, ed. Geoffrey Wainwright and Karen Westerfield-Tucker (Oxford/New York: Oxford University Press, 2006), 131–69; Lucas Van Rompay, "Excursus: The Maronites," in ibid., 170–74; and Alexander Rentel, "Byzantine and Slavic Orthodoxy," in ibid., 254–306. See also Paul Naaman, *The Maronites: The Origins of an Antiochene Church*, Cisterican Studies 243 (Collegeville, MN: Liturgical Press, 2009). On Eastern Christianity in general see Mahmoud Zibawi, *Eastern Christian Worlds* (Collegeville, MN: Liturgical Press, 1995); and for Egypt specifically, see Massimo Capuani, *Christian Egypt: Coptic Art and Monuments Through Two Millennia* (Collegeville, MN: Liturgical Press, 2002).

Euchologion 336 (hereafter, *Barberini gr. 336*),[2] is the dominant, largest, and most influential liturgical tradition of and in the Christian East. The rite or liturgy itself is that which emerged from the great Byzantine liturgical synthesis of Antiochene, Jerusalem, and local liturgical practice—both parochial/cathedral and monastic—in Constantinople[3] and which today includes some twenty-eight Orthodox Churches (e.g., Greek, Russian, Ukrainian, and Serbian Orthodox) and at least ten Eastern Catholic Churches (e.g., Melkite, Ruthenian, Ukrainian, and Bulgarian) among its practitioners.[4] It was this tradition that in 988 was adopted as the rite of what eventually was to become Russia, after emissaries of Prince Vladimir experienced the eucharistic liturgy in the great sixth-century Justinian church of Hagia Sophia in Constantinople and reported that "we knew not whether we were in heaven or on earth."[5]

The East Syrian Rite, centered originally in the region of Nisibis (Nusyabin, Syria) and in Edessa (Urfa, Turkey), beyond the borders and influence of the dominant Roman Empire, is also sometimes referred to as "The Assyro-Chaldean Rite," "The Assyrian or Chaldean Rite," or as part of the "Persian Family" of rites. More properly, it is the rite celebrated by the Ancient (Assyrian) Church of the East, the Chaldean Catholic Church, and the Syro-Malabar Catholic Church in

---

[2] See the critical edition of this document, *L'Eucologio Barberini gr. 336*, 2nd ed. rev. with Italian translation, ed. Stefano Parenti and Elena Velkovska, Bibliotheca Ephemerides Liturgicae "Subsidia" 80 (Rome: CLV-Edizioni Liturgiche, 2000).

[3] For overall introductions to the Byzantine liturgical tradition see Robert Taft, *The Byzantine Rite: A Short History* (Collegeville, MN: Liturgical Press, 1992); and Hans-Joachim Schulz, *The Byzantine Liturgy* (Collegeville, MN: Liturgical Press, Pueblo, 1986).

[4] For listings and names of the various churches and their respective rites see the excellent study by Ronald Roberson, *The Eastern Christian Churches: A Brief Survey*, 6th ed. (Rome: Edizioni "Orientalia Christiana," 2006). See also, more recently, Johannes Oeldemann, *Die Kirchen des christlichen Ostens: Orthodoxe, orientalische und mit Rom unierte Ostkirchen* (Kevelaer: Verlagsgemeinschaft Topos Plus, 2006).

[5] S. H. Cross and O. P. Sherbowitz-Weltzor, *The Russian Primary Chronicle, Laurention Text* (Cambridge, MA: The Medieval Academy of America, 1953), 110–11, as quoted by Robert Taft, "The Spirit of Eastern Christian Worship," in *idem, Beyond East and West: Problems in Liturgical Understanding*, 2nd ed. (Rome: Pontificio Istituto Orientale, 1997), 144.

India. Because the Ancient Assyrian Church of the East at the Synod of Seleucia-Ctesiphon (ca. 410) had adopted the Christology of Nestorius, a split between this church and the rest of both Eastern and Western Christianity resulted after the Council of Ephesus (431) and has remained so for centuries, with members of this ancient tradition often called in the past by the pejorative term "Nestorian." Liturgically, this rite, with some medieval additions, was codifed in the mid-seventh-century liturgical reforms of Patriarch Isho'yabh III (ca. 650–60). Nevertheless, it also displays several ancient Syrian elements and is in broad continuity with the witness of those early Syrian documents we have already encountered, the *Didascalia Apostolorum* and the Syrian *Acts*, and the great East Syrian fathers, Aphrahat, Ephrem, and Narsai.[6]

The West Syrian Rite or family, sometimes also called "Antiochene" or "Syro-Antiochene," stems from the ancient patriarchate of Antioch, Syria. Celebrated today by the Syrian Orthodox Church, the Syrian Catholic Church, the Malankara Othodox Syrian Church (India), and the Syro-Malankara Catholic Church (India), the West Syrian Rite is that rite reflected in its earliest stages in the *Apostolic Constitutions*, the homilies of St. John Chrysostom from his time as a presbyter in Antioch, and from the catecheses of Theodore of Mopsuestia. It has also been influenced by the early liturgical practices of Jerusalem. Ephrem Carr summarizes West Syrian Christianity thus:

> Syrian Christians became divided by reason of the council of Chalcedon [451] into Melkites, who were loyal to the council and the emperor (*malko* = "ruler" or "king"), and the anti-chalcedonians. The Melkites gradually accepted also the liturgy of the imperial capital and became by the twelfth century part of the Byzantine rite. The Syrian faithful who rejected the council slowly formed their own church, a move fostered by Jacob Baradai (+578) and his establishment of an independent hierarchy from 543 onward. Thus the Syrian church came to be called Jacobite. During the upheavals over Christology in the fifth and sixth centuries the Antiochene liturgy was revised and augmented. An important role was played by Patriarch Severus (512–518, +538), who reformed the ritual of baptism and composed a Hymn Book (ὀκτώηχος) with some of his own liturgical poetry.[7]

---

[6] See above, 35–38, 115–20.
[7] Carr, "Liturgical Families in the East," 15.

Within the overall West Syrian family or rite the Maronites might also be placed, though because their liturgy also has several ancient features in common with East Syria one must not push this designation too far. Stemming originally from the Monastery of St. Maron in Lebanon (the exact location of which is still uncertain), the Maronites became an autonomous church in Lebanon in the eighth century and have been in communion with Rome since their origins.[8]

The Coptic Rite, celebrated by both Coptic Orthodox and Catholics, and the Ethiopian Rite, celebrated by both Ethiopian Orthodox and Catholics and now also by the churches of Eritrea, are two distinct rites with two distinct histories and developments. The Coptic Rite, of course, derives from the ancient patriarchate of Alexandria, Egypt, and also from the distinctive monastic practices of the surrounding desert, which exert a greater influence after 451. This rite was celebrated originally in Greek but from the seventh century on in Coptic, both in the Sahidic and (later) Bohairic dialects. As for West Syrian Christianity, so also for Coptic Christianity was the Council of Chalcedon (451) both a decisive and divisive event, with the result that the Coptic Orthodox Church became and has remained non-Chalcedonian or, better, Miaphysite, in its Christology. The Ethiopian Rite has traditionally been interpreted as coming almost exclusively from the Coptic Rite of Alexandria. And while it is certainly true that the Ethiopian Orthodox Church (also Miaphysite in Christology) had been from the fourth until the mid-twentieth century dependent on Alexandria and its patriarch, scholars today point to the influence of Syrian monastic evangelization in Ethiopia from earliest times onward.[9] Hence, the Ethiopian Rite

[8] It was William Macomber who first made the strong case that the Maronite Rite is a distinct rite. See William Macomber, "A Theory on the Origins of the Syrian, Maronite, and Chaldean Rites," OCP 39 (1973): 235–42.

[9] On Ethiopian Christianity see Hebtemichael Kidane, "Ethiopian (Ge'ez) Worship," in *The New Westminster Dictionary of Liturgy & Worship*, ed. Paul F. Bradshaw (Louisville, KY: Westminster John Knox Press, 2002), 169–72; Aziz S. Atiya, *History of Eastern Christianity* (Notre Dame, IN: University of Notre Dame Press, 1968), 146–66; Adrian Hastings, *The Church in Africa: 1450–1950* (Oxford: Clarendon Press, 1994), chaps. 1, 4, and 6; Elizabeth Isichei, *A History of Christianity in Africa from Antiquity to the Present* (London: SPCK, 1995). See also Gabriele Winkler's recent work on the Sanctus in the eucharistic prayer, in which she directs our attention to Syrian influence in Ethiopia: *Das Sanctus. Über den Ursprung und die Anfänge des Sanctus und sein Fortwirken*, OCA 267 (Rome: Pontificio Istituto Orientale, 2002).

is better understood as the synthesis of much wider and more diverse liturgical influences than has been previously maintained.

The rite of the oldest Christian nation in history, Armenia (traditionally dated 301 but certainly by 314), celebrated by both the Armenian Apostolic Orthodox Church and the Armenian Catholic Church, was long thought to be but a modified or even simplified version of the Byzantine Rite. Recent scholarship, however, especially on the *Badarak* (Divine Liturgy), has shown that Byzantine influence dates only from the turn of the first millennium.[10] More fundamental is an earlier Cappadocian-Caesarean stratum,[11] as well as, thanks to the work of Gabriele Winkler, a decidedly Syrian core.[12] Although later influences are certainly present in the current shape of the Armenian Rite, including both Byzantine and Latin (due to Dominican missionaries in the twelfth century), it is also becoming increasingly clear that the Armenians developed their earlier rites in close connection with Jerusalem, expressed, as we have seen already above in this study, in the fifth-century *Armenian Lectionary*. Some mention here must also be made of the Orthodox Church of Georgia in the Caucasus Mountains on the east of the Black Sea. While the Orthodox Church of Georgia has followed the Byzantine Rite since the eleventh century, its earlier liturgical tradition, somewhat like that of Armenia, with whom it also shares an early relationship with Jerusalem, is more akin to East rather than West Syria.[13]

THE RITES

The eucharistic liturgies of the churches of the Christian East are known by a variety of titles, each title emphasizing a particular liturgical understanding of the Mystery being celebrated.[14] The Byzantine

---

[10] See Charles Renoux, "Un bilan proviso ire sur l'héritage grec du rite arménien," *Le Muséon* 116 (2003): 53–69.

[11] See M. Daniel Findikyan, *The Commentary on the Armenian Daily Office by Bishop Step'anos Siwnec'I (d. 735): Critical Edition and Translation with Textual and Liturgical Analysis*, OCA 270 (Rome: Pontificio Istituto Orientale, 2004), 511–15.

[12] See Gabriele Winkler, *Das armenische Initiationsrituale. Entwicklungsgeschichtliche und liturgievergleichende Untersuchung der Quellen des 3. Bis 10. Jahrhunderts*, OCA 217 (Rome: Pontificio Istituto Orientale, 1982).

[13] See Gabriele Winkler, "Baptism 2: Eastern Churches," in *The New Westminster Dictionary of Liturgy & Worship*, ed. Bradshaw, 38.

[14] See the classic study of Irenée-Henri Dalmais, *Eastern Liturgies*, Twentieth-Century Encyclopedia of Catholicism, vol. 112 (New York: Hawthorne Books, 1960), 75–95.

Rite uses the terminology of "the Divine Liturgy." Among the Syrians, Armenians, and Copts the title of the liturgy underscores its sacrificial or offering character with the use of *Qurbana* (Syriac), *Badarak* (Armenian), or *Prosfora* (Coptic). For the East Syrians and Ethiopians the titles *Qedussah* or *Keddase* reflect the overall influence of the *Sanctus* and the process of the sanctification of the eucharistic gifts and communicants.[15] In chapter 3 we presented the concept of liturgical "soft spots"[16] and their propensity to attract various additional elements to themselves, often with the result of making the earlier liturgical units at the entrance, transfer of the eucharistic gifts to the altar, and at the time of communion (all actions accompanied by chants and concluded by collects) difficult to uncover or discern. Stefano Parenti has noted that in comparison with Western liturgies, particularly that of the Roman Rite, the Eastern liturgies differ primarily in the various verbal elements added to these "soft spots."[17] With the addition of the Liturgies of the Word and the various Eastern anaphoras, our presentation of the Eastern Rites here will follow the "soft spots" primarily. Because, as noted, the Byzantine Rite is the dominant, largest, and most influential liturgical tradition of and in the Christian East, it will often be our point of reference and model for our comparative presentation.

1. Preliminary Rites and the Liturgy of the Word

Before the liturgies proper begin with elements such as opening blessings, hymns, and litanies immediately before the Liturgy of the Word, all of the Eastern Rites have elaborate rites of preparation (called the *Prothesis* in the Byzantine Rite) of the eucharistic gifts of bread (leavened bread, except for the Armenians and Maronites) and wine as well as for the ministers (prayers for vesting and private prayers of unworthiness similar to the various *apologiae* often noted with regard to Gallican influence on the Roman Rite[18]). In the Coptic and Ethiopic Rites the bread and wine are prepared at the altar, and

---

[15] For the Ethiopian title especially, see Winkler, *Das Sanctus*, 196ff.

[16] See above, 72.

[17] Stefano Parenti, "The Eucharistic Liturgy in the East: Various Orders of Celebration," in *Handbook for Liturgical Studies*, vol. 3: *The Eucharist*, ed. Anscar J. Chupungco (Collegeville, MN: Liturgical Press, Pueblo, 1999), 62. Parenti's essay has served here as a guide for portions of this chapter.

[18] See below, 221.

the East Syrian Rites include a presentation of the bread and wine at the altar during the entrance rite of the liturgy itself. The East Syrians even include as part of these rites the baking of the bread, into which is added the *Malka*, or holy leaven, a powdery substance renewed every year on Holy Thursday and understood as having been made from the bread actually used at the Last Supper, thus perpetuating it in historic continuity.[19] In the Armenian, Byzantine, and West Syrian (Maronite, at least) Rites, the bread and wine are prepared at a side table (behind the iconostasis or "icon screen" for the Byzantines) and are solemnly transferred to the altar after the Liturgy of the Word during what is called (for Armenians and Byzantines) the Great Entrance. In Constantinople at Hagia Sophia, the eucharistic gifts were prepared in a separate building altogether—the *Skeuophylakion*—from where they were transferred to the altar with a great degree of solemnity during the Great Entrance.[20] Of particular interest is the fact that in many of these rites the bread that has been prepared is referred to even at this point as the "Lamb of God who takes away the sins of the world."

The rites of entrance or the beginning of the liturgy in the Byzantine Rite (called the *Enarxis*), as table 5.1 below shows, consists now of an opening blessing ("Blessed is the kingdom of the Father and of the Son and of the Holy Spirit now and forever and unto the ages of ages. Amen"), a long litany called the "Grand Synapte" or "Synapte of Peace"[21] (beginning, "in peace, let us pray to the Lord," with the response, "Kyrie Eleison"), followed by a prayer and antiphon, a short

---

[19] See Bryan Spinks, "The Mystery of the Holy Leaven (*Malka*) in the East Syrian Tradition," in *Issues in Eucharistic Praying in East and West: Essays in Liturgical and Theological Analysis*, ed. Maxwell E. Johnson (Collegeville, MN: Liturgical Press, Pueblo, 2011), 63–70.

[20] See Thomas F. Matthews, *The Early Churches of Constantinople: Architecture and Liturgy* (University Park: Pennsylvania State University Press, 1971); and Robert Taft, *A History of the Liturgy of St. John Chrysostom*, vol. 2: *The Great Entrance: A History of the Transfer of Gifts and other Pre-anaphoral Rites*, 4th ed., OCA 200 (Rome: Pontificio Istituto Orientale, 2004).

[21] The "Grand Synapte" was originally attached to the prayers of the faithful after the readings and homily. See Juan Mateos, *La celebration de la parole dans la liturgie Byzantine: Étude historique*, OCA 191 (Rome: Pontificio Istituto Orientale, 1971), 29–31. See also the recent essay by Peter Jeffery, "The Meanings and Functions of *Kyrie Eleison*," in *The Place of Christ in Liturgical Prayer: Trinity, Christology, and Liturgical Theology*, ed. Bryan D. Spinks (Collegeville, MN: Liturgical Press, Pueblo, 2008), 127–94, here at 156–73.

litany (*Mikra* or "Little Synapte"), followed by a prayer and antiphon, and, finally, another "Little Synapte," followed by a prayer and antiphon to which has been attached the hymn, *Hō Monogenēs*:

> Only-Begotten Son and Word of God, immortal as you are, You condescended for our salvation to be incarnate from the Holy Theotokos and ever-virgin Mary, and without undergoing change, You became Man; You were crucified O Christ God, and you trampled death by your death; You are One of the Holy Trinity; equal in glory with the Father and the Holy Spirit: save us!

Juan Mateos demonstrated several years ago, however, that the original beginning of the Byzantine Divine Liturgy is to be seen in what is now called the Little Entrance, where the presiding minister takes the gospel book from the altar and processes out the north door of the iconostasis (icon screen), through the body of the church and back to the altar through the royal doors in front of the altar.[22] Originally, claimed Mateos, this procession would have taken place as the opening procession of the liturgy from the entrance of the church itself to the altar during the chanting of the *Trisagion* as the entrance antiphon: "Holy God, Holy Mighty One, Holy Immortal One, have mercy on us!"[23] In fact, it is still only during this chant that a bishop actually enters the church and goes to the altar, thus underscoring Mateos' point. The Prayer of the Entrance in the Byzantine Rite demonstrates this clearly:

> Master Lord our God, who established in the heavens the orders and hosts of angels and archangels to minister to your glory: Make our entrance to be united with the entrance of the holy angels, that together we may serve and glorify your goodness. For to you belong all glory, honor, and worship, to the Father and to the Son and to the Holy Spirit, now and forever and to the ages of ages. Amen.[24]

---

[22] Ibid., 71–90.

[23] On the *Trisagion*, in addition to ibid., 91–110, see Sebastià Janeras, "Les byzantins et le *trisagion* christologique," in *Miscellanea liturgica in onore di Sua Eminenza il Cardinale Giacomo Lercaro*, vol. 2 (Rome: Desclée, 1967), 469–99; and *idem*, "Le trisagion : Une formule brève en liturgie comparée," in *Comparative Liturgy Fifty Years after Anton Baumstark (1872–1948)*, ed. Robert F. Taft and Gabriele Winkler, OCA 265 (Rome: Pontificio Istituto Orientale, 2002), 495–562.

[24] Greek text in F. E. Brightman, *Liturgies Eastern and Western*, vol. 1: *Eastern Liturgies* (London: Oxford, 1896), 312.

Hence, the *Trisagion*, originating at Constantinople during the reign of Proclus in the fifth century, was moved to its present location only after other seasonal hymns or entrance antiphons related to various feasts were added, a process beginning already there in the sixth century.

But if the original function of the *Trisagion* is masked by its current location and other seasonal hymns and antiphons, so also is the actual beginning of the Byzantine Divine Liturgy at the Little Entrance obscured by the three litanies, prayers, and antiphons that now precede it. This Office of the Three Antiphons, as it is called, has its origins, according to Mateos,[25] in the various stational liturgies of Constantinople during the reign of Justinian. That is, this reflects various processions from stational churches to Hagia Sophia, during which psalms and litanies, and, later, nonbiblical refrains or antiphons were sung, one of which is the *Hō Monogenēs* (added in the year 528) described above. Hence, the Office of the Three Antiphons appears as a vestige of liturgical processions from elsewhere in Constantinople, now moved indoors and codified as a part of Byzantine liturgy.

Because the *Trisagion* appears also in every other Eastern eucharistic liturgy, scholars have customarily interpreted its presence therein as functioning originally in the same way as it did in the Byzantine Rite, namely as an introit or entrance chant. This is not, however, self-evident. M. Daniel Findikyan has argued[26] that because the Armenian and East Syrian Rites already had their own entrance psalms (Ps 92 for the Armenians and the hymn *Laku Mara*, "To You, Lord," for the East Syrians)[27] *before* they adopted the *Trisagion* from Constantinople, the chant has a different function in those rites and is not part of a now deteriorated entrance rite. According to Findikyan, that function in the Armenian and East Syrian Rites is in relationship to the Liturgy of the Word and precisely in connection to the reading and procession of the

---

[25] In addition to Mateos, *La liturgie*, 34–45, see also *idem*, "The Evolution of the Byzantine Liturgy," *John XXIII Lectures*, 1 (New York: John XXIII Center For Eastern Christian Studies, Fordham University, 1965), 76–112.

[26] Findikyan, *Commentary*, 456ff.

[27] "You, Lord of all, we confess: you, Jesus Christ, we glorify: for you are the life-giver of our bodies and you are the Savior of our souls." ET adapted from Brightman, *Liturgies Eastern and Western*, 249. See H. Jammo, *La structure de la messe chaldéene du début jusqu'à l'anpaphore; Étude historique*, OCA 207 (Rome: Pontifico Istituto Orientale, 1979), 97–99.

Table 5.1
Liturgy of the Word

Armenian	Byzantine	Coptic	Ethiopic	East Syrian	West Syrian
– *Hō monogenēs* or seasonal hymn – blessing – four prayers said by priest while choir sings the proper psalm and hymn – *trisagion* – litany	– initial blessing *enarxis* long litany, prayer, and antiphon – short litany, prayer, and antiphon – second short litany, prayer and antiphon *Hō monogenēs* – Little Entrance – seasonal hymns – *trisagion*	– incensation of altar three times with prayers	– invitation to stand – peace – invitation to worship of Trinity	– *Lakho Mara* hymn of praise to Christ the Lord – *trisagion*	– *trisagion* (in Aramaic)

146

Armenian	Byzantine	Coptic	Ethiopic	East Syrian	West Syrian
– Epistle Reading	– Epistle Reading – Gospel Reading	Reading from Paul + prayer Reading from Catholic Epistles + prayer Reading from Acts + prayer petitions, reverences, and processions around altar offering of incense	Epistle Readings Praises of Mary	– two Readings (Malabar) or four Readings (Chaldean)	– *mazmooro* a psalm chanted by the assembly and priest – one or two readings
– Gospel Reading		*trisagion* Gospel and procession	*trisagion* Gospel reading	[Gospel reading included] – [prayer of the faithful (Malabar)] – Creed	– Gospel reading – brief seasonal response
	– litany	prayer of the Gospel			– Creed
– Creed – litany	– prayer for and dismissal of catechumens				
– blessing – dismissal of catechumens					

147

gospel. The very location of the *Trisagion* in the Coptic and Ethiopic Rites in relationship to the gospel would tend to support Findikyan's conclusion. Hence, if the *Trisagion* was part of the original beginning of the Byzantine Rite, it is connected more closely to the Liturgy of the Word in all other Eastern Rites.

The location and function of the *Trisagion* is not the only difference between the Byzantine Rite and the others: its theological interpretation is also a key distinction. In the Byzantine Rite the *Trisagion* is interpreted as a trinitarian hymn, while in all of the other rites it is viewed christologically, especially with the addition of the clause, "who was crucified for us," added to its conclusion by Patriarch Peter the Fuller at Antioch in 468.[28] Viewed by the Byzantines as a heretical (i.e., Monophysite) insertion, this so-called Theopaschite clause underscored the christological interpretation of the *Trisagion* and contributed to its function as one of a "solemnization of the gospel reading, the high point of the Eucharistic Synaxis."[29]

With regard to the biblical readings themselves, as table 5.1 above also shows, the Copts, Ethiopians, and East and West Syrians have retained the older pattern of several readings before the gospel, while the Armenians and Byzantines have only an epistle reading.[30] In comparison with earlier centuries, however, the Eastern Rites as well as those of the West will see the further development of complete lectionaries for the eucharistic liturgies. One of the most prominent of these is included in the tenth-century *typicon* of Constantinople, edited by Juan Mateos,[31] which still functions in the Byzantine Rite today. Finally, while both the Armenian and Byzantine Rites still keep prayers for and dismissals of catechumens at the end of the Liturgy of the Word, the initiation of infants (baptism, chrismation, and communion) became the norm in all of the Eastern Rites, and, hence, there are seldom any real catechumens present to be dismissed from the liturgical assembly.

[28] See the discussion of this in Schulz, *The Byzantine Liturgy*, 22–25; and see the work of Janeras in note 23 above.

[29] Findikyan, *Commentary*, 456. On the Theopaschite controversy, see Schulz, *The Byzantine Liturgy*, 22–25, 161–63.

[30] For details on the Liturgy of the Word in general, see Mateos, *La liturgie de la parole*, 127–47.

[31] Juan Mateos, *Le typicon de la grande Église*, 2 vols., OCA 165, 166 (Rome: Pontifico Istituto Orientale, 1962–63).

2. Pre-anaphoral Rites

The term "pre-anaphoral rites" is customary in Eastern Christian liturgical study for describing the various rites and ceremonies that take place between the Liturgy of the Word and the anaphora itself. As table 5.2 shows, these rites include elements such as the transfer of the eucharistic gifts (with the exception of the Coptic[32] and Ethiopian Rites), the recitation of the Creed (with the exception of the Armenians and Syrians, where it occurs earlier), and the kiss of peace (still in its classic Eastern, and originally Western, position before the Eucharist proper).

In the Byzantine Rite the transfer of the eucharistic gifts to the altar, the Great Entrance, became and has remained clearly one of the more visible and dramatic moments of the entire Divine Liturgy. This action, including a solemn procession through the church with candles and incense among both the Byzantines and Armenians, is accompanied by the chant known as the *Cherubic Hymn*:

> We who mystically represent the Cherubim, who sing to the life-giving Trinity the thrice-holy hymn, let us now lay aside all earthly care that we may welcome the king of All, invisibly escorted by angel hosts. Alleluia! Alleluia! Alleluia![33]

Anton Baumstark, the father of comparative liturgiology (the method of study employed in this work), articulated as one of his "laws of liturgical development" that "certain actions which are purely utilitarian by nature may receive a symbolic meaning either from their function in the liturgy as such or from factors in the liturgical texts which accompany them."[34] There is probably no better example of this than the rite of the Great Entrance. The utilitarian action of transferring the bread and wine from either the old Constantinopolitan *Skeuophylakion* or from a side table, from the time of Maximus the Confessor (628–30) through Symeon of Thessalonica in the fourteenth century, became interpreted as related symbolically or allegorically either to heavenly spiritual realities or to various moments in

---

[32] On the Coptic pre-anaphoral rites, see Maxwell E. Johnson, *Liturgy in Early Christian Egypt*, Alcuin/GROW Joint Liturgical Studies 33 (Cambridge: Grove Books, 1995), 17–21.

[33] For the Greek text, see Brightman, *Liturgies Eastern and Western*, 377–79.

[34] Anton Baumstark, *Comparative Liturgy* (Westminster, MD: The Newman Press, 1958), 59–60, 130.

Table 5.2
Pre-Anaphoral Rites

Armenian	Byzantine	Coptic	Ethiopic	East Syrian	West Syrian
	– prayer of access to the altar – prayer of the faithful	– prayer of veil (prayer of access) Intercessions		– access to the altar	– prayer of access to the altar
			– prayer of blessing and intercession – Creed – prayer of purification – doxology		
– proclamation "the Body of our Lord, and the Blood of our Redeemer are about to be present. . . ." – *hagiology* of the day – removal of vestments of honor from clergy					

– transfer of gifts with Cherubic hymn with corresponding prayer	– "Great Entrance" with Cherubic hymn			– transfer of gifts (Chaldean) or presentation and preparation of gifts (Malabar)	– transfer of gifts to the altar
– incensation of gifts	– incensation	– incensation			
– diaconal admonition					
– prayer of oblation	– litany of offering			– prayer of gratitude on the part of the ministers	– prayer of offering
– benediction					– general incensation
– peace greeting	– kiss of peace			– greeting of peace	– peace
	– Creed	– Creed		– unveiling of gifts	
		– peace	– kiss of peace	– incensing of gifts	

151

Christ's passion (e.g., being carried to his burial) or other events in his life, even his Palm Sunday entrance into Jerusalem or his second coming (see table 5.4 below). While the Armenians and Maronites do have offertory prayers at this point in their rites, probably adopted under Latin influence, Robert Taft, in his definitive study of this rite,[35] has demonstrated that the Great Entrance is in no way equivalent to Western offertory rites. Rather, the eucharistic offering takes place within the anaphora—the Prayer of Offering—itself! The Great Entrance and other pre-anaphoral rites, in other words, are entirely preparatory for that event.

The entrance of the Nicene-Constantinopolitan Creed into Eastern eucharistic liturgies is dated to the patriarchate of Timothy (511–17) at Constantinople,[36] from where it spread elsewhere throughout the Christian East, though, as we see in table 5.2, its location in those rites varies. In the Armenian Rite, for example, the location of the Creed immediately following the gospel has its only close parallel with the Roman Rite. While this has sometimes been interpreted as the result of Latin influence, Findikyan has shown that it was already there prior to the time of Latinization in the twelfth century.[37]

The exchange or kiss of peace in its traditional location has remained a characteristic liturgical element in all of the Eastern Rites. Until only recently, however, with contemporary attempts at its restoration in various places,[38] that action, as in the Roman Rite before the reforms of the Second Vatican Council, had been either suppressed altogether or had become shared only among the clergy and other liturgical ministers at the altar.

3. The Anaphoras

In chapter 3 we indicated that the major anaphoral traditions of the Christian East divided into Antiochene or West Syrian, East Syrian,

[35] Taft, *The Great Entrance*.
[36] See Parenti, "The Eucharistic Liturgy in the East," 68. See also the work of Gabriele Winkler on the Eastern Creeds, *Über die Entwicklungsgeschichte des armenische Symbolums: Ein Vergleich mit dem syrischen und griechischen Formelgut unter Einbezug der relevanten georgischen und äthiopischen Quellen*, OCA 262 (Rome: Pontificio Istituto Orientale, 2000).
[37] Findikyan, *Commentary*, 466.
[38] See *The Divine Liturgy: An Anthology for Worship*, ed. Peter Galadza et al. (Ottawa: Metropolitan Andrey Sheptytsky Institute of Eastern Christian Liturgical Studies, 2004), 138.

and Alexandrian with regard to overall structure or pattern. Since the Antiochene or West Syrian pattern becomes, via the anaphoras ByzBAS and CHR, the pattern of the Byzantine Rite, its anaphoral structure is also termed by scholars as "Syro-Byzantine." These patterns, of course, are characteristic of the diverse Eastern eucharistic rites we have been studying in this chapter, though among the Copts, anaphoras reflecting both the Alexandrian and Syro-Byzantine (EgBAS) patterns are employed.

A characteristic of eucharistic praying in the East, as also in the West, is that beginning in the sixth century (East) we begin to get references to the anaphora being prayed silently during the liturgy. While the reasons for this are not clear, this tendency would become a characteristic of all of the Eastern Rites, with the anaphora being prayed behind the royal doors of the iconastasis (Byzantine) or behind a veil drawn across the front of the altar (Syrian). At the same time, it is often the case that both the narrative of institution and the epiclesis of the Holy Spirit are recited or sung aloud so that, unlike the West, the anaphora itself is never completely in silence.[39]

While it is certainly true that the *Armenian Rite* at one time did know and use versions of BAS—and according to Gabriele Winkler,[40] versions that reflect Syriac sources and predate EgBAS—the only anaphora used in the Armenian Rite today is known as "St. Athanasius," also sometimes referred to as the "Liturgy of St. Gregory the Illuminator," and is dependent in part on those earlier Armenian versions of BAS.[41]

[39] See Robert Taft, "Was the Eucharistic Anaphora Recited Secretly or Aloud? The Ancient Tradition and What Became of It," in *Worship Traditions in Armenia and the Neighboring Christian East,* ed. Roberta Ervine, AVANT: Treasures of the Armenian Christian Tradition 3 (Crestwood, NY: St. Vladimir Seminary Press, St. Nersess Armenian Seminary, 2006), 15–58.

[40] See G. Winkler, *Die Basilius-Anaphora: Edition der beiden armenischen Redaktionen und der relevanten Fragmente, Übersetzung und Zusammenschau aller Versionen im Licht der orientalischen Überlieferungen,* Anaphorae Orientales 2 (Rome: Pontificio Istituto Orientale, 2005); and *idem,* "Armenia's Liturgy at the Crossroads of Neighbouring Traditions," OCP 74, no. 2 (2008): 363–87.

[41] The critical edition of this anaphora with commentary is H.-J. Feulner, *Die armenische Athanasius-Anaphora. Kritische Edition, Übersetzung und liturgievergleichender Kommentar,* Anaphorae Orientales 1 - Anaphorae Armeniacae 1 (Rome: Pontificio Istituto Orientale, 2001).

The Priest: ✛ The grace, the love and the divine sanctifying power of the Father and of the Son and of the Holy Spirit be with you all.
The Choir: Amen. And with your spirit.
The Deacon: The doors, the doors! With all wisdom and good heed lift up your minds in the fear of God.
The Choir: We have them lifted up to you, O Lord almighty.
The Deacon: And give thanks to the Lord with the whole heart.
The Choir: It is proper and right.

The Priest: It is truly proper and right with most earnest diligence always to adore and glorify you, Father almighty, who did remove the hindrance of the curse by your imponderable Word, your co-creator, who, having taken the Church to be a people to himself, made his own those who believe in you, and was pleased to dwell among us in a ponderable nature, according to the dispensation through the Virgin, and as the divine master-builder building a new work, he thereby made this earth into heaven. For he, before whom the companies of vigilant angels could not bear to stand, being amazed at the resplendent and unapproachable light of his divinity, even he, becoming man for our salvation, granted to us that we should join the heavenly ones in spiritual choirs, And in one voice with the seraphim and the cherubim, we should sing holy songs and make melodies and, boldly crying out, shout with them and say:
The Choir: Holy, holy, holy Lord of hosts; Heaven and earth are full of your glory. Praise in the highest. Blessed are you who did come and are to come in the name of the Lord. Hosanna in the highest. Blessed [are] you who did come and are to come in the name of the Lord. Hosanna in the highest.

The Priest: Holy, holy, holy are you truly and all-holy; and who is he that will presume to contain in words the outpouring of your infinite loving kindness to us? From the very beginning you did care for him who had fallen into sin and did comfort him in diverse manners by the prophets, by the giving of the law, by the priesthood and by the prefigurative offering of animals. And at the end of these days, tearing up the sentence of condemnation for all our debts, you gave us your only-begotten Son, both debtor and debt, immolation and anointed, lamb and heavenly bread, high priest and sacrifice; for he is distributor and he himself is distributed always in our midst without ever being consumed. For having become man truly and without illusion, and having become incarnate, through union without confusion, through the Mother of God, the holy Virgin Mary, he journeyed through all the passions of our human life without sin and came willingly to the world-saving cross, which was the occasion of our redemption.

Taking the bread in his holy, divine, immortal, spotless and creative hands, he blessed it, gave thanks, broke it and gave it to his chosen, holy disciples, who were seated, saying: Take, eat; this is my body, which is distributed for you and for many, for the expiation and remission of sins.
The Choir: Amen.

The Priest: Likewise taking the cup, he blessed it, gave thanks, drank and gave it to his chosen, holy disciples, who were seated, saying: Drink this all of you. This is my blood of the new covenant, which is shed for you and for many for the expiation and remission of sins.
The Choir: Amen.

The Choir: Heavenly Father, who did give your Son to death for us, debtor for our debts, by the shedding of his blood, we beseech you, have mercy upon your rational flock.

The Priest: And your only-begotten beneficent Son gave us the commandment that we should always do this in remembrance of him. And descending into the lower regions of death in the body which he took of our kinship, and mightily breaking asunder the bolts of hell, he made you known to us the only true God, the God of the living and of the dead. And now, O Lord, in accordance with this commandment, bringing forth the saving mystery of the body and blood of your Only-begotten, we remember his redemptive sufferings for us, his life-giving crucifixion, his burial for three days, his blessed resurrection, his divine ascension and his enthronement at your right hand, O Father; his awesome and glorious second coming, we confess and praise. And we offer to you yours of your own from all and for all.
The Choir: In all things blessed are you, O Lord. We bless you, we praise you; We give thanks to you; We pray to you, O Lord our God.

The Priest: We do indeed praise you and give thanks to you at all times, O Lord our God, who, having overlooked our unworthiness, have made us ministers of this awesome and ineffable mystery. Not by reason of any good works of our own, of which we are always altogether bereft and at all times find ourselves void, but ever taking refuge in your overflowing forbearance, we make bold to approach the ministry of the body and blood of your Only-begotten, our Lord and Savior Jesus Christ, to whom is befitting glory, dominion and honor, now and always and unto the ages of ages. Amen.

The Priest: ✠ Peace to all.
The Choir: And with your spirit.
The Deacon: Let us bow down to God.
The Choir: Before you, O Lord.

The Choir: Son of God, who are sacrificed to the Father for reconciliation, bread of life distributed among us, through the shedding of your holy blood, we beseech you, have mercy on your flock saved by your blood.

The Priest: We bow down and beseech and ask you, beneficent God, send to us and to these gifts set forth, your co-eternal and co-essential Holy Spirit.
The Deacon: Amen. Bless, Lord.
The Priest: Whereby blessing this bread, make it truly the body of our Lord and Savior Jesus Christ. *[He repeats this three times.]* And blessing this cup, make it truly the blood of our Lord and Savior Jesus Christ. *[He repeats this three times.]* Whereby blessing this bread and this wine, make them truly the body and blood of our Lord and Savior Jesus Christ, changing them by your Holy Spirit. *[He repeats this three times.]* So that for all of us who approach it, this may be for acquittal, for expiation and for remission of sins.

The Choir: Spirit of God, who, descending from heaven, accomplishes through us the mystery of him who is glorified with you, by the shedding of his blood, we beseech you, grant rest to the souls of those of ours who have fallen asleep.

The Priest: Through this grant love, stability and desirable peace to the whole world, to the holy Church and to all orthodox bishops, to priests, to deacons, to kings, to the princes of the world, to peoples, to travelers, to seafarers, to prisoners, to those who are in danger, to the weary and to those who are at war with barbarians. Through this grant also seasonableness to the weather and fertility to the fields and a speedy recovery to those who are afflicted with diverse diseases. Through this give rest to all who long ago have fallen asleep in Christ: to the forefathers, the patriarchs, the prophets, the apostles, martyrs, bishops, presbyters, deacons and the whole company of your holy Church and to all the laity, men and women, who have ended their life in faith. With whom, O beneficent God, visit us also, we beseech you. . . .

[The Intercessions continue.]

The Priest: . . . And having cleansed our thoughts, make us temples fit for the reception of the Body and Blood of your Only-begotten and our Lord and Savior Jesus Christ, with whom to you, O Father almighty, together with the life-giving and liberating Holy Spirit, is befitting glory, dominion and honor, now and always and unto the ages of ages. Amen.[42]

---

[42] Text is adapted from *The Divine Liturgy of the Armenian Church*, ed. M. Daniel Findikyan (New York: St. Vartan Press, 1999), 28–39.

The *Byzantine Rite*, of course, uses those anaphoras ByzBAS and CHR together with, on rare occasions, the Greek anaphora of St. James (hereafter, JAS)[43] and another called St. Gregory, which is the only Byzantine anaphora addressed directly to Christ. In *Barberini gr. 336* the Divine Liturgy of St. Basil appears before that of St. John Chrysostom, demonstrating that prior to the adoption of CHR, the Liturgy of Basil had been the preferred and traditional usage of Constantinople. This earlier usage is confirmed by another of Anton Baumstark's liturgical laws which asserts that "primitive conditions are maintained with greater tenacity in the more sacred seasons of the liturgical year,"[44] since the complete Liturgy of St. Basil is celebrated in the Byzantine Rite only on the Sundays in Lent, Holy Thursday, Holy Saturday (the original Constantinopolitan Paschal Vigil), the Christmas Vigil, the Epiphany Vigil, and on January 1 (the Feast of St. Basil of Caesarea). Apart from this and from those rare anaphoral exceptions noted above, the Liturgy of St. John Chrysostom is always used, having taken precedence over that of Basil in the ninth century during what has been called the Post-iconoclast Reform.[45] The texts of both ByzBAS and CHR appear in chapter 3 above and so are not presented here again.[46]

As previously noted, the *Coptic Rite* employs anaphoras of both the Alexandrian and Syro-Byzantine types. The primary anaphora used is EgBAS with Coptic Mark (also known as "St. Cyril") used on occasion, and another later, and less used, West Syrian imported text named for St. Gregory Nazianzus. Since both EgBAS and Coptic Mark were presented in chapter 3 above, those texts do not appear here.

The *Ethiopian Rite* uses at least twenty-two different anaphoras, generally of the Alexandrian type, the most commonly used being a version of St. Mark closely resembling the one used on occasion in the Coptic Rite. Another of these, called The Anaphora of Mary of Hereyaqos of

[43] On JAS see below, 161–66.

[44] Baumstark, *Comparative Liturgy*, 27ff.

[45] See Stefanos Alexopoulos, "The Influence of Iconoclasm on Liturgy: A Case Study," in *Worship Traditions in Armenia and the Neighboring Christian East*, ed. Ervine, 127–37. See also Stefano Parenti, "La 'vittoria' nella Chiesa di Constantinopoli della Liturgia di Crisostomo sulla Liturgia di Basilio," in *Comparative Liturgy Fifty Years after Anton Baumstark (1872–1948)*, ed. Taft and Winkler, 907–28.

[46] See above, 89–93, 98–101.

Behensa, is addressed directly to the Virgin Mary,[47] underscoring the high Mariology of the Ethiopian Church, although the rich and poetic text is quite clear in not ascribing attributes to Mary belonging to God alone. We present a portion of this prayer from its post-*Sanctus* section:

> O Virgin, full of glory, with whom and with what likeness shall we liken you? You are the loom from which Emannuel took his ineffable garment of flesh. He made the warp from the same flesh as that of Adam, and the woof is your flesh. The shuttle is the Word himself, Jesus Christ. The length of the warp is the shadow of God the Most High. The weaver is the Holy Spirit. How marvelous and wonderful is this thing! O bridge over which the ancient fathers crossed from death to life! O ladder from earth to heaven, through you the first creation was renewed!
>
> [. . .]
>
> O Virgin, you were not wed to Joseph for coming together, but in order that he might keep you in purity, and so was it fulfilled. When God the Father saw your purity he sent to you his radiant angel, whose name is Gabriel, and he said to you: The Holy Spirit shall come upon you, and the power of the Most High shall overshadow you. The Word came to you without being separated from the bosom of his Father; you conceived him without his being limited, and he stayed in your womb without making subtraction from above or addition from beneath. In your womb there dwelt the inestimable and unsearchable fire of the Godhead. It is not just to compare him with earthly fire. Fire has measurement and volume, but of the Deity it cannot be said that it is like this, or even seems to be like this. . . .
>
> . . . O Virgin, when there dwelt in your womb the fire of the Godhead, whose face is fire, whose clothes are fire, whose covering is fire, how did it not burn you? In what part of your womb were the seven curtains of the flame of the fire prepared and spread? Were they in the right or the left side while you were but a child? In what part of your womb was the glittering cherubic throne, compassed by the flame of fire, prepared and planted while you were a young bride? How wonderful it is! A mother and a maid; the narrowness of the womb and the infinite; conception without intercourse, as a bee conceives, from

[47] See David K. Glenday, "Mary in the Liturgy: An Ethiopian Anaphora," *Worship* 47 (1973): 222–26; Getachew Haile, "A Hymn to the Blessed Virgin from Fifteenth-Century Ethiopia," *Worship* 65 (1991): 445–50; idem, "On the Identity of Silondis and the Composition of the Anaphora of Mary Ascribed to Hereyaqos of Behensa," *OCP* 49 (1983): 366–89; and idem, "On the Writings of Abba Giyorgis Saglawi from Two Unedited Miracles of Mary," *OCP* 48 (1982): 65–91.

the voice of a word; milk with virginity! When I think of this my mind likes to swim in the depth of your Son's seas, and the billows from the hiding-place of your Beloved seep across it. . . .

. . . O Virgin who gives the fruit that can be eaten, and the spring which can be drunk: O Bread got from you, that gives life and salvation to those who eat of it in faith. O Bread got from you, that is as hard as the stone of "Admas," which cannot be chewed, to those who do not eat of it in faith. O Cup got from you, that helps those who drink of it in faith to incline to wisdom, and that gives them life. O Cup got from you, that intoxicates those who do not drink of it in faith and causes them to stumble and fall and adds sin to them instead of the remission of sin![48]

What has captured the attention of recent liturgical scholarship, however, is the Ethiopian Anaphora of the Apostles, a fourteenth-century text that includes an Ethiopian translation of the anaphora of chapter 4 of the so-called *Apostolic Tradition*, as well as a concluding *Benedictus* doxology from the Ethiopic version of the late fourth- or early fifth-century church order, the *Testamentum Domini*. While the overall pattern appears to reflect a more Alexandrian structure with intercessions in the preface and the post-*Sanctus* connected to the *Sanctus* by means of "full," there is no explicit post-*Sanctus* epiclesis of the Holy Spirit upon the gifts but, rather, a consecratory epiclesis in the Syro-Byzantine position after the anamnesis. Recent work on the *Sanctus* and *Benedictus* in this anaphora also suggests early Syrian influence by means of a document of Syrian origin, but in its Ethiopian translation, namely, the Book of Enoch. So, while the text in its present shape may be from the fourteenth century, it is quite plausible that some very early elements are represented within it.[49]

The Ethiopian Anaphora of the Apostles

Preface

Priest: We give thanks to you, O Lord, through your beloved Son our Lord Jesus, who in the last days you sent to us, your Son, the Savior and

---

[48] ET adapted from *The Liturgy of The Ethiopian Church*, trans. Marcos Daoud, rev. Marsie Hazen (Cairo: The Egyptian Book Press, 1959), 134–36, 141–42.

[49] See Winkler, *Das Sanctus*, 96ff., 143ff. See also, Maxwell Johnson, "Recent Research on the Anaphoral *Sanctus*: An Update and Hypothesis," in *Issues in Eucharistic Praying*, ed. idem, 161–88. For recent work on the *Testamentum Domini* see Gabriele Winkler, "Über das christliche Erbe Henochs und einige Probleme des *Testamentum Domini*," *Oriens Christianus* 93 (2009): 201–47.

Redeemer, the messenger of your counsel. This Word is he, who is from you, and through whom you made all things according to your will.

[Intercessions]

Introduction to the *Sanctus* and *Sanctus*

Priest: There stand before you a thousand thousands and ten thousand times ten thousand, both the holy angels and archangels and your honorable beasts, each with six wings. [*Deacon:* Look to the east.] With two of their wings they cover their face, with two of their wings they cover their feet, and with two of their wings they fly from end to end of the world. [*Deacon:* Let us be attentive.] And they all constantly hallow and praise you, with all of those who hallow and praise you. Receive also our hallowing, which we utter to you: Holy, holy, holy, perfect Lord of hosts. [*Deacon:* Answer you all.]

People: Holy, holy, holy, perfect Lord of hosts, heaven and earth are full of the holiness of your glory.

Post-*Sanctus*

Priest: Truly heaven and earth are full of the holiness of your glory, through our Lord, God, and Savior Jesus Christ, your holy Son. He came and was born of a virgin, so that he might fulfill your will and make a people for yourself.

People: Remember us all in your kingdom; remember us, Lord, Master, in your kingdom; remember us, Lord, in your kingdom, as you remembered the thief on the right hand when you were on the tree of the holy cross.

Priest: He stretched out his hands in the passion, suffering to save the sufferers that trust in him; he, who was delivered to the passion that he might destroy death, break the bonds of Satan, tread down hell, lead forth the saints, establish a covenant and make known his resurrection.

Institution Narrative

Priest: In the same night that they betrayed him. . . . As often as you do this, do it in remembrance of me.

People: We proclaim your death, Lord, and your holy resurrection; we believe in your ascension and your second advent. We glorify you, and confess you, we offer our prayer to you and supplicate you, our Lord and our God.

Anamnesis

Priest: Now, Lord, we remember your death and your resurrection. We confess you and we offer to you this bread and this cup, giving thanks to you; and thereby you have made us worthy of the joy of standing before you and ministering to you.

Epiclesis

Priest: We pray and beseech you, O Lord, that you would send the Holy Spirit and power upon this bread and upon this cup. May he make them the body and blood of our Lord, God, and Savior Jesus Christ, unto the ages of ages.

People: Amen. Lord pity us, Lord spare us, Lord have mercy on us.

Deacon: With all our heart let us beseech the Lord our God that he grant to us the good communion of the Holy Spirit.

People: As it was, is and shall be unto generations of generations, world without end.

Priest: Grant it together to all of them that partake of it, that it may be to them for sanctification and for filling with the Holy Spirit and for strengthening of the true faith, that they may hallow and praise you and your beloved Son, Jesus Christ with the Holy Spirit.

People: Amen.

Priest: Grant us to be united through your Holy Spirit, and heal us by this oblation, that we may live in you for ever. [*The people repeat his words.*]

Priest: Blessed be the Name of the Lord, and blessed be he that comes in the Name of the Lord, and let the Name of the Lord, and let the Name of his glory, be blessed. So be it. So be it. So be it blessed. [*The people repeat his words.*]

Priest: Send the grace of the Holy Spirit upon us. [*The people repeat his words.*] [50]

Like the Ethiopians, the *West Syrians* employ several different anaphoras, including a Syriac version of JAS,[51] *Twelve Apostles* (discussed in chapter 3), and several others in current usage.[52] JAS is

---

[50] ET adapted from Daoud, *The Liturgy of the Ethiopian Church*, 69–76. A critical edition of the Ethiopian text is in preparation by Reinhard Meßner and Martin Lang. See their study, "Ethiopian Anaphoras: Status and Tasks in Current Research Via an Edition of the Ethiopian Anaphora of the Apostles," in *Jewish and Christian Liturgy and Worship: New Insights into its History and Interaction*, ed. Albert Gerhards and Clemens Leonhard, Jewish and Christian Perspectives 15 (Leiden/Boston: Brill, 2007), 185–206.

[51] On Syriac JAS see Baby Varghese, *The Syriac Version of the Liturgy of St. James: A Brief History for Students*, Alcuin/GROW Joint Liturgical Studies 49 (Cambridge: Grove Books, 2001). See also Phillip Tovey, *The Liturgy of St. James As Presently Used*, Alcuin/GROW Joint Liturgical Studies 40 (Cambridge: Grove Books, 1998).

[52] For current texts in Syriac and English translation see *Anaphoras: The Book of the Divine Liturgies according to the Rite of the Syrian Orthodox Church of*

connected to early Jerusalem liturgy, especially to the *Mystagogical Catecheses* of Cyril (John) of Jerusalem, and the text also bears some relationship to the anaphoral tradition of BAS. Following Geoffrey Cuming, John R. K. Fenwick argued, in fact, that the core of JAS was the result of an amalgamation made in the late fourth century between the prayer described in the *Mystagogical Catecheses* and EgBAS and was then subject to several considerable later influences.[53] More recently, while noting some relationship between JAS and EgBAS, Winkler has suggested in a preliminary way a much closer relationship with the first Armenian version of BAS, a relationship noted above also with the Anaphora of St. Athanasius.[54] We present the anaphora of JAS here with what have been identified to be the later Greek insertions in brackets, after the translation of Jasper and Cuming.[55]

Anaphora of Saint James

The bishop: The love of God the Father, the grace of our Lord [and] God and Savior Jesus Christ, and the fellowship [and the gift] of the [all-] Holy Spirit be with you all.
People: And with your spirit.
The Bishop: Let us lift up our minds and hearts.
People: We have them with the Lord.
The Bishop: Let us give thanks to the Lord.
People: It is fitting and right.

The bishop, bowing, says:
It is truly fitting and right, suitable and profitable, to praise you, [to hymn you,] to bless you, to worship you, to glorify you, to give thanks to you, the creator of all creation, visible and invisible, [the treasure of eternal good things, the fountain of life and immortality, the God and Master of all]. You are hymned by [the heavens and] the heavens of heavens and all their powers; the sun and moon and all the choir of

---

Antioch, trans. Murad Sallba Barsom, ed. Mar Athanasius Yeshue Samuel (Lodi, NJ: Mar Athanasius Yeshue Samuel, 1991).

[53] See J. R. K. Fenwick, *The Anaphoras of St Basil and St James: An Investigation into their Common Origin*, OCA 240 (Rome: Pontificio Istituto Orientale, 1992); John Witvliet, "The Anaphora of St. James," in *Essays in Early Eastern Eucharistic Prayers*, ed. Paul F. Bradshaw (Collegeville, MN: Liturgical Press, Pueblo, 1997), 153–72.

[54] Gabriele Winkler, "Preliminary Observations About the Relationship Between the Liturgies of St. Basil and St. James," OCP 76 (2010): 5–55.

[55] ET from PEER, 90–99.

stars; earth, sea, and all that is in them; the heavenly Jerusalem, [the assembly of the elect,] the church of the first-born written in heaven, [the spirits of righteous men and prophets, the souls of martyrs and apostles;] angels, archangels, thrones, dominions, principalities and powers, and awesome virtues. The cherubim with many eyes and seraphim with six wings, which cover their own faces with two wings, and their feet with two, and fly with two, cry one to the other with unwearying mouths and never-silent hymns of praise, *(aloud)* *[singing]* with clear voice the triumphal hymn of your magnificent glory, proclaiming, praising, crying, and saying:

People: Holy, holy, holy, Lord of Sabaoth; heaven and earth are full of your glory. Hosanna in the highest. Blessed is he that comes and will come in the name of the Lord. Hosanna in the highest.

And the bishop, standing up, seals the gifts, saying privately: Holy you are, King of the ages and [Lord and] Giver of all holiness; holy too is your only-begotten Son, our Lord Jesus Christ, [through whom you made all things;] and holy too is your [all-]Holy Spirit, who searches out all things, even your depths, O God and Father. *(He bows and says:)* Holy you are, almighty, omnipotent, awesome, good, [compassionate,] with sympathy above all for what you fashioned.

You made man from the earth [after your image and likeness,] and granted him the enjoyment of paradise; and when he transgressed your commandment and fell, you did not despise him or abandon him, for you are good, but you chastened him as a kindly father, you called him through the law, you taught him through the prophets.

Later you sent your only-begotten Son, [himself, our Lord Jesus Christ,] into the world to renew [and raise up] your image [by coming himself.] He came down [from heaven] and was made flesh from the Holy Spirit and Mary, the Holy [ever-]Virgin Mother of God. He dwelt among men and ordered everything for the salvation of our race.

And when he was about to endure his voluntary [and life-giving] death [on the cross], the sinless for us sinners, in the night when he was betrayed, [or rather handed himself over,] for the life and salvation of the world. *(He stands up, takes the bread, seals it, and says:)* he took bread in his holy, undefiled, blameless [and immortal] hands, [looked up to heaven, and] showed it to you, his God and Father; he gave thanks, blessed, sanctified, and broke it, and gave it to his [holy and blessed] disciples and apostles, saying, *(he puts the bread down, saying aloud:)* "Take, eat; this is my body, which is broken and distributed for you for the forgiveness of sins." *People:* Amen.

(*He takes the cup, seals it, and says privately:*) "Likewise after supper [he took] the cup, he mixed wine and water, [he looked up to heaven and showed it to you, his God and Father; he gave thanks,] blessed, and sanctified it, [filled it with the Holy Spirit,] and gave it to his [holy and blessed] disciples and apostles, saying, (*he puts it down, saying aloud:*) "Drink from it, all of you; this is my blood of the new covenant, which is shed and distributed for you and for many for forgiveness of sins." *People:* Amen.

(*Then he stands and says privately:*) "Do this for my remembrance; for as often as you eat this bread and drink this cup, you proclaim the death of the Son of Man and confess his Resurrection, until he comes."

(*And the deacons present answer:*) We believe and confess.

People: Your death, Lord, we proclaim and your Resurrection we confess.

Then he makes the sign of the cross, bows, and says: We [sinners,] therefore, [also] remembering [his life-giving suffering and his saving cross and] his death [and his burial] and his Resurrection from the dead on the third day and his return to heaven and his session at your right hand, his God and Father, and his glorious and awesome second coming, when he [comes with glory to] judge the living and the dead, when he will reward each according to his works [—spare us, Lord our God (*thrice*)—or rather according to his compassion], we offer you, [Master,] this awesome and bloodless sacrifice, [asking you] that you "deal not with us after our sins nor reward us according to our iniquities," but according to your gentleness and [unspeakable] love for man to [pass over and] blot out [the handwriting that is against us] your suppliants, [and grant us your heavenly and eternal gifts, "which eye has not seen nor ear heard nor have entered into the heart of man, which you, O God, have prepared for those who love you." And do not set at naught your people on account of me and my sins, O Lord, lover of men (*thrice*),] (*aloud*) for your people and your Church entreats you.

People: Have mercy on us, [Lord, God,] Father, the almighty.

And the bishop stands up and says privately: Have mercy on us, [Lord,] God the Father, almighty; [have mercy on us, God, our Savior. Have mercy on us, O God, according to your great mercy,] and send out upon us and upon these [holy] gifts set before you your [all-]Holy Spirit, (*he bows*) the Lord and giver of life, who shares your throne and the kingdom with you, God the Father and your [only-begotten] Son, consubstantial and co-eternal, who spoke in the law and the prophets and in your new covenant, who descended in the likeness of a dove upon our Lord Jesus

Christ in the river Jordan [and remained upon him,] who descended upon your holy apostles in the likeness of fiery tongues [in the Upper Room of the holy and glorious Zion on the day of the holy Pentecost; (*he stands up and says privately:*) send down, Master, your all-Holy Spirit himself upon us and upon these holy gifts set before you,] (*aloud*) that he may descend upon them, [and by his holy and good and glorious coming may sanctify them,] and make this bread the holy body of Christ, (*People:* Amen.) and this cup the precious blood of Christ. (*People:* Amen.)

The bishop stands up and says privately: that they may become to all who partake of them [for forgiveness of sins and for eternal life] for sanctification of souls and bodies, for bringing forth good works, for strengthening your holy, [catholic, and apostolic] Church, which you founded on the rock of faith, that the gates of hell should not prevail against it, rescuing it from heresy and from the stumbling-blocks of those who work lawlessness, [and from the enemies who rose and rise up] until the consummation of the age.

The clerics alone answer: Amen.

Then he makes the sign of the cross, bows, and says: We offer to you, [Master,] for your holy places also, which you glorified by the theophany of your Christ [and the descent of your all-Holy Spirit;] principally for [holy and glorious] Zion, the mother of all the churches, and for your holy, [catholic, and apostolic] Church throughout the world: even now, Master, grant it richly the gifts of your [all-]Holy Spirit.

Remember, Lord, also our holy [fathers and] bishops [in the Church,] who [in all the world] divide the word of truth [in orthodoxy]; principally our holy Father N., [all his clergy and priesthood]: grant him an honorable old age; preserve him to shepherd your flock in all piety and gravity for many years.

Remember, Lord, the honorable presbytery here and everywhere, the diaconate in Christ, all the other ministers, every ecclesiastical order, [our brotherhood in Christ, and all the Christ-loving people.

Remember, Lord, the priests who stand around us in this holy hour, before your holy altar, for the offering of the holy and bloodless sacrifice; and give them and us the word in the opening of our mouths to the glory and praise of your all-holy name.]

[The Intercessions continue.]

The bishop says aloud: Through whom, [as a good God and a Master that loves men,] to us and them (*People:*) remit, forgive, pardon, O God, our transgression, voluntary and involuntary, witting and unwitting.

The bishop alone says: By the grace and compassion and love for men of your Christ, with whom you are blessed and glorified, with your all-Holy and life-giving Spirit, now and always and to the ages of ages. Amen.

As noted above, the *Maronites* are often associated with the West Syrian Rite, but several of their liturgies—including their rites of Christian initiation—also have close affinities with East Syrian liturgy. One of these is the Third Anaphora of St. Peter, which is commonly referred to as *Sharar*, from its first word in Syriac. Thanks to the initial work of William Macomber,[56] liturgical scholars now see this text as sharing a common source with Addai and Mari,[57] discussed above in chapter 2, and reflecting not a West but an East Syrian structure, with the epiclesis of the Holy Spirit coming after rather than before the intercessions, although, unlike Addai and Mari, *Sharar* does include a narrative of institution. After the *Sanctus*, *Sharar*, like Addai and Mari throughout, is addressed directly to Christ, a sure sign of its antiquity, and it may actually preserve in some instances (e.g., in the epiclesis) an earlier version of the text than does Addai and Mari. Scholars have also noted in *Sharar* the influence of another East Syrian anaphora called Theodore the Interpreter.[58]

Third Anaphora of Saint Peter (Sharar)

Deacon: Let us stand aright.

Priest: We offer to you, God, our Father, Lord of all, an offering and a commemoration and a memorial in the sight of God, living and from the beginning and holy from eternity, for the living and for the dead, for the near and for the far, for the poor and for travelers, for the churches and monasteries which are here and in every place and in

---

[56] William Macomber, "The Maronite and Chaldean Versions of the Anaphora of the Apostles," OCP 37 (1971): 55–84; and *idem*, "A Theory on the Origins of the Syrian, Maronite, and Chaldean Rites."

[57] See Bryan Spinks, *Addai and Mari—The Anaphora of the Apostles: A Text for Students*, Grove Liturgical Study 24 (Cambridge: Grove Books, 1980); and Anthony Gelston, *The Eucharistic Prayer of Addai and Mari* (Oxford: Oxford University Press, 1992).

[58] See Bryan Spinks, *Mar Nestorius and Mar Theodore the Interpreter: The Forgotten Eucharistic Prayers of East Syria*, Alcuin/GROW Joint Liturgical Studies 45 (Cambridge: Grove Books, 1999).

all regions; and for me, unworthy and a sinner, whom you have made worthy to stand before you (remember me in your heavenly kingdom); and for the souls and spirits whom we commemorate before you, Lord, mighty God, and for this people which is in the true faith and awaits your abundant mercy; and for the sins, faults, and defects of us all, we offer this pure and holy offering.

People: It is fitting and right.

Priest: It is fitting and right, our duty and our salvation, natural and good. Let our minds ever be lifted up to heaven, and all our hearts in purity.

People: To you, Lord, God of Abraham, Isaac, and Israel, O King glorious and holy for ever.

Priest: To you, Lord, God of Abraham, savior of Isaac, strength of Israel, O King glorious and holy forever. The Lord is worthy to be confessed by us and adored and praised.

(Here the priest blesses the people, and says a prayer relating to the incense and a number of commemorations, after which he begins the anaphora.)

Priest (bowing): Glory to you, adorable and praiseworthy name of the Father and of the Son and of the Holy Spirit. You created the world through your grace and all its inhabitants by your mercy and made redemption for mortals by your grace.

Your majesty, O Lord, a thousand thousand heavenly angels adore; myriad myriads of hosts, ministers of fire and spirit, praise you in fear. With the cherubim and the seraphim, who in turn bless, glorify, proclaim, and say, let us also, Lord, become worthy of your grace and mercy, to say with them thrice, "Holy, holy, holy . . ."

(bowing) We give thanks to you, Lord, we your sinful servants, because you have given your grace which cannot be repaid. You put on our human nature to give us life through your divine nature; you raised our lowly state; you restored our Fall; you gave life to our mortality; you justified our sinfulness; you forgave our debts; you enlightened our understanding, conquered our enemies, and made our weak nature to triumph.

(aloud) And for all your grace towards us, let us offer you glory and honor, in your holy Church before your altar of propitiation . . .

(bowing) You, Lord, through your great mercy, be graciously mindful of all the holy and righteous Fathers, when we commemorate your body and blood, which we offer to you on your living and holy altar, as you, our hope, taught us in your holy gospel and said, "I am the living bread who came down from heaven that mortals may have life in me."

(aloud) We make the memorial of your Passion, Lord, as you taught us. In the night in which you were betrayed to the Jews, Lord, you took bread in your pure and holy hands, and lifted your eyes to heaven to your glorious Father; you blessed, sealed, sanctified, Lord, broke, and gave it to your disciples the blessed Apostles, and said to them, "This bread is my body, which is broken and given for the life of the world, and will be to those who take it for the forgiveness of debts and pardon of sins; take and eat from it, and it will be to you for eternal life."

(He takes the cup) Likewise over the cup, Lord, you praised, glorified, and said, "This cup is my blood of the new covenant, which is shed for many for forgiveness of sins; take and drink from it, all of you, and it will be to you for pardon of debts and forgiveness of sins, and for eternal life." Amen.

"As often as you eat from this holy body, and drink from this cup of life and salvation, you will make the memorial of the death and resurrection of your Lord, until the great day of his coming."

People: We make the memorial, Lord, of your death . . .

Priest: We adore you, only begotten of the Father, firstborn of creation, spiritual Lamb, who descended from heaven to earth, to be a propitiatory sacrifice for all men and to bear their debts voluntarily, and to remit their sins by your blood, and sanctify the unclean through your sacrifice.

Give us life, Lord, through your true life, and purify us through your spiritual expiation; and grant us to gain life through your life-giving death, that we may stand before you in purity and serve you in holiness and offer that sacrifice to your Godhead, that it may be pleasing to the will of your majesty, and that your mercy, Father, may flow over us all. . . .

We ask you, only-begotten of the Father, through whom our peace is established; Son of the Most High, in whom highest things are reconciled with lower; Good Shepherd, who laid down your life for your sheep and delivered them from ravening wolves; merciful Lord, who raised your voice on the cross and gathered us from vain error; God, the god of spirits and of all flesh; may our prayers ascend in your sight, and your mercy descend on our petitions, and let that sacrifice be acceptable before you; we offer it as a memorial of your Passion on your altar of propitiation.

May it please your Godhead, and may your will be fulfilled in it; by it may our guilt be pardoned and our sins forgiven; and in it may our dead be remembered. Let us praise you and adore you, and the father who sent you for our salvation, and your living and Holy Spirit now. . . .

By it may the glorious Trinity be reconciled, by the thurible and the sacrifice and the cup; by it may the souls be purified and the spirits sanctified of those for whom and on account of whom it was offered and sanctified; and for me, weak and sinful, who offered it, may the mercy of the glorious Trinity arise, Father. . . .

(The priest bows and says a prayer to the Mother of God.)

We offer before you, Lord, this sacrifice in memory of all righteous and pious fathers, of prophets, apostles, martyrs, confessors, and all our patriarchs, and the pope of the city of Rome and metropolitan bishops, area bishops, visitors, priests, deacons, deaconesses, young men, celibates, virgins, and all sons of holy Church who have been sealed with the sign of saving baptism, and whom you have made partakers of your holy body.

(privately) First and especially we commemorate the holy and blessed and saintly Virgin, the Blessed Lady Mary.

Deacon: Remember her, Lord, God, and us through her pure prayers.

Priest (bowing): Remember, Lord God, at this time the absent and the present, the dead and the living, the sick and the oppressed, the troubled, the afflicted, and those who are in various difficulties.

Remember, Lord God, at this time, our fathers and brothers in spirit and in body; and forgive their offences and sins.

Remember, Lord God, at this time, those who offer sacrifices, vows, firstfruits, memorials; grant to their petitions good things from your abundant store.

Remember, Lord God, at this time, those who join in commemorating your mother and your saints; grant them recompense for all their good works; and for all who communicated in this eucharist which was offered on this holy altar; grant them, Lord God, a reward in your kingdom; and for all who have said to us, "pray for us in your prayers before the Lord." Remember them, Lord God, and purge their iniquities.

Remember, Lord God, at this time, my miserableness, sinfulness, importunity, and lowliness; I have sinned and done evil in your sight consciously or not, voluntarily or not. Lord God, in your grace and mercy pardon me and forgive whatever I have sinned against you; and may this eucharist, Lord, be as a memorial of our dead and for the reconciliation of our souls.

Remember, Lord God, at this time, your weak and sinful servant George, who wrote this, and pardon him and forgive him his offences and sins, and forgive his fathers. Amen.

(kneeling) Hear me, Lord *(thrice)*, and let your living and Holy Spirit, Lord, come and descend upon this offering of your servants, and may it be to those who partake for remission and forgiveness of sins, for a blessed resurrection from the dead, and for new life in the kingdom of heaven for ever.

(aloud) And because of your praiseworthy dispensation towards us, we give thanks to you, we your sinful servants redeemed by your innocent blood, with eloquent mouth in your holy Church before your altar of propitiation. . . . [59]

The most famous anaphora used by the *East Syrian Rite* is that of Addai and Mari. It is still used by the Ancient (Assyrian) Church of the East without the narrative of institution, though in the versions used by the Chaldean Catholics and by the Syro-Malabars in India the narrative appears. Beginning in 1994 with a *Common Christological Declaration between the Catholic Church and the Assyrian Church of the East*, continued ecumenical dialogue and convergence led in 2001 to a document titled *Guidelines for Admission to the Eucharist between the Chaldean Church and the Assyrian Church of the East*. There is no question but that this is a highly significant liturgical-ecumenical development. What makes it so is that it now allows Chaldean Catholics to receive Holy Communion in liturgies celebrated in assemblies of the Assyrian Church of the East, even when Addai and Mari is used *without the explicit recital of the Words of Institution*. That is, Addai and Mari is recognized by Rome as a valid prayer of eucharistic consecration, and eucharistic celebration within the Assyrian Church of the East is acknowledged as constituting a *Catholic* Eucharist in the full sense of the word. Chaldean Catholics receiving communion in such eucharistic celebrations are assured that they are indeed receiving the body and blood of Christ. The implications of this are mind-boggling on several levels, not the least of which is the now-official recognition of what liturgical scholars have been saying for years, namely, that it is the *entire* eucharistic prayer itself,

---

[59] Text from PEER, 46–51.

and not various "formulas" within eucharistic prayers (i.e., institution narrative or epiclesis), that "consecrate" the Eucharist.[60]

In addition to Addai and Mari, the East Syrians, with the exception of the Syro-Malabars, also make use of two other anaphoras, namely, Mar Nestorius, named, of course, for the fifth-century patriarch whose views against the term *Theotokos* were condemned by the Council of Ephesus, and Mar Theodore the Interpreter, named for Theodore of Mopsuestia. These two anaphoras, called by Bryan Spinks "the forgotten Eucharistic prayers of East Syria," are often claimed to be but "compilations based on the two Byzantine anaphoras"[61] (i.e., BAS and CHR). They are actually, however, both mid-sixth-century redactions, probably by Mar Aba (d. 553), Catholicos (i.e., Patriarch) of the East Syrians from 540 to 552, making use of earlier Greek liturgical sources such as BAS and CHR, as well as earlier East Syrian anaphoral traditions (Addai and Mari) and other sources, and reflecting the strongly Antiochene theology of Theodore of Mopsuestia himself.[62]

4. Communion and Dismissal Rites

Many of the rites often referred to as post-anaphoral or pre-communion, culminating in the distribution and reception of Holy Communion itself, were already in place by the end of the fourth and beginning of the fifth century. *Mystagogical Catechesis* 5.11–20 of Cyril (John) of Jerusalem describes the recitation of the Lord's Prayer immediately after the eucharistic prayer, followed by an invitation to communion ("Holy things for the holy") coupled with the elevation of the gifts, as table 5.3 shows, and with the congregational response, "One is holy, one Lord, Jesus Christ"—what Robert Taft calls the "ancient

---

[60] On all of this see Robert Taft, "Mass without Consecration? The Historic Agreement on the Eucharist between the Catholic Church and the Assyrian Church of the East Promulgated 26 October 2001," *Worship* 77 (2003): 482–509. For a more recent assessment, see Nicholas Russo, "The Validity of the Anaphora of *Addai and Mari*: Critique of the Critiques," in *Issues in Eucharistic Praying in East and West*, ed. Johnson, 21–62. On the question of eucharistic consecration in the Christian East see below, 181–84.

[61] Enzo Lodi, "The Oriental Anaphoras," in *Handbook for Liturgical Studies*, vol. 3: *The Eucharist*, ed. Chupungco, 95.

[62] For texts of these prayers and commentary, see Spinks, *Mar Nestorius and Mar Theodore the Interpreter*.

communion call and its response" of Eastern liturgies.[63] Early references to this also appear in Egypt with the earliest being the *De Trinitate* 3.13 of Didymus the Blind and *In Johannis Evangelium* 4.7, 12 of Cyril of Alexandria. There was also a prayer of thanksgiving after communion in *Mystagogical Catechesis* 5.22, the equivalent of Western post-communion prayers. These elements are paralleled in some other early Eastern sources. Theodore of Mopsuestia, for example, already makes reference to a "fraction" rite, as well as describing a commixture or commingling of the bread and wine before communion (*Baptismal Homily* 5.15–20), a similar invitation to communion ("Holy things for the holy"), and a prayer of thanksgiving after communion (*Baptismal Homily* 5.22–23, 29). As we saw in chapter 3, a prayer of inclination before communion, a thanksgiving prayer after communion, and a final inclination prayer at the dismissal were becoming characteristic structures in the late fourth century among the Copts (including the *Prayers of Sarapion of Thmuis*) and the East and West Syrians (including *Apostolic Constitutions* 8).

While all of the Eastern Rites, with the exception of the Armenians, regularly use a mixed chalice containing both wine and water prepared earlier in the liturgy, only the Byzantine Rite maintains in current usage the addition of hot water (the *zeon*) poured into the chalice immediately after the fraction and the commixture (the comingling of the body and blood of Christ). According to Robert Taft,[64] however, evidence from the Byzantine liturgical manuscripts demonstrates that beginning in the sixth century this action took place during the preparation of the bread and wine before the liturgy (at the *Prothesis*). Later in history, in order to have a warm chalice for communion, the *zeon* began to be added immediately before the Great Entrance. But it was not until the eleventh century that the current practice developed and became normative. By that time, various theological interpretations had arisen as to the meaning of this action. As Alex Rentel has noted:

> Byzantine liturgical commentators will . . . see what transpires at the epiclesis, with the descent of the Holy Spirit, as completed only at the addition of hot water, the *zeon*, to the chalice directly after the fraction

---

[63] See Robert Taft, *A History of the Liturgy of St. John Chrysostom*, vol. 5: *The Precommunion Rites*, OCA 261 (Rome; Pontificio Istituto Orientale 2000), 231ff. See also his essay, "'Holy Things for the Saints': The Ancient Call to Communion and Its Response," in *Fountain of Life*, ed. Gerard Austin (Washington, DC: Pastoral Press, 1991), 87–102.

[64] See Taft, *The Precommunion Rites*, 441–502.

and commixture. This ritual vividly portrays Christ's resurrected body and blood being enlivened by the warmth and "fullness of the Holy Spirit" [*Barberini gr. 336*].[65]

Together with this resurrection imagery others began to interpret the *zeon* as indicative of Christ's living *warm* blood (and water) flowing from his side after his death on the cross.[66]

With regard to the distribution and reception of holy communion itself, while every Eastern Rite came to have a stylized fraction (*melismos*) and commixture, and every rite distributes communion (*comminution*) under both bread and wine, only the Copts and East Syrians have retained the practice of distributing the bread and cup separately, while the other rites use forms of intinction, with the Byzantines since the eleventh century using a spoon.[67] Again, it is Taft who has argued that:

> the distinction between melismos and comminution [has] validity only in the later stages of liturgical development, when the ritualization of the manual acts symbolizing the rejoining of Christ's body and blood (intinction, consignation, commixture) forces a distinction in the fraction between the "symbolic" melismos that precedes these rites, and the "practical" comminution that follows.[68]

He notes further:

> Just when and how this comminution took place is not indicated in the early sources. Van de Paverd has suggested "that a piece of bread was broken off for each individual communicant so that for all practical purposes the fraction took place during communion." This solution seems to fit the evidence best. First, the main celebrant at the altar broke off particles for himself and his fellow ministers. Then the gifts were brought out and a piece was broken off and placed in the hand of each communicant as he or she approached in the communion procession. Communion is still given this way in the Coptic Orthodox service.[69]

---

[65] Alexander Rentel, "Byzantine and Slavic Orthodoxy," 295.

[66] On this, as well as controversies with the Armenians over the use of a mixed chalice or water alone and its christological arguments, see Schulz, *The Byzantine Liturgy*, 39–43.

[67] Robert Taft, *A History of the Liturgy of St. John Chrysostom*, vol. 6: *The Communion, Thanksgiving, and Concluding Rites*, OCA 281 (Rome: Pontificio Istituto Orientale, 2008), 281–315.

[68] Robert Taft, "Melismos and Comminution: The Fraction and Its Symbolism in the Byzantine Tradition," *Studia Anselmiana* 95 (1988): 531–52, here at 541.

[69] Ibid., 538–39.

All of the Eastern Rites also have one or more prayers of preparation for the worthy reception of communion called "inclination" prayers. In the Byzantine and Armenian Rites, however, this prayer probably functioned originally in the time of John Chrysostom, as we also saw in chapter 3, as a prayer for the solemn "dismissal" of non-communing faithful who, in the context of the post-Constantinian influx of converts and the gradual decline in the reception of communion in general, were leaving the Eucharist at this point. This type of "dismissal prayer" seems to be related as well to the discipline of public penance. In some places (e.g., Asia Minor and Constantinople), certain penitents known as "bystanders without offering" were dismissed from the Eucharist with a special blessing before communion was then distributed.[70] In this context, we might also note the penitential character of many of the Eastern pre-communion rites, including prayers of absolution in some rites, especially among the Copts and Ethiopians.

In addition to a final inclination prayer of blessing and dismissal at some point in all of the rites, the Armenians and Byzantines distribute to all in attendance the bread which is known in the churches of the Byzantine Rite as *antidoron* ("instead of the gift"). This is the remainder of the bread prepared at the *Prothesis* but not consecrated or used for communion. Having its origins in early Christian customs, perhaps even as the vestige of a full Christian meal, such distribution of unconsecrated leftover bread was a common practice at one time in churches of both the West[71] and the East. It appears that the *antidoron* grew in importance, at least among the Byzantines, at a time in which both frequent communion was in decline and the *Prothesis* itself was developing into a more elaborate rite.[72]

Of all the Eastern Rites, only the West Syrians and the Maronites have a prayer of "farewell" addressed to the altar by the priest. The Maronite version reads:

> Remain in peace, O altar of God, and I hope to return to you in peace. May the sacrifice which I have offered upon you forgive my sins, help me to avoid faults, and prepare me to stand blameless before the throne

---

[70] On all of this, see Robert Taft, "The Inclination Prayer before Communion in the Byzantine Liturgy of St. John Chrysostom: A Study in Comparative Liturgy," *Ecclesia Orans* 3 (1986): 29–60, here at 42–48.

[71] See Joseph Jungmann, *The Mass of the Roman Rite* (New York: Benziger, 1955) 2:453–55.

[72] See Robert Taft, *The Communion, Thanksgiving, and Concluding Rites*, 699–719.

of Christ. I know not whether I will be able to return to you again to offer sacrifice. Guard me, O Lord, and protect your holy Church, so that she may remain the way of salvation and the light of the world.[73]

While this prayer undoubtedly originates in Jerusalem and/or Palestinian usage, it is clearly an addition to an earlier Antiochene-type concluding rite that would have ended the liturgy with a simple prayer of blessing and dismissal.

To the Byzantine Rite was added a final prayer called the *Opisthambonos*, Prayer Behind the Ambo.[74] Originally prayed by the clergy at Hagia Sophia in Constantinople during the recession to the *Skeuophylakion*, with another prayer said therein at their arrival, this Prayer Behind the Ambo, was moved to its current location *after* the dismissal by the tenth century. And only the Armenians, under the influence of the Dominican Order in the twelfth century, have incorporated the "Last Gospel," John1:1-14, a characteristic of various Latin medieval, eventually including the Tridentine, rites of the Mass.

5. *Liturgy of the Pre-Sanctified*

Several of the Eastern liturgical traditions also have a rite for the distribution of communion separate from the eucharistic liturgy, known as the Liturgy of the Pre-Sanctified (PRES). Technically speaking, the PRES is not a "liturgy"—a term often reserved in the East for the Divine Liturgy—but an office of communion attached to Vespers; therefore, its central prayer is *not* an anaphora. As Stefanos Alexopoulos has shown,[75] it is structured around and combines various pre-communion and other elements from ByzBAS. Its origins lay in the fourth and fifth centuries, within the context of incidents of abuse in, and eventual suppression of, private reservation of the Eucharist and private communion; fears of heresy; a move toward liturgical uniformity; and increased clericalization of the liturgy. It should also be noted that the PRES appears in

---

[73] ET from the Liturgical Commission of the Diocese of St. Maron, USA, *Anaphora Book of the Syriac-Maronite Church of Antioch* (Youngstown, OH: Catholic Publishing Co., 1978), 30–31.

[74] On dismissal and final prayers, especially in Byzantine usage, see Taft, *The Communion, Thanksgiving, and Concluding Rites*, 565–644.

[75] Stefanos Alexopoulos, *Presanctified Liturgy in the Byzantine Rite: A Comparative Analysis of Its Origins, Evolution, and Structural Components*, Liturgia Condenda 21 (Leuven: Peeters, 2009). This section is based on Alexopoulos' definitive study.

Table 5.3
Communion and Dismissal Rites

Armenian	Byzantine	Coptic	Ethiopic	East Syrian	West Syrian
– Lord's Prayer	– litany of supplication – Lord's Prayer	– Lord's Prayer – several prayers of remembrance – prayer of absolution	– thanksgiving prayer – Lord's Prayer – prayers of blessing, absolution, and remembrance		
	– preparation prayer			– proclamation of faith in the life-giving bread of heaven	
– incensation – prayer of penitence addressed to Holy Spirit – elevation – fraction	– elevation – fraction – *Zeon* – communion of clergy	– elevation – fraction	– fraction – elevation	– fraction and signing – elevation – litany prayer for forgiveness	– fraction and signing
– priest's communion with accompanying prayers – communion of people	– communion of people	– preparation prayers and communion	– preparation prayers – communion	– Lord's Prayer – communion	– Lord's Prayer – penitential rite – elevation – communion

– thanksgiving prayer – "last gospel" (John 1:1-14) – prayer for peace – final blessing and distribution of *antidoron*	– litany – thanksgiving prayer – dismissal – prayer behind the ambo – final blessing and distribution of *antidoron*	– thanksgiving prayer – blessing – dismissal	– thanksgiving prayer – blessing of people – final blessing and dismissal	– thanksgiving prayer – blessing – dismissal	– prayer of thanksgiving – final blessing – "farewell" prayer addressed to the altar

places where the celebration of the full Eucharist was prohibited on fasting days; in places where the full Eucharist was allowed on fasting days, however, the PRES either never appeared or appeared only momentarily in history.

The earliest manuscript evidence for the Byzantine PRES comes from *Barberini gr. 336*, where the PRES already appears in a rather developed form. Our first reference to a PRES in the Byzantine Rite, however, comes from the beginning of the seventh century. The original simple form of the PRES would have included the reservation of the gifts from a previous full liturgy, the transfer of the gifts to the altar, and communion. It is upon this basic structure that the PRES expanded. According to Alexopoulos, three dynamics fueled its development: (1) imitation, as the communion part of the PRES grew, copying structures, actions, and elements of the full liturgy; (2) conservatism, as the PRES preserved elements of the cathedral Office of daily prayer otherwise lost, or elements that were dropped from the full liturgy; and (3) differentiation, in that we see in the PRES an effort to halt the imitation of the full liturgy and the attempt to create its own identity.[76]

Currently the PRES in the Byzantine liturgical tradition is celebrated on Wednesdays and Fridays of Lent and Holy Monday, Holy Tuesday, and Holy Wednesday in Great Week. Originally, it could be celebrated on every Wednesday and Friday of the year; Wednesday and Friday of Cheesefare Week (the week before the beginning of Lent); all weekdays of Lent; Holy Monday, Tuesday, Wednesday, and Friday; and possibly September 14, as well as in the context of coronations, appointments of civil servants, and weddings. The PRES, however, is not unique to the Byzantine liturgical tradition. In fact, there are three other types in the Christian East: Syrian (i.e., West Syrian and Maronite); Jerusalem (e.g., Armenian); and Nubian (a variation of the Ethiopic Rite). With the exception of the Nubian tradition, each of these types can further be divided into two categories: cathedral and monastic.[77] In all Eastern liturgical traditions only consecrated bread was originally reserved, the cup being sanctified by the signing of the chalice/commingling, that is, the adding of the consecrated bread to unconsecrated wine. In the Syrian tradition, in fact, the PRES is called the Signing of the Chalice.[78]

[76] Ibid., 294.
[77] Ibid., 95–127.
[78] For examples of this rite see ibid., 95–107.

178

Not all of the Eastern Churches today, however, have the practice either of the PRES or even of reserving the Eucharist.[79] The Coptic Orthodox, Ethiopian Orthodox, and the Ancient (Assyrian) Church of the East still do not reserve the Eucharist, though, as we have seen, the East Syrians have the practice of reserving and adding the *Malka* to the eucharistic bread during its preparation.[80] And what is fascinating about this is that these churches are all recognized by Rome as having authentically *Catholic* eucharistic doctrine and practice. Hence, to reserve or not to reserve the Eucharist cannot be the question or litmus test with regard to individual churches and their theology of the real presence of Christ in the Eucharist. Together with this it should also be noted that, unlike the later Western medieval period wherein devotion to the Eucharist outside of the liturgy became a popular practice (including, for example, the development of the feast of Corpus Christi in the thirteenth century), the Christian East never developed any equivalent devotional practices separate from its liturgical context. Where the Eucharist is reserved in the Christian East, as in early Christianity, it is for the communion of the sick or for the PRES during Lent. Many Eastern Christians greet and venerate icons when they enter a church building, not the eucharistic Host reserved in a tabernacle on a main or side altar.

EUCHARISTIC THEOLOGY

Before moving into a discussion of eucharistic theology in these liturgical traditions specifically, it is necessary to touch upon a theological topic related to Eastern Christianity in general. The Armenian Apostolic Church, like the Coptic, Ethiopian, and Syrian Orthodox Churches, was and has remained Miaphysite in its Christology, just as the Ancient (Assyrian) Church of the East was and has remained non-Ephesine in its Christology. In the past these churches were often called by what today can only be considered derogatory designations—"Monophysite" or "Nestorian"—terms one unfortunately still encounters on occasion in scholarly literature.[81] The use of such

---

[79] On Eastern practices of reservation and veneration of the Eucharist apart from the liturgy, see Taft, *The Communion, Thanksgiving, and Concluding Rites*, 415–53.

[80] See above, 143.

[81] See Sebastian Brock, "The 'Nestorian' Church: A Lamentable Misnomer," in *idem*, *Fire from Heaven: Studies in Syriac Theology and Liturgy* (Aldershot/Burlington, VT: Ashgate, 2006), 1–14.

designations to identify a church based on what another church views as a heretical doctrinal position is unacceptable today, as is also the pejorative term "uniate" to describe an Eastern Church in communion with Rome. In fact, ecumenical dialogue between the Eastern and Oriental Orthodox Churches[82] and between many of these churches and the West has led to greater understanding and progress toward Christian unity. For example, the 1994 *Common Christological Declaration between the Catholic Church and the Assyrian Church of the East*, leading in 2001 to the document titled *Guidelines for Admission to the Eucharist between the Chaldean Church and the Assyrian Church of the East*,[83] as we discussed above, is a hopeful ecumenical sign of things to come. And although eucharistic hospitality is not regularly practiced by the Eastern Rites with regard to Roman Catholics, the Roman Catholic Church does welcome Eastern Orthodox and Oriental Orthodox Christians to the reception of Holy Communion in Roman Catholic eucharistic liturgies, an invitation not generally accepted.

With specific regard to eucharistic theology, it is safe to say that within the Christian East there appears to be a more consistent theological-historic continuity with the previous centuries, especially the fourth and fifth centuries, than took place, as we shall see, in the West. Nathan Mitchell has noted that "medieval Latin theology's preoccupation with the sacrificial aspects of Eucharist developed in part from a tendency to separate 'sacrifice' from 'sacrament,' and 'consecration' from the church's 'offering' and communion."[84] But Taft has shown, with particular reference to the anaphoral oblation in the Byzantine Rite, that such separation and compartmentalization of the Eucharist does not take place in the Eastern liturgical traditions:

> There is one single offering of the Church within which several things happen. These things are expressed in various ways and moments according to the several pre-reformation traditions of East and West, all of which agree on the basic ritual elements of their traditions. These classical anaphoras express that the Eucharist is a sacrifice, the sacramental memorial of Christ's own sacrifice on the cross, in which the

---

[82] See several documents listed by the "Orthodox Unity" web site: http://www.orthodoxunity.org/statements.html.

[83] See above, 170–71.

[84] Nathan Mitchell, "Eucharistic Theologies," in *The New Westminster Dictionary of Liturgy & Worship*, ed. Bradshaw, 200.

Church, repeating what Jesus did at the Last Supper, invokes God's blessing on bread and wine so that it might become Jesus' body and blood, our spiritual food and drink. . . . All attempts to squeeze more out of the words of the prayer . . . is an inference that can only be made by imposing on the text the results of later theological reflection and/or polemics. . . . So the most one can say is that the "offering" expressions that fall between institution and epiclesis in BAS and CHR neither confirm nor exclude any particular theological thesis of when or by what particular part of the anaphoral prayer the consecration is effected, or just *what*, beyond the Eucharistic service in its most general sense of the Church's offering of the memorial Jesus is believed to have commanded the Church to repeat, is offered: bread and wine, body and blood, the "reasonable and unbloody sacrifice" of the Church, the sacrifice of Christ represented in its sacrament. . . . My own view is that later precisions, in the sense in which they are sometimes posed today as the result of confessional disputes, are sterile and point-less. . . . I would prefer that the earlier liturgical language, which is metaphorical and evocative, not philosophical and ontological, in-cludes *all these "offerings,"* if implicitly and not self-consciously.[85]

This does not mean, however, that various positions on when and how consecration takes place did not develop in the Christian East. To that we now turn.

1. Eucharistic Consecration
    It is often assumed by Western Christians, though not exclusively by them, that as the West came to focus on the narrative of institution as the "moment" of eucharistic consecration of the bread and wine into the body and blood of Christ, so the Eastern Rites focused and continue to focus that "moment" on the epiclesis of the Holy Spirit fol-lowing that narrative. And it is certainly true that a variety of liturgical texts and commentaries could be listed as supporting such a view. This becomes especially the case, for example, in the liturgical writings of the fourteenth-century Byzantine lay theologian and mystic Nicho-las Cabasilas (d. ca. 1363), who in his influential *Commentary on the Divine Liturgy* claims:

[85] Robert Taft, "Understanding the Byzantine Anaphoral Oblation," in *Rule of Prayer, Rule of Faith: Essays in Honor of Aidan Kavanagh, O.S.B.*, ed. Nathan D. Mitchell and John F. Baldovin (Collegeville, MN: Liturgical Press, Pueblo, 1996), 32–55, here at 53–54.

When these words have been said [i.e., the words of the epiclesis], the whole sacred rite is accomplished, the offerings are consecrated, the sacrifice is complete; the splendid Victim, the Divine oblation, slain for the salvation of the world, lies upon the altar. For it is no longer the bread, which until now has represented the Lord's Body, nor is it a simple offering, bearing the likeness of the true offering, carrying as if engraved on it the symbols of the Savior's Passion; it is the true Victim, the most holy Body of the Lord, which really suffered the outrages, insult and blows; which was crucified and slain, which under Pontius Pilate bore such splendid witness; that Body which was mocked, scourged, spat upon, and which tasted gall. In like manner the wine has become the blood which flowed from that Body. It is that Body and Blood formed by the Holy Spirit, born of the Virgin Mary, which was buried, which rose again on the third day, which ascended into heaven and sits on the right hand of the Father.[86]

Cabasilas claimed that the Roman *canon missae* could be brought to bear here as well since he interpreted the post–institution narrative *Supplices te rogamus* portion of the Canon, in which the angel is asked to take the offerings to God's altar in heaven and the faithful receive Christ's body and blood, as an equivalent consecratory epiclesis.

The view of Cabasilas and other theologians on the importance of the epiclesis of the Holy Spirit was seriously challenged at the Council of Florence (1438–45), called initially to bring about union between the Church at Constantinople, needing assistance against the invading Turks, and Rome, together with other Eastern Rites (Coptic, Armenian, and, eventually, West Syrian). With regard to eucharistic theology, the representatives of the Byzantine East, with the notable exception of Mark Eugenikos, Metropolitan of Ephesus, all signed an agreement (*Laetetus Coeli*, 1439), which asserted—among other controversial things like acceptance of the *filioque* clause in the Nicene Creed and the doctrine of purgatory—that it is the narrative of institution alone that consecrates the Eucharist. It was, however, the position of Mark of Ephesus (now venerated by the Orthodox as *Saint* Mark of Ephesus),

---

[86] Cabasilas, *Commentary on the Divine Liturgy*, chap. 27, as quoted in Schulz, *The Byzantine Liturgy*, 129. On Cabasilas' theology see Schulz, *The Byzantine Liturgy*, 124–32.

in agreement with that of Cabasilas, that eventually won the day in the Byzantine East after the ill-fated Florentine attempt at union fell apart.[87]

Even so, however, eucharistic consecration by means of the epiclesis of the Holy Spirit is not the only Eastern Christian position on the transformation of the bread and wine into the body and blood of Christ. In a recent essay, Russian Orthodox scholar Michael Zheltov has demonstrated that, at least for the Byzantines, a variety of differing opinions has existed historically and even today still exist on this question.[88] These positions include the narrative of institution, the elevation of the gifts with the invitation "Holy things for the holy," as the moment when the Holy Spirit descends, the dropping of the consecrated bread into the unconsecrated wine in the PRES (= consecration without an epiclesis), the *Prothesis* rite at the beginning of the Divine Liturgy, and other acts of the priest during the liturgy (e.g., priestly blessings). Zheltov's conclusion is important in drawing attention to the *why* of eucharistic consecration in the first place:

> [W]ith respect to a "moment" of the Eucharistic consecration, the Byzantines by no means limited themselves to the epiclesis. But the most distinct feature of their approach seems to be not their preference for one set of words over another but their reverence toward the manual acts of the Eucharistic celebration—be it the priestly blessing, the elevation, or the immersion of the Lamb into the chalice. However strange this attitude may seem, there is some logic behind it. It stresses the unity of the liturgical text and ritual action behind it and, in the case of the elevation, the importance of experiencing the whole Divine Liturgy in its entirety—the gifts are not "complete" until they are needed for communion. Such a perception of the liturgy reveals its holistic and integral character and does not allow its reduction to the recitation of a "sacramental formula."[89]

Along similar lines Alex Rentel has written of the internal logic of the Divine Liturgy:

---

[87] See Michael Zheltov, "The Moment of Eucharistic Consecration in Byzantine Thought," in *Issues in Eucharistic Praying in East and West*, ed. Johnson, 263–306, here at 276–81.

[88] See ibid. See also the important essay by Robert Taft, "Ecumenical Scholarship and the Catholic-Orthodox Epiclesis Dispute," *Ostkirchliche Studien* 45 (1996): 201–26.

[89] Zheltov, "Moment of Eucharistic Consecration," 305–6.

The ritual of the Divine Liturgy . . . already in the preparatory rites, points to the bread as the "Lamb of God who takes away the sins of the world" and who is "sacrificed for the life of the world and its salvation" and whose side is pierced where "straightway there came forth blood and water and he who saw bore witness and his witness is true." The theme of the lamb being sacrificed is only resumed again later, right before communion at the fraction, when the priest says, "Broken and divided is the Lamb of God, who is broken, but not disunited, who is ever-eaten, but never consumed, but sanctifies all the faithful." Here there is no movement, no intervening climax; the liturgy began where it ends. Obviously, according to the Orthodox Church, something does happen in the liturgy that changes the bread and wine into the body and blood of Christ, but this something cannot be reduced to an efficacious word or phrase or a single moment or even the arc of a series of moments. It is simply a mystery effected by the power of God. If there is an overarching unidirectional moment, it is intended to be on the part of believers, who in one unitary contemplation of salvation offered by God, with many voices proclaiming it and many layers enriching it and giving it depth, move toward union with him.[90]

The purpose of the consecration of the Eucharist into the body and blood of Christ is for the communion of the faithful. *When* and *where* this occurs in the liturgy matters less in the East than *why*—the reason for which this occurs!

Before leaving this section on eucharistic consecration, one more point is especially important to make, particularly for Western readers. That is, while there is no question about Eastern Christian belief in the real presence of Christ in the Eucharist, including even at times apparition conversion stories with a little Child (Lamb of God) seen as being sacrificed and divided on the *diskos* (paten), rivaling Western stories of bleeding Hosts for their realism,[91] Eastern eucharistic theology, with the exception of those churches in full communion with Rome, does not accept the terminology of *transubstantiation*.[92] Even so, words like "transformation," "conversion," "change," and others are used to speak of what happens at the consecration. But the East does not appeal to the Aristotelian framework used by Western Scholastic

---

[90] Rentel, "Byzantine and Slavic Orthodoxy," 294.

[91] See Schulz, *The Byzantine Liturgy*, 66–67.

[92] See John A. McGuckin, *The Orthodox Church: An Introduction to Its History, Doctrine, and Spiritual Culture* (Oxford: Blackwell Publishing, 2008), 291.

theology, in terms of substance and accidents, to explain or undergird this reality. In other words, as the Christian East demonstrates clearly, neither terms like transubstantiation nor practices like the reservation of the Eucharist are necessary in order to demonstrate a belief in or theology of the real presence of Christ in the Eucharist.

2. Liturgical Commentaries

Liturgical theology in the Christian East is based not only on the rites themselves but also on the numerous liturgical commentaries that have been produced over the ages. Such approaches to liturgical theology are certainly in harmony and continuity with the great Eastern mystagogues of the fourth and fifth centuries, namely, Cyril (John) of Jerusalem, John Chrysostom, and Theodore of Mopsuestia. The particular style of those commentaries, however, is often seen as beginning with the description of Theodore, who, as we saw in chapter 3, viewed the whole eucharistic liturgy as a ritual allegory reenacting the events of Jesus' passion, death, burial, and resurrection, with the bringing up of the bread and wine by the deacons symbolizing Christ being led to his passion, the cloths on the altar as his burial cloths in the tomb, and the climax of the rite occurring at the epiclesis of the Holy Spirit when the bread and wine become Christ's *risen* body.[93] While what began with Theodore continued in all of the Eastern traditions,[94] and Theodore himself, of course, is representative of early

---

[93] See above, 67–68.
[94] The primary study for the Byzantine commentaries is R. Bornert, *Les commentaires byzantins de la Divine Liturgie du VIIe au XVe siècle*, Archives de l'orient chrétien 9 (Paris: Institut Français d'études byzantines, 1966). For East Syrian commentaries, see Sebastian Brock, "An Early Syriac Commentary on the Liturgy," in *idem, Fire From Heaven*, 387–403; and *idem*, "Gabriel of Qatar's Commentary on the Liturgy," in ibid., 1–25. See also Paul Maniyattu, "East Syriac Theology of Eucharist," in *idem, East Syriac Theology: An Introduction* (Satna, India: Ephrem's Publications, 2007), 320–44. For Armenian commentaries see A. Renoux, "Les commentaires liturgiques arméniens," in *Mytsagogie: Pensé liturgique d'augord'hui et liturgie ancienne. Conferences Saint-Serge XXXIXe semaine d'études liturgiques*, ed. A. M. Triacca and A. Pistoia (Rome; CLV-Edizioni Liturgiche, 1993), 276–308; and Michael Daniel Findikyan, "Christology in Early Armenian Liturgical Commentaries," in *The Place of Christ in Liturgical Prayer: Trinity, Christology, and Liturgical Theology*, ed. Bryan D. Spinks (Collegeville, MN: Liturgical Press, Pueblo, 2008), 197–221. For some Ethiopic sources see Habtemichael Kidane, "The Holy Spirit in the Ethiopian Orthodox

Syrian rather than Byzantine theology, again it is the dominance and influence of the Byzantine Rite that leads us to limit our presentation here to two representative examples from within that tradition.

First of all, we present the comments of Germanus (d. 733), patriarch of Constantinople from 715 to 730, on the Great Entrance of the Divine Liturgy as it existed in the eighth century:

> 37. By means of the procession of the deacons and the representation of the fans, which are in the likeness of the seraphim, the Cherubic Hymn signifies the entrance of all the saints and righteous ahead of the cherubic powers and the angelic host, who run invisibly in advance of the great king, Christ, who is proceeding to the mystical sacrifice, borne aloft by material hands. Together with them comes the Holy Spirit in the unbloody and reasonable sacrifice. The Spirit is seen spiritually in the fire, incense, smoke, and fragrant air: for the fire points to His divinity, and the fragrant smoke to His coming invisibly and filling us with good fragrance through the mystical, living, and unbloody service and sacrifice of burnt-offering. In addition, the spiritual powers and the choirs of angels, who have seen His dispensation fulfilled through the cross and death of Christ, the victory over death which has taken place, the descent into hell and the resurrection on the third day, with us exclaim the alleluia.
>
> It is also in imitation of the burial of Christ, when Joseph took down the body from the cross, wrapped it in clean linen, anointed it with spices and ointment, carried it with Nicodemus, and placed it in a new tomb hewn out of a rock. The altar is an image of the holy tomb, and the divine table is the sepulcher in which, of course, the undefiled and all-holy body was placed.
>
> 38. The discos [= paten] represents the hands of Joseph and Nicodemus, who buried Christ. The discos on which Christ is carried is also interpreted as the sphere of heaven, manifesting to us in miniature the spiritual sun, Christ, and containing Him visibly in the bread.
>
> 39. The chalice corresponds to the vessel, which received the mixture, which poured out from the bloodied, undefiled side and from the hands and feet of Christ. . . .

Täwahedo Church Tradition," in *The Spirit in Worship—Worship in the Spirit*, ed. Teresa Berger and Bryan Spinks (Collegeville, MN: Liturgical Press, Pueblo, 2009), 179–205.

40. The cover on the discos corresponds to the cloth which was on Christ's head and which covered His face in the tomb.

41. The veil, or the aer, corresponds to the stone which Joseph placed against the tomb and which the guards of Pilate sealed. . . .
. . . Thus Christ is crucified, life is buried, the tomb is secured, the stone is sealed. In the company of the angelic powers, the priest approaches, standing no longer as on earth, but attending at the heavenly altar, before the altar of the throne of God, and he contemplates the great, ineffable, and unsearchable mystery of God.[95]

Such an obvious allegorical focus on the eucharistic liturgy as representative of the life of Christ has often been referred to as "Antiochene" in approach rather than "Alexandrian," an approach more concerned with the liturgy viewed as mediating the heavenly realities in commentaries such as those of the fifth-century *Ecclesiastical Hierarchy* of Pseudo-Dionysius and the sixth-century *Mystagogy* of Maximus the Confessor.[96] While it is certainly true that this so-called Alexandrian approach is never completely replaced in Byzantine liturgical mystagogy, the fourteenth-century commentary of Nicholas Cabasilas certainly demonstrates the overall normativity of this "life of Christ" approach to the Divine Liturgy.

There is another way in which these forms, like all the ceremonies of the Holy Sacrifice, sanctify us. It consists in this: that in them Christ and the deeds he accomplished and the sufferings he endured for our sakes are represented. Indeed, it is the whole scheme of the work of redemption which is signified in the psalms and readings, as in all the actions of the priest throughout the liturgy; the first ceremonies of the service represent the beginnings of this work; the next, the sequel; and the last, its results. Thus, those who are present at these ceremonies have before their eyes all these divine things. The consecration of the elements—the sacrifice itself—commemorates the death, resurrection, and ascension of the Saviour, since it transforms these precious gifts into the very Body of the Lord, that Body which was the central figure in all these mysteries, which was crucified, which rose from the dead, which ascended into heaven. The ceremonies, which precede the act

[95] Germanus of Constantinople, *On the Divine Liturgy*, 37–41 in Paul Meyendorff, *St. Germanus of Constantinople: On the Divine Liturgy* (Crestwood, NY: St. Vladimir's Seminary Press, 1984), 87–89.
[96] On these see Schulz, *The Byzantine Liturgy*, 25–28, 43–49.

of sacrifice symbolize the events which occurred before the death of Christ: his coming on earth, his first appearance and his perfect manifestation. Those which follow the act of sacrifice recall "The promise of the Father," as the Saviour himself called it: that is, the descent of the Holy Spirit upon the apostles, the conversion of the nations which they brought about, and their divine society. The whole celebration of the mystery is like a unique portrayal of a single body, which is the work of the Saviour; it places before us the several members of this body, from beginning to end, in their order and harmony. That is why the psalmody, as well as the opening chants, and before them all that is done at the preparation of the offerings, symbolize the first period of the scheme of redemption. That which comes after the psalms—readings from Holy Scriptures and so on—symbolizes the period which follows. . . .

. . . Because the Holy Scriptures contain divinely-inspired words and praises of God, and because they incite to virtue, they sanctify those who read or chant them. But, because of the selection, which has been made, and the order in which the passages are arranged, they have another function; they signify the coming of Christ and his work. Not only the chants and readings but the very actions themselves have this part to play; each has its own immediate purpose and usefulness. But at the same time each symbolizes some part of the works of Christ, his deeds or his sufferings. For example, we have the bringing of the Gospel to the altar, then the bringing of the offerings. Each is done for a purpose, the one that the Gospel may be read, the other that the sacrifice may be performed; besides this, however, one represents the appearance and the other the manifestation of the Saviour; the first obscure and imperfect, at the beginning of his life; the second, the perfect and supreme manifestation. There are even certain ceremonies, which fulfill no practical purpose, but have only a figurative meaning; such as the action of piercing the Host, and tracing thereon the pattern of a cross, or again the fact that the metal instrument used for the perforation is shaped like a lance; there is also the ceremony which takes place near the end, of mixing a little warm water with the wine. . . .

. . . As far as the ceremonies performed in the eucharistic liturgy are concerned, they all have some connection with the scheme of the work of redemption. Their purpose is to set before us the Divine plan, that by looking upon it our souls may be sanctified, and thus we may be made fit to receive these sacred gifts.[97]

[97] Nicholas Cabasilas, *A Commentary on the Divine Liturgy*, trans. J. M. Hussey and P. A. McNulty (London: SPCK, 1960), 26–28.

As table 5.4 shows, one can actually trace the historical development of the Divine Liturgy by means of these mystagogical commentaries, all the way from Maximus the Confessor in the sixth century until Symeon of Thessalonica in the fourteenth, whose writings, according to Hans-Joachim Schulz, "represent the canonization of liturgical interpretation in the manner of Germanus, . . . which had by now become customary in Byzantium."[98]

As we saw in chapter 3, there was already in the fourth and fifth centuries a tendency toward the dramatic, the development of what Alexander Schmemann called a "mysteriological piety" divorced increasingly from true liturgical symbolism toward making Christianity a "Mystery Religion,"[99] infrequent reception of communion, and the liturgy increasingly viewed as an object of devotion to be gazed upon from afar. That tendency has clearly continued in the Eastern Rites. As Stefano Parenti concludes succinctly:

> The process of development was . . . marked in both East and West by regressive features . . . ; for example, the shortening of the biblical readings, the atrophy or elimination of the psalmody, the decline in the prayer of the faithful, the suppression or clericalization of the sign of peace, and the recitation of the celebrant's prayers, including the anaphora, in a low voice. . . . The gradual loss of a clear understanding of the structure of the liturgical action led to compositions in the genre seen in the medieval liturgical commentaries. The Eucharistic celebration which is a *re-presentation* to the Father of the redemptive economy of Christ, this being rendered actual by the action of the Holy Spirit, becomes in the literary genre of the liturgical commentaries, a *representation* of the life of Christ for the sake of the faithful.[100]

This is precisely what we have seen.

SUMMARY
1. The eucharistic liturgies of the Christian East develop into distinct rites associated with the ancient Patriarchal Sees of Alexandria and Antioch as well as with the new See of Constantinople and the honorific See of Jerusalem.

---

[98] Schulz, *The Byzantine Liturgy*, 114. For understanding this entire development in Byzantine Eucharist theology Schulz's book is indispensable.

[99] Schmemann, *Introduction to Liturgical Theology*, 81–86.

[100] Parenti, "The Eucharistic Liturgy in the East," 62.

Table 5.4: "Life of Christ" Symbolism in the Byzantine Liturgy: Comparative Table[1]

	Prothesis	Enarxis	First Entrance	Ascent to Throne	Epistle	Gospel
Maximus the Confessor			First coming of Christ in the flesh, Passion and Resurrection	The Ascension of Christ	Instruction in the Christian life	The end of the world and the Second Coming of Christ to judge the world
Germanos of Constantinople	The sacrifice of Christ: Passion and Death	Prophetic foretelling of the Incarnation	Coming of the Son of God into the world	Completion of salvation and Ascension	Prokeimenon (psalm or canticle) and Alleluia = Prophecies of the coming of Christ	Revelation of God brought by Christ Bishop's blessing after Gospel = Second Coming
Nicholas of Andida	The Virgin Birth and hidden life of Christ before his baptism	Prophetic foretelling of the Incarnation and the ministry of John the Baptist	Manifestation of Christ at his Baptism in the Jordan	Passage from the Law and the Old Covenant to the beginning of divine grace	The calling of the Apostles	The teaching of Christ
Nicholas Cabasilas	The Incarnation and early years of Christ; his Passion and Death foreshadowed	Prophetic witness to the coming of Christ: the time before the Baptist	Manifestation of Christ to the crowds at his Baptism		Manifestation of Christ in his teaching to the Apostles	Manifestation of Christ in his teaching to the crowds
Symeon of Thessalonike	The Incarnation of Christ; his Passion and Death foreshadowed	The Incarnation and the work of the incarnate Word	The resurrection and ascension of Christ The coming of the Spirit	Christ's sitting at the right hand of the Father	Mission of the Apostles to the Gentiles	Proclamation of the Gospel in all the world

	Dismissal of Catechumens	Great Entrance	Placing of Gifts on Holy Table	Anaphora	Elevation	After Communion
Maximus the Confessor	The entrance of those worthy into the bridal chamber of Christ	Revelation of the mystery of salvation hidden in God		Our future union with the spiritual powers of heaven	The union of all the faithful with God in the age to come	
Germanos of Constantinople		Christ proceeding to his mystical sacrifice	The burial of Christ in the tomb	The Resurrection of Christ		
Nicholas of Andida		The Lord's journey to Jerusalem on Palm Sunday	The upper room made ready	The Last Supper	Christ's Crucifixion, Death, and Resurrection	The Ascension of Christ and the coming of the Spirit
Nicholas Cabasilas		Christ's journey to Jerusalem and his entry on Palm Sunday		Christ's Death, Resurrection, and Ascension	The *Zeon* = The coming of the Holy Spirit	
Symeon of Thessalonike	The end of the world and final consummation	The final coming of Christ			The elevation of Christ on the Cross	The Ascension of the Lord and the proclamation of the Gospel in all the world

[1] This comparative table is adapted from Hugh Wybrew, *The Orthodox Liturgy: The Development of the Eucharistic Liturgy in the Byzantine Rite* (Crestwood, NY: St Vladimir's Seminary Press, 1990), 182–83.

2. In further development of the eucharistic liturgies of the fourth and fifth centuries, discussed in chapter 3, these Eastern Rites all expand especially at what have been called "soft spots," namely, at the entrance or beginning of the liturgy, the transfer of the gifts to the altar in preparation for the anaphora, the time of communion, and after communion to the end of the liturgy.

3. Characteristic hymns, such as the *Trisagion*, *Hō Monogenēs*, and the "Cherubic Hymn," are added and eventually become permanent elements of the liturgy at those soft spots in various rites.

4. The anaphoras assume their final fixed forms in all of the Eastern Rites and serve to characterize those rites, often by the use of their titles for the entire liturgy (e.g., the Liturgy of St. Basil and the Liturgy of St. John Chrysostom).

5. Theologically, while greater attention is given to what "consecrates" the Eucharist as the body and blood of Christ—whether narrative of institution or epiclesis of the Holy Spirit, the latter of which becomes rather explicitly "consecratory" in emphasis— Eastern eucharistic theology is able to maintain a more holistic and integral view of the importance of the entire liturgy instead of focusing on particular "moments" in the liturgy. Such includes also no real separation or compartmentalization of the theological categories of "presence," "sacrifice," and "consecration."

6. Eucharistic theology continues to build upon the various dramatic, architectural, and ritual aspects noted in chapter 3 and is shaped by the genre of mystagogical commentaries on the liturgies, leading toward an understanding of those liturgies in a representational or allegorical sense of presenting the life of Christ from his incarnation to his coming again as reenacted before the faithful as an object of liturgical contemplation.

Chapter 6

The Medieval West

The so-called Middle Ages in the Christian West are normally understood as beginning with the death of Gregory I (604 CE) and concluding with the beginnings of the Protestant Reformation (October 31, 1517).[1] The period begins with several different liturgical traditions in use throughout the Western Christian world: the Gallican Rites in Gaul (France and Germany); the "Mozarabic" (or "false Arabic") Rite in Spain, so named because of the Islamic Moors who governed Spain through much of the medieval period, and sometimes otherwise referred to as the Visigothic or Hispanic Rite; the rite used in the Archdiocese of Milan, known as the Milanese or Ambrosian Rite (even though there is no evidence that it was the composition of Ambrose of Milan); the Celtic Rite (a variation of the Gallican) in the British Isles; and, of course, the Roman Rite itself, that particular local rite of the diocese of Rome. While this period begins with all of these distinct Western Rites, it will end with the Roman Rite itself essentially having become *the* rite of Western Christianity, although not everywhere.

Just as it is impossible to understand the liturgical shifts of the fourth and fifth centuries without paying attention to the changed social and political context brought about by the "conversion" of Constantine and its aftermath, so the context of what is called, after the emperor Charlemagne, the Carolingian Reform of the ninth century is equally important for understanding liturgical change in the medieval west. For it is with Charlemagne himself that *the* liturgy of Rome was to become normative and paradigmatic for Western Christianity in general.

Gary Macy describes this period in the following manner:

---

[1] For good summaries of the history and theologies of the church throughout the Middle Ages, see R. W. Southern, *Western Society and the Church in the Middle Ages* (Harmondsworth: Penguin, 1970); and Jaroslav Pelikan, *The Christian Tradition: A History of the Development of Doctrine*, vol. 3: *The Growth of Medieval Theology (600–1300)* (Chicago: University of Chicago Press, 1978).

The year 800 marks a turning point in the history of western Europe. First of all, for the first time since the Roman Empire had come under attack in the fifth century, a kind of unity and peace had been enforced on central Europe by the powerful warlord and leader of the Franks, Charles the Great (or in French, Charlemagne). Secondly, in a dramatic move, the west officially and formally broke diplomatic ties with the east when Pope Gregory III crowned a reluctant and astounded Charlemagne emperor on Christmas Day, 800. Charlemagne was not just crowned emperor in the west, but the true Roman emperor, successor to Julius Caesar and Caesar Augustus. Needless to say, this did not go down well in Constantinople, but by this time, there was little empress Irene could do. The west turned traitor to the old empire and began to chart an independent course. . . . Charlemagne was chosen by the papacy to restore order and Christianity to western Europe. Even before his coronation, Charles had set about the reformation of his empire with the same vigor and resourcefulness that he once used to smash his enemies. One of Charlemagne's first orders of business was the preaching and teaching of Christianity to his people. For this purpose, he imported to his court the best scholars to be had and even borrowed the pope's own mass book so that copies could be made and sent out to all the bishops. To an illiterate people the liturgy was extremely important, as here the common folk could see the central mysteries of Christianity acted out in a kind of pantomime.[2]

Charlemagne found little resistance to such an attempt at liturgical or ecclesiastical uniformity throughout the empire, even if absolute liturgical uniformity was never really attained in the West. Nevertheless, it is important to note that this attempt was imperial and *not* the result of the papacy trying to impose Roman usage universally on the West. No such papal involvement, in fact, was really needed. Rather, it was quite natural in the West for pilgrims to go to Rome, visit the holy places, attend papal liturgies in the great Roman basilicas, and begin copying at home what they had seen and experienced there. In other words, Western Europe was quite favorably disposed toward Rome and its liturgy in general, even before Charlemagne sought to make Roman practice normative for all. As James White has written,

[2] Gary Macy, *The Banquet's Wisdom: A Short History of the Theologies of the Lord's Supper* (New York: Paulist Press, 1992), 68–69. See also Timothy Thibodeau, "Western Christendom," in *The Oxford History of Christian Worship*, ed. Geoffrey Wainwright and Karen B. Westerfield Tucker (Oxford/New York: Oxford University Press, 2006), 216–53, here at 227–28.

The liturgical role of Rome was far from deliberate. Because of the prestige accorded the holy city as the resting place of the martyrs, Roman ways of worship were widely imitated even though Rome rarely sought to promote them outside of nearby regions of Italy. . . . *Romanitas* or the imitation of Rome as the most impressive model for liturgy became a common western practice. . . . But for the most part, Rome took a hands off approach. Its influence was largely from respect not from coercion. Charlemagne tried to use liturgy as a means of unifying his empire in the ninth century but with little cooperation from Rome. Gregory VII interfered in the worship of the Spanish churches in the eleventh century by trying to force relinquishment of the Mozarabic rite in favor of the Roman rite but with only partial success. . . . Liturgical centralization was impossible in any case before the invention of the printing press. As late as 1549, Cranmer noted England still had various uses: "some following Salisbury use, some Hereford use, some of the use of Bangor, some of York, and some of Lincoln."[3]

LITURGICAL BOOKS

As we saw in the previous chapter, parts of the eucharistic rite began to assume a fixed—and written—form from at least the middle of the fourth century. But the liturgical books that are extant in the West all date from the end of the sixth century onward. These are of several different kinds. Chief among them are sacramentaries—books containing the various prayers that the bishop or priest presiding over the rite needed for particular celebrations of the Eucharist throughout the year. The oldest of these is the Verona Sacramentary (named after the city in which the only known manuscript of it exists), often called the Leonine Sacramentary, although it is certainly not the work of Pope Leo the Great (d. 461) and strictly speaking not a sacramentary in the sense of a book that was actually used in the celebration of the Eucharist. Instead, it is a private collection of older *libelli*—shorter, pamphlet-like texts from Rome containing the prayers for one or more Masses. The oldest sacramentary proper of Roman origin with texts for the whole liturgical year is the Old Gelasian, again improbably attributed to Pope Gelasius I (d. 496). Dating from the middle of the eighth century, it contains liturgical material a century or more older that had first been used by Roman presbyters but then had been taken

---

[3] James F. White, *A Brief History of Christian Worship* (Nashville, TN: Abingdon Press, 1993), 78–79.

to Gaul, where it was supplemented with elements from local practice while in use there. Alongside this stands the Gregorian Sacramentary. Although its attribution to Pope Gregory can no longer be accepted, it too probably originated in the eighth century but contained the papal rather than presbyteral form of the Roman liturgy. When taken to Gaul, it was adapted for presbyteral use, and later versions combined elements from both the Gelasian and Gregorian types of book together with other material from the Gallican tradition.

Other liturgical books included *ordines*—sets of detailed directions for the order and ceremonial to be followed in a liturgical celebration; capitularies (from the Latin, *capitulum*, "a chapter") containing the opening words (*incipit*, literally, "it begins") and endings (*explicit*, "it ends") of each reading to be used on a particular occasion, necessary for finding it in the Bible before the more modern division of the biblical books into chapters and verses, and later replaced by books containing the full texts of the readings in the order of the liturgical year; and various books containing the different chants to be sung by the choir or a soloist on each occasion.[4]

THE RITES

From these books it is possible to reconstruct the pattern of the Eucharist as it would have been celebrated at Rome in the eighth century. From the Gallican interpolations in them and from other books of Gallican origin we can also learn much about the liturgical practices and prayer texts that were being used in that region before they were superseded by the hybrid Romano-Gallican version. There are in existence also liturgical books containing the Ambrosian and Mozarabic Rites.[5] Table 6.1 outlines the forms that these various regional rites outside Rome came to take. A form not unlike the Roman rite also would have been used originally in North Africa, but aside from syn-

[4] For further information concerning liturgical books, see Cyrille Vogel, *Medieval Liturgy: An Introduction to the Sources*, trans. and rev. William Storey and Niels Rasmussen (Washington, DC: Pastoral Press, 1986); Eric Palazzo, *A History of Liturgical Books from the Beginning to the Thirteenth Century* (Collegeville, MN: Liturgical Press, Pueblo, 1998), esp. 19–110.

[5] See W. C. Bishop, *The Mozarabic and Ambrosian Rites* (London: Mowbray; Milwaukee, WI: Morehouse, 1924); Cesare Alzati, *Ambrosianum mysterium: The Church of Milan and Its Liturgical Tradition*, Alcuin/GROW Liturgical Study 44, 47–48 (Cambridge: Grove Books, 1999–2000).

odal documents and homiletic evidences, all trace of it was obliterated after the Islamic invasion of the territory in the seventh century. Similarly, our knowledge of the Celtic Rite is too fragmentary to attempt a confident reconstruction.[6]

Table 6.1

Medieval Western [Non-Roman] Eucharistic Liturgies[7]		
Gallican	*Hispano-Mozarabic*	*Ambrosian*
Antiphona ad praelegendum with psalm	*Praelegendum* with psalm *Trisagion*	*Ingressa*
Call for silence and greeting	Greeting	
Trisagion and *Kyrie*		*Kyrie* or *Gloria*
Prophetia (= *Benedictus* or hymn)		
Collectio post Prophetiam		*Oratio super populum*
Old Testament reading	Old Testament reading	Old Testament reading
Responsorium	Psalm	Psalm
Epistle	Epistle	Epistle
Canticle (Dan 3:35-66)		
Trisagion ante Evangelium		Alleluia with verse
Gospel	Gospel	Gospel
Sanctus post Evangelium	*Laudes*	
Homily		Homily
Preces		
Collectio post precem		
Dismissal of catechumens	Dismissal of catechumens	Dismissal of catechumens
Intercessions		*Kyrie* and *Antiphona post Evangelium*
Presentation of gifts with *sonus*	*Sacrificium* (with verses for offertory procession)	Peace
Praefatio missa and *collectio*	*Missa* (= bidding)	*Oratio super sindonem*

Table 6.1 continued on next page.

[6] See Neil Xavier O'Donoghue, *The Eucharist in Pre-Norman Ireland* (Notre Dame, IN: University of Notre Dame Press, 2011).

[7] This outline of the rites has been adapted from John Brooks-Leonard, "Traditions, Liturgical, in the West: Pre-Reformation," in *The New Dictionary of Sacramental Worship*, ed. Peter Fink (Collegeville, MN: Liturgical Press, Michael Glazier, 1990), 1282–93.

Medieval Western [Non-Roman] Eucharistic Liturgies		
Gallican	*Hispano-Mozarabic*	*Ambrosian*
Names and *collectio post nomina*	*Alia orati* *Nomina offerentium*	Offertory procession
	Diptychs *Post-nomina*	Nicene Creed
Collectio ad pacem	*Ad pacem*	*Oratio super oblata*
Peace	Peace	
Eucharistic prayer	Eucharistic Prayer	Eucharistic prayer
Confractionem	*Laudes ad Confractionem*	*Fractio*
	[Nicene Creed] *Ad orationem Dominicam*	
Lord's Prayer	Lord's Prayer	*Commixtio*
	Commixtio and *Trisagion*	Lord's Prayer
Episcopal benediction	*Benedictio*	
	Invitation to communion	
	Ad Accentes (Pss 33, 34, etc.)	
Communion and *Trecanum*	Communion	Communion and *Transitorium Oratio*
Post Eucharisticam and *Collectio post communionem*	*Completuria*	*post communionem*
		Kyrie
Dismissal	Dismissal	Dismissal

As space does not permit a detailed study of all of these, we must content ourselves with noting a few characteristics of the Gallican eucharistic rite. It is distinctive for its tendency to address some prayers to Christ rather than to the Father, for the inclusion of both the hymn known as the *Trisagion* ("Holy God, Holy Strong, Holy Immortal, have mercy on us") and the Canticle of the Three Young Men (Dan 3:35-66) in the Liturgy of the Word, and for extensive variations in the texts during the changing seasons of the liturgical year. Rather than a fixed eucharistic prayer, only the *Sanctus* and institution narrative were stable throughout the year; what elsewhere would be known as the *Praefatio*, "preface"[8] (but here called the *Contestatio* or *Immolatio*), and the

[8] On the origin and use of this term, which does *not* mean preface in the English sense of the word, see Enrico Mazza, *The Eucharistic Prayers of the Roman Rite* (New York: Pueblo, 1986), 36–41.

post-*Sanctus* prayer and prayer after the institution narrative (known as the Post-*mysterium* or Post-*secreta* because the narrative itself came to be said silently out of reverence) all varied from occasion to occasion. As an example of the prayer style, what follows is the eucharistic prayer for an ordinary Sunday. It will be seen that it inclines toward prolix and florid language in the preface, in contrast to the rather brief and sober language of the prefaces to the Roman Canon that we will examine later; what follows the *Sanctus*, however, is extremely terse and restrained in comparison with its Roman counterpart.

Contestatio/Immolatio *(variable)*

It is fitting and right, right and just, here and everywhere to give you thanks, Lord, holy Father, eternal God; you snatched us from perpetual death and the last darkness of hell, and gave mortal matter, put together from the liquid mud, to your Son and to eternity. Who is acceptable to tell your praises, who can make a full declaration of your works? Every tongue marvels at you, all priests extol your glory.

When you had overcome chaos and the confusion of the beginning and the darkness in which things swam, you gave wonderful form to the amazed elements: the tender world blushed at the fires of the sun, and the rude earth wondered at the dealings of the moon. And lest no inhabitant should adorn the world and the sun's orb shine on emptiness, your hands made from clay a more excellent likeness, which a holy fire quickened within, and a lively soul brought to life throughout its idle parts. We may not look, Father, into the inner mysteries. To you alone is known the majesty of your work: what there is in man, that the blood held in the veins washes the fearful limbs and the living earth, that the loose appearances of bodies are held together by tightening nerves, and the individual bones gain strength from the organs within them.

But whence comes so great a bounty to miserable men, that we should be formed in the likeness of you and your Son, that an earthly thing should be eternal? We abandoned the commandments of your blessed majesty; we were plunged, mortal once more, into the earth from which we came, and mourned the loss of the eternal comfort of your gift. But your manifold goodness and inestimable majesty sent the Word of salvation from heaven, that he should be made flesh by taking a human body, and should care for that which the age had lost and the ancient wounds. Therefore all the angels, with the manifold multitude of the saints, praise him with unceasing voice, saying:

(people:) Holy, holy, holy, Lord God of Sabaoth. Heaven and earth are full of your glory. Hosanna in the highest. Blessed is he who comes in the name of the Lord. Hosanna in the highest.

Post-Sanctus *(variable)*

As the supernal creatures resound on high the praise of your glory, your goodness wished that it should be known also to your servants; and this proclamation, made in the starry realms, was revealed to your servants by the gift of your magnificence, not only to be known but also to be imitated.

Secreta *(fixed)*

Who, the day before he suffered for the salvation of us all, standing in the midst of his disciples and apostles, took bread in his holy hands, looked up to heaven to you, God the Father almighty, gave thanks, blessed, and broke it, and gave it to his disciples, saying, "Take, eat from this, all of you; for this is my body, which shall be broken for the life of the age." Likewise after supper he took the cup in his hands, looked up to heaven to you, God the Father almighty, gave thanks, blessed it, and handed it to his apostles, saying, "Take, drink from this, all of you; for this is the cup of my holy blood, of the new and eternal covenant, which is shed for you and for many for the forgiveness of sins." In addition to these words he said to them, "As often as you eat from this bread and drink from this cup, you will do it for my remembrance, showing my passion to all, (and) you will look for my coming until I come (again)."

Post-Secreta *(variable)*

Therefore, most merciful Father, look upon the commandments of your Son, the mysteries of the Church, (your) gifts to those who believe: they are offered by suppliants, and for suppliants they are to be sought; through Jesus Christ your Son, our God and Lord and Savior, who, with you, Lord, and the Holy Spirit, reigns for ever, eternal Godhead, to the ages of ages.[9]

We will focus in greater detail on the Roman Rite because it became the basis of all the variant local forms of eucharistic liturgy celebrated in the later Middle Ages in the West. By the time that its extant liturgical books appear, various additions had been made to the core rite described above in chapter 3. Table 6.2 lists the most important of these, which are also commented on immediately below. The subsequent developments will either also be mentioned there or referred to later in this chapter. This table alone, however, does not capture the style of celebration of the Eucharist that had become the norm

[9] ET from PEER, 148–50.

whenever the pope presided at it. We possess the detailed ceremonial directions for the papal liturgy stemming from around the year 700 in a document known as *Ordo Romanus Primus*.[10] From this it is clear not only that every detail of the papal liturgy was minutely regulated but also that its whole manner was elaborate and ornate, resembling the court ceremonial of the emperor. While celebrations by other bishops and priests would not have been on such a scale, it did leave its mark on the ceremonial style of the later Roman Rite.

Table 6.2

Roman Eucharistic Liturgy in Development		
by the fourth century	*by the eighth century*	*later in the Middle Ages*
	Introit psalm *Kyries* *Gloria in excelsis*	Preparatory prayers [Shortened]
Greeting		

Readings	Collect
	(Old Testament
	  reading)
	(Responsorial psalm)
	Epistle
	Gradual and alleluia
	  or tract
	(Dismissal of
	  catechumens?)
	Gospel	

		Sequence
Homily	[Sometimes]	
		Creed
Intercessions	[Disappeared]	
Kiss of peace	[Moved to a later point]	

Bread and wine
  presented
	Offertory psalm
	Prayer over the gifts
		[Shortened]
		Offertory prayers and
		  ceremonies

Eucharistic prayer	Fixed form called *Canon missae*	

Table 6.2 continued on next page.

[10] Text and ET in E. G. Cuthbert F. Atchley, *Ordo Romanus Primus* (London: Moring, 1905); ET also in Alan Griffiths, *Ordo Romanus Primus: A Text for Students*, Alcuin/GROW Joint Liturgical Study 73 (Norwich: Canterbury Press, 2012).

Roman Eucharistic Liturgy in Development		
by the fourth century	*by the eighth century*	*later in the Middle Ages*
	Lord's Prayer	
	Kiss of peace	
	Fraction rite	
	Agnus Dei	
	Commixture	
		Private prayers of priest
Communion	Communion psalm	[Shortened]
Collection for the poor		Private prayers of priest
	Post-communion prayer	
	Dismissal	
		Blessing
		Last Gospel (John 1:1-14)

1. The Liturgy of the Word and the Prayers

The introit, offertory, and communion psalms had emerged to provide musical cover for processional movements within the liturgy in the large basilicas of the city, the particular psalms being chosen when possible for their appropriateness to the occasion being celebrated.

The repeated chanting of *Kyrie eleison* and *Christe eleison* ("Lord, have mercy," "Christ, have mercy") is the remnant of a processional litany copied from Eastern practice that once used to be sung on the way to the church. Although at this time the refrains or acclamations alone were sung by the choir as many times as needed to cover movement, eventually their number was fixed at nine: *Kyrie eleison* three times, *Christe eleison* three times, and *Kyrie eleison* again three times.[11]

The hymn *Gloria in excelsis* ("Glory to God in the highest") is a festal addition to the rite, again derived from Eastern practice, where it forms the final canticle at Morning Prayer, and hence the "hinge" to the Eucharist when that is celebrated immediately afterward. At first

---

[11] See John F. Baldovin, "Kyrie Eleison and the Entrance Rite of the Roman Eucharist," *Worship* 60 (1986): 334–47; also Peter Jeffery, "The Meaning and Functions of *Kyrie eleison*," in *The Place of Christ in Liturgical Prayer*, ed. Bryan D. Spinks (Collegeville, MN: Liturgical Press, Pueblo, 2008), 127–94, who argues that its immediate ancestor in the Roman Rite is the litany of saints rather than a litany of an intercessory kind.

it was used in the Roman Rite only by bishops on Sundays and feasts, but later its use was extended on those occasions to priests as well.

The sacramentaries provide a specific short opening prayer for every Sunday and feast in the year, some of them thematically related to the occasion but many of a more general kind. This prayer was later known as the "collect," *collecta* and *collectio* being Gallican terms used to denote a concluding prayer that gathered up or collected the preceding prayers of the people.[12]

Although it has commonly been believed that Rome, like many other places, at one time would have had three readings every Sunday (Old Testament, epistle, and gospel), with a responsorial psalm after the first, there is no extant evidence for this except on rare occasions in the year, and it seems at least as likely that there had generally never been more than two, the first usually from the epistles and the second a gospel reading. Nonetheless, a psalm still followed the first reading, known here as the gradual psalm (from the Latin *gradus*, "step"), as it was sung from the steps to the ambo by a soloist with the congregation responding with a refrain after each verse. The increasing tendency toward greater elaboration of the chant, however, eventually led both to its being sung by the choir alone and to its abbreviation to a single verse and the musically prolix refrain.

The gradual was immediately followed by another chant with an Alleluia response, except during penitential seasons when that response was replaced by a refrain known as the Tract. It was also because of the increasing elaboration of the Alleluia chant that the hymn known as the sequence was later added to the rite. The final "a" of the last Alleluia was sung with a lengthy and embellished neum. As an aid to memory, in the ninth century words began to be supplied with one syllable for each note in the neum, and by the eleventh century these started to be developed into metrical hymns. So popular were these that by the end of the Middle Ages five thousand such sequences existed in various dioceses throughout Europe.

Because the unbaptized were not permitted to share in prayer or the Eucharist with the baptized, in ancient times they were dismissed at the end of the Liturgy of the Word in most places. No trace of this practice remains in the extant Roman sources, except for a directive in the seventh-century *Ordo Romanus* 11, prescribing that the catechumens are

[12] See Joseph Jungmann, *The Mass of the Roman Rite* (New York: Benziger, 1951) 1:359–90.

to be dismissed *prior* to the reading of the gospel on the three Sundays in Lent when the prebaptismal scrutinies took place. Could this be the remains of an old tradition that precluded catechumens from hearing the gospel on every Sunday in the year?[13]

Although in other parts of the world recitation of the Nicene Creed had become a regular part of the eucharistic liturgy from quite early times, this had not been so at Rome. When Emperor Henry II was crowned there in 1014, however, he inquired why it had been omitted; as a consequence, Pope Benedict VIII ordered that it should be included after the sermon on all Sundays and feasts.

Perhaps out of a desire to shorten the service, sermons were now rarely preached and the prayers of intercession had fallen out of use, except on Good Friday when their archaic form was retained.[14] Although the kiss of peace is found at the conclusion of the prayers in every other church, uniquely in the Roman Rite it has been moved to a position immediately before the reception of communion. The reason for this is unknown, although it has been suggested that it may be copied from the practice in the city churches of Rome where presbyters presided over a rite at which there was no eucharistic prayer, but communion was distributed with bread and wine that were understood to have been consecrated through contact with the *fermentum*—a piece of consecrated bread sent by the pope to each church in the city from the Eucharist he was celebrating that day. In this situation, the service of the word and prayers would have ended with the kiss, and communion would have followed immediately.[15]

2. The Eucharistic Action

In many places, it was customary for the people to bring their offerings of bread and wine directly to the altar themselves. This was not so at Rome, where the ministers collected the gifts instead. The pope and his assistants went to the nobility and received their offerings of bread

[13] See Paul F. Bradshaw, *Reconstructing Early Christian Worship* (London: SPCK 2009; Collegeville, MN: Liturgical Press, Pueblo, 2011), 61.

[14] Text and commentary in Paul De Clerck, *La prière universelle dans les liturgies latines anciennes* (Münster: Aschendorff, 1977), 125–44, 168–87; ET in Gordon P. Jeanes, *The Origins of the Roman Rite*, Alcuin/GROW Liturgical Study 20 (Nottingham: Grove Books, 1991), 21–23.

[15] See John F. Baldovin, "The *Fermentum* at Rome in the Fifth Century: A Reconsideration," *Worship* 79 (2005): 38–53.

while the archdeacon followed and received the wine, pouring it into a large vessel. Other ministers did the same for the rest of the congregation (the choirboys offering water as their gift, which was then mixed with the wine). What was not needed for the service was set aside for the poor.[16]

After the elements had been prepared on the altar, just a single prayer was said: the *oratio super oblata*, "prayer over the offerings," with a different one being provided for each Sunday and feast in the year (as also in the case of the collect). The contents of their petition vary. Some speak only of prayers or the sacrifice of praise that the worshipers are offering, while others refer more specifically to the eucharistic elements and employ stronger sacrificial imagery, thus suggesting that a gradual shift in focus had taken place in the course of time as these were composed.[17]

The Roman eucharistic prayer, the *canon missae* or "Canon of the Mass" as it is usually called, is first known to us in full in the sacramentaries, although, as we saw in chapter 3, a version of part of it was quoted by Ambrose of Milan in the fourth century; there are also allusions to it in some other writings of the same period[18] that have enabled tentative attempts at reconstruction of its form at this early date. The text below reflects the form that it had reached for use on an ordinary day in about the seventh century, based on that in the Gregorian Sacramentary, without the minor verbal changes and additions that were made later. Although its overall structure had become firmly fixed by this date, parts of it remained variable from occasion to occasion. Thus, the *Sanctus* was now a permanent part of the prayer, but the "preface" preceding it varied according to the feast or season, giving expression to the particular themes of thanksgiving appropriate to the occasion. The Verona Sacramentary has 267 prefaces, even though that does not cover the whole year. Later books have considerably fewer—the Gregorian only fourteen. The form reproduced here is the common preface used on "ordinary" days rather than one of the "proper prefaces" for particular occasions. The Roman Canon hence

[16] See Jungmann, *The Mass of the Roman Rite*, 2:1–8.

[17] See Kenneth Stevenson, *Eucharist and Offering* (New York: Pueblo, 1986), 85–89.

[18] See Mazza, *The Eucharistic Prayers of the Roman Rite*, 57–58; Gordon P. Jeanes, *The Day Has Come! Easter and Baptism in Zeno of Verona*, Alcuin Club Collections 73 (Collegeville, MN: Liturgical Press, 1995), 7–17, 191–96.

differed from Eastern prayers, which told the whole story of salvation each time they were used, and so it considerably reduced the element of praise and anamnesis in the prayer. This transformation of its character became even more marked when in later centuries the canon came to be thought of as beginning *after* the *Sanctus*, making it simply a prayer of offering, consecration, and intercession. The break was made clear in the liturgical books themselves when the initial "T" in *Te igitur* (the first words of the part of the prayer following the *Sanctus*) began to be elaborated into a picture of Christ on the cross and later in the twelfth century turned into a full-page illustration between the *Sanctus* and the rest of the prayer.[19]

Other parts of the Canon also remained variable. The form of the *Hanc igitur* differed according to the needs of the particular occasion. The Verona Sacramentary contains ten versions of it, the Gelasian no less than forty-one, but the Gregorian only six. Special forms of the *Communicantes* were also provided for certain feasts in the year, and because the commemoration of the dead (*Memento etiam*) is not included in several of the eighth-century Gelasians and some of the best manuscripts of the Gregorian Sacramentary, this suggests that it too was used only on appropriate occasions and not on a regular basis. It has therefore been placed in brackets here.[20]

The Roman Canon (seventh century)

Preface

It is truly fitting and right, our duty and our salvation, that we should always and everywhere give you thanks, Lord, holy Father, almighty and everlasting God, through Christ our Lord; through whom angels praise your majesty, dominions adore, powers fear, the heavens and the heavenly hosts and the blessed seraphim celebrate together in exultation. We pray you, bid our voices also to be admitted with theirs, beseeching, confessing, and saying:

(*people:*) Holy, holy, holy, Lord God of Sabaoth. Heaven and earth are full of your glory. Hosanna in the highest. Blessed is he who comes in the name of the Lord. Hosanna in the highest.

---

[19] See Jungmann, *The Mass of the Roman Rite*, 2:101–6; also the comment by Innocent III, below, page 217.

[20] For a more detailed study of the Canon, see Jungmann, *The Mass of the Roman Rite*, 2:101–274; Mazza, *The Eucharistic Prayers of the Roman Rite*, 49–87.

Te Igitur

We therefore pray and beseech you, most merciful Father, through your Son Jesus Christ our Lord, to accept and bless these gifts, these offerings, these holy and unblemished sacrifices, which we offer to you above all for your holy catholic church; vouchsafe to grant it peace, protection, unity, and guidance throughout the world, together with your servant N. our pope.

Memento, Domine

Remember, Lord, your male and female servants, and all who stand around, whose faith and devotion are known to you, who offer to you this sacrifice of praise for themselves and for all their own, for the redemption of their souls, for the hope of their salvation and safety, and pay their vows to you, the living and true eternal God.

Communicantes

In fellowship with and venerating above all the memory of the glorious ever-Virgin Mary, mother of God and our Lord Jesus Christ, and also of your blessed apostles and martyrs Peter and Paul, Andrew, James, John, Thomas, James, Philip, Bartholomew, Matthew, Simon and Thaddeus, Linus, Cletus, Clement, Sixtus, Cornelius, Cyprian, Lawrence, Chrysogonus, John and Paul, Cosmas and Damian, and all your saints; by their merits and prayers grant us to be defended in all things by the help of your protection; through Christ our Lord.

Hanc igitur

Therefore, Lord, we pray you graciously to accept this offering made by us your servants, and also by your whole family; and to order our days in peace; and to command that we are snatched from eternal damnation and numbered among the flock of your elect; through Christ our Lord.

Quam oblationem

Vouchsafe, we beseech you, O God, to make this offering wholly blessed, approved, ratified, reasonable, and acceptable; that it may become to us the body and blood of your dearly beloved Son Jesus Christ our Lord; . . .

Qui pridie

. . . who, on the day before he suffered, took bread in his holy and reverend hands, lifted up his eyes to heaven to you, O God, his almighty Father, gave thanks to you, blessed, broke, and gave it to his disciples, saying, "Take and eat from this, all of you; for this is my body." Likewise after supper, taking also this glorious cup in his holy and reverend hands, again he gave thanks to you, blessed and gave it to his disciples, saying, "Take and drink from it, all of you; for this is the cup of my blood, of the new and eternal covenant, the mystery of faith, which will be shed for you and for many for forgiveness of sins. As often as you do this, you will do it for my remembrance."

Unde et memores

Therefore also, Lord, we your servants, but also your holy people, having in remembrance the blessed passion of your Son Christ our Lord, likewise his resurrection from the dead, and also his glorious ascension into heaven, do offer to your excellent majesty from your gifts and bounty a pure victim, a holy victim, an unblemished victim, the holy bread of eternal life and the cup of everlasting salvation.

Supra quae

Vouchsafe to look upon them with a favorable and kindly countenance, and accept them as you vouchsafed to accept the gifts of your righteous servant Abel, and the sacrifice of our patriarch Abraham, and that which your high priest Melchizedek offered to you, a holy sacrifice, an unblemished victim.

Supplices te

We humbly beseech you, almighty God, bid these things be borne by the hands of your angel to your altar on high, in the sight of your divine majesty, that all of us who have received the most holy body and blood of your Son by partaking at this altar may be filled with all heavenly blessing and grace; through Christ our Lord.

[Memento etiam]

[Remember also, Lord, your male and female servants who have gone before us with the sign of faith, and sleep in the sleep of peace. We beseech you to grant to them and to all who rest in Christ a place of refreshment, light and peace; through Christ our Lord.]

Nobis quoque

To us sinners your servants also, who trust in the multitude of your mercies, vouchsafe to grant some part and fellowship with your holy apostles and martyrs, with John, Stephen, Matthias, Barnabas, Ignatius, Alexander, Marcellinus, Peter, Felicity, Perpetua, Agatha, Lucy, Agnes, Caecilia, Anastasia, and all your saints; into whose company we ask that you will admit us, not weighing our merit, but bounteously forgiving; through Christ our Lord.

Per ipsum

Through him, Lord, you ever create, sanctify, quicken, bless, and bestow all these good things upon us. Through him, and with him, and in him, all honor and glory is yours, O God the Father almighty, in the unity of the Holy Spirit, through all the ages of ages. Amen.

3. Communion and After

Although the use of the Lord's Prayer in the Eucharist is mentioned by Augustine, the earliest direct reference to it at Rome is in a letter of Pope Gregory the Great, where he defends his action in moving it from immediately before communion to a position immediately after the canon. In contrast to some other traditions, it is said by the presiding bishop or priest alone. In the sacramentaries it includes a fixed embolism immediately following the final petition "but deliver us from evil":

Deliver us, we beseech you, O Lord, from all evils past, present and to come; and at the intercession of the blessed and glorious ever-virgin Mother of God Mary with your blessed Apostles Peter and Paul and Andrew and all the saints, favorably grant peace in our days, that assisted by the help of your mercy, we may be both ever free from sin and safe from all distress; through the same.[21]

During the breaking of the bread into pieces for communion, or fraction as it is commonly called, which naturally took some time, a chant was introduced by Pope Sergius I (687–701), *Agnus Dei, qui tollis peccata mundi, miserere nos*, "Lamb of God, that takes away the sins of the world, have mercy on us," repeated as many times as was necessary to cover the action of the breaking. In the East, the fraction was understood as a symbolic representation of Christ's passion and death and the eucharistic bread as the sacrificial "Lamb"; it appears that Sergius, himself Syrian in origin, wished to introduce an allusion to that here.[22]

By the eighth century, just before communion the pope would break off a small piece of the bread he was about to consume and drop it into

[21] See Jungmann, *The Mass of the Roman Rite*, 2:277–93.
[22] Ibid., 303–11, 332–40.

. No explanation is given for this ceremony of commixture, omewhat later this prayer was attached to it: "May the com- nd consecration of the body and blood of our Lord Jesus me to us who receive it unto eternal life." It has been sug- gested that the intention was to represent the resurrection reunion of the body and blood of Christ that had been separated at the Lord's death.[23]

After communion, there remained at first only a single post-commu- nion prayer before the dismissal, again varying according to the occa- sion and usually containing some reference to the sacred mysteries in which the congregation had just participated (or more specifically to the reception of communion) and praying for God's continuing favor upon them. The pope was accustomed to bestow his blessing informally on groups of people as he left the church, however, and over the course of time there developed out of this custom in many places—though not ev- erywhere—a final blessing of the congregation within the rite. The reci- tation of John 1:1-14—always a popular passage—was not added until the thirteenth century. In some cases it was said by the priest while re- turning from the altar to the sacristy, in others while removing his vest- ments, but increasingly in many places at the altar before departing.[24]

THE PARTICIPATION OF THE PEOPLE

From as early as the late fourth century the tendency had existed among some people not to receive communion on every occasion that they attended the Eucharist, and as the centuries passed this trend increased, not least because worshipers were taught that eating and drinking the body and blood of the Lord unworthily could lead to one's damnation (see 1 Cor 11:27-32); hence, it was necessary to prepare carefully for the reception of communion by purifying one's life, confessing one's sins, and receiving absolution first. It therefore seemed safer to restrict oneself most of the time to what became known as "spiritual communion"—attending the rite but not consum- ing the sacred elements.[25]

[23] Ibid., 311–21.
[24] Ibid., 419–25, 432–37, 439–51.
[25] For a discussion of spiritual communion, see Charles Caspers, "The West- ern Church during the Late Middle Ages: *Augenkommunion* or Popular Mysti- cism?," in *Bread of Heaven: Customs and Practices Surrounding Holy Communion*, ed. Charles Caspers, Gerard Lukken, and Gerard Rouwhorst, Liturgia Con- denda 3 (Kampen: Kok Pharos, 1995), 83–97.

In the course of time this practice received theological justification, which naturally encouraged it to spread more widely. In the twelfth century a more precise vocabulary for discussing sacraments began to emerge among theologians. Most notable of these was an Augustinian canon, Hugh, who taught from 1127 to his death in 1142 in the school of St. Victor that would eventually form part of the University of Paris. Although he continued to use the word _sacramentum_ in the broader sense it had been used by earlier writers,[26] as denoting any action that mediated the union between God and human beings, he distinguished between the outward sign alone of that action (_sacramentum tantum_), the thing that was signified by it (_res tantum_), and that which both signified and was signified by it (_sacramentum et res_). Thus, in the case of the Eucharist, the signs were the bread and wine, the thing signified was union with God, and that which was both signified by the bread and wine and which signified the union was the real presence of the Lord. Because, therefore, it was the union with God that was ultimately of most importance in the Eucharist, such theologians argued that the reception of the sign was not absolutely essential and taught that substituting some other devotional practice in place of the physical reception of the sacrament was just as effective for the believer's salvation.[27] Moreover, the priest was now understood to receive communion on behalf of the people.

As a result, many Christians did not receive communion more than a few times a year, and the Fourth Lateran Council in 1215 had to include among its canons an insistence on the minimum of once a year: "all the faithful of both sexes, after they have reached the age of discretion, shall faithfully confess to their own priest all their sins at least once a year and perform to the best of their ability the penance imposed on them, receiving reverently the sacrament of the Eucharist at least at Easter, unless it happens that on the counsel of their own priest they are to abstain for a time from its reception for some reasonable cause."[28] At the same period, however, blessed bread began to be distributed to the worshipers at the end of Mass as a sort of substitute

---

[26] It was Peter the Lombard later in the century who introduced the limitation of the term sacrament to just seven ritual actions of the church, which became standard thereafter.

[27] See Macy, _The Banquet's Wisdom_, 85–88.

[28] Latin text in Heinrich Denzinger-Adolfus Schönmetzer, _Enchiridion Symbolorum_, 32nd ed. (Freiburg: Herder, 1963) no. 812.

for the sacrament, and spiritual benefits from receiving it were promised. Moreover, the practice of giving communion itself *after* Mass was ended rather than during the rite also began to appear, as a way of dealing with the large numbers who presented themselves on major festivals.[29]

Those who did not receive communion consequently no longer participated in another way in the eucharistic action, namely, by bringing gifts of bread and wine from home. In any case, even for those who did receive communion, this practice eventually ceased because from the ninth century onward unleavened bread, specially prepared in monastic houses, began to replace the ordinary bread previously used, so that it would correspond more exactly with the kind of bread that Jesus was believed to have used at the Passover meal that was the Last Supper. This also led in time to the baking of separate individual wafers for communicants so that they no longer shared in part of a common loaf.[30] Naturally, the fraction rite in the Mass consequently became a purely symbolic act and not a utilitarian one for the people's communion, but although no longer needed to cover that lengthy action, the *Agnus Dei* continued to be sung or said.

Even when people did receive communion, there were changes in the manner of reception, some of which arose out of a concern about accidental spillage of the sacred elements. From the ninth century onward the bread began to be placed on people's tongues instead of into their hands (though whether this was to avoid crumbs failing to be consumed, or because of fears that the bread might be carried away for sacrilegious purposes, or because the people were thought unworthy to touch the sacred object is not clear), the practice of kneeling to receive communion began to be introduced from the eleventh century onward (this certainly for reasons of reverence), and by the thirteenth century in some places acolytes were holding a cloth (known in English as a houseling cloth) in front of each communicant to catch anything that might fall from their mouths.[31]

[29] See Eamon Duffy, *The Stripping of the Altars: Traditional Religion in England 1400–1580* (New Haven, CT: Yale University Press, 1992), 125–27; Nathan Mitchell, *Cult and Controversy: The Worship of the Eucharist Outside Mass* (New York: Pueblo, 1982), 90–92; Miri Rubin, *Corpus Christi: The Eucharist in Late Medieval Culture* (Cambridge: Cambridge University Press, 1991), 73–74.

[30] See Jungmann, *The Mass of the Roman Rite*, 2:31–37.

[31] For further details, see ibid., 374–82; Mitchell, *Cult and Controversy*, 86–88.

As early as the eighth century there is evidence for the existence of the *fistula*, a special communion tube made of precious metal through which communicants might suck the wine, in order to lessen the risk of drops being spilled by drinking directly from the chalice. Because its use did not apparently entirely solve the problem of spillage, however, in the centuries that followed the laity were increasingly permitted to receive only the bread and not the consecrated wine, although they were still given a drink of unconsecrated wine afterward to wash down the bread. This trend, however, was not universal and in some places communion in both kinds did linger on.[32]

The restriction of the chalice increased especially after the theory of concomitance (or "association") was adopted in the late twelfth century. It was argued that because a body cannot exist without its blood, Christ's blood was present concomitantly as soon as the bread was consecrated and hence communicants who received the bread alone still received the whole Christ. Thus the cup was unnecessary for them, even though Christ's blood was also present in a different mode by direct conversion when the wine was consecrated. This doctrine also led to the eventual abandonment in the West of the practice of intinction—the dipping of the consecrated bread in wine so that a communicant might receive both elements together.[33]

Because the words of the prayer over the offerings, the *oratio super oblata*, and of the Canon were considered the most sacred part of the rite, from the late eighth century onward in Gaul they began to be said in a low voice, so that only ministers standing close by could hear them. Within a hundred years, they were recited in complete silence everywhere. The prayer over the offerings even became known as the *secreta*.[34] Thus, laypeople would neither see what was happening on the altar, because it was against the east wall with the priest standing on its west side, nor hear the central part of the rite, and because the whole Mass, including the readings, was in Latin, they would not be able to understand even the parts which they did hear. They would be further cut off from the action at the high altar at Sunday Mass by the large chancel screens that became increasingly common in churches from the twelfth century onward.

[32] See Jungmann, *The Mass of the Roman Rite*, 2:382–86, 411–14; Mitchell, *Cult and Controversy*, 92; Rubin, *Corpus Christi*, 72.
[33] See Mitchell, *Cult and Controversy*, 92–96, 157–62.
[34] See Jungmann, *The Mass of the Roman Rite*, 2:90–93.

prayer over offerings most important from 8th c. on said lowly

It would be easy to conclude from all this that the laity had become almost entirely passive and distant in eucharistic worship, even alienated from it, by the end of the Middle Ages. And certainly they were encouraged to pursue their own devotions while the rite was being celebrated (except at the moment of the elevation of the consecrated bread, about which more will be said later). Those with wealth and education were able to purchase and use books of prayers that were being produced for this purpose by this time, while the rest simply repeated from memory brief formulae that they had been taught.[35] But Eamon Duffy warns against making too hasty a negative judgment. While admitting that Sunday Mass would be obscured from view by the screen to some extent, and completely in Lent when a veil was suspended right across the sanctuary, he asserts:

> We need to grasp that both screen and veil were manifestations of a complex and dynamic understanding of the role of both distance and proximity, concealment and exposure, within the experience of the liturgy. Both screen and veil were barriers, marking boundaries between the people's part of the church and the holy of holies, the sacred space within which the miracle of transubstantiation was effected, or, in the case of the veil, between different types of time, festive and penitential. The veil was there precisely to function as a temporary ritual deprivation of the sight of the sacring. Its symbolic effectiveness derived from the fact that it obscured for a time something which was normally accessible; in the process it heightened the value of the spectacle it temporarily concealed.
>
> The screen itself was both a barrier and no barrier. It was not a wall but rather a set of windows, a frame for the liturgical drama, solid only to waist-height, pierced by a door wide enough for ministers and choir to pass through and which the laity themselves might penetrate on certain occasions. . . . Even the screen's most solid section, the dado, might itself be pierced with elevation squints, to allow the laity to pass visually into the sanctuary at the sacring.[36]

Duffy goes on to remind his readers that Sunday Mass was not the only nor even perhaps the most common lay experience of the Eu-

---

[35] See Duffy, *The Stripping of the Altars*, 117–23; David N. Power, *The Eucharistic Mystery: Revitalizing the Tradition* (Dublin: Gill & Macmillan, 1992), 187–95; Rubin, *Corpus Christi*, 156–63.

[36] Duffy, *The Stripping of the Altars*, 111–12.

charist, as many attended Mass on some weekdays as well—"lo\ Masses, which were often not concealed behind screens or out of shot but celebrated at "side altars" in chantries, transepts, niches, ᵜ the like, and thus close at hand.

We should also note two ways in which the degree of active participation actually increased during the later Middle Ages, at least at Mass on Sunday. The first was the introduction from the ninth century onward of the "Bidding of the Bedes," variable prayers of intercession said in the vernacular. These were originally located before the offertory and thus in the position occupied by the traditional intercessory prayers in earlier centuries but were later incorporated into a larger vernacular unit known as Prone, placed after the offertory and also including other prayers, preaching, catechetical instruction and announcements.[37] The second was the use from the eleventh century onward of the *pax* or *"pax-brede,"* usually a smooth round disk made of wood or precious metal and like the eucharistic bread in appearance, on which was painted a sacred emblem such as the Lamb of God or a crucifix. This was passed around the congregation for the people to kiss and thus functioned as a substitute for the reception of communion and as a means of uniting individuals in a corporate body.[38]

Participation or, rather, "hearing Mass" attentively and devotedly was also encouraged—for those fortunate enough to be able to read, by means of various commentaries on the Mass, including what came to be known as *expositiones missae*, expositions of the Mass.[39] Amalarius, the ninth-century bishop of Metz, Germany, in his *Liber officialis* provides the following allegorical description of the reading of the gospel at Mass:

> The deacon goes to the altar where he picks up the gospel book from which he will read. The altar can stand for Jerusalem since, according to the Scriptures, the proclamation of the Gospel comes from this city: "For from Zion will come the Law, and from Jerusalem the word of the Lord" [Isa 2:3]. The altar can also stand for the body of the Lord himself, in whom are the words of the Gospel, namely, the Good News.

[37] See ibid., 124.
[38] See ibid., 125; Rubin, *Corpus Christi*, 74–76.
[39] See Gary Macy, "Commentaries on the Mass During the Early Scholastic Period, " in *Medieval Liturgy: A Book of Essays*, ed. Lizette Larson-Miller (New York: Garland, 1997), 25–59; Thibodeau, "Western Christendom," in *The Oxford History of Christian Worship*, 237–42.

It is Christ who ordered the apostles to preach the Gospel to every creature; it is Christ who said: "my words are spirit and life" [Isa 6:64]. His words are contained in the Gospel. The deacon who carries the book is, as it were, the feet of Christ. He carries the book upon his right shoulder; this evokes the life of this world in which the Gospel must be announced.

When the deacon greets the people, it is fitting that all turn toward him. The priest and the people are in fact facing the East till the moment when the Lord speaks through the deacon, and they sign themselves on their foreheads. . . . And why on this particular part of the body? The reason is that the forehead is the seat of shame. If the Jews were ashamed to believe in the one whom they desired to crucify, as the Apostle says—"We proclaim Christ crucified, a stumbling block to the Jews" [1 Cor 1:23]—we believe that we are saved by the Crucified One. The Jews were ashamed of his name, whereas we believe that this name protects us. This is why we make the sign of the cross on the forehead, which is the seat of shame, as we have said.

. . . The two candles carried before the gospel book stand for the Law and the Prophets which preceded the gospel teaching. The censer evokes all the virtues that flow from the life of Christ. The censerbearer ascends the ambo before the gospel so as to spread the odor of perfume, thus showing that Christ did good before announcing the Gospel, as Luke in the Acts of the Apostles attests: "All that Jesus did and taught" [Acts 1:1]. He first acted and then taught.

The elevated place from which the Gospel is read shows the superiority of the teaching of the Gospel and its great authority of judgment. The location of the candles shows that the Law and the Prophets are inferior to the Gospel. And when the book, after the reading, is returned to its place, the candles are extinguished since it is the preaching of the Gospel that continues, the Law and the Prophets speaking no longer. . . .

The rites before the gospel stand for Christ's preaching up to the hour of his passion as well as that of those who preach to the end of the world and beyond. The rites after the gospel reveal what has been brought about by Christ's passion, resurrection, and ascension into heaven, and likewise the sacrifice, mortification, and resurrection of his disciples who profess the faith.[40]

[40] Amalarius, *Liber officialis* 3.18; ET from Robert Cabié, *History of the Mass* (Portland, OR: Pastoral Press, 1992), 72–73.

Similarly, at the end of the twelfth century, Pope Innocent III offers this "Passion of Christ" interpretation of the text of, and gestures during, the canon of the Mass:

The Eucharistic Prayer: The sacred words must not be profaned. If everyone knows these words because all have heard them, then these words can be repeated in public and in profane places. This is why the church has decreed that the priest is to say the prayer secretly, a prayer having the appearance of a mystery. It is said that some shepherds, at a time before this custom was established, repeated these words in the fields and thus were struck down by God.

In the Mysteries we make memory of the passion, namely, of what occurred during the week before the Passover, from the tenth day of the first lunar month when Jesus entered Jerusalem, till the seventeenth day when he was raised from the dead. This is why most sacramentaries contain a picture of Christ's image between the preface and the canon; we are not merely to understand the text but also to contemplate the image, which inspires the memory of the Lord's passion. Perhaps it is the result more of providence than of human art that the Canon begins with the letter T, a letter whose form is that of a cross and which symbolizes a cross. In fact, the T recalls the mystery of the cross since God says through the prophet: "Mark with a tau the foreheads of those who lament and cry" [Ezek 9:4].

Te igitur clementissime Pater: The true Lamb entered Jerusalem on the very day when the crowds acclaimed Christ. This was the tenth day of the first lunar month, the day when the Law called for Hebrews to take into their homes the symbolic lamb. Spied upon by those men, full of hate, men who stirred up the people, he was threatened by the snares intended to cause his death. There were three who handed Christ over: God, Judas, and the Jew. . . . To express this the priest makes three crosses over the gifts as he says: *Haec dona, haec munera, haec sacrificial illibata*. He was handed over by God like a gift, by Judas on behalf of those who were present, by the Jew as a sacrifice without stain. It was unto "death, death on a cross" [Phil 2:8] that he was handed over by each of the three.[41]

Thus, in the West, as in the East, an allegorical or representative symbolism comes to be imposed on the words, acts, and gestures of the Eucharist. Each element of the Mass is therefore interpreted as

[41] Innocent III (1198), *De sacro alteris mysterio*, liber 3.1–3; ET from Cabié, *History of the Mass*, 82.

having a particular meaning, often in relationship to the life and death of Christ being presented dramatically by means of the rite. As we shall see, such is also connected to the liturgical developments related to the articulation of Christ's real presence.

EUCHARISTIC SACRIFICE AND THE PRIVATE MASS

A small but significant change to the Roman Canon was made in some manuscripts of the Gregorian Sacramentary when to the words in the commemoration of the living, *qui tibi offermius hoc sacrificium laudis* ("who offer to you this sacrifice of praise"), were prefixed an alternative phrase, *pro quibus offerimus* ("for whom we offer"). This became a standard part of later versions of the text. When this alternative was used, it changed the men and women just mentioned from being those who *themselves* offered to those *for whom* the Mass was offered. Although the idea that the clergy were the ones who offered on behalf of the laity, rather than the whole assembly offering together, went back at least to Cyprian in the third century, this understanding was now embodied in the Roman liturgical text itself. From this it was only a small step for the presence of any laypeople at the rite to be viewed as inconsequential and the way opened for "private" Masses—celebrations at which only a priest, and perhaps a server, were present.[42]

The practice seems to have originated first in monasteries in the seventh century, where in contrast to earlier centuries the community might include a substantial number of priests. Because priesthood was now being defined primarily in terms of the power of celebrating the Eucharist, it is not surprising that these priests desired to exercise that power daily, and it was not long before secular (diocesan) priests began to follow their example.[43] Other factors also encouraged this trend. Although throughout the Middle Ages theologians almost without exception continued to hold that the Mass was not a new sacrifice but was called a sacrifice because it commemorated the passion of Christ, this was not true of popular imagination, which thought more in terms of it being an addition to or repetition of the sacrifice on Calvary. More-

[42] See Thomas O'Loughlin, "The *Commemoratio pro vivis* of the Roman Canon: A Textual Witness to the Evolution of Western Eucharistic Theologies?," forthcoming in *Studia Patristica* 53 (2012).

[43] See Power, *The Eucharistic Mystery*, 164–71; Thomas O'Loughlin, "Treating the 'Private Mass' as Normal: Unnoticed Evidence from Adomnán's *De locis sanctis*," *Archiv für Liturgiewissenschaft* 51 (2009): 334–44.

over, the "fruits" of the Mass—the benefits which it brought—were commonly understood in a quantitative sense, so that two Masses were believed to bring twice as many benefits as one Mass, and this led to a dramatic increase in the number of celebrations. Paying a stipend to a priest to celebrate one or more Masses on one's behalf became one of the accepted ways in which a sinner might seek to expiate his or her fault, and doing the same on behalf of a deceased person in order to purge their sins and secure their salvation also became widespread. The very wealthy would leave money in their wills so that the same might be done for them after their demise. Offering the sacrifice for particular purposes—a "votive Mass"—was what the Eucharist came to be thought of as being all about.[44] It was no wonder, therefore, that the offertory part of the rite, originally having just the single *oratio super oblata*, soon became subject to an explosion of additional prayers and ceremonial acts, resulting in the later Middle Ages in what the liturgical scholar Joseph Jungmann described as "a veritable jungle."[45] The following example well illustrates the character of these prayers, especially as this one is written in the first-person singular, leaving no doubt as to who is regarded as the subject of the eucharistic action:

> Receive, Holy Father, almighty, eternal God, this unblemished offering which I, your unworthy servant, present to you, my living and true God, for my innumerable sins, offences and negligences; for all who stand round, for all faithful Christians, alive and dead; that it may avail for my salvation and theirs to eternal life.[46]

Inevitably such prayers anticipated and to a considerable extent duplicated the contents of the Canon itself, so much so that in the late

---

[44] See William R. Crockett, *Eucharist: Symbol of Transformation* (New York: Pueblo, 1989), 120–25; Macy, *The Banquet's Wisdom*, 114–20; Enrico Mazza, *The Celebration of the Eucharist: The Origin of the Rite and the Development of Its Interpretation* (Collegeville, MN: Liturgical Press, Pueblo, 1999), 162–81, 210–14; Power, *The Eucharistic Mystery*, 226–30, 248–49; Stevenson, *Eucharist and Offering*, 116–19. On Mass stipends, see Edward J. Kilmartin, *The Eucharist in the West: History and Theology* (Collegeville, MN: Liturgical Press, Pueblo, 1998), 109–15.

[45] Jungmann, *The Mass of the Roman Rite*, 2:41. See also ibid., 41–100, for commentary on the various prayers and ceremonial acts.

[46] ET from PEER, 163, where examples of other prayers can also be found, 162–63. See also Stevenson, *Eucharist and Offering*, 112–16.

Middle Ages the term "little canon" began to be applied to the offertory rites.

The emergence of the private Mass led to other substantial changes in the ceremonial that had been used hitherto. Since there were no other ministers present to read the readings or choir to sing the chants, the priest read all these texts himself. Because there was no congregation, it was pointless for the priest to move away from the altar to proclaim the readings, although a token change in position was retained, with the epistle being read on the right side of the altar and the gospel on the left. Similarly, because there was no solemn procession bringing the eucharistic elements to the altar, they were simply taken from a small table beside the altar when needed. In the course of time, the need to have the various books containing the parts of the Mass originally assigned to different ministers became inconvenient in such a celebration, and so embryonic forms of the Missal—a book containing all the texts needed in one volume—began to emerge from the ninth century onward and came into common use everywhere from the thirteenth century.[47]

These were not the only changes that resulted from this development. Because of the need for multiple celebrations of the Eucharist on the same day in order that each priest could fulfill what was seen as his primary function, it was often necessary to allow for a number of secondary altars in a church building in addition to the principal one. Because these altars were commonly situated quite close to one another, the Masses were said rather than sung, usually in a low voice so as not to disturb others celebrating nearby. And because eventually an altar might be used several times a day, it became customary for the priest himself to carry in at the beginning the vessels he was to use and to carry them out afterward rather than their being at the altar in advance. Later, the wealthy would endow special "chantry chapels" in churches, just large enough for a priest and a small altar, together with a regular stipend for the priest to say Mass each day after the donor's death and thus seek forgiveness for sins committed in her or his lifetime.[48] Because by the later Middle Ages some priests ended up with the obligation to say a number of Masses each day for different people,

[47] See Theodor Klauser, *A Short History of the Western Liturgy* (London: Oxford University Press, 1969), 101–8.

[48] For details of the control of laypeople over the practices associated with such chapels, see Duffy, *The Stripping of the Altars*, 114. As an indication of how

a strange custom that used the *missa sicca* or "dry Mass" emerged. This was a rite in which all the Mass texts were said, except for what one might think were the vital parts: the offertory, consecration, and communion. Although a priest was ordinarily forbidden to say more than one Mass a day, this restriction did not apply to the *missa sicca*, and so the priest might repeat that part of the rite numerous times for different intentions (receiving a stipend each time), while completing it with the rest of the Mass only once—which gives a new meaning to the expression "Mass production"!

Some of the practices associated with the private Mass also began to affect the way the Eucharist was celebrated on other occasions too. Because there were no longer time-consuming movements at the introit, offertory, and communion at regular Masses as well as the private celebration, the psalms appointed for these points in the liturgy became abbreviated—eventually to the antiphon (refrain), a single verse of the psalm, the "Glory to the Father," and the repetition of the antiphon. This abbreviation sometimes resulted in omission of the very verse for which the psalm had been chosen in the first place.[49] Similarly, beginning in the ninth century it became usual by the thirteenth century for priests themselves to recite silently the various texts that were being sung by the choir. Some preparatory prayers, originally said by the priest while vesting or on the way to the altar, began to be said after arrival, just as in the private Mass, and other originally informal devotional prayers said by the priest at what we have referred to in an earlier chapter as "soft spots" in the rite—not only at the offertory, as we have already seen in this chapter, but also before the gospel, before and after communion, and after the dismissal—became a formal part of what had to be said. Many of these prayers entered the liturgy from Gallican sources, with a good number of them being in the first-person singular, being frequently known as *apologiae* because of their self-deprecatory nature.[50]

---

widespread they were, it is worth noting that Henry VIII suppressed 2,374 chantries in England shortly before his death in 1547.

[49] So, for example, on the feast of the Epiphany the first verse of Psalm 72, "Give the King your judgments, O God," was retained rather than verses 10-11: "The kings of Tharsis and of the isles shall give presents."

[50] See Jungmann, *The Mass of the Roman Rite*, 1:272–311, 343–50, 400–406, 437–39; Joanne M. Pierce, "The Evolution of the *Ordo Missae* in the Early Middle Ages," in *Medieval Liturgy*, ed. Larson-Miller, 3–24, especially 8–10; *eadem*,

EUCHARISTIC PRESENCE AND THE MOMENT OF CONSECRATION

We have seen that in the early centuries of Christianity there was a general acceptance that Christ was in some way present in the eucharistic bread and wine—that they were his body and blood. Exactly in what sense this was so was apparently not explored, and it did not become a topic of philosophical debate among Western theologians until the ninth century. As William Crockett has observed, the terms of the debate

> reflect two fundamental liturgical and cultural shifts that had taken place since the fourth century. In the first place, the unity between symbol and reality, which was characteristic of the ancient world, is beginning to dissolve. The symbol is no longer seen as the means of participating in the reality, but is on the way to becoming a mere sign or pointer that is separated from the reality that it signifies. It is against the background of this fundamental cultural shift that symbolical and realist language run into conflict with each other. As long as the symbol is the means by which the community participates in the reality that it signifies, there is no problem in using symbolical and realist language simultaneously. Once the unity between the symbol and the reality begins to dissolve, however, the presence of the reality seems to be threatened when symbolical language is used.
>
> The other fundamental change that is beginning to take place in the ninth century is the loosening of the unity between the Christological and the ecclesiological meanings of the "body of Christ." In Paul and in Augustine, the body of Christ in the eucharist is understood in both its Christological and its ecclesiological senses. Participation in the eucharist means both participation in Christ himself and in his body the Church. . . . In the patristic period, the term "body of Christ" meant primarily the Church, in the tradition of Paul and Augustine. In the Middle Ages, the term "body of Christ" came to mean primarily the sacramental presence of Christ in the elements of bread and wine on the altar.[51]

"Early Medieval Vesting Prayers in the *Ordo Missae* of Sigebert of Minden (1022–1036)," in *Rule of Prayer, Rule of Faith: Essays in Honor of Aidan Kavanagh, OSB,* ed. Nathan Mitchell and John F. Baldovin (Collegeville, MN: Liturgical Press, Pueblo, 1996), 80–105. For examples of prayers before communion, see Mitchell, *Cult and Controversy,* 104–7.

[51] Crockett, *Eucharist: Symbol of Transformation,* 106–7.

Some time between 831 and 833 Paschasius Radbertus, a monk at the monastery of Corbie in northern France, wrote a treatise *De Corpore et Sanguine Domini* ("On the Body and Blood of the Lord") that attempted to explain the nature of Christ's presence in the Eucharist for the benefit of his fellow monks. He asserted that it was the same body which had been born of Mary, suffered on the cross, and rose from the tomb that Christians received in the Eucharist, though veiled from their sight under the outward forms of bread and wine, and that through consuming it, their human nature was joined to Christ's nature. How that body could be in more places than one at the same time Paschasius attributed to God's omnipotence.

By 844 Paschasius had become abbot of Corbie and he then sent a special copy of his treatise to the new king of West Francia, Charles the Bald, at his coronation. Soon afterward Charles wrote a letter to Ratramnus, Paschasius' fellow monk and former abbot, requesting the answer to two questions: Did communicants receive the body and blood of Christ in truth or in mystery, and was that the same body and blood that had been born of Mary? Historians presume that it must have been his reading of Paschasius' treatise that prompted these questions. Ratramnus then wrote his own treatise, with the same title as that of Paschasius, in which he took a very different position. While agreeing that communicants do really receive the body and blood of Christ, he insisted that this was a spiritual reality, invisible to the senses and perceived only by faith, and not the same body born of Mary.

Although each of the two theologians approached the matter from opposite points—Paschasius insisting that it had to be the same body and blood as the risen Lord if it was to have the power to save, and Ratramnus denying that what was received could possibly be equated with the physical body with its flesh, bones, and sinews—yet both spoke of it as the "spiritual" body and blood of Christ and both regarded the presence as "real." Thus their disagreement does not seem to have been quite as polarized as later ages made it, and the two appear to have continued to live together in harmony in the same monastery.[52]

---

[52] On their dispute, see further Crockett, *Eucharist: Symbol of Transformation*, 106–9; Kilmartin, *The Eucharist in the West*, 82–89; Mazza, *The Celebration of the Eucharist*, 182–87; Macy, *The Banquet's Wisdom*, 68–74; Mitchell, *Cult and Controversy*, 73–86; Thibodeau, "Western Christendom," in *The Oxford History of Christian Worship*, 232–33.

It was, however, Paschasius' "realist" understanding that slowly came to be generally accepted in the centuries that followed, and it was not until the eleventh century that the contrary view was revived by Berengarius,[53] a canon of the cathedral at Tours in France and head of its school. He drew an even sharper distinction between a physical and a spiritual presence than Ratramnus had done. For Berengarius, it was impossible to imagine that actual pieces of Christ's flesh could be eaten in communion. Thus, the bread and wine remained bread and wine but became sacramental signs of Christ's spiritual presence to be apprehended in the mind by faith. He immediately encountered condemnation for these views from opponents who thought that he was thereby denying the reality of Christ's presence, and especially from Lanfranc, prior of the Abbey of Bec in Normandy and later archbishop of Canterbury. Pope Leo IX excommunicated Berengarius and summoned him to appear at the Synod of Vercelli in 1050. Passing through Paris on his way to the synod, he sought permission to attend from King Henry I of France, who was titular abbot of Tours. The king, however, imprisoned him, and he was condemned *in absentia*, as was Ratrammus' work, but under the supposed authorship of Johannes Scotus Erigena. Even after his release from prison, he continued to be pursued by his opponents. In 1059 he was forced to take an oath that contained a definition of eucharistic presence in the most crudely physical terms. It stated that "the bread and wine which are placed on the altar are after consecration not only a sacrament but also the true body and blood of our Lord Jesus Christ, and with the senses not only sacramentally but in truth are taken and broken by the hands of the priests and crushed by the teeth of the faithful."[54]

Nearly twenty years later, at the Synod of Rome in 1079, he was required to take another oath in similar terms. It read:

[53] On the Berengarian controversy, see Charles M. Radding and Francis Newton, *Theology, Rhetoric, and Politics in the Eucharistic Controversy, 1078–1079: Alberic of Monte Cassino Against Berengar of Tours* (New York: Columbia University Press, 2003), 1–31, 86–107; Thibodeau, "Western Christendom," in *The Oxford History of Christian Worship*, 233–34.

[54] Latin text in Denzinger–Schönmetzer, *Enchiridion Symbolorum*, no. 690. On Berengarius, see further Crockett, *Eucharist: Symbol of Transformation*, 109–12; Macy, *The Banquet's Wisdom*, 75–81; Kilmartin, *The Eucharist in the West*, 97–102; Mazza, *The Celebration of the Eucharist*, 190–92; Mitchell, *Cult and Controversy*, 137–51.

I, Berengarius, believe in my heart and openly profess that the bread and wine that are placed on the altar are through the mystery of the sacred prayer and the words of our Redeemer substantially changed into the true and proper and life-giving flesh and blood of Jesus Christ our Lord; and that after the consecration is the true body of Christ, which was born of the Virgin, as an offering for the salvation of the world hung on the cross, and sits at the right hand of the Father; and (is) the true blood of Christ which flowed from his side; not only through the sign and power of the sacrament but in his proper nature and true substance; as it is set down in this summary and as I read it and you understand it. Thus I believe, and I will not teach any more against this faith. So help me God and this holy Gospel of God.[55]

Although similar to the earlier oath, there is one important difference. It introduces the words "substantially" and "substance." This was the result of the recent recovery of the philosophy of Aristotle (d. 322 BCE) in the medieval schools. In Aristotle's terminology, "substance" was the fundamental essence of a thing or a person and quite distinct from the "accidents," which were the physical properties that could be apprehended through the five senses. So, for example, while a table might be said to possess various accidents, such as color, hardness, and so on, there was beyond those properties an inner essence or reality, which the mind alone grasped, that made it a table and not, for instance, a stool. Nevertheless, even when the term "transubstantiation" (*transsubstantiatio*) entered the theological vocabulary to denote the change of the bread and wine into the body and blood of Christ in the first half of the twelfth century and was incorporated in the official teaching of the church in the first canon of the Fourth Lateran Council in 1215, it was not at first linked exclusively to a particular understanding of the manner of Christ's presence by theologians, and a more crass materialistic view of the nature of that presence still tended to dominate people's thinking.[56] It was only later that Aristotle's way of understanding objects was to be developed and so opened up the possibility of talking about a change of essence or substance that was

[55] Latin text in Denzinger–Schönmetzer, *Enchiridion Symbolorum*, no. 700.
[56] See Joseph Goering, "The Invention of Transubstantiation," *Traditio* 46 (1991): 147–70; James F. McCue, "The Doctrine of Transubstantiation from Berengar Through the Council of Trent," *Harvard Theological Review* 61 (1968): 385–430.

real and yet not discernible by physical examination of external properties or accidents.

The Dominican theologian Thomas Aquinas (ca. 1225–74) was the first to apply the Aristotelian categories in this way, understanding transubstantiation to be a change in the substance of the bread and wine into the substance of the body and blood of Christ, while all the accidents of bread and wine remained as exactly as before. This meant that Christ's substantial presence was not by way of a physical change that could be known in any way through the senses, but only grasped by the mind. This did not, however, make it less "real," because for Aristotle and for Thomas, what the mind grasped was what was most real. "Substance as such cannot be seen by the bodily eye, nor is it the object of any sense, nor can it be imagined; it is only open to the intellect, the object of which is the essence of things, as Aristotle says. Hence, properly speaking, the body of Christ, according to the mode of existence which it has in this sacrament, can be reached neither by sense nor by imagination; it is open only to the intellect which may be called a spiritual eye."[57]

Thomas rejected all alternative understandings of Christ's presence as erring either in being too physical or in being purely symbolic. Yet it was not without its own intellectual difficulties, because Aristotle had asserted that accidents could not exist without substance or substance without accidents. In saying that the substance of one thing could be combined with the accidents of another, Thomas had to resort to the category of pure miracle. And while the term transubstantiation passed into common usage in the later Middle Ages as denoting not just how Christ was really present in the eucharistic elements but also

---

[57] Thomas Aquinas, *Summa Theologiae* 3a.76.7; ET from the Blackfriars edition (Oxford, 1963) 58:117. On Aquinas and transubstantiation, see further S. L. Brock, "St. Thomas and the Eucharistic Conversion," *The Thomist* 65 (2001): 529–66; Crockett, *Eucharist: Symbol of Transformation*, 113–20; Macy, *The Banquet's Wisdom*, 104–9; Kilmartin, *The Eucharist in the West*, 143–53; Power, *The Eucharistic Mystery*, 219–26; Liam Walsh, "An Ecumenical Reading of Aquinas on the Eucharist," in *Liturgia et Unitas: Liturgiewissenschaft und ökumenische Studien zur Eucharistie und zum Gottesdienstlichen in der Schweiz: in honorem Bruno Bürki*, ed. Martin Klöckener and Armand Join-Lambert (Freiburg: Univ.-Verlag.; Geneva: Labor et Fides, 2001), 226–40, esp. 232–40; Joseph P. Wawrykow, "Transubstantiation," in *The Westminster Handbook to Thomas Aquinas*, ed. *idem* (Louisville, KY: Westminster John Knox Press, 2005), 159–61.

that this was so, not all theologians understood it in exactly the same way as Thomas.

In particular, there was a disagreement over what happened if a mouse were able to eat a piece of the consecrated bread (apparently a not uncommon problem in the period). According to his principles, Thomas had to insist that transubstantiation resulted in a permanent change and so the substance of Christ's body would remain in the mouse (even if it did not benefit the creature) until the accidents had disappeared. But his Franciscan contemporary Bonaventure, following his teacher Alexander of Hales, rejected that explanation: "the body of Christ in no way descends into the stomach of a mouse because Christ is only under this sign [*sacramentum*] in so far as it is destined for human use, of course for eating. But when a mouse gnaws it, it becomes unusable and the sign ceases to exist, and the body of Christ also ceases to exist here, and the substance of the bread returns."[58]

Challenges to the theory of transubstantiation came from other theologians too, and especially from among the Franciscans. John Peter Olivi claimed that, according to a proper understanding of Aristotle, the eucharistic body of Christ must possess quantity, or the risen Christ would have been merely a spirit, and that was heretical. John Duns Scotus, writing at the very beginning of the fourteenth century, some fifty years after Thomas, argued that the latter had been wrong in asserting that transubstantiation was the most reasonable explanation of Christ's presence in the Eucharist: it faced several difficult philosophical problems, and God's omnipotence could have enabled him to choose other modes of presence instead that were more reasonable. Nevertheless, it seemed that transubstantiation was the mode he had freely selected. Finally, Robert Holcot, a student of Scotus, pointed out that because God can apparently make one thing exist under the appearance of another, this must mean that God could change the entire world, and so human beings could never have any certitude about the truth of their own experience. Thus, although by the end of the Middle Ages transubstantiation was the most commonly held explanation for Christ's presence in the Eucharist, it continued to be seen as problematic by some.[59]

---

[58] Bonaventure, *Commentary on the Sentences*, L. 4, dist. 13; ET from Macy, *The Banquet's Wisdom*, 111. See also Mazza, *The Celebration of the Eucharist*, 215–22.

[59] See Macy, *The Banquet's Wisdom*, 112–14; Power, *The Eucharistic Mystery*, 245–48; Marilyn McCord Adams, *Some Later Medieval Theories of the Eucharist:*

Alongside these debates on the nature of the real presence, there were also conflicting views among medieval theologians as to the precise moment in the eucharistic prayer when the change from bread and wine to body and blood occurred. Since the time of Ambrose, consecration had been linked in Western thought principally with the narrative of institution (although some Western patristic and medieval commentators did continue to acknowledge the part played by the Holy Spirit as well, in spite of the fact that the Roman Canon made no reference to it[60]). But did the consecration take place only after that whole narrative was finished, or were the bread and wine each consecrated separately when Christ's respective sayings over bread and cup were repeated? This question occupied the minds of several theologians in the twelfth century.[61] But it was not merely an academic discussion, because it was connected with the emerging practice of the priest elevating the bread during the narrative of institution in order to show it to the people so that they might adore it.[62] If the priest lifted up the bread immediately after saying the words of Jesus about it being his body, was it already consecrated or were the worshipers guilty of idolatry in adoring what was still only bread?

The issue was finally dealt with by a synod convoked in Paris sometime between 1205 and 1208, which apparently accepted the majority view that there was a separate consecration of bread and wine, as it resolved that "in the canon of the mass, when they begin the words, 'On the day before . . . ,' presbyters are ordered not to elevate the host immediately so that it may be seen by all the people; rather, they are to hold it just in front of their chest until they have said the words, 'This is my body.' At that point, they elevate the host so that all may see it."[63] It appears that a second elevation, of the cup, did not become

---

Thomas Aquinas, Giles of Rome, Duns Scotus, and William Ockham (Oxford: Oxford University Press, 2010).

[60] For examples of this, see Yves Congar, *I Believe in the Holy Spirit* (New York: Seabury; London: Chapman, 1983) 3:250ff.

[61] For details, see V. L. Kennedy, "The Moment of Consecration and the Elevation of the Host," *Medieval Studies* 6 (1944): 121–50; Mitchell, *Cult and Controversy*, 151–54.

[62] In earlier centuries the custom had been for the consecrated elements to be lifted up and shown to the people after the eucharistic prayer and before communion: see Mitchell, *Cult and Controversy*, 47–49.

[63] Quoted from Mitchell, *Cult and Controversy*, 156.

common until the fourteenth century. William Durandus (1230–96) insisted that for the sake of symmetry and respect for Scripture, "although the blood cannot be seen, the elevation of the chalice is not superfluous," but others did not agree, both because of the greater risk of spillage and because the cup did not capture public imagination in the same way as the host.[64] Even some missals of the early sixteenth century do not mention the ceremonial gesture.

Because most people in the late Middle Ages were reluctant to take the risk of receiving communion more than a few times a year and because they believed that the eucharistic bread was truly the body of Christ, being able to gaze at it and adore at the elevation became for them the devotional climax of the rite. By the thirteenth century a small bell, known in England as the sacring bell, would be rung to warn them when it was about to happen so that they might look up from their devotions, and the church bells themselves might also be rung to alert passers by.[65] Prayers originally intended as preparation for communion were recommended to be used at this moment in the rite,[66] and preachers would elaborate on the spiritual and physical benefits that would result for those who beheld and adored their Lord in this way, among them the weakening of sinful lusts, the strength of the soul to endure, restoration of sight to the blind, and freedom from sudden death.[67] People would dash from altar to altar and from church to church in order to catch a glimpse of the consecrated host more than once; they might even pay the priest to repeat the elevation two or three times; and they would commonly feel free to leave Mass immediately after the elevation had taken place. To encourage them to stay to the end of the service, however, they were taught that particular graces would then attach to them, and they would receive an indulgence if they heard the final element in every Mass, the reading of the last gospel (John 1:1-14). To gain that indulgence, they had to kiss a text, an image, or even their own thumbnail at the words, "The Word became flesh."[68]

[64] Rubin, Corpus Christi, 55–56.
[65] See ibid., 56–60.
[66] See Power, The Eucharistic Mystery, 187–92.
[67] For examples, see Duffy, The Stripping of the Altars, 100–101.
[68] See E. G. C. Atchley, "Some Notes on the Beginning and Growth of the Usage of a Second Gospel at Mass," Transactions of the St Paul's Ecclesiological Society 4 (1900): 161–76; also Rubin, Corpus Christi, 152.

Although the critical remarks of the sixteenth-century archbishop of Canterbury, Thomas Cranmer, may contain some element of exaggeration, they surely catch the general tenor of late medieval eucharistic devotion:

> What made the people to run from their seats to the altar, and from altar to altar, and from sacring (as they call it) to sacring, peeping, tooting and gazing at that thing which the priest held up in his hands, if they thought not to honour the thing which they saw? What moved the priests to lift up the sacrament so high over their heads? Or the people to say to the priest "Hold up! Hold up!"; or one man to say to another "Stoop down before"; or to say "This day have I seen my Maker"; and "I cannot be quiet except I see my maker once a day"? What was the cause of all these, and that as well the priest and the people so devoutly did knock and kneel at every sight of the sacrament, but that they worshipped that visible thing which they saw with their eyes and took it for very God?[69]

SUMMARY

1. There were different forms of eucharistic rites in the various regions of the West, but it was the Roman Rite that came to form the foundation of all later medieval practices and which, by the eighth century, had acquired substantially the pattern that it was to retain until the end of the Middle Ages and beyond.
2. Most subsequent changes to the liturgy took the form of abbreviation of certain parts of the rite (principally the psalm chants) and the addition of personal prayers of devotion of the priest or bishop celebrating the rite.
3. The active participation of the laity declined as they ceased to receive communion on most occasions in the year or to bring their gifts of bread and wine anymore.
4. The corporate celebration by the assembly was superseded by concept of the priest or bishop offering the eucharistic sacrifice on behalf of the people, and often specifically for the spiritual benefit of certain individuals, who did not need to be present for the rite to be thought effective for them.

[69] *Miscellaneous Writings and Letters of Thomas Cranmer*, ed. J. E. Cox, Parker Society (Cambridge: Cambridge University Press, 1846), 442. For further details, see Duffy, *The Stripping of the Altars*, 95–102.

5. The evolution of the "private Mass" brought about significant changes in the style of celebration of all forms of Mass in the course of the Middle Ages.
6. When laypeople attended the Eucharist, their devotion centered upon seeing and adoring Christ present in the consecrated bread (and wine).
7. The nature of that presence gradually came to be defined by theologians through the philosophical term of transubstantiation.

Chapter 7

The Protestant and Catholic Reformations

Both ecclesial and social life in the late or high Western Middle Ages were ripe for some kind of far-reaching reform and renewal, one that would reach down to the very roots of Western society and culture. As Herman Wegman notes:

> People were deeply disappointed in both church and state. The call for reform was widespread, especially for reform of the church. In making such a call people looked to the past. The early church was the ideal from which the church had now strayed, so far that nothing seemed to remain from that early period. Holiness, purity, poverty, zealous faith had all disappeared, or so it was thought. The humanists with their growing historical insight had a distaste for what we now call "the Middle Ages." They saw it as a barbaric time of bad Latin and impossible metaphysics. Especially the clergy and the pope were responsible for these ills. At the Councils of Constance and Basel this dissatisfaction and a certain kind of antipapalism had already appeared, but now this tendency was becoming much more evident. Certain forms of anticlericalism were to be found not only in the scholarly circles but also among the faithful. Savanarola brought the city of Florence into revolt against the pope and his "clique," i.e., the Curia, which consisted mostly of the pope's relatives. The people began to criticize just like the learned. The development of printing brought books onto the market and many people learned to read them. Once people began to pore over the works of someone like Erasmus, it was not long before they too became reform-minded. The church, which had for many years looked upon learning and scholarship as its monopoly, now lost the claim and became the object of a bitter critique carried on by learning, once the church's handmaid.[1]

Nationalism, the increasing loss of ecclesiastical and/or papal control of Western Europe, the biting critiques of Humanist scholars and

---

[1] Herman A. J. Wegman, *Christian Worship in East and West: A Study Guide to Liturgical History*, trans. Gordon W. Lathrop (New York: Pueblo, 1985), 298.

others, and the so-called Gutenberg Revolution (i.e., the invention of the moveable-type printing press and with it the possibility of mass-produced pamphlets and books) all contributed to bringing about and fostering the sixteenth-century Reformation. In such a changed historical context, the eucharistic liturgies inherited from the Middle Ages would themselves either become drastically reformed and re-shaped, according to various theological perspectives, or, as in the case of the Roman Catholic Church, lead to a new *Missale Romanum* (1570) viewed as canonically binding, with notable exceptions, throughout the Catholic world until the early 1960s.

It was not only the various forms of Protestantism that emerged as the result of the sixteenth-century Reformation, nor only those known as the "Protestant" Reformers who were concerned about reform and renewal within the Western Church. As much as the Lutheran, Reformed, Anglican, and other churches owe their immediate origins to the various sixteenth-century reforming movements, so also does the particular shape and self-understanding of the Roman Catholic Church itself as it emerged from the late Middle Ages. As Gary Macy states so clearly:

> Different churches retained different customs of the old medieval church, to be sure, and some of the churches, especially the Roman Catholic and Anglican churches, treasured their continuity with the medieval centuries. Yet it is important to remember that *none* of the churches which emerged from this great upheaval can claim the past exclusively their own. *The modern Roman Catholic Church started in the sixteenth century just as surely as the Lutheran and Calvinist churches.* . . . [B]efore the reformation there were no Protestants, no Anglicans, no Roman Catholics. Christians were simply Christians—eastern and western Christians sometimes, but mostly simply Christians.[2]

It is thus important to realize that just as there was a Protestant Reformation so also was there a decidedly Catholic Reformation, that is, an internal reform of the Roman Church itself, quite apart from the challenges posed to it by the various Protestant movements. While a significant part of this Catholic Reformation was indeed what has often been called the "Counter-Reformation,"[3] in response to Protes-

---

[2] Gary Macy, *The Banquet's Wisdom: A Short History of the Theologies of the Lord's Supper* (New York: Paulist Press, 1992), 135. Emphasis added.

[3] This helpful distinction between "Catholic" and "Counter" Reformations is that of Hubert Jedin. See his four-volume study: *A History of the Council of*

tantism, the mere fact that among Roman Catholic concerns was the reform of liturgical books, liturgical and devotional life, and the catechetical education of clergy and laity alike, demonstrates that far more was at stake than simply responding to Protestantism. Both "Counter" Reform and "Catholic" Reform were the concerns of the Council of Trent, which met in some twenty-five sessions over three separate periods (1545–47, 1551–52, and 1562–63).

THE EUCHARIST OR "LORD'S SUPPER" IN THE PROTESTANT REFORMATION

The origin of critiques of the Eucharist in the Protestant Reformation is to be found in the first detailed attack against the medieval sacramental system of the Western Church in general, namely, Martin Luther's 1520 treatise titled *The Babylonian Captivity of the Church*. In this polemical and lengthy treatise, Luther—Augustinian friar, biblical scholar, and university professor—claimed that just as the Jews had been captive in Babylon in the sixth-century BCE, so the true meaning of the sacraments and Christian freedom itself had been held captive by Rome. In this he laid the foundation for almost all subsequent Protestant sacramental theology. Inheriting the traditional medieval scholastic definition of the necessary elements (e.g., matter, form, minister, and dominical institution), which constituted a sacrament, Luther wrote:

> To begin with, I must deny that there are seven sacraments, and for the present maintain that there are but three: baptism, penance, and the bread. All three have been subjected to a miserable captivity by the Roman curia, and the church has been robbed of all her liberty. Yet, if I were to speak according to the usage of the Scriptures, I should have only one single sacrament [i.e., Christ; 1 Tim 3:16], but with three sacramental signs, of which I shall treat more fully at the proper time.[4]

But later in this same treatise he backed away from identifying penance as a specific "sacrament," saying:

> It has seemed proper to restrict the name of sacrament to those promises which have signs attached to them. The remainder, not being

---

Trent, trans. Ernest Graf (St. Louis, MO: Herder, 1957); as well as his *Ecumenical Councils of the Catholic Church*, trans. Ernest Graf (New York: Herder and Herder, 1960).

[4] Martin Luther, *The Babylonian Captivity of the Church* (1520), LW 36, 18.

bound to signs, are bare promises. Hence, there are, strictly speaking, but two sacraments in the church of God—baptism and the bread. For only in these two do we find both the divinely instituted sign and the promise of forgiveness of sins.[5]

James F. White is absolutely correct in pointing out that in his limiting of the church's genuine sacraments to baptism and Eucharist alone, Luther "brings to a logical conclusion one possible development of the late-medieval concept of the number of sacraments."[6] That is, if sacraments themselves are defined according to what scholastic theology considered to be the necessary elements, then based on the command and institution of Christ, as that command is recorded in the New Testament, the reduction from seven to two "dominical sacraments" is perfectly logical.

To be completely fair, however, neither Luther's approach to the sacraments nor that of Protestant sacramental theology in general is based simply on those scholastic categories of matter, form, intention, and dominical institution. Rather, instead of focusing exclusively on what scholasticism considered to be the "form" of the sacraments, i.e., the "formulas" recited in their administration, Luther considered the dominical "words of institution" to be the very key and central element in the sacraments, the very "promise" of God to do what the "formulas" in the sacraments *proclaim* that God does. And, since it is

faith alone for Luther which justifies and saves, that saving faith is trust not in the sacramental *rite* itself but in the divine promise proclaimed in and by the sacrament. Hence, as White says, "Luther's theology of salvation shapes his theology of the sacraments. Since salvation is a divine gift, not a human work, the sacraments are subject to the same order of salvation. They are signs and promises of what God does for humans and, like redemption, can only be received in faith."[7]

Luther's reduction from seven to two sacraments, based biblically on the command of Christ ("Go . . . baptize," and "Do this in memory of me") and the promise of Christ ("The one who believes and is baptized shall be saved," and "This is my Body . . . my Blood, [given and] shed for you for the forgiveness of sins"), was inherited in

[5] Ibid., 127.
[6] James White, *Protestant Worship: Traditions in Transition* (Louisville, KY: Westminster John Knox Press, 1989), 38.
[7] Ibid., 38.

some way by all of the Protestant Reformers. Although the Lutheran tradition itself never has come to a consensus on the precise number of genuine "sacraments" in the church (with penance, called "absolution," ordination, and even prayer itself appearing in some lists),[8] other traditions developing out of the Protestant Reformation tended to limit the sacraments, or dominical "ordinances," as some came to call them, to baptism and Eucharist ("Lord's Supper") alone.

Before entering into the specific approaches of the Protestant Reformers, focusing in this chapter primarily on Luther, Ulrich Zwingli, John Calvin, and Thomas Cranmer, it is necessary to indicate a change in our approach from previous chapters. That is, while we have been able to separate "rite" from "eucharistic theology" in our preceding presentations of the various rites of East and West in their development and interpretation, that is no longer possible here. What happens in the reform of various rites, including that of the 1570 *Missale Romanum*, is that various theologies come to shape and prescribe what is to be done liturgically. In other words, where in preceding centuries, and especially in the early church, theological reflection and formulation of the *lex credendi*, or "law of belief," generally tended to *follow* upon the experience of encountering God in worship (i.e., the *lex orandi* or "law of prayer"), beginning in the sixteenth century we see the *lex credendi* shaping the *lex orandi*, rather than the other way around. Thus, while both *lex orandi* and *lex credendi* are always a two-way street of mutual influence, it is clear in this Reformation period that it is the *lex credendi* which emerges as the primary catalyst for liturgical and ecclesial reform.

Martin Luther (1483–1546) and the Lutheran Churches
As noted, it was Luther's *Babylonian Captivity of the Church* (1520) that provided the foundation for Protestant theologies of the sacraments in general. Hence, dealing with Luther in some detail is justified here in light of the influence he was to have. With regard to the Eucharist specifically, Luther claimed that it had been subject to three captivities in the late medieval church:

---

[8] See the *Apology of the Augsburg Confession* and *The Smalcald Articles*, in *The Book of Concord: The Confessions of the Evangelical Lutheran Church*, ed. Robert Kolb and Timothy Wengert (Minneapolis, MN: Fortress Press, 2000), 185ff., and 319.

The first captivity of this sacrament, therefore concerns its substance or completeness, which the tyranny of Rome has wrestled from us. . . . But they are the sinners, who forbid the giving of both kinds [bread and wine] to those who wish to exercise this choice. The fault lies not with the laity, but with the priests. The sacrament does not belong to the priests but to all men. The priests are not lords, but servants in duty bound to administer both kinds to those who desire them, as often as they desire them. . . .

The second captivity of this sacrament [transubstantiation] is less grievous as far as the conscience is concerned, yet the gravest of dangers threatens the man who would attack it, to say nothing of condemning it. . . .

We have to think of real bread and real wine, just as we do of a real cup (for even they do not say that the cup was transubstantiated). Since it is not necessary, therefore, to assume a transubstantiation effected by divine power, it must be regarded as a figment of the human mind, for it rests neither on the Scriptures nor on reason, as we shall see. . . .

And why could not Christ include his body in the substance of the bread just as well as in the accidents? In red-hot iron, for instance, the two substances, fire and iron, are so mingled that every part is both iron and fire. Why is it not even more possible that the body of Christ be contained in every part of the substance of the bread? . . .

What shall we say when Aristotle and the doctrines of men are made to be the arbiters of such lofty and divine matters? Why do we not put aside such curiosity and cling simply to the words of Christ, willing to remain in ignorance of what takes place here and content that the real body of Christ is present by virtue of the words? Or is it necessary to comprehend the manner of the divine working in every detail? . . .

Both natures are simply there in their entirety, and it is truly said: "This man is God; this God is man." Even though philosophy cannot grasp this, faith grasps it nonetheless. And the authority of God's Word is greater than the capacity of our intellect to grasp it. In like manner, it is not necessary in the sacrament that the bread and wine be transubstantiated and that Christ be contained under their accidents in order that the real body and real blood may be present. But both remain there at the same time. . . .

The third captivity of this sacrament is by far the most wicked abuse of all. . . . The holy sacrament has been turned into mere merchandise, a market, and a profit-making business. . . .

238

It is certain, therefore, that the mass is not a work which may be communicated to others, but the object of faith (as has been said), for the strengthening and nourishing of each one's own faith.

Now there is yet a second stumbling block that must be removed, and this is much greater and the most dangerous of all. It is the common belief that the mass is a sacrifice, which is offered to God. Even the words of the canon seem to imply this, when they speak of "these gifts, these presents, these holy sacrifices," and further on "this offering." Prayer is also made, in so many words, "that the sacrifice may be accepted even as the sacrifice of Abel," etc. Hence Christ is termed "the sacrifice of the altar." Added to these are the sayings of the holy fathers, the great number of examples, and the widespread practice uniformly observed throughout the world.

Over against all these things, firmly entrenched as they are, we must resolutely set the words and example of Christ. For unless we firmly hold that the mass is the promise or testament of Christ, as the words clearly say, we shall lose the whole gospel and all its comfort. Let us permit nothing to prevail against these words—even though an angel from heaven should teach otherwise [Gal. 1:8]—for they contain nothing about a work or a sacrifice. Moreover, we also have the example of Christ on our side. When he instituted this sacrament and established this testament at the Last Supper, Christ did not offer himself to God the Father, nor did he perform a good work on behalf of others, but, sitting at the table, he set this same testament before each one and proffered to him the sign. Now, the more closely our mass resembles that first mass of all, which Christ performed at the Last Supper, the more Christian it will be. But Christ's mass was most simple, without any display of vestments, gestures, chants, or other ceremonies, so that if it had been necessary to offer the mass as a sacrifice, then Christ's institution of it was not complete.[9]

With regard to the first of these "captivities," the restoration of the cup to the laity had already been a hallmark of Reforming movements in Bohemia in the fifteenth century (the *Utraquists*),[10] and Luther was certainly in line with those concerns. Concerning the captivity of the

---

[9] Luther, *Babylonian Captivity*, LW 36, 27; 28; 31–33; 35; 51–52.
[10] See David Holeton, "The Bohemian Eucharistic Movement in Its European Context," *Bohemian Reformation and Religious Practice* 1 (1996): 23–47; also *idem, Infant Communion–Then and Now*, Grove Liturgical Study 27 (Cambridge: Grove Books, 1981), 9ff.

doctrine of transubstantiation as well, Luther was also in line with several late medieval theologians, who much preferred the theology of "consubstantiation" but considered themselves bound by the accepted terminology of transubstantiation.[11] Luther's own theology, however, is not properly called "consubstantiation" since he would have repudiated the use of the Aristotelian categories undergirding this as much as he denied transubstantiation for the same reason. It is *not* that transubstantiation incorrectly describes the change of bread and wine into the real presence of Christ, his body and blood truly present and distributed in the Eucharist, but that the concept depends on the philosophy of Aristotle and *not* on the words of Jesus alone to explain that presence.

Luther's theology of real presence has to do with the Chalcedonian doctrine of the two natures of Christ. That is, just as Christ is completely human and completely divine in his personal (hypostatic) union, so is the Eucharist completely the body and blood of Christ *and* completely bread and wine at the same time. This is brought about by what is often referred to as a "sacramental union," articulated in categories derived from Augustine: "let the word come to the element, and the sacrament will come to be" (*Tractatus in Ioh. Evang.*, 80.3). In the Eucharist, the word of Christ (the "narrative of institution") is connected to the elements of bread and wine and the sacrament results from this union.[12] Elsewhere in *The Babylonian Captivity* Luther underscores this christologically based approach to eucharistic presence:

> Thus, what is true in regard to Christ is also true in regard to the Sacrament. In order for the divine nature to dwell in him bodily, it is not necessary for the human nature to be transubstantiated and the divine nature contained under the accidents of the human nature. Both natures are simply there in their entirety, and it is truly said; "This man is God; this God is man." Even though philosophy cannot grasp this, faith grasps it nonetheless.[13]

[11] On this, see James F. McCue, "The Doctrine of Transubstantiation from Berengar through the Council of Trent," in *Lutherans and Catholics in Dialogue III: The Eucharist as Sacrifice*, ed. Paul C. Empie and T. Austin Murphy (Minneapolis, MN: Augsburg Publishing House, 1967), 102.

[12] See Arthur Carl Piepkorn, "Digests of Recent American and European Lutheran Discussions of the Sacrament of the Altar," in *Lutherans and Catholics in Dialogue III*, ed. Empie and Murphy, 125–47.

[13] Luther, *Babylonian Captivity*, LW 36, 35.

And as he explains in his *Large Catechism* of 1529:

> Now, what is the Sacrament of the Altar? *Answer:* It is the true body
> and blood of the Lord Christ in and under the bread and wine, which
> we Christians are commanded by Christ's word to eat and drink. As
> we said of Baptism that it is not mere water, so we say here that the
> sacrament is bread and wine, but not mere bread or wine such as is
> served at the table. It is bread and wine comprehended in God's Word
> and connected with it.[14]

Indeed, Roman Catholic eucharistic theology would not—and did
not—have any problems with the way that Christ's real presence is
articulated in the primary confessional document of the Lutheran
movement, the *Confessio Augustana* or *Augsburg Confession* of 1530,
clearly reflecting Luther's theology. Article 10 of this *Confession* states,
"It is taught among us that the true body and blood of Christ are really
present in the Supper of our Lord under the form of bread and wine
are there distributed and received."[15]

What Luther and the other Protestant Reformers did *not* do, however, was to continue the practice of the reservation of the Eucharist
or the various devotional practices associated with the cult of the Eucharist outside the context of the eucharistic liturgy. In relationship
to Corpus Christi processions, for example, article 22 of the *Augsburg
Confession* states, "Because the division of the sacrament [i.e., the with-
drawal of the cup] is contrary to the institution of Christ, the customary carrying about of the sacrament in processions is also omitted by
us."[16] If this article might be interpreted as but critiquing a "mis-use"
or "abuse" of the sacrament, the *Formula of Concord, Solid Declaration*
(1580) is much stronger in its approach. In its rejection of the doctrine
of transubstantiation, article 7 states:

> [T]hey assert that under the species of the bread, which they allege has
> lost its natural substance and is no longer bread, the body of Christ
> is present even apart from the action of the sacrament (when, for in-
> stance, the bread is locked up in the tabernacle or is carried about as
> a spectacle and for adoration). For nothing can be a sacrament apart

---

[14] Martin Luther, *The Large Catechism*, in *The Book of Concord*, trans. and ed.
Theodore G. Tappert (Philadelphia, PA: Fortress Press, 1959), 447.

[15] *The Augsburg Confession*, article 10, in ibid., 34.

[16] Ibid., 51.

from God's command and the ordained use for which it is instituted in the Word of God.[17]

Without the sacramental "action," the "ordained use" of the Eucharist, frequently, though incorrectly, interpreted as the "reception" or *"sumptio"* of the body and blood of Christ in communion (often times called "receptionism"), the Eucharist is not the Eucharist and the body and blood of Christ are not present.

But what really is intended by "use" or "sacramental action" in this context? Herman Sasse, in his classic study of Luther's eucharistic theology, *This Is My Body*, critiques the idea of "receptionism":

> Luther and the early Lutheran Church avoided forming any theory about the "moment" when the Real Presence begins and the "moment" when it ceases. Some later orthodox theologians advanced the theory that Christ's body and blood are present only at the "moment" when they are being received. This is frequently regarded, within and without the Lutheran Church, as the genuinely Lutheran doctrine. . . . [But] as far as Luther himself is concerned, there cannot be the slightest doubt that he never did limit the Real Presence to the instant of distribution and reception. He never abandoned the view that by the words of consecration bread and wine "become" the body and blood of Christ. Otherwise neither the elevation, which was in use at Wittenberg up to 1542, nor the adoration of Christ, who is present in the elements, could have been justified. He always regarded it as Zwinglianism to neglect the difference between a consecrated and an unconsecrated host, and it has always been the custom of the Lutheran Church to consecrate the new supply of bread or wine or both if more is needed than originally was provided for. The rule that Luther, like Melanchthon and the Lutheran Confessions, followed was that that there is no sacrament, and consequently no presence of the body and blood of Christ, "apart from the use instituted by Christ" or "apart from the action divinely instituted." Since the word "usus" is explained by "action" it cannot mean the same as "sumptio." If it has sometimes been understood in this way, it must be said that neither Luther nor the Formula of Concord . . . identified the "sumptio" (eating and drinking) with the use or action of the sacrament.[18]

[17] Ibid., 588.

[18] Herman Sasse, *This Is My Body: Luther's Contention for the Real Presence of Christ in the Sacrament* (Minneapolis, MN: Augsburg Publishing House, 1959), 173–74.

In a related footnote Sasse adds:

> Luther demanded the dismissal of a pastor who had given to a communicant an unconsecrated host instead of a consecrated one, which had been dropped. This unfortunate man was imprisoned. Luther does not approve of such punishment, but he thinks him unfit for the Lutheran ministry: "He should go to his Zwinglians" (Letter of Jan. 11, 1546; WA Br 11, No. 4186). In 1543 Luther and Bugenhagen gave their opinion in a controversy about the question whether consecrated hosts could be preserved together with unconsecrated ones for another consecration. Luther criticizes this. Nothing of the consecrated elements should be saved, but must be consumed. In this connection he gives a clear definition of the sacramental "time" or "action": "sic ergo definiemus tempus vel actionem sacramentalem, ut incipiat ab initio orationis dominicae et duret, donec omnes communicaverint, calicem ebiberunt, particulas comederint, populus dimissus et ab altari descessum sit" (WA Br 10, No. 3894, lines 27ff.). In a Table Talk of 1540 Luther goes so far as to allow the blessed sacrament to be carried to another altar (in the same church) or even, as was still customary in some churches, to be brought to the sick in their home (WA TR 5, No. 5314), provided this could be regarded as part of the "action." This was tolerated as an exception. However, a reservation of the sacrament was not allowed. The remnants of the elements should be either consumed or burned.[19]

If there was at least general agreement on the real presence of Christ in the Eucharist with Rome (and with the Christian East, for that matter), the third captivity of the Eucharist, that of Eucharist as "sacrifice," proved to be an insurmountable obstacle and problem.[20] In previous chapters we have already seen that an unfortunate development in the West was the tendency to separate sacrifice from sacrament and consecration from the church's offering and communion, and such a

---

[19] Ibid.,174. The Latin phrase quoted above can be translated as: "In this way, therefore, let us define sacramental 'time' or 'action': that it might begin at the prayer of the Lord [*orationis dominicae*] and remain until all will have communed, the chalice will have been drunk, the particles [of bread] will have been eaten, and the people dismissed and left the altar." It is difficult to know if *orationis dominicae* here means the Lord's Prayer (= Our Father) or is a reference to the institution narrative.

[20] The best overall treatment of the Reformation debates and polemics over the question of eucharistic sacrifice is Frank Senn, *Christian Liturgy: Evangelical and Catholic* (Minneapolis, MN: Fortress Press, 1997), 267–98, 448–79.

separation was clearly inherited by Luther and other Reformers. What had been forgotten is that for Thomas Aquinas these concepts had been held together and that for Thomas the eucharistic sacrifice took place not at the offering but at the consecration; they were two sides of the same single dynamic event, seen from two different angles.[21] By the late Middle Ages this separation had become more exaggerated and was expressed increasingly by the various *expositiones missae* (expositions of the Mass) that were circulating and being studied. John Jay Hughes describes a view of the sacrificial understanding of the Mass current in these *expositiones* at the time of Luther:

> The celebrant first "brings about the miracle of transubstantiation," causing Christ's body and blood to be really and objectively present under the outward forms of bread and wine. And then he offers the body and blood of Christ (or sometimes simply Christ himself) to God the Father in sacrifice. This is the teaching of a pre-Reformation theologian like Gabriel Biel, whose *Exposition of the Canon of the Mass* was in its day a standard work of theology, which was studied closely by Luther before his first mass. . . . Biel explains that the prayer, *Unde et memores*, following the consecration, which speaks about offering "to your glorious majesty, from your gifts and presents, a pure, holy, and immaculate victim, the bread of eternal life and the cup of everlasting salvation," refers to the priest's offering of the flesh and blood of Jesus Christ—or simply Christ himself.[22]

Given Luther's theological position on justification by grace alone, for the sake of Christ alone, received by faith alone, and the fact that, increasingly, this "sacrifice of the Mass" was offered for the living and for the dead in purgatory alike, it is no wonder that he responded to this view with such vehemence and vitriol:

> Do you not hear? Christ has sacrificed himself once; henceforth he will not be sacrificed by anyone else. He wishes us to remember his sacrifice. Why are you then so bold as to make a sacrifice out of this remembrance? Is it possible that you are so foolish as to act upon your own devices, without any scriptural authority? If you make a sacrifice out of the remembrance of his sacrifice, and sacrifice him once more, why

[21] See John Jay Hughes, "Eucharistic Sacrifice Transcending the Reformation Deadlock," *Worship* 43 (1969): 541.

[22] Ibid., 537.

do you not also make another birth out of the memory of his   ʟ
that he may be born once more?[23]

And further:

> The Mass in the papacy must be regarded as the greatest and
> rible abomination. . . . It is held that this sacrifice or work of the Mass
> (even when offered by an evil scoundrel) delivers men from their sins,
> both here in this life and yonder in purgatory, although in reality this
> can and must be done by the Lamb of God alone.[24]

To the Mass as sacrifice Luther juxtaposed what became the classic Lutheran emphasis on the Eucharist or Lord's Supper as the "Last
Will and Testament of Christ," and that "will" and "testament" are,
precisely, what is promised by the narrative of institution, those words
which constituted for Luther "the sum total of the whole Gospel,"[25]
i.e., the Gospel in a nutshell. The reception of this testament and
promise of Christ in communion is antithetical to any view of the
Mass as sacrifice or some kind of good work performed by humans to
merit justification:

> Now if we properly understood . . . that the mass is nothing else than
> a testament and sacrament in which God makes a pledge to us and
> gives us grace and mercy, I think it is not fitting that we should make
> a good work or merit out of it. For a testament is *non beneficium accep-
> tum, sed datum*; it does not take benefit from us, but brings benefit to
> us. Who has ever heard that he who receives an inheritance has done
> a good work? He simply takes for himself a benefit. Likewise in the
> mass we give nothing to Christ, but only receive from him; unless they
> are willing to call this a good work, that a person sits still and permits
> himself to be benefitted, given food and drink, clothed and healed,
> helped and redeemed.[26]

Hence, since what becomes of the utmost importance is communion,
Luther may be said to have restored the "meal character" of the

[23] Martin Luther, *The Misuse of the Mass* (1521) in LW, 36, 147.
[24] Martin Luther, *The Smalcald Articles* (1537), II, in *The Book of Concord*, trans.
and ed. Tappert, 536–37.
[25] Luther, *Babylonian Captivity*, LW 36, 56.
[26] Martin Luther, *Treatise on the New Testament, That Is, The Holy Mass* (1520),
LW 35, 86–87.

ᴜcharist and, without the presence of communicants to hear the Word of promise and to receive the testament, there would be no Mass celebrated whatsoever in Lutheran circles. This principle was followed by all of the Protestant Reformers over and against Masses at which only the priest communed or private Masses offered for the various intentions of the living and the dead. It is thus no surprise that, while terms like "Mass" or "Sacrament of the Altar" continued in use, Lutherans and others came to prefer the terminology of "Lord's Supper," stressing its meal character.

This last will and testament of Christ "*pro nobis* [for us] and *pro me* [for me]" approach in his eucharistic theology clearly shapes Luther's two major liturgical reforms of the Mass in 1523 (Latin) and 1526 (German). The first of these, his Latin *Formula Missae et Communionis* for the church at Wittenberg retained much of the classic Western liturgical tradition, since he believed that "the service now in common use everywhere goes back to genuine Christian beginnings."[27] Hence, the classic structure of the Western liturgy, including the introits, graduals, and communion antiphons, together with the lectionary cycle, and the Ordinary of the Mass itself (*Kyrie, Gloria in excelsis, Credo, Sanctus,* and *Agnus Dei*) continued to shape Lutheran liturgy. But if Luther's reform of the Latin Mass was conservative in what it retained, it was also radical in what it deleted, namely, the offertory prayers and the *canon missae*:

> . . . that utter abomination follows which forces all that precedes in the mass into its service and is, therefore, called the offertory. From here on almost everything smacks and savors of sacrifice. And the words of life and salvation [the Words of Institution] are imbedded in the midst of it all, just as the ark of the Lord once stood in the idol's temple next to Dagon [1 Sam 5:2]. And there was no Israelite who could approach or bring back the ark until it "smote his enemies in the hinder parts, putting them to a perpetual reproach" [Ps 78:66], and forced them to return it—which is a parable of the present time. Let us, therefore, repudiate everything that smacks of sacrifice, together with the entire canon and retain only that which is pure and holy, and so order our mass.
>
> I. After the Creed or after the sermon let bread and wine be made ready for blessing in the customary manner. I have not yet decided

---

[27] Martin Luther, *Concerning the Order of Public Worship* (1523), LW 53, 11.

whether or not water should be mixed with the wine. I rather incline, however, to favor pure wine without water; for the passage, "Thy wine is mixed with water," in Isaiah 1:22 gives the mixture a bad connotation.

Pure wine beautifully portrays the purity of gospel teaching. Further, the blood of Christ, whom we here commemorate, has been poured out unmixed with ours. Nor can the fancies of those be upheld who say that this is a sign of our union with Christ; for that is not what we commemorate. In fact, we are not united with Christ until he sheds his blood; or else we would be celebrating the shedding of our own blood together with the blood of Christ shed for us. Nonetheless, I have no intention of cramping anyone's freedom or of introducing a law which might again lead to superstition. Christ will not care very much about these matters, nor are they worth arguing about. Enough foolish controversies have been fought on these and many other matters by the Roman and Greek churches. And though some direct attention to the water and blood which flowed from the side of Jesus, they prove nothing. For that water signified something entirely different from what they wish that mixed water to signify. Nor was it mixed with blood. The symbolism does not fit, and the reference is inapplicable. As a human invention, this mixing [of water and wine] cannot, therefore, be considered binding.

II. The bread and wine having been prepared, one may proceed as follows:

The Lord be with you.
Response: *And with thy spirit.*

Lift up your hearts.
Response: *Let us lift them to the Lord.*

Let us give thanks unto the Lord our God.
Response: *It is meet and right.*

It is truly meet and right, just and salutary for us to give thanks to Thee always and everywhere, Holy Lord, Father Almighty, Eternal God, through Christ our Lord . . .

III. Then: . . . *Who the day before he suffered, took bread, and when he had given thanks, brake it, and gave it to his disciples, saying, Take, eat; this is my body, which is given for you.*

After the same manner also the cup, when he had supped, saying, This cup is the New Testament in my blood, which is shed for you and for many, for the remission of sins; this do, as often as ye do it, in remembrance of me.

I wish these words of Christ—with a brief pause after the preface—to be recited in the same tone in which the Lord's Prayer is chanted elsewhere in the canon, so that those who are present may be able to hear them, although the evangelically minded should be free about all these things and may recite these words either silently or audibly.

IV. The blessing ended, let the choir sing the Sanctus. And while the Benedictus is being sung, let the bread and cup be elevated according to the customary rite for the benefit of the weak in faith who might be offended if such an obvious change in this rite of the mass were suddenly made. This concession can be made especially where through sermons in the vernacular they have been taught what the elevation means.

V. After this, the Lord's Prayer shall be read. Thus, *Let us pray: Taught by thy saving precepts.* . . . The prayer which follows, *Deliver us, we beseech thee,* . . . is to be omitted together with all the signs they were accustomed to make over the host and with the host over the chalice. Nor shall the host be broken or mixed into the chalice. But immediately after the Lord's Prayer shall be said, *The peace of the Lord*, etc., which is, so to speak, a public absolution of the sins of the communicants, the true voice of the gospel announcing remission of sins, and therefore the one and most worthy preparation for the Lord's Table, if faith holds to these words as coming from the mouth of Christ himself. On this account I would like to have it pronounced facing the people, as the bishops are accustomed to do, which is the only custom of the ancient bishops that is left among our bishops.

VI. Then, while the Agnus Dei is sung, let him [the liturgist] communicate, first himself and then the people. But if he should wish to pray the prayer, *O Lord Jesus Christ, Son of the Living God, who according to the will of the Father*, etc., before the communion, he does not pray wrongly, provided he changes the singular *mine* and *me* to the plural *ours* and *us*. The same thing holds for the prayer, *The body of our Lord Jesus Christ preserve my (or thy) soul unto life eternal*, and *The blood of our Lord preserve thy soul unto life eternal*.

VII. If he desires to have the communion sung, let it be sung. But instead of the *complenda* or final collect, because it sounds almost like a sacrifice, let the following prayer be read in the same tone: *What we have taken with our lips, O Lord.* . . . The following one may also be read: *May thy body which we have received* . . . (changing to the plural number) . . . *who livest and reignest world without end. The Lord be with you*, etc. In place of the *Ite missa*, let the *Benedicamus domino* be said, adding Alleluia according to its own melodies where and when it is desired. Or the *Benedicamus* may be borrowed from Vespers.

VIII. The customary benediction may be given; or else the one from Numbers 6:24-27, which the Lord himself appointed:

The Lord bless us and keep us. The Lord make his face shine upon us and be gracious unto us. The Lord lift up his countenance upon us, and give us peace.

Or the one from Psalm 67:6-7:

God, even our own God shall bless us. God shall bless us; and all the ends of the earth shall fear him.

I believe Christ used something like this when, ascending into heaven, he blessed his disciples (Luke 24:50-51).[28]

Luther's apparent "deletion" of the Roman Canon in his *Formula Missae* needs to be nuanced rather carefully. Some scholars have argued that for Luther it is not simply the *canon* as such but *any* eucharistic prayer that should be omitted in Lutheran liturgy in order to avoid the danger of confusing the gift character of the Eucharist with any human action toward God, even an action of *eucharistia*, thanksgiving.[29] Bryan Spinks, however, has demonstrated that what Luther actually did in the *Formula Missae* was to keep the narrative of institution in a traditional *prayer* form by attaching it to the short incipit of the eucharistic preface by the *qui pridie* ("who, the day before he suffered") clause.[30] By doing this and by concluding this structure with the *Sanctus* as a response, Luther here retained what can only be called a short eucharistic prayer at the traditional location of the Roman *canon missae*, what Spinks refers to as Luther's "mini-anaphora of praise." While Luther's contemporaries would have understood the *Sursum Corda*, preface, and *Sanctus* as only preliminary to the *canon* beginning after the *Sanctus* with the words *Te igitur*, a common misunderstanding supported, as we have seen, by the prominence given to the initial "T" in *Te igitur* within liturgical manuscripts since the

---

[28] Martin Luther, *An Order of Mass and Communion for the Church at Wittenberg* (1523), LW 53, 25–28, as appearing in PEER, 191–94.

[29] Oliver K. Olson, "Contemporary Trends in Liturgy Viewed from the Perspective of Classic Lutheran Theology," *Lutheran Quarterly* 26 (1974): 110–57.

[30] Bryan D. Spinks, *Luther's Liturgical Criteria and His Reform of the Canon of the Mass*, Grove Liturgical Study 30 (Cambridge: Grove Books, 1982). See also *idem*, "Berakah, Anaphoral Theory, and Luther," *Lutheran Quarterly* 3 (1989): 267–80.

eighth century,[31] modern liturgical scholarship correctly understands the eucharistic prayer as beginning at the *Sursum Corda*. In other words, what Luther did was to move the narrative of institution, the *Verba*, from its post-*Sanctus* position to a new and central position in the anaphoral preface before the *Sanctus*. And, in so doing he did not "eliminate" the Canon, as is often asserted; he altered it by composing a "new canon," one that rather unconsciously, according to Spinks, mimics those short ascriptions of praise and thanksgiving concluding with doxologies that characterized very early eucharistic praying.[32] What is of equal interest here is that by keeping all of this in Latin and by retaining the elevation of the Host at its medieval location during the *Benedictus*, the very experience of the *Formula Missae et communionis* would not have been much different from the regular experience of the Mass in the sixteenth century, its radical revisions apparent only to those who knew Latin well.[33]

Other Lutheran Reformers did not consider Luther's deletion of the Roman *canon missae* to be simultaneously a theologically or doctrinally normative statement about the use of a eucharistic prayer in general, something clearly born out by Lutheran liturgical revisions elsewhere. Philip Melanchthon in the *Apology of the Augsburg Confession*, article 24, speaks approvingly of the "Greek canon" (= ByzBAS and CHR), including its theology of offering.[34] Modeled on the *Quam oblationem* of the Roman Canon, the *Pfalz-Neuburg Church Order* of 1543, for example, contained the following consecratory petition in prayer form immediately before the narrative of institution:

> O Lord Jesus Christ, thou only true Son of the living God, who hast given thy body unto bitter death for us all, and hast shed thy blood for the forgiveness of our sins, and hast bidden all thy disciples to eat that same thy body and to drink thy blood whereby to remember thy death; we bring before thy divine Majesty these thy gifts of bread and wine and beseech thee to hallow and bless the same by thy divine grace, goodness

[31] See above, 205–6.

[32] See G. Cuming, "Four Very Early Anaphoras," *Worship* 58 (1984): 168–72; and above, 111–12.

[33] See Frank Senn, "Martin Luther's Revision of the Eucharistic Canon in the Formula Missae of 1523," *Concordia Theological Monthly* 44 (1973): 101–18. See also *idem, Christian Liturgy*, 278–79.

[34] *Apology of the Augsburg Confession*, in *The Book of Concord*, trans. and ed. Tappert, 265.

and power and ordain [*schaffen*] that this bread and wine may be [*sei*] thy body and blood, even unto eternal life to all who eat and drink thereof.[35]

And, of course, one must not neglect the liturgical reforms of the Lutheran Church in Sweden, where in 1531, under the leadership of Olavus Petri (student at Wittenberg from 1516–18), an Order of Mass was produced that contained a much-expanded version of Luther's "mini-anaphora of praise" from the *Formula Missae*. Still culminating in the *Sanctus*, this particular prayer included a longer christological thanksgiving before introducing the narrative of institution.[36] Olavus Petri's attempt here was but the first in a long line of Swedish liturgical ventures, which resulted throughout Sweden, according to Frank Senn, in "a church life that was both catholic and evangelical, embracing the whole population of the country and maintaining continuity with pre-Reformation traditions, but centered in the Bible's gospel."[37] Such "pre-Reformation traditions" included, in Sweden especially, more of an openness to speak of the Eucharist in sacrificial terms as the actualization of Christ's once-for-all sacrifice. Laurentius Petri, the brother of Olavus and archbishop of Upsala, whose own 1571 "High Mass" Church Order is still influential today in Sweden, could even say that it is the sacrifice of Christ in the Eucharist that is held by the priest and people between them and God's wrath.[38]

Luther's other major eucharistic liturgical reform was his German vernacular Mass, the *Deutsche Messe* of 1526. As table 7.1 indicates, this particular Mass took as one of its principles the substitution of German hymns for the Ordinary of the Mass, including the Creed. Prior to the narrative of institution (the *Verba*), now clearly separated from any prayer but sung in German, a paraphrase of the Our Father was inserted. In time those Lutheran churches following the *Deutsche Messe* tradition tended to delete this paraphrase and admonition, substituting instead a sung Lord's Prayer. It is important to note, however, that Luther continued to favor the elevation of the Host during the *Sanctus* in whatever version it might be sung. His rationale for this

[35] Luther Reed, *The Lutheran Liturgy* (Philadelphia, PA: Fortress Press, 1947), 753.
[36] See PEER, 202–3.
[37] Senn, *Christian Liturgy*, 394. On the Reformation in Scandinavia, see 393–447.
[38] See ibid., 467–77.

Table 7.1

Formula Missae 1523	Deutsche Messe 1526
[Sermon][39]	
Introit	Hymn or Psalm
Kyrie (ninefold)	*Kyrie* (threefold)
Gloria	
Collect	Collect
Epistle	Epistle
Gradual (Sequence)	Hymn (by choir)
Gospel	Gospel
Nicene Creed	Creed (German Hymn, "In one true God we all believe")
[Sermon]	Sermon
Preface (with *Verba* attached)	Lord's Prayer paraphrase/admonition
Sanctus (with elevation)	
Lord's Prayer	*Verba* (with possibility of distribution of Bread after the Words over the Bread and the Cup after the words over the Cup)
	Sanctus Hymn (with elevation)
Pax	
	Distribution (Hymn or German *Agnus Dei* during)
Communion (Agnus Dei during)	
Communio	
Final Collect	Post-Communion collect
Benedicamus	
Benediction	Benediction (Num 6)

demonstrates again that his view of eucharistic presence was not limited to the reception of communion:

> We do not want to abolish the elevation, but retain it because it goes well with the German Sanctus and signifies that Christ has commanded us to remember him. For just as the sacrament is bodily elevated, and yet Christ's body and blood are not seen in it, so he is also remembered and elevated by the word of the sermon and is confessed and adored in the reception of the sacrament. In each case he is ap-

[39] The location of the sermon or homily was not fixed in the Western liturgy and could take place even apart from the liturgy itself.

prehended only by faith, for we cannot see how Christ gives his body and blood for us and even now daily shows and offers it before God to obtain grace for us.[40]

And with regard to this retention of what would have been a prolonged elevation in its traditional Western location in both of these Masses, there is no question but that Luther continues liturgically the "Host piety" that had become dominant in the late Middle Ages. It is for this reason that Louis Bouyer once remarked, especially with regard to the *Deutsche Messe*, that Luther had invented "Benediction of the Blessed Sacrament" long before the Roman Catholic Church did.[41] In addition, in a suggestion that was to have far-reaching consequences later in liturgical history, Luther also stated his preference for a freestanding altar so that the "priest should always face the people as Christ doubtlessly did in the Last Supper."[42]

The story of Lutheran eucharistic liturgy in Europe following the publication of Luther's two Masses is the story of these two forms being adopted or adapted in what are called the *Kirchenordnungen*, the German Church Orders. These orders, prepared for various churches, cities, and states, number over 135 for the years between 1523 and 1555 and are concerned mostly, notes Frank Senn, with what is to be used and not used from the pre-Reformation liturgical books, since it is precisely those books (e.g., the Roman Missal and *Graduale*) that were needed for elements such as the chants, prefaces, etc., in the celebration of the Eucharist.[43] As a general characteristic, these orders tended to follow either the *Formula Missae* or the *Deutsche Messe* tradition, and occasionally a combination of them both.

For those who want to champion Luther as the great advocate of the vernacularization of Christian worship, Luther's *Deutsche Messe* serves as the primary model. But one must not forget that this Mass was developed specifically for "unlearned lay folk,"[44] and Luther

---

[40] PEER, 198.

[41] Louis Bouyer, *Eucharist: Theology and Spirituality of the Eucharistic Prayer* (Notre Dame, IN: University of Notre Dame Press, 1968), 388n14.

[42] Martin Luther, *The German Mass*, LW 53, 69.

[43] Senn, *Christian Liturgy*, 332–38. For the texts of these orders, see Emil Sehling, *Die evangelischen Kirchenordnungen des XVI. Jahrhunderts* 5 vols., Institut für Evangelisches Kirchenrecht (Aalen: Scientia Verlag, 1970–).

[44] Luther, *The German Mass*, 63.

never intended it to replace his *Formula Missae*, especially in cities and university settings. In fact, in the introduction to the *Deutsche Messe* he says explicitly:

> It is not now my intention to abrogate or to change this service [the Latin *Formulae Missae* of 1523]. It shall not be affected in the form which we have followed so far; but we shall continue to use it when or where we are pleased or prompted to do so. For in no wise would I want to discontinue the service in the Latin language because the young are my chief concern. And if I could bring it to pass, and Greek and Hebrew were as familiar to us as the Latin and had as many melodies and songs, we would hold Mass, sing, and read on successive Sundays in all four languages, German, Latin, Greek, and Hebrew. I do not at all agree with those who cling to one language and despise all others.[45]

Such an attitude clearly marked the early Lutheran liturgical tradition, with article 24 of the *Augsburg Confession* stating:

> Our churches are falsely accused of abolishing the Mass. Actually, the Mass is retained among us and is celebrated with the greatest reverence. Almost all the customary ceremonies are also retained, except that German hymns are interspersed here and there among the parts sung in Latin.[46]

As James White noted,[47] this normative pattern of Sunday eucharistic liturgy continued among the Lutheran churches for a good two centuries in Germany. At Leipzig, Sunday Mass might even have taken four hours because of the number of communicants, as well as the length of Lutheran sermons! If this practice disappeared in Leipzig in the eighteenth century, largely, according to White, as the result of the Enlightenment, it still continued in Sweden through the nineteenth. Unlike those attempts at more frequent communion within the Reformed tradition, as we shall see below, the Lutheran Reform of the Eucharist, including its location at the center of Sunday worship, was a success, at least for a time.

---

[45] Ibid., 62–63.
[46] *The Book of Concord*, trans. and ed. Tappert, 56.
[47] James White, *The Sacraments in Protestant Practice and Faith* (Nashville, TN: Abingdon Press, 1999), 85.

With regard to the liturgical ceremonies referred to immediately above, Lutherans came to regard many of these as *"adiaphora,"* that is, as "something that makes no difference," things that may or may not be done liturgically in the overall context of evangelical freedom. While an intra-Lutheran "Adiaphoristic Controversy" took place in the middle of the sixteenth century leading to the Peace of Augsburg in 1555, this controversy was more about what Roman Catholic practices (e.g., the seven sacraments, the Mass according to the Roman Rite, and veneration of the saints) could be accepted by Lutherans in Leipzig for the sake of peace and unity in the empire.[48] In 1577 the *Formula of Concord, Solid Declaration*, article 10, stated the normative Lutheran position on this question:

> Ceremonies neither commanded nor forbidden in God's Word, but instituted alone for the sake of propriety and good order, are not even a part of the service of God. The Church of every time and place has the power to change such ceremonies, as may be most useful and edifying. In time of persecution, we should not yield to the enemies in regard to such adiaphora. No church should condemn another because one has less or more external ceremonies not commanded by God than the other, if otherwise there is agreement among them in doctrine and in the right use of the Holy Sacraments.[49]

But what is fascinating in this regard is the evidence of Lutherans as late as the eighteenth century in some places retaining some very "Catholic" eucharistic practices. Edward Trail Horn in the late nineteenth century collated these practices reflected in the German Church Orders and elsewhere as follows:

> According to the Brunswick Agenda of Duke Augustus, 1657, the pastors went to the altar clad in alb, chasuble, and mass vestments. Sacristans and elders held a fair cloth before the altar during the administration, that no particle of the consecrated Elements should fall to the ground. The altar was adorned with costly stuffs, with lights and fresh flowers. "I would," cries [Christian] Scriver, "that one could make the whole church, and especially the altar, look like a little Heaven." Until the nineteenth century the ministers at St. Sebald in Nuremberg wore chasubles at the administration of the Holy Supper.

---

[48] See Senn, *Christian Liturgy*, 325–27.
[49] *The Book of Concord*, trans. and ed. Tappert, 611–12.

The alb was generally worn over the Talar, even in the sermon. [Valerius] Herberger calls it his natural Säetuch [seed-cloth], from which he scatters the seed of the Divine Word. The alb was worn also in the Westphalian cities. At Closter-Lüne in 1608 the minister wore a garment of yellow gauze, and over it a chasuble on which was worked in needlework a "Passion." The inmates and abbesses, like Dorothea von Medine, were seen in the costume of the Benedictines. The "Lutheran monks" of Laccuna until 1631 wore the white gown and black scapular of the Cistercian order. Still later they sang the Latin Hours. The beneficiaries of the Augustinian Stift [monastery] at Tübingen wore the black cowl until 1750. The churches stood open all day. When the Nuremberg Council ordered that they should be closed except at the hours of service, it aroused such an uproar in the city that the council had to yield. In 1619 all the churches in the Archbishopric of Magdeburg were strictly charged to pray the Litany. In Magdeburg itself there were in 1692 four Readers, two for the Epistle, two for the Gospel. The Nicene Creed was intoned by a Deacon in Latin. Then the sermon and general prayer having been said, the Deacon with two Readers and two Vicars, clad in Mass garment and gowns, went in procession to the altar, bearing the Cup, the Bread, and what pertained to the preparation for the Holy Supper, and the Cüster [verger] took a silver censer with glowing coals and incense, and incensed them, while another (the Citharmeister?) clothed and arranged the altar, lit two wax candles, and placed on it two books bound in red velvet and silver containing the Latin Epistles and Gospels set to notes, and on festivals set on the altar also a silver or golden crucifix, according to the order of George of Anhalt in 1542. The Preface and Sanctus were in Latin. After the Preface the communicants were summoned into the choir by a bell hanging there. The Nuremberg Officium Sacrum (1664) bids all the ministers be present in their stalls, in white chorrocken [surplices], standing or sitting, to sing after the Frühmesse [morning Mass], "Lord, keep us steadfast." The minister said his prayer kneeling with his face to the altar, with a deacon kneeling on either side. He arranged the wafers on the paten in piles of ten, like the shewbread, while the Introit and Kyrie were sung. The responses by the choir were in Latin. Up to 1690 the Latin service was still said at St. Sebald's and St. Lawrence's. Throughout this (eighteenth) century we find daily Matins and Vespers, with the singing of German psalms. There were sermons on weekdays. There were no churches in which they did not kneel in confession and at the Consecration of the Elements.[50]

---

[50] Edward T. Horn, "Ceremonies in the Lutheran Church," *Lutheran Cyclopedia* (New York: Charles Scribner's Sons, 1899), 82–83.

Ulrich Zwingli (1484–1531), John Calvin (1509–64),
and the Reformed Churches

If Luther and the subsequent Lutheran tradition represent a r.
conservative approach to the Western liturgical tradition, as wel.
retaining an objective understanding of Christ's eucharistic presence,
Ulrich Zwingli, the Reformer and parish priest of the Great Minster
in Zurich, Switzerland, from 1523 until his death in battle in 1531,
represents another side and another approach altogether, giving rise
to what has come to be known, especially through John Calvin, as
the Reformed tradition.[51] Sacraments, for Zwingli, did not convey the
grace that they signify "for by that argumentation restriction would
have been placed on the liberty of the divine Spirit, who distributes to
every one as he will, that is, to whom and when and where he will."[52]
Nowhere, however, is Zwingli more different from Luther—or from
Rome—than in his theology of the Eucharist. In his 1526 treatise *On the
Lord's Supper* this distinction is evident:

> For it is clear that if they insist upon a literal interpretation of the word
> "is" in the saying of Christ: "This is my body," they must inevitably
> maintain that Christ is literally there, and therefore they must also
> maintain that he is broken, and pressed with the teeth. Even if all the
> senses dispute it, that is what they must inevitably maintain if the
> word "is" is taken literally, as we have already shown. Hence they
> themselves recognize that the word "is" is not to be taken literally. . . .

> This [human] nature was a guest in heaven, for no flesh had ever pre-
> viously ascended up into it. Therefore when we read in Mark 16 that
> Christ was received up into heaven and sat on the right hand of God
> we have to refer this to his human nature, for according to his divine
> nature he is eternally omnipresent, etc. . . . . The proper character of
> each nature must be left intact, and we ought to refer to it only those
> things which are proper to it. . . . . The Ascension can be ascribed
> properly only to his humanity. . . .

> And this he signified by the words: "This is (that is, represents) my
> body," just as a wife may say: "This is my late husband," when she
> shows her husband's ring. And when we poor creatures observe this
> act of thanksgiving amongst ourselves, we all confess that we are of

---

[51] On Zwingli in general, see White, *Protestant Worship*, 59–63.
[52] Cited in J. C. D. Fisher, *Christian Initiation: The Reformation Period* (London: SPCK, 1970), 129.

> those who believe in the Lord Jesus Christ, and seeing this confession is demanded of us all, all who keep the remembrance or thanksgiving are one body with all other Christians. Therefore if we are the members of his body, it is most necessary that we should live together as Christians, otherwise we are guilty of the body and blood of Christ, as Paul says.[53]

As the above quotations make abundantly clear, the issues at stake for Zwingli, as for Luther, were decidedly christological in focus. Christ could be and is present "spiritually" in the Eucharist according to his divine nature, but he is not *bodily* present, since his "body" or human nature is located in heaven and could not be in two places at once. Such unity of the two natures as taught by Luther was for Zwingli tantamount to "Monophysitism," the blurring of Christ's humanity and divinity into a single nature, but this unity Luther understood by the traditional christological concept of the *communicatio idiomatum* (what is said of one nature is said equally of the other) and by appeal, in this case, to the ubiquitous presence of Christ—human and divine—everywhere, but by promise and Word in the Eucharist *pro nobis* in a saving way.[54] For Luther, alternatively, Zwingli's separation of those two natures was the equivalent of "Nestorianism," creating by this separation the equivalent of two distinct persons of Christ. And, indeed, what is behind Zwingli's christological approach is his strict separation of "matter" from "spirit" in terms of what grants or brings about salvation. As Gary Macy says: "the linchpin of Zwingli's theology was his radical separation of spirit and matter. Only spirit, God, could save human beings, and nothing in the material realm could effect salvation."[55]

Further, as is also demonstrated in the above quotations, for Zwingli, the word "is" in the narrative of institution ("This *is* my body . . . *is* my blood") is to be interpreted as "signifies" or "represents": it does not mean that the bread and wine literally *are* or become the body and blood of Christ in the Eucharist. Rather, as James White has written:

[53] Ulrich Zwingli, *On the Lord's Supper*, trans. G. W. Bromiley, LCC, XXIV, 195, 213, 234–35.

[54] For Luther's understanding of "ubiquity" in relationship to Christology and the Eucharist, see his treatise, *The Sacrament of the Body and Blood of Christ—Against the Fanatics*, LW 37, 212.

[55] Gary Macy, *The Banquet's Wisdom*, 151.

For Zwingli, the center of attention was not "this is," but "do this": what the community does in the Lord's Supper. Luther was traditional in focusing on the elements; Zwingli did indeed represent a new spirit in his focus on the community. What Luther did not appreciate was that Zwingli was stating in new way the reality of Christ's presence as a transubstantiation of the congregation rather than of the elements.[56]

With the exception of White's erroneous use of "transubstantiation" in this comment, since Zwingli himself would have abhorred such terminology, there is no question but that Zwingli does underscore the liturgical action and identity of the celebrating community in the Lord's Supper. With regard to this, Gary Macy notes correctly that:

> Zwingli's insistence on a spiritual presence of Christ in the sacrament might seem completely new in the sixteenth century, especially considering the emphasis that the later middle ages had placed on miracle hosts and the feast of Corpus Christi—all proofs of the real physical presence of the Lord. Yet Zwingli's theology has a certain medieval ring to it. . . . [T]he medieval theologians . . . had argued that the real point of the Eucharist, the *res tantum*, was the participation in the life of the church and in the life of the risen Lord. This union could be achieved apart from sacramental communion through "spiritual communion." Coupled with Zwingli's insistence that only Spirit mattered, the teaching on "spiritual communion" as the most important aspect of the sacrament could easily lead one to think that spiritual reception was the *only* reception.[57]

The apparently irreconcilable theological approaches of Luther and Zwingli and their supporters led to a colloquy in 1529 at Marburg, Germany, where, in an attempt toward negotiation and unity in the context of ecclesiastical and political threats and challenges, the Reformers met together in the hopes of producing an agreed-upon theological statement or confession. While several issues, in fact, were agreed upon, the "Lutherans" and "Zwinglians," as called by the Lutherans, failed to reach agreement on the bodily presence of Christ in the Eucharist. Even as nuanced by Zwingli's supporter, Martin Bucer at Strassbourg (1491–1551), that in the Eucharist we receive the "signs" of bread and wine outwardly while receiving Christ inwardly

[56] White, *Protestant Worship*, 59.
[57] Macy, *The Banquet's Wisdom*, 154.

259

by faith,[58] this did not meet the Lutheran position adequately since it did not safeguard that real presence "in, with, and under" the forms of bread and wine. Indeed, during the debate at Marburg, Luther had taken chalk and written on the library table in front of him, "Hoc est corpus meum" ("This is my body"), as an indication that there would be no compromise on the literal meaning of these words of Christ.[59] Consequently, the Marburg Colloquy represents the great split of the Protestant Reformation over the question of the eucharistic presence of Christ. For the most that could be agreed upon concerning the Eucharist, thanks really to the mediating influence of Bucer, was the following:

> [W]e all believe and hold concerning the Supper of our dear Lord Jesus Christ that both kinds should be used according to the institution by Christ; [also that the Mass is not a work with which one can secure grace for someone else, whether he is dead or alive;] also that the Sacrament of the Altar is a sacrament of the true body and blood of Jesus Christ and that the *spiritual partaking* of the same body and blood is especially necessary for every Christian. Similarly, that the use of the sacrament, like the word, has been given and ordained by God Almighty in order that weak consciences may thereby be excited to faith by the Holy Spirit. And although at this time, *we have not reached an agreement as to whether the true body and blood of Christ are bodily present in the bread and wine*, nevertheless, each side should show Christian love to the other side insofar as conscience will permit, and both sides should diligently pray to Almighty God that through his Spirit he might confirm us in the right understanding. Amen.[60]

But, in spite of this "agreement," it was clear that such a position was not acceptable to Luther himself and he responded to Bucer by saying, "Our spirit is different from yours; it is clear that we do not possess the same spirit."[61] The position of Zwingli on the presence of Christ in the Eucharist was similar ultimately to that of the Anabaptists, who for the Lutherans were known as the *Schwärmer*, or *Enthusiasts*, for whom the Eucharist was only an "ordinance" and little other than a

---

[58] See Senn, *Christian Liturgy*, 310–12; and White, *Sacraments*, 76–79.
[59] On this see Sasse, *This Is My Body*, 232, 294.
[60] *The Marburg Articles* (1529). Article XV, LW, 38, 88–89, emphasis added.
[61] Ibid., 70–71.

"memorial" of Christ's death. As Balthasar Hübmaier, an early Ana-
baptist leader notes:

> the Supper is nothing other than a memorial of the suffering of Christ
> who offered his body for our sake and shed his crimson blood on the
> cross to wash away our sins. But up to the present we have turned this
> Supper into a bear's mass, with mumbling and growling. We have
> sold the mass for huge amounts of possessions and money and, be it
> lamented to God, would gladly henceforth continue with it.[62]

It is precisely against this type of "memorialism" and eucharistic symbolism that the Lutheran tradition will become entrenched.

Like Luther, Zwingli also composed two different liturgical forms
of the Mass for use in Zurich: one in 1523, his *De Canone Missae Epicheiresis* ("Attack on the Canon of the Mass"), which was a very traditional form in Latin, including the replacement of the Roman Canon
with four Latin prayers of his own composition before the narrative
of institution; and one in 1525, the more radical *Action oder Bruch des
Nachtmahls* ("Action or Use of the Lord's Supper"). In the first of these
liturgical reforms, the continued use of elements such as the traditional distribution formula ("The body/blood of our Lord Jesus Christ
preserve you to everlasting life") might suggest some kind of acknowledgment of Christ's bodily presence. But the second of Zwingli's four
prayers makes it abundantly clear that Christ's true presence can only
be spiritual:

> O God, you fed not only man from his youth but also every living crea-
> ture. Feed our hungry souls, we pray, with heavenly food: for you are
> he who fills the hungry with good things. Our souls are spiritual, made
> in your image; therefore they can only be refreshed with spiritual food,
> *and that food can only be given by your word. Your word is truth: for you
> are truth, and from you nothing can come save that which is genuine, holy,
> steadfast and unspotted. Never deprive us of the food of your word, but ever
> feed us in your goodness. That is the true bread, which gives life to the world.*
> We would eat the flesh and drink the blood of your Son in vain, if we
> did not firmly believe above all things through the faith of your word,
> that your Son our Lord Jesus Christ was crucified for us and atoned for

---

[62] Balthasar Hübmaier, *Summa of the Entire Christian Life* (1525), in *Balthasar
Hübmaier: Theologian of Anabaptism*, trans. and ed. H. Wayne Pipkin and John
Howard Yoder (Scottdale, PA: Herald Press, 1989), 88.

s of the whole world. *He himself said that the flesh profits nothing,* *the Spirit which gives life. Quicken us, therefore, by your Spirit and deprive us of your word;* for your word is the vehicle of your Spirit, *surely it will never return to you empty.* By that one thing, and that alone, is the human mind set free, for it is the truth; and you have promised through your Son that if the truth sets us free, then indeed we shall be truly free. So we pray that we may never lack the food of your word, for by that one thing we are granted the freedom and security of salvation. Through your Son, Jesus Christ our Lord, who is alive and reigns with you in the unity of the Holy Spirit, God through all the ages of ages. Amen.[63]

While Zwingli's first reform met with little success, his 1525 *Action oder Bruch des Nachtmahls* was received well, though its influence on Reformed worship in general was minimal. In this *Action* almost all traditional liturgical texts and ceremonies have disappeared in favor of a radical simplicity, with communion itself being brought to and received by the congregation in their places. Not even does a formula of distribution remain in this rite.

[Nicene Creed, recited antiphonally between men and women.]

Then the server [i.e., minister, pastor] says:
Dear brothers, in keeping with observance and institution of our Lord Jesus Christ, we now desire to eat the bread and drink the cup which He has commanded us to use in commemoration, praise and thanksgiving that He suffered death for us and shed His blood to wash away our sin. Wherefore, let everyone call to mind, according to Paul's word, how much comfort, faith and assurance he has in the same Jesus Christ our Lord, lest anyone pretend to be a believer who is not, and so be guilty of the Lord's death. Neither let anyone commit offense against the whole Christian communion, which is the body of Christ.

Kneel, therefore, and pray:
Our Father, which art in heaven, hallowed be thy name. Thy kingdom come. Thy will be done, in earth as it is in heaven. Give us our daily bread. Forgive us our debts, as we forgive our debtors. And lead us not into temptation, but deliver us from evil.

The people say: Amen.

[63] PEER, 184 (emphasis added).

262

Now the server [minister, pastor] prays further as follows:
O Lord, God Almighty, who by thy Spirit hast brought us together into thy one body, in the unity of faith, and hast commanded that body to give thee praise and thanks for thy goodness and free gift in delivering thine only begotten Son, our Lord Jesus Christ, to death for our sins: grant that we may do the same so faithfully that we may not, by any pretense or deceit, provoke thee who art the truth which cannot be deceived. Grant also that we may live as purely as becometh thy body, thy family and thy children, so that even the unbelieving may learn to recognize thy name and glory. Keep us, Lord, that thy name and glory may never be reviled because of our lives. O Lord, ever increase our faith, which is trust in thee, thou who livest and reignest, God for ever and ever. Amen.

THE WAY CHRIST INSTITUTED THE SUPPER
The server [minister, pastor] reads as follows:
"On the night in which He was betrayed and given up to death, Jesus took bread: and when he had given thanks, he brake it, and said, take, eat; this is my body: do this in remembrance of me. After the same manner also, he took the cup after supper, said thanks, and gave it to them, saying, Drink ye all of this: this cup is the new testament in my blood. This do ye, as oft as ye do it, in remembrance of me. For as often as ye shall eat this bread and drink this cup, ye should shew forth and glorify the Lord's death."

Then the designated servers [ministers] carry round the unleavened bread, from which each one of the faithful takes a morsel or mouthful with his own hand, or has it offered to him by the server [minister] who carries the bread around. And when those with the bread have proceeded so far that everyone has eaten his small piece, the other servers [ministers] then follow with the cup, and in the same manner give it to each person to drink. And all of this takes place with such honor and propriety as well becomes the Church of God and the Supper of Christ.

Afterwards, the people having eaten and drunk, thanks is given according to the example of Christ, by the use of Psalm 112 [113].[64]

Coupled with the radical iconoclasm that characterized the Reformation in Zurich in general, Zwingli was quite content to have the Lord's Supper celebrated only on the traditional four occasions of the year

---

[64] ET from *Liturgies of the Western Church*, ed. Bard Thompson (New York: The World Publishing Co., Meridian, 1961), 153–54.

faithful of Zurich had been accustomed to receive com-
n the past: Christmas, Easter, Pentecost, and September 11,
ad been the local patronal feast of Saints Felix and Regula.[65]
larterly communions would come to be a hallmark of many
Prote..ant traditions.

After Zwingli's death in battle in 1531, the leadership of the Reformed movement passed to the great Reformer of Geneva, John
Calvin, often called the first systematic theologian of the Protestant
Reformation due to his multivolume *Institutes of the Christian Religion*
(originally published in 1536 with the final version appearing in 1559).
In contrast to Zwingli, Calvin had a much higher appreciation for the
sacraments as vehicles of God's grace and mercy for human beings.
James White summarizes Calvin's overall understanding of church
and sacraments, saying:

> Calvin's understanding of people is central to his whole approach to
> worship, and it is best to begin with this aspect of his thought and its
> consequences. No one had a dimmer view of the prospect of human-
> ity left to itself than Calvin, a view summed up in his view that "no
> part [of man] is immune from sin and all that proceeds from him is to
> be imputed to sin." Not only is humanity perverse but also ignorant
> of its own good. Such perversity and stupidity can be overcome only
> by God's grace, and God out of mercy has chosen to liberate a select
> number from the limitations of their humanity. God has gathered all
> the chosen in the church, where they might be instructed, disciplined,
> and joined together in praising their Redeemer for gratuitous mercy
> in choosing them. . . . But the mercy of God does not end there. The
> Creator, knowing even better than humans their capacity, "so tempers
> himself to our capacity," providing for the elect visible means to help
> them know God's mercies. The institution of sacraments provided
> those visible signs of God's love whereby God "imparts spiritual
> things under visible ones." There is a world of difference between
> Calvin's concept of the importance of signs, for humans to experience
> God's self giving, and Zwingli's dualism between nature and spirit.
> Calvin had recovered the biblical mentality that God uses material
> things to give us spiritual things. . . . Calvin saw the necessity of the
> church as the visible embodiment of God's will to save the elect. . . .
> The church was essential to salvation, and baptism was the entrance to
> the church.[66]

[65] See White, *Protestant Worship*, 62.
[66] Ibid., 64.

264

both and?

According to Calvin, a sacrament may be defined as a "testim[ony] divine grace toward us, confirmed by an outward sign, with m[...] attestation of our piety toward God."[67] Contrary to Zwingli, who arg[ued] that the sacraments are, primarily, signs of the church's "pledge" toward God, Calvin focused on their God-to-us direction. He continued:

> It is therefore certain that the Lord offers us mercy and the pledge
> of his grace both in his Sacred Word and in his sacraments. But it is
> understood only by those who take the Word and sacraments with
> sure faith, just as Christ is offered and held forth by the Father to all
> unto salvation, yet not all acknowledge and receive him.[68]

Indeed, based on the sacramental vocabulary of Augustine, the sacraments for Calvin were "visible Words," visible testimonies, or demonstrations of what God did and does for human salvation. This approach is shown clearly in his *Short Treatise on the Holy Supper of Our Lord and Only Saviour Jesus Christ* in 1541:

> We have already seen how Jesus Christ is the only provision by which
> our souls are nourished. But because it is distributed by the Word of
> the Lord, which he has appointed as instrument to this end, it is also
> called bread and water. Now what is said of the Word fitly belongs also
> to the sacrament of the Supper, by means of which our Lord leads us
> to communion with Jesus Christ. For seeing we are so foolish, that we
> cannot receive him with true confidence of heart, when he is presented
> by simple teaching and preaching, the Father, of his mercy, not at all
> disdaining to condescend in this matter to our infirmity, has desired to
> attach to his Word a visible sign, by which he represents the substance
> of his promises, to confirm and fortify us, and to deliver us from all
> doubt and uncertainty. Since then it is a mystery so high and incom-
> prehensible, when we say that we have communion with the body and
> blood of Jesus Christ, and since we on our side are so rude and gross
> that we cannot understand the smallest things concerning God, it was
> of consequence that he give us to understand, according as our capac-
> ity can bear it.
>
> For this reason, the Lord instituted for us his Supper, in order to sign
> and seal in our consciences the promises contained in his gospel

[67] Calvin, *Institutes of the Christian Religion*, 4.14.1, LCC, XXI, as cited in White, *Documents of Christian Worship*, 132.
[68] White, *Documents of Christian Worship*, 133.

concerning our being made partakers of his body and blood; and to give us certainty and assurance that in this consists our true spiritual nourishment; so that, having such an earnest, we might entertain a right assurance about salvation. Second, for the purpose of inciting us to recognize his great goodness towards us, so that we praise and magnify it more fully. Third, to exhort us to all sanctity and innocence, seeing that we are members of Jesus Christ, and particularly to unity and brotherly charity, as is specially recommended to us. When we have noted well these three reasons, which our Lord imposed in ordaining his Supper for us, we shall be in a position to understand both what benefits accrue to us from it, and what is our duty in its right use.[69]

It is in his *Institutes of the Christian Religion*, however, where Calvin attempts to balance the divisive theological positions of Luther and Zwingli seeking to refine them theologically:

5. Now here we ought to guard against two faults. First, we should not, by too little regard for the signs, divorce them from their mysteries, to which they are so to speak attached. Secondly, we should not, by extolling them immoderately, seem to obscure somewhat the mysteries themselves. . . .

7. Moreover, I am not satisfied with those persons who, recognizing that we have some communion with Christ, when they would show what it is, make us partakers of the Spirit only, omitting mention of flesh and blood. As though all these things were said in vain: that his flesh is truly food, that his blood is truly drink [John 6:55]; that none have life except those who eat his flesh and drink his blood [John 6:53]; and other passages pertaining to the same thing! Therefore, if it is certain that an integral communion of Christ reaches beyond their too narrow description of it, I shall proceed to deal with it briefly, in so far as it is clear and manifest, before I discuss the contrary fault of excess.

For I shall have a longer disputation with the extravagant doctors, who, while in the grossness of their minds they devise an absurd fashion of eating and drinking, also transfigure Christ, stripped of his own flesh, into a phantasm—if one may reduce to words so great a mystery, which I see that I do not even sufficiently comprehend with my mind. I therefore freely admit that no man should measure its sublimity by the little measure of my childishness. Rather, I urge my readers not

<hr />

[69] John Calvin, *Short Treatise on the Holy Supper of Our Lord and Only Saviour Jesus Christ* (1541), trans. J. K. S. Reid, LCC, XXII, 143–44.

to confine their mental interest within these too narrow limits, but to strive to rise much higher than I can lead them. For, whenever this matter is discussed, when I have tried to say all, I feel that I have as yet said little in proportion to its worth. And although my mind can think beyond what my tongue can utter, yet even my mind is conquered and overwhelmed by the greatness of the thing. Therefore, nothing remains but to break forth in wonder at this mystery, which plainly neither the mind is able to conceive nor the tongue to express. . . .

10. Even though it seems unbelievable that Christ's flesh, separated from us by such great distance, penetrates to us, so that it becomes our food, let us remember how far the secret power of the Holy Spirit towers above all our senses, and how foolish it is to wish to measure his immeasurableness by our measure. What, then, our mind does not comprehend, let faith conceive: that the Spirit truly unites things separated in space. . . .

19. But when these absurdities have been set aside, I freely accept whatever can be made to express the true and substantial partaking of the body and blood of the Lord, which is shown to believers under the sacred symbols of the Supper—and so to express it that they may be understood not to receive it solely by imagination or understanding of mind, but to enjoy the thing itself as nourishment of eternal life. . . .

26. Not Aristotle, but the Holy Spirit teaches that the body of Christ from the time of his resurrection was finite, and is contained in heaven even to the Last Day [cf. Acts 3:21]. . . .

30. Unless the body of Christ can be everywhere at once, without limitation of place, it will not be credible that he lies hidden under the bread in the Supper. To meet this necessity, they [i.e., Luther] have introduced the monstrous notion of ubiquity. . . .

32. Now, if anyone should ask me how this takes place, I shall not be ashamed to confess that it is a secret too lofty for either my mind to comprehend or my words to declare. And, to speak more plainly, I rather experience than understand it. Therefore, I here embrace without controversy the truth of God in which I may safely rest. He declares his flesh the food of my soul, his blood its drink [John 6:53-56]. I offer my soul to him to be fed with such food. In his Sacred Supper he bids me take, eat, and drink his body and blood under the symbols of bread and wine. I do not doubt that he himself truly presents them, and that I receive them.[70]

[70] John Calvin, *Institutes of the Christian Religion*, IV, 17 (1559), trans. Ford Lewis Battles, LCC, XXI, 1364–1404.

Like Luther, but unlike Zwingli, the above statements demonstrate that Calvin taught clearly that in the Lord's Supper communicants receive a "true and substantial partaking of the body and blood of the Lord" for the right assurance of salvation. That is, there can be no question but that Calvin affirmed the "Real Presence" of Christ in the Eucharist! At the same time, like Zwingli, Calvin also questioned the Christology of the Lutheran movement, especially Luther's notion of the ubiquity of both human and divine natures, claiming instead that Christ's human nature is finite and in heaven alone. If for Zwingli this was not a problem since communion was only "spiritual," Calvin had to find a mediating position since he affirms both the reception of Christ's body and blood in the Eucharist *and* the location of Christ's human body in heaven. Calvin's solution to this is ingenious. Whether he developed this from reading the early Eastern fathers (especially John Chrysostom) or through other contemporary Reformers, Calvin argued that what brings about this real communion with the flesh and blood of Christ in the Lord's Supper is the activity of the Holy Spirit.[71] As we read above:

> Even though it seems unbelievable that Christ's flesh, separated from us by such great distance, penetrates to us, so that it becomes our food, let us remember how far the secret power of the Holy Spirit towers above all our senses, and how foolish it is to wish to measure his immeasurableness by our measure. What, then, our mind does not comprehend, let faith conceive: that the Spirit truly unites things separated in space.

Calvin's solution, called by some a "pneumatological instrumentalism," in his attempt to find middle ground between the positions of Luther and Zwingli has been described as steering the course between "the Scylla of Luther's sacramental realism and the Charybdis

---

[71] The best treatment of Calvin's eucharistic theology to date is Sue A. Rozeboom, *The Provenance of John Calvin's Emphasis on the Role of the Holy Spirit Regarding the Sacrament of the Lord's Supper* (PhD dissertation, University of Notre Dame, August 2010), 154–74. See also the classic study of Killian McDonnell, *John Calvin, the Church and the Eucharist* (Princeton, NJ: Princeton University Press, 1967); and Hughes Oliphant Old, *The Patristic Roots of Reformed Worship*, Züricher Beiträge zur Reformatsgeschichte, vol. 5 (Zürich: Theologisches Verlag, 1970), 289–305.

of Zwingli's spiritualistic symbolism."[72] But with some exce
his attempt did not succeed in bringing about any large-sca
ment between the Reformed and Lutheran Reformations. In
to the Reformed christological position, which continued to
Lutherans as "Nestorian," as much as the Lutheran position ᴄᴏɴᴛɪɴᴜᴇᴅ
to strike the Reformed as "Monophysite," or even "Docetic" (the denial of Christ's real human body), the eucharistic question came down
to the problem of what the faithless or unworthy recipient of communion receives in the Lord's Supper. For the Lutherans, unworthy
reception (*communicatio impiorum*) still meant that Christ's body and
blood are received "in, with, and under" the forms of bread and wine
since they are there objectively by the Word. Hence, the faithless or
unworthy received them to their own condemnation (see 1 Cor 11:29).
For Calvin and the Reformed it is also important to discern the body
of Christ at communion and so avoid condemnation, as Paul says in
1 Corinthians 11:29, but since that presence of Christ is not *objectively*
connected to the bread and wine themselves, the body and blood of
Christ are not "here" but can only be received in faith by the activity
of the Holy Spirit simultaneously with (i.e., at the same time as) the
bread and wine as the communicants are lifted up to heaven where
Christ dwells. Hence, for Calvin, the unworthy, without faith, receive
only bread and wine. On this very issue Lutherans and Reformed have
remained divided until only quite recently.

It is often lamented by liturgical scholars that Calvin's theological
insights about the role of the Holy Spirit, as well as his theology of the
real presence, did not find expression in his liturgical reforms, though
a prayer invoking the Holy Spirit before the reading and proclamation
of the Scriptures did find a permanent place in Reformed worship,
and other Reformed theologians did try to incorporate such an approach in their own liturgical books.[74] In addition to having to settle
for a quarterly practice of the Lord's Supper in Geneva (in spite of the
fact that Calvin, like Luther, wanted it to be held every Sunday), the
liturgy itself became highly penitential in character. James White has
summarized this well:

[72] See Rozeboom, *The Provenance*, 305–6.
[73] See especially Senn, *Christian Liturgy*, 310ff.
[74] See Rozeboom, *The Provenence*, 342–82.

Parents who failed to raise their children in the faith, along with other transgressors, could be refused communion by a process known as "fencing the tables." This direct connection of worship and morality was to have a long, if not happy, legacy, for it gave worship a social function quite distinct from the glorification of God. . . . [I]t was felt necessary to use every opportunity to instruct and to reprimand; worship became the chief opportunity for this. Calvin's liturgy of 1542 strongly reflects the moral demands for righteousness. Its opening confession reminds worshipers that they are "incapable of any good and that in our depravity we transgress thy holy commandments without end or ceasing." To remove any doubt, the Ten Commandments were sung, a practice probably originating with Bucer in Strasbourg. At communion a long list of sins was read and everyone guilty of them categorically excommunicated. . . . The tone of the service is prolix and verbose, never lacking a chance to instruct, whether in the form of a prayer, spoken rubric, or exhortation. In fact, much of the instruction is addressed to the Almighty in the form of a prayer intended to be edifying to the congregation. So great was the imperative to teach that each service contains a condensed course in theology and ethics. This became a lasting characteristic of Reformed worship, contributing to its overwhelmingly cerebral character. . . . Calvin's is basically a penitential eucharist, serving the purpose of two sacraments, that of penance and that of the eucharist. For him, it seems more a case of being forgiven *in order* to receive the eucharist than being forgiven *through* receiving the eucharist.[75]

With the exception of any reference to the Holy Spirit lifting up our hearts and spirits on high, the following section from Calvin's influential liturgy at Geneva, *The Form of Church Prayers*, 1542, illustrates perfectly his eucharistic theology:

> Above all, therefore, let us believe those promises which Jesus Christ, who is the unfailing truth, has spoken with His own lips: He is truly willing to make us partakers of His body and blood, in order that we may possess Him wholly and in such wise that He may live in us and we in Him. And though we see but bread and wine, we must not doubt that he accomplishes spiritually in our souls all that He shows us outwardly by these visible signs, namely, that He is the bread of heaven to feed and nourish us unto eternal life. So let us never be unmindful of the infinite goodness of our Saviour who spreads out all

---

[75] White, *Protestant Worship*, 65–66.

His riches and blessings on this Table, to impart them to us that all that He has is ours. Therefore, let us receive this Sacrament as a pledge that the virtue of His death and passion is imputed to us for righteousness, even as though we had suffered them in our own persons. May we never be so perverse as to draw away when Jesus Christ invites us so gently by His Word. But accounting the worthiness of this precious gift which He gives, let us present ourselves to Him with ardent zeal, that He may make us capable of receiving it.

To do so, let us lift our spirits and hearts on high where Jesus Christ is in the glory of His Father, whence we expect Him at our redemption. Let us not be fascinated by these earthly and corruptible elements which we see with our eyes and touch with our hands, seeking Him there as though He were enclosed in the bread or wine. Then only shall our souls be disposed to be nourished and vivified by His substance when they are lifted up above all earthly things, attaining even to heaven, and entering the Kingdom of God where he dwells. Therefore let us be content to have the bread and wine as signs and witnesses, seeking the truth spiritually where the Word of God promises that we shall find it.[76]

THOMAS CRANMER AND THE LITURGICAL REFORMS IN ENGLAND

The eucharistic theologies and liturgical reforms of the three great European Reformers studied so far in this chapter, namely, Luther, Zwingli, and Calvin (the latter especially as mediated by Martin Bucer),[77] came to have far-reaching influences in the English reform under Thomas Cranmer.[78] During the reign of Henry VIII those eager

---

[76] John Calvin, *The Form of Church Prayers, Geneva, 1542; Strassburg, 1542*, in Thompson, *Liturgies of the Western Church*, 207.

[77] See E. C. Whitaker, ed., *Martin Bucer and the Book of Common Prayer*, Alcuin Club Collections 55 (Great Wakering, Essex: Mayhew-McCrimmon, 1974).

[78] On matters covered in this section, see Colin O. Buchanan, *What Did Cranmer Think He Was Doing?* Grove Liturgical Study 7 (Nottingham: Grove Books, 1976); Geoffrey J. Cuming, *A History of Anglican Liturgy*, 2nd ed. (London: Macmillan, 1982); Horton Davies, *Worship and Theology in England*, 5 vols. (London: Oxford University Press; Princeton, NJ: Princeton University Press, 1961–75); Gordon Jeanes, "Cranmer and Common Prayer," in *The Oxford Guide to The Book of Common Prayer: A Worldwide Survey*, ed. Charles Hefling and Cynthia Shattuck (New York: Oxford University Press, 2006), 21–38; and *idem,*

to pursue Protestant revisions to the liturgy—among them Cranmer, whom Henry had appointed as archbishop of Canterbury in 1533— were restrained by the king's conservatism. All that was allowed to happen was that readings from the Bible in English at Morning and Evening Prayer were authorized in 1543 and a form of litany in the vernacular in 1544. It was not until after the king's death in 1547, when his young son Edward VI came to the throne, that restraint on reformation was removed. It was then ordered that the readings at the Eucharist should be in English and that one of the homilies from a collection of twelve prepared by Cranmer some years earlier was to be read every Sunday. Later in the same year, it was directed that communion be received by the people in both kinds, bread and wine; to facilitate this and encourage more frequent reception of the sacrament, in March 1548, "The Order of the Communion" was authorized. This was not a complete eucharistic rite but merely a set of prayers of preparation and words for the distribution of communion which were to be inserted into the Latin Mass.[79]

In 1549 the first *Book of Common Prayer* (often simply called the "Prayer Book") was produced, with Cranmer as its chief architect; it was prescribed for use from Whitsunday (Pentecost) of that year onward. It contained a full set of services, including the Eucharist, titled "The Supper of the Lord and Holy Communion Commonly Called the Mass," which incorporated the material from the 1548 Order. Because the priest's vestments, the altar, and other church furnishings were left untouched, and the general pattern of the traditional eucharistic rite retained, congregations might well have imagined that it was simply a translation of the medieval service with which they were familiar. In reality, however, various parts of the rite were carefully worded so as to permit a wider interpretation of eucharistic doctrine. All reference to the sacrifice of the Mass was eliminated; the offertory rite focused instead on almsgiving; the only offering mentioned in the prayers was of "ourselves, our souls and bodies," and of the "sacrifice of praise." Any elevation of the consecrated bread and wine was forbidden, as was private Mass: the Eucharist was not to proceed beyond the offer-

---

Signs of God's Promise: Thomas Cranmer's Sacramental Theology and the Book of Common Prayer (London: Continuum, 2008).

[79] See PEER, 228–31; also Colin O. Buchanan, ed., *Background Documents to Liturgical Revision 1547–1549*, Grove Liturgical Study 35 (Nottingham: Grove Books, 1983).

tory when there were none present willing to receive communion with the priest.

Within three years, however, a second *Book of Common Prayer* was produced and replaced the first from All Saints' Day 1552. Scholars are divided over whether Cranmer had planned this version from the outset,[80] always intending the 1549 Book to serve merely as an interim measure to introduce the process of reform, or whether this later book only came into being as a reaction to certain conservative bishops— among them Stephen Gardiner, bishop of Winchester, who found that the first book was just about compatible with Catholic teaching—and under pressure for more radical reform from the likes of John Hooper, bishop of Gloucester. Be that as it may, the eucharistic rite in this new book admitted none of the ambiguity of the earlier version but was a thoroughgoing presentation of the belief that the essence of the Eucharist was intended to be the eating of bread and drinking of wine in grateful remembrance of Christ's death.

The word "Mass" disappeared from the title, it now being called "The Order for the Administration of the Lord's Supper or Holy Communion," and no worshiper entering the church the first time that it was used can have been in any doubt that something quite different was going on than before. The clergy were to wear only cassock and surplice, the stone altar had disappeared from the east end of the building, and a large wooden dining table was set up lengthwise in the chancel or in the body of the church, covered with a white linen cloth and with the priest standing on its north side to conduct the service. There was to be no singing, except for the *Gloria in excelsis* (which was moved to the end of the service as an expression of the praise that those who had received communion were now made worthy to offer), and the recitation of the Ten Commandments was introduced near the beginning, all of which contributed to imbuing the rite with a strongly penitential flavor.

[80] See Nathan D. Mitchell, "Reforms, Protestant and Catholic," in *The Oxford History of Christian Worship*, ed. Geoffrey Wainwright and Karen B. Westerfield-Tucker (Oxford and New York: Oxford University Press, 2006), 307–50, esp. 325–26.

Table 7.2

1549 and 1552 Liturgies Compared (Elements based on the 1548 "Order of the Communion" are indicated by asterisks)	
1549	*1552*
Lord's Prayer	Lord's Prayer
Collect for Purity	Collect for Purity
Introit Psalm	[omitted]
Kyries	Ten Commandments (with *Kyrie* responses)
Gloria in excelsis	[moved]
Collect of the day	Collect of the day
Collect for the King	Collect for the King
Epistle	Epistle
Gospel	Gospel
Nicene Creed	Nicene Creed
Sermon or Homily	Sermon or Homily
*Exhortation to communion	[moved]
Offertory Sentences	Sentences
	Prayer for the Church Militant
	*Exhortation to communion
	*Invitation to confession
	*Confession
	*Absolution
	*Comfortable Words
Eucharistic Prayer:	
Preface	Preface
Sanctus	*Sanctus*
Prayer for the Church Militant	*Prayer of Humble Access
Prayer for consecration	Prayer for worthy reception
(including institution narrative)	(including institution narrative)
Prayer of oblation	[moved]
Lord's Prayer	[moved]
Peace	[omitted]
*Invitation to confession	[moved]
*Confession	[moved]
*Absolution	[moved]
*Comfortable Words	[moved]
*Prayer of Humble Access	[moved]
*Communion (with *Agnus Dei*)	Communion
Post-communion sentences	Lord's Prayer
Prayer of Thanksgiving	Prayer of Oblation *or* Prayer of Thanksgiving
	Gloria in excelsis
*Blessing	*Blessing

As can be seen from table 7.2, other changes were also made to the order, particularly to the eucharistic prayer. The intercessions, called the "Prayer for the Church Militant," were removed and placed earlier in the service, and what had been the final part of the eucharistic prayer was deferred until after communion to become a prayer of oblation by those made worthy to offer themselves and their praise through their reception of the bread and wine. Now the eucharistic prayer terminated abruptly after the narrative of institution, without even an "Amen," so that the worshipers immediately did what the Lord had commanded them to do on that occasion and received communion straightaway. Moreover, the character of what was left in the prayer was altered significantly. It continued to affirm the once-for-all nature of Christ's sacrifice on the cross as in the first Prayer Book, but it no longer asked God "with thy Holy Spirit and word vouchsafe to bless and sanctify these thy gifts and creatures of bread and wine that they may be unto us the body and blood of thy most dearly beloved Son Jesus Christ"[81]—a petition that was capable of being interpreted as referring to either an objective or a subjective presence of Christ. Instead, it became merely a petition for the communicants, as indicated in italics below:

> Almighty God, our heavenly Father, which of thy tender mercy didst give thine only Son Jesus Christ to suffer death upon the cross for our redemption; who made there, by his one oblation of himself once offered, a full, perfect, and sufficient sacrifice, oblation, and satisfaction for the sins of the whole world; and did institute, and in his holy gospel command us to continue, a perpetual memory of that his precious death until his coming again; Hear us, O merciful Father, we beseech thee; and *grant that we, receiving these thy creatures of bread and wine, according to thy son our Saviour Jesus Christ's holy institution, in remembrance of his death and passion, may be partakers of his most blessed body and blood;* who, in the same night that he was betrayed, took bread; and when he had given thanks, he brake it, and gave it to his disciples, saying, Take, eat; this is my body which is given for you. Do this in remembrance of me. Likewise after supper he took the cup; and when he had given thanks, he gave it to them, saying, Drink ye all of this; for this is my blood of the New Testament, which is shed for you and for many, for remission of sins: do this, as oft as ye shall drink it in remembrance of me.[82]

---

[81] PEER, 239.
[82] Ibid., 248.

The words said at the distribution of the bread and wine were also changed to avoid the possibility that they too might be understood as referring to a localized presence of Christ in the bread and wine:

Book of Common Prayer, 1549
The body of our Lord Jesus Christ, which was given for thee, preserve thy body and soul unto everlasting life.
The blood of our Lord Jesus Christ, which was shed for thee, preserve thy body and soul unto everlasting life.[83]

Book of Common Prayer, 1552
Take and eat this in remembrance that Christ died for thee, and feed on him in thy heart by faith with thanksgiving.
Drink this in remembrance that Christ's blood was shed for thee, and be thankful.[84]

Not only that, but the instructions concerning the bread and wine at the end of the service made it clear that the bread was to "be such as is usual to be eaten at the table with other meats, but the best and purest wheat bread that conveniently may be gotten," and that "if any of the bread or wine remain, the Curate shall have it to his own use"—further reinforcing the understanding that they were not in any way changed by their use in this service.

The directions in the service concerning the manner of receiving communion had stated that the bread was to be placed in the communicants' hands (rather than directly in their mouths as in 1549 and in medieval practice) while they knelt. At the last minute it must suddenly have occurred to someone that kneeling for communion might be interpreted as evidence for a continuing belief in the presence of Christ in the eucharistic elements, and so an addendum was hastily inserted at the end of the service even while it was already being printed. Often called "The Black Rubric" because it was printed in black rather than in the red type used for the other rubrics (a sign of its last-minute addition), it is not really a rubric or direction at all but rather an assertion of the lack of doctrinal significance in the practice of kneeling for communion:

Although no order can be so perfectly devised, but it may be of some, either for their ignorance and infirmity, or else of malice and obstinacy,

[83] Ibid., 242.
[84] Ibid., 248.

misconstrued, depraved, and interpreted in a wrong part: And yet because brotherly charity willeth, that so much as conveniently may be, offences should be taken away: therefore we willing to do the same. Whereas it is ordained in the Book of Common Prayer, in the administration of the Lord's Supper, that the communicants kneeling should receive the Holy Communion, which thing being well meant, for a signification of the humble and grateful acknowledging of the benefits of Christ, given unto the worthy receiver, and to avoid the profanation and disorder, which about the Holy Communion might else ensue: Lest yet the same kneeling might be thought or taken otherwise, we do declare that it is not meant thereby, that any adoration is done, or ought to be done, either unto the sacramental bread or wine there bodily received, or unto any real and essential presence there being of Christ's natural flesh and blood. For as concerning the sacramental bread and wine, they remain still in their very natural substances, and therefore may not be adored, for that were idolatry to be abhorred of all faithful Christians. And as concerning the natural body and blood of our Saviour Christ, they are in heaven and not here. For it is against the truth of Christ's true natural body to be in more places than in one at one time.

Sometimes unfairly referred to as espousing "the doctrine of the real absence," this declaration on kneeling is concerned to assert that Christ's presence is a spiritual one that benefits only the *worthy* receiver and does not involve any change of *substance* in the bread and wine.

The 1552 Prayer Book was short-lived, however, as within a few months of its authorization Edward VI died (July 1553) and his Roman Catholic half-sister Mary came to the throne, throwing the whole reform movement into reverse, returning the English church to papal obedience and restoring the Latin Mass. Nevertheless, when Mary died and her Protestant half-sister Elizabeth inherited the crown in 1558, a reversion to something like the 1552 book, rather than attempting a major revision, seemed to be the safer course in order to promote political stability. Thus, although Cranmer had been put to death under Queen Mary, his liturgical composition lived on in the Church of England, with just a few small—though significant—changes, to make its doctrine less narrow. In the Eucharist of the Prayer Book of 1559, just two noteworthy changes were made: the complete elimination of the "Black Rubric" and the combining of the words of administration at communion from the 1549 book with those from the 1552 book, creating a rather lengthy formula to be said to each communicant but permitting the 1552 words to be interpreted in the light of the 1549 words (or, of course, vice-versa). One other change was made elsewhere in the book with relevance to the celebration of the Eucharist: at the beginning of Morning and Evening Prayer a note stated that "the Minister at the time of the Communion, and at all other times in his ministration, shall use such ornaments in the church as were in use by authority of Parliament in the second year of the reign of Edward the Sixth." Just what vestments and other ornaments were legal in that year is unclear, and it has been concluded that the statement may have been intended to be deliberately vague in order to permit some variation in practice.

Further changes in practice, however, were introduced by royal injunctions: when it was not being used for the eucharistic service, the communion table might be placed where the altar used to stand, and unleavened wafer-bread was prescribed for communion, in spite of the Prayer Book's direction to the contrary. This latter became a matter of some contention throughout the realm, until the Canons of 1604 resolved the question by ordering the use of "fine white bread."

It was always Cranmer's intention that the Eucharist should be celebrated every Sunday, but he was thwarted by the refusal of the laity in most places to change their ingrained habits of receiving communion only a few times each year. In the 1549 Prayer Book he had made efforts to encourage more frequent reception by providing an exhortation to be read to the congregation when the minister saw them reluctant to receive communion and by directing that at the time of the offertory the members of the congregation should go into the chancel to deposit their alms in the "poor men's box" set up there, apparently in the hope that they would then choose to remain in that place and become communicants rather than be seen by their neighbors walking back out of church. But his efforts were in vain, and without a sufficient number of communicants, a weekly Eucharist became an impossibility. In the Elizabethan period and for centuries afterward, therefore, the normal Sunday morning pattern in the Church of England became Morning Prayer, Litany, and Ante-Communion (the first half of the eucharistic rite up to the end of the "Prayer for the Church Militant").

In Scotland, meanwhile, reform had taken a different course. There the formal break with the papacy came in 1560, and under the leadership of John Knox Calvinism was established. The *Book of Common Order*, which Knox had drawn up while living with English Protestant exiles in Geneva, was adopted in 1562, with a revised and enlarged revision replacing it in 1564. The order for the Lord's Supper, which was to be preceded by a service of the word, began with an exhortation that included the quotation of 1 Corinthians 11 as a warrant for the celebration and stressed the need for penitence by intending communicants. There followed a substantial prayer of thanksgiving and the distribution of the bread and wine, during which a passage of Scripture was to be read. Then came a further prayer of thanksgiving, and the service concluded with the singing of a psalm of thanksgiving (Psalm 103 was recommended) and a blessing.

When James VI of Scotland became also king of England on the death of Elizabeth I in 1603, many Puritans in England hoped that he would be favorable to their desire to reform the English liturgy further toward this model. This did not happen,[85] and during the subsequent reign of his son Charles I, English practice tended to move in a more high-church direction, including the greater use of vestments for the clergy, candles, and even incense. The holy table was frequently left in its "altar" position even during the celebration of the Eucharist and was covered with a rich cloth down to the floor on all sides (later known as a "Laudian frontal" after William Laud, the archbishop of Canterbury at the time); the priest, however, still followed the Prayer Book rubric requiring him to stand on its north side. Although Laud and the other high-church bishops and clergy would have desired to revise the English Prayer Book to reflect their own eucharistic doctrine, they recognized the political dangers inherent in that from the Puritans and refrained from doing so. They did, however, attempt to foist something similar on the church in Scotland in a new Prayer Book in 1637.[86] Its eucharistic rite reinstated some of the features of the 1549 Prayer Book: after the *Sanctus* what was now called "The Prayer

[85] See Colin O. Buchanan, ed., *The Hampton Court Conference and the 1604 Book of Common Prayer*, Alcuin/GROW Joint Liturgical Study 68 (Norwich: Hymns Ancient and Modern, 2009); also Bryan D. Spinks, *From the Lord and "the Best Reformed Churches": A Study of the Eucharistic Liturgy in the English Puritan and Separatist Traditions, 1550–1633* (Rome: CLV-Edizioni Liturgische, 1984).

[86] For text, see *The Book of Common Prayer and Administration of the Sacraments and Other Parts of Divine Service for the Use of the Church of Scotland: Commonly Known as Laud's Liturgy (1637)*, ed. James Cooper (Edinburg: William Blackwood and Sons, 1904).

of Consecration" closely followed the 1549 form, including the Prayer of Oblation at its end. The Lord's Prayer and Prayer of Humble Access were moved from their 1552 positions and came after this, leading into the distribution, at which the 1549 forms of words were adopted. The book was firmly rejected by the Scots and never used at the time.[87]

In England too the subsequent outbreak of civil war led to Elizabeth's Prayer Book being outlawed by Parliament in 1645 and replaced with the Westminster Directory of Public Worship. Although its directions for "the celebration of the Communion, or Sacrament of the Lord's Supper" were broadly similar to those in the Scottish *Book of Common Order*, they reflect a somewhat "higher" doctrine than was expressed in that book, speaking of the minister "sanctifying and blessing the elements of bread and wine," this being accomplished "by the word of institution and prayer." In the prayer God is to be asked to "vouchsafe his presence, and the effectual working of his Spirit in us, and so to sanctify these elements both of bread and wine, and to bless his own ordinance, that we may receive by faith the body and blood of Jesus Christ crucified for us." The words used at the distribution were to be: "Take ye, eat ye; this is the body of Christ which is broken for you. Do this in remembrance of him." "This cup is the New Testament in the blood of Christ, which is shed for the remission of the sins of many; drink ye all of it."[88]

When Charles II regained the English throne in 1660, there were hopes that a liturgical compromise might be found between the wishes of the Anglicans and the desires of the Puritans,[89] but hardly any concessions were made to the latter, and the Eucharist in the revised *Book of Common Prayer* authorized in 1662 was still basically the service from the Elizabethan Book with a few small though significant changes to the rubrics. As in the ill-fated Scottish liturgy of 1637, the prayer before communion was now titled "The Prayer of Consecra-

---

[87] See Gordon Donaldson, *The Prayer Book in Scotland 1549–1949* (Dundee: Winter, 1949); Duncan Forrester and Douglas Murray, eds., *Studies in the History of Worship in Scotland* (Edinburgh: T & T Clark, 1984); Bryan D. Spinks, *Sacraments, Ceremonies and the Stuart Divines: Sacramental Theology and Liturgy in England and Scotland 1603–1662* (Aldershot: Ashgate, 2002).

[88] See Ian Breward, ed., *The Westminster Directory*, Grove Liturgical Study 21 (Nottingham: Grove Books, 1980), 21–23.

[89] See Colin O. Buchanan, ed., *The Savoy Conference Revisited*, Alcuin/GROW Joint Liturgical Studies 54 (Cambridge: Grove Books, 2002).

tion," and the priest was directed not only to take the bread and wine into his hands while saying the equivalent words in the institution narrative (as in the 1549 and 1637 books) but also to break the bread at the mention of Jesus doing so. None of the other alterations to the order from the Scottish book were adopted, but the final rubrics were amended so that they directed that it was only "unconsecrated" bread and wine that the Curate was to have to his own use. Perhaps somewhat surprisingly, the "Black Rubric" from the 1552 book, struck out in 1559, was reinstated, but with a single change of wording that significantly altered its meaning: "corporal" replaced "real and essential" so that all it was denying was that adoration was being done to any *corporal* presence of Christ's natural flesh and blood. Though the rite as it stood probably did not fully satisfy anyone's eucharistic theology, it was a workable compromise and one that has continued to serve the Church of England down to the present day. For, while alternative forms of eucharistic celebration have been authorized in recent years, the 1662 rite continues to be established by law and used, at least on some occasions, in a good number of parish churches and cathedrals.[90]

The service in the 1662 Prayer Book also became the basis, adapted to a greater or lesser extent, for those used in other provinces throughout the worldwide Anglican Communion as they emerged in subsequent centuries,[91] and its influence extended even outside Anglicanism, with some Free Church traditions sometimes drawing upon it as well as creating forms of their own.[92] Nor did the 1637 Scottish rite disappear without trace. While the Church of Scotland itself reverted to its Calvinist and Presbyterian roots after the accession of William of Orange in 1688, the minority Scottish Episcopal Church adopted a variant of the 1637 Eucharist in its 1764 "Communion-Office," which was more "Eastern" in shape, locating the epiclesis after the institution narrative and anamnesis, and strengthened the language of oblation

[90] For the later history of the rite, in addition to Cuming, *History of Anglican Liturgy*, see also Ronald C. D. Jasper, *The Development of the Anglican Liturgy 1662–1980* (London: SPCK, 1989).
[91] See Bernard Wigan, ed., *The Liturgy in English*, Alcuin Club Collections 43 (London: Oxford University Press, 1962; 2nd ed. 1964).
[92] See, for example, Alexander Elliott Peaston, *The Prayer Book Tradition in the Free Churches* (London: Clarke, 1964); Bryan D. Spinks, *Freedom or Order? The Eucharistic Liturgy in English Congregationalism 1645–1980* (Allison Park, PA: Pickwick, 1984).

and consecration. As a result of the consecration in Scotland of Samuel Seabury as the first American bishop in 1784, this Scottish Eucharist strongly influenced the American rite of 1789 and subsequent American Prayer Books, as well as those in some other parts of the Anglican Communion.

John Wesley extended the use of the 1662 Prayer Book service into Methodism. He himself valued the Eucharist very highly, either celebrating or receiving communion more than once a week, in contrast to the infrequent celebrations more usual among Anglicans at the time. He regarded it as a "converting ordinance" for those with some faith who were seeking full assurance, and when he took the step of ordaining elders to serve in the United States, he encouraged them to celebrate it every Sunday. For that purpose, he included in *The Sunday Service of the Methodists in North America* an Order for the Lord's Supper that was simply an abbreviated version of the Anglican service: "elder" replaced "priest," the Collect for the King, the Creed, the Exhortations, and the alternative post-communion Prayer of Thanksgiving were omitted, and a new rubric permitted extempore prayer at the end. This rite continued to provide the basic framework for subsequent eucharistic services in most forms of Methodism down into the twentieth century.[93]

THE COUNCIL OF TRENT AND THE MISSALE ROMANUM OF PIUS V (1570)

As noted above, both "Counter" Reform and "Catholic" Reform were the concerns of the Council of Trent, which met in some twenty-five sessions over three separate periods (1545–47, 1551–52, and 1562–63).[94] With regard to eucharistic theology and liturgy leading to the eventual reform of the *Missale Romanum* in 1570 under Pope Pius V, three of the council's sessions are significant: Session Thirteen (October 11, 1551); Session Twenty-One (July 16, 1522); and Session Twenty-Two (September 17, 1562). The dates here reflect the acceptance of the various canons and decrees of these sessions by the council fathers.

---

[93] See John C. Bowmer, *The Sacrament of the Lord's Supper in Early Methodism*, (London: Dacre, 1951); *idem, The Lord's Supper in Methodism 1791–1960* (London: Epworth Press, 1961); James F. White, *John Wesley's Sunday Service of the Methodist in North America* (Nashville, TN: United Methodist Publishing House, 1984); and Karen Westerfield-Tucker, *American Methodist Worship* (New York: Oxford University Press, 2001).

[94] See above, note 3.

Session Thirteen: The Holy Eucharist

The "Decree Concerning the Most Holy Sacrament of the Eucharist" contained eight chapters and eleven canons.[95] Of particular significance in the doctrinal section, first of all, is the strong stance taken against the Reformed approach of both Zwingli and Calvin in asserting that while Christ "sits always at the right hand of the Father in heaven according to the natural mode of existing [*juxta modum existendi naturalem*]," he also exists in many places "sacramentally [*sacramentaliter*] present to us in His own substance by a manner of existence . . . we can scarcely express in words" (chap. 1). This substantial presence of Christ is underscored in chapter 3 where it is noted that "immediately after the consecration the true body and blood of our Lord, together with His soul and divinity exist under the form of bread and wine." Second, in addition to maintaining the doctrine of concomitance (chap. 3), the doctrine of transubstantiation is upheld: the conversion of bread and wine into the body and blood of Christ "is conveniently [*convenienter*] and properly [*proprie*] called transubstantiation" (chap. 4). Related to this, the decree notes in chapters 5 and 6 that the highest form of worship (*latria*) is due to the Eucharist, that eucharistic processions and feasts are to be maintained, and that reservation for the communion of the sick is to be retained. Finally, the last two chapters (7 and 8) are concerned with preparation for the reception of communion and the proper use of this sacrament.

Within the canons condemning the theological positions of the Protestant Reformers, many of these same elements appear. Against Zwingli, Calvin, and others, in canons 1 and 8, for example, Christ's presence as only "in a sign, or figure, or force" is rejected in favor of his true, real, and substantial (*vere, realiter, et substantialiter*) presence, as well his being received sacramentally and "really," as opposed to "spiritually" (*spiritualiter*) alone. And in canon 2, transubstantiation is again defended, this time with the word *aptissime* ("most aptly"), that is, the conversion of the bread and wine "the Catholic Church most aptly [*aptissime*] calls transubstantiation."

What strikes one as quite surprising is the rather general way in which transubstantiation appears to be treated in the canons and decrees of this session. The doctrinal chapter on real presence (chap. 1)

[95] ET here and throughout from *The Canons and Decrees of the Council of Trent*, trans. H. J. Schroeder (St. Louis, MO: B. Herder Book Co., 1950). Decrees will be identified in the text simply by chapter or canon.

is in fact *separate* from that on transubstantiation itself (chap. 4), and, as we have seen, description of transubstantiation as the process of eucharistic transformation is limited to words like "fitting" and "appropriate" (*convenienter; proprie*) and "most apt" (*aptissime*). Hence, real presence and transubstantiation are not treated as equivalent. As Piet Schoonenberg once noted, the dominant intention at Trent "was to affirm and safeguard the belief in the real presence" itself—the "what" and not the "how" of that presence![96] In other words, while transubstantiation is certainly defended against the Reformers, the language used suggests that there could be other proper, convenient, and apt possibilities for interpreting the eucharistic conversion. In fact, as James McCue has noted, there were those at the council who suggested that transubstantiation not be used at all since the doctrine of the real presence had already been asserted clearly in chapter 1 of the decree.[97]

Session Twenty-One: Holy Communion

Although chapter 2 of the decree in Session Thirteen had underscored the reason for Christ's real presence in the Eucharist as "the spiritual food of souls" in the reception of communion, the discussion of the necessity of communion under both species (*sub utraque specie*) and related topics had been postponed at the end of Session Thirteen, out of respect for the Protestants of the "glorious province of Germany" to whom had been promised safe passage, that they might come to Trent to express their views. It took eleven years for this discussion to resume—and then without the presence of Protestants from Germany—and "The Doctrine of Communion under Both Kinds and the Communion of Little Children," with its four chapters and four canons, is easily summarized. Against all the Reformers, the *divine necessity* of communion under both species is denied for both laity and non-offering clergy in that communion with bread alone is not an error, that each species is in accord with Christ's institution, and that "Christ, whole and entire [*totum atque integrum*]" is received in either form alone (chap. 3). Similarly, children are not bound to receive the Eucharist prior to reaching the "age of discretion." Finally, while concomitance is clearly defended, the door is left open to making a

---

[96] Piet Schoonenberg, "Transubstantiation: How Far Is This Doctrine Historically Determined?" *Concilium* 24 (New York: Paulist Press, 1967), 78–91, here at 85.

[97] McCue, "The Doctrine of Transubstantiation," 119.

possible concession on the use of the chalice for the communion of the laity "under certain conditions," although this issue is to be examined and defined at another time. That other time would appear to have been in Session Twenty-Two where, in response to a petition made by the German Protestants, the question was referred to the pope.

Session Twenty-Two: The Mass
Two emphases regarding the Eucharist and its liturgical celebration appear in this session: first, the "Doctrine Concerning the Sacrifice of the Mass," with its nine chapters and canons, and, second, a decree "Concerning the Things to be Observed and Avoided in the Celebration of Mass." In addition to underscoring the desirability of frequent communion reception by the faithful (chap. 6) and frequent preaching by clergy (chap. 7), the major focus here, against the theological positions of all the Reformers, is on the Mass as a propitiatory sacrifice. Hence, the Mass is called "a visible sacrifice" whereby Christ's "bloody sacrifice . . . might be represented [*repraesentaretur*] . . . and its salutary effects applied" (chap. 1). Further, Christ is "immolated [*immolandum*] under visible signs by the Church through the priests in memory of his own passage . . . to the Father" (chap. 1). In this sacrifice Christ "is contained and immolated in an unbloody manner" with the result that it is propitiatory, "for the victim is one and the same, the same now offering by the ministry of priests who then offered Himself on the cross, the manner alone of offering being different [*sola offerendi ratione diversa*]" (chap. 2). Since these, along with real presence in Session Thirteen, are the two key doctrinal or theological emphases of Trent on the Eucharist, some additional comment is necessary.

While Francis Clark[98] argued that official Catholic teaching on the eucharistic sacrifice was clear all along, the fact of the matter is that Trent is the first council to define the Eucharist as a sacrifice. John Jay Hughes (in disagreement with Clark's position) notes that in the centuries preceding Trent, as we saw in chapter 6 above, the primary theological focus had been on real presence and not on sacrifice. So, when Luther first launched his attack on the sacrificial understanding of the Mass, he caught the Catholic theologians somewhat off-guard.[99] And not finding Aquinas' use of representation adequate to their needs (since

---

[98] See Francis Clark, *Eucharistic Sacrifice and the Reformation* (Westminster: The Newman Press, 1960).
[99] Hughes, "Eucharistic Sacrifice," 536.

representation tended now not to be understood objectively), the Catholic Apologists went beyond this and posited an offering "subsequent to and separate from the consecration,"[100] now narrowly associated with the recitation of the narrative of institution. While in Aquinas Christ's immolation was not separate from the consecration—the sacrifice *is* the presence of his body and blood offered—Trent inherited and fostered (especially through its *Catechism* in 1566) the separation of sacrament, communion, and sacrifice and so could not interpret all three as part of an integral unitary reality in relationship to what might be called a commemorative actual presence of the total Christ event.[101]

The second primary emphasis in Session Twenty-Two concerns the liturgical celebration of the Mass, especially with regard to what the Catholic Reformers themselves had uncovered as the rather dismal state of liturgical life in the late sixteenth century. What the decree "Concerning the Things to be Observed and Avoided in the Celebration of Mass" reveals is but a short summary of the kinds of things that the Tridentine Commission on Mass Abuses had uncovered.[102] The council's decree itself refers to abuses related to "avarice" (e.g., problems with Mass stipends), "irreverence" (e.g., clerical immorality, wandering priests, and "lascivious or impure music"), and "superstition" (e.g., fixed numbers of votive Masses for particular intentions, numbers of candles, and the need for the use of only approved prayers and Mass formulas). This decree, above all, paves the way toward the publication of the new Missal, which appeared finally in 1570, several years after the Council of Trent itself was over.

Calls for and attempts at liturgical reform of the various Missals in use had been made beginning in the late fifteenth and early sixteenth centuries, at least at the diocesan and synodal level.[103] But the Council

---

[100] Ibid., 537.

[101] See David Power, *The Sacrifice We Offer: The Tridentine Dogma and Its Reinterpretation* (New York: Crossroad, 1987); and E. Kilmartin, *The Eucharist in the West*, ed. Robert Daly (Collegeville, MN: Liturgical Press, Pueblo, 1998), 169–78.

[102] The report of this commission is available in *Concilium Tridentinum: Diariorum, Actorum Epistularum, Tractatuum nova collectio*, vol. 8 (Freiburg: Herder, 1901), 916–21. See also Reinhold Theisen, *Mass Liturgy and the Council of Trent* (Collegeville, MN: Saint John's University Press, 1965); and *idem*, "The Reform of Mass Liturgy and the Council of Trent," *Worship* 4 (1966), 565–83.

[103] The best guide to this development is Hubert Jedin, "Das Konzil von Trient und die Reform der liturgischen Bücher," in *idem*, *Kirche des Glaubens, Kirche der Geschichte* (Freiburg: Herder, 1966), 499–525.

of Trent itself was unable to accomplish the needed liturgical reforms of the books and so in 1563 this task was commended to Pope Pius V, under whose pontificate was produced both the *Breviarium Romanum* (Roman Breviary) in 1568 and the *Missale Romanum* in 1570. Pope Pius' promulgation of this Missal, *Quo primum*, on July 14, 1570, describes the process by which the experts or "learned men" (*eruditis delectis viris*) in his employ accomplished their work:

> The Council of Trent reserved to us the publication and correction of the holy books, of the catechism, the missal, and the breviary; once, thanks to God, the catechism for the formation of the people, and the corrected breviary for the celebration of the praise due to God were published, it appeared necessary for us to consider immediately what remained to be done in this area, namely, the publication of the missal so that it correspond to the breviary, as is right and fitting, just as it is desirable that in the church of God there be one manner of saying the office and one single rite for celebrating Mass. This is why we entrusted this work to men chosen for their learning. They closely compared everything with the ancient manuscripts, corrected and incorrupt, collected from all over; they consulted the writings of those ancient and trustworthy authors who have left us information concerning the holy arrangement of these rites, and they restored the rites of the Mass to the form received from the holy Fathers. Having examined and checked this, and after full consideration, we have ordered that the Missal be published at Rome as soon as possible . . . so that the usages of the holy Roman Church, mother and teacher of all other churches, be adopted and observed by all. . . . We prescribe and order by this declaration, whose force is perpetual, that all the churches relinquish the use of their proper missals . . . ; exceptions are made for a rite approved at its origin by the Apostolic See or for a custom faithfully observed by these churches for at least two hundred years for the celebration of Mass; it is not our intention to suppress in any way such a rite or custom.[104]

This new Missal, a sixteenth-century *Novus Ordo*, was clearly that— not a mere codification or reprinting of what had come before, but a new publication with the clear attempt at *restoring* and *correcting* late medieval eucharistic liturgy according to what was then believed to be the "form received from the holy Fathers" (*ad pristinam Missale*

---

[104] Pope Pius V, *Quo primum tempore*; ET in R. Cabié, *History of the Mass* (Portland, OR: The Pastoral Press, 1990), 87.

ipsum sanctorum Patrum normam ac ritum restituerunt). Indeed, among the council fathers themselves were those who thought that the *canon missae* had been composed either by St. Peter or St. James, the apostles.[105] But, of course, as we saw in chapter 6 above, the *Roman* Rite by this point had become such a synthesis of essentially Roman and Gallican elements that any kind of true restoration of *the* Roman Rite was not really possible. Nor was the liturgical scholarship available at that time to undertake such a process.

Furthermore, it is important not to overlook Pius V's concession to other approved rites or liturgical customs that had been used for at least two hundred years. What this meant, of course, is that older religious orders (e.g., Benedictines, Cistercians, Dominicans, Franciscans, etc.) could and did continue to use their own Missals for the celebration of the Eucharist, and it is not insignificant to note that Pius V was himself a Dominican. Theoretically, it also meant that almost any diocese could make a similar claim to continue using its own diocesan Missals. But the liturgical chaos of this period[106] made the use of the new Missal of Pius V quite welcome in most areas. Nevertheless, there is to be noted a significant shift here from the authority of the local bishop regulating liturgical affairs in his diocese to a now more centralized approach coming from Rome. That is, if in the past the Missal in use might reflect the name of the diocese in which it was used and developed, e.g., the *Missale Aboense* for the diocese of Åbo (or Turku), Finland, or the *Missale Benentanum* for the diocese of Benevento, Italy, or even the influential *Missale Romanum* of 1474 for the diocese of Rome, now the term *Romanum* indicates a more universal shift: *everyone* (with, of course, notable exceptions) is now to use *the* Missal of *Rome*. And, to underscore and ensure a type of liturgical uniformity, although never really accomplished fully, the Congregation of Sacred Rites (later the Sacred Congregation of Rites, now the Congregation for Divine Worship and the Sacraments) was established in 1588 as a curial congregation, whose task it was to pronounce judgments on what is lawful or not in liturgical usage—texts, ceremonies, vestments, and other usages—around the Catholic world.[107]

---

[105] See Theisen, *Mass Liturgy*, 22ff.
[106] See Jedin, "Das Konzil von Trient," 515ff.
[107] See Frederick R. McManus, *The Congregation of Sacred Rites* (Washington, DC: Catholic University of America Press, 1954).

During the next two centuries after Trent, a period that Nathan Mitchell refers to as the "reform of [the] reform"[108] of Trent, and that Theodor Klauser once termed the age of "rigid unification and rubricism,"[109] at least two developments stand out, although neither of these reflects much change in the liturgical texts of the Mass, apart from the regular additions of new feasts or adjustments to liturgical rubrics. These two developments concern, first, the cult of the real presence of Christ both within and apart from the eucharistic liturgy and, second, the continued attempts theologically to interpret and explain the sacrificial character of the Eucharist. With regard to the first, it is certainly correct to say that in response to what was considered to be a denial of Christ's real presence in the Eucharist on the part of the Protestant Reformation, Roman Catholics came to emphasize that presence in a variety of ways: (1) tabernacles for the reserved Eucharist were now to be placed on the high altar itself rather than in sacristy aumbries or side chapels (from 1614 on this was mandated by law); (2) increased devotions to the reserved and/or exposed Eucharist continued to develop (e.g., Exposition and Benediction of the Blessed Sacrament, Forty Hours devotions, and *even* the celebration of Mass *in the presence of* the exposed Eucharist);[110] and (3) especially through the leadership of the newly founded Society of Jesus, the "Jesuits," church architecture from the late sixteenth century on came to be modeled on the great Jesuit church in Rome, the *Gesu*, which, as in the Baroque period in general, tended to turn the church into a throne room for the Blessed Sacrament reserved or exposed on the altar, which was now the focus of the church building. One cannot emphasize this too much, for in spite of Trent's own call for more frequent communion by the faithful, an attempt also thwarted in the seventeenth century by the rise of the rigorist Jansenist movement in France with great influence elsewhere,[111] there is no question but that, in the words of Klauser, it

---

[108] Nathan Mitchell, *The Mystery of the Rosary: Marian Devotion and the Reinvention of Catholicism* (New York: New York University Press, 2009), 45.

[109] Theodor Klauser, *A Short History of the Western Liturgy: An Account and Some Reflections*, 2nd ed. (Oxford: Oxford University Press, 1979), 117–52.

[110] See Joseph Jungmann, *The Mass of the Roman Rite* (New York: Benziger, 1951) 1:122.

[111] On Jansenism, see F. Ellen Weaver, *The Evolution of the Reform of Port-Royal: From the Rule of Citeaux to Jansenism* (Beauchesne, 1978).

was "the cult of the Sacrament which had swallowed up and subordinated the liturgy to its own purposes."[112]

Concerning the second point above, namely, further attempts to speak theologically about the eucharistic sacrifice, at least two general approaches will characterize theological thought on this until the early twentieth century. The first of these has been called the "theory of oblation," and the second, the "theory of destruction." These are summarized as follows:

> The theory of oblation holds that the offering of a gift is the essence of sacrifice. In the case of the Eucharistic sacrifice, influenced by the order of treatment of the sacraments of the somatic real presence of the whole Christ and the Eucharistic sacrifice, the offering of the gift of Christ was depicted as conditioned by the prior conversion of the bread and wine. Here, generally speaking, the conversion was conceived as occurring simultaneously with the sacrificial offering, but according to the priority of nature and not as priority of time. . . .
> . . . The theory of destruction was based on the principle that a change of the gift is the essence of sacrifice. Therefore, some theologians attempted to identify what it was in which this destruction of the victim of the Eucharistic sacrifice might consist. The idea of "virtual death" through the separate consecration of the Eucharistic gifts was often proposed. Robert Bellarmine taught that the destruction of the victim through the priest's eating of the Eucharistic body and blood constituted an essential aspect of the Eucharistic sacrifice.[113]

Further reflection on the integral connection of real presence, eucharistic sacrifice, and the reception of communion would have to wait until much later in history.

The doctrinal and theological decisions of Trent on the Eucharist and on the Mass were unacceptable to the Protestant Reformers and their descendants,[114] and from this point on until the twentieth and twenty-first centuries, Catholicism and Protestantism went their separate ways, engaged in an uneasy relationship based often on polemics, accusations, and mutual condemnations. What such an approach did do, however, was to drive both back to the sources of the Christian

---

[112] Klauser, *A Short History*, 139.

[113] Kilmartin, *The Eucharist in the West*, 184–85.

[114] For Protestant responses, especially that of the Lutheran leader, Martin Chemnitz, see Senn, *Christian Liturgy*, 458–67.

liturgical traditions, many of which were unknown in the sixteenth century, as these became ever-more readily available in critical editions. Hence, what began often as studying the sources in order to find support for one position against the other will end up in a new and common appropriation of several elements leading to a new ecumenical focus on liturgy in the contemporary churches.

SUMMARY

1. The sixteenth century brought about both a Protestant and a Catholic Reformation.

2. In common with other Protestant Reformers, Martin Luther believed that there were only two sacraments, baptism and the Lord's Supper (possibly penance, understood as "absolution"), and that communion should be administered with both species of bread and wine. He rejected the understanding of the Eucharist as a sacrifice, but, while also rejecting the doctrine of transubstantiation because of its philosophical rather than biblical foundations, he continued to believe in the real presence of Christ in, with, and under the forms of bread and wine and produced orders for the Mass that reflected these beliefs.

3. Ulrich Zwingli, on the other hand, did not regard the Lord's Supper as a sacrament that conveyed grace. He believed that the bread and wine only signified or represented Christ's body and blood and that Christ was present only in a spiritual and not a bodily sense. For this reason, he was content that communion should continue to be offered and received only four times a year. He also drew up forms of service that reflected his beliefs.

4. John Calvin had a higher view than did Zwingli of the sacraments as signs and means of God's grace and of Christ's presence in the Eucharist. He believed that worthy communicants received Christ's body and blood through being lifted up into heaven by the action of the Holy Spirit. This latter point failed to find liturgical expression in the forms of service he produced, however, and his desire for weekly celebrations in Geneva was frustrated by the opposition of the local authorities, so that he had to settle for four times a year.

5. The liturgical reforms in England at first produced a eucharistic rite that was able to be interpreted variously in terms of Catholic or Lutheran doctrine; shortly thereafter, it was replaced with one that reflected a theology close to that of Zwingli. Successive

minor revisions to the rite enabled those with a higher doctrine of the sacrament to find their beliefs in it. It became the basis for Anglican rites throughout the world and for those of the Methodist Churches too.

6. The Roman Catholic Church's Council of Trent condemned the positions taken by the Protestant Reformers. It affirmed the real presence of Christ in the bread and wine, most appropriately understood as transubstantiation. It denied the necessity for laypeople to receive the cup in addition to the bread and asserted that the Mass was a propitiatory sacrifice. It reformed abuses in the celebration of Mass and paved the way for the production of a new Missal by Pius V in 1570 that would continue in use with very little change for some four hundred years.

Chapter 8

The Modern Period

The twentieth century witnessed unprecedented change, recovery, renewal, and ecumenical convergence in the eucharistic liturgies and their interpretation within several churches throughout the world, a process that is continuing in the present. The earliest major example illustrating both such ecumenical rapprochement and liturgical reform comes not from Europe or the Americas, however, but from the Church of South India (CSI), which merged Anglican, Methodist, Presbyterian, and Congregationalist Christians together in a new "united church" beginning in 1947.[1] While from its beginning a stated intention was that the CSI "will aim at conserving for the common benefit whatever of good has been gained in the separate history of those churches . . . and therefore in its public worship will retain for its congregations freedom either to use historic forms or not to do so,"[2] a mounting need for a common eucharistic liturgy to be used on diocesan occasions was almost immediately recognized. Thus, in 1948 a liturgy committee was formed, charged with the task of preparing just such a liturgy. The committee drew elements of worship from the denominational

---

[1] On the history of the Church of South India and the development of its liturgy, see Leslie W. Brown, "The Making of a Liturgy," *Scottish Journal of Theology* 4 (1951): 55–63; Colin Buchanan, "The Legacy of the Church of South India," in *The Oxford Guide to the Book of Common Prayer*, ed. Charles Hefling and Cynthia Shattuck (Oxford: Oxford University Press, 2006), 244–48; John R. K. Fenwick and Bryan D. Spinks, *Worship in Transition: The Liturgical Movement in the Twentieth Century* (New York: Continuum, 1995), 53–59; T. S. Garrett, *Worship in the Church of South India* (Richmond: John Knox, 1958); Samson Prabhakar, "The Church of South India," in *The Oxford History of Christian Worship*, ed. Geoffrey Wainwright and Karen B. Westerfield Tucker (Oxford and New York: Oxford University Press, 2006), 534–40; and M. Thomas Thangaraj, "Worship and Unity in the Church of South India, " in *Worship Today: Understanding, Practice, Ecumenical Implications*, ed. Thomas F. Best and Dagmar Heller (Geneva: WCC Publications, 2004), 158–65.

[2] *The Constitution of the Church of South India* (Madras: CLS, 1952), 11, Article 12.

traditions represented in the CSI, as well as from the local East-Syrian Rite St. Thomas Christians' liturgy (i.e., JAS),[3] and made use of the best liturgical scholarship stemming from the international Liturgical Movement available at the time. The "Order for the Lord's Supper" was introduced in 1950 at the CSI Synod in Madras, and, after a trial period and upon slight revision, it was approved in 1954 and published in 1963 with other rites in the *Book of Common Worship* of the CSI.[4]

A number of characteristics made this new eucharistic liturgy remarkable—aside, of course, from the unprecedented union of Christians from which it emerged and from its being the *first* liturgy developed in light of scholarship arising from within the Liturgical Movement. Among these features we would note the following that, originating in the CSI liturgy, were widely adopted and became standard in the liturgical reforms of many churches later in the century, including those considered throughout this chapter: (1) recommended presidency from "behind the Holy Table, facing the people";[5] (2) provision of readings from both the Old and New Testaments before the proclamation of the gospel for each Sunday and major feast; (3) options for general intercessions in litany forms, based on Anglican and East-Syrian Rite models, with congregational responses; (4) reintroduction of a congregational sign of peace for the first time in *any* liturgy since the Reformation; and (5) a full anaphora based loosely on the West-Syrian (Syro-Byzantine) pattern, incorporating historically Anglican and Reformed textual elements and, interestingly, including two internal acclamations for the assembly (in addition to the *Sanctus* and final Amen) based again on Eastern Rite forms. Such acclamations were a novelty to Christians from a primarily Western liturgical heritage but became widespread as many churches followed the lead in liturgical reform first taken by the CSI and later (and on a much larger scale) by the Roman Catholic Church.

In response to the mandate of the Constitution on the Sacred Liturgy of the Second Vatican Council (1963–65) that the Roman eucharistic liturgy be restored,[6] the Roman Catholic Church, under Pope Paul VI,

---

[3] Fenwick and Spinks, *Worship in Transition*, 55–56.

[4] Church of South India, *The Book of Common Worship: As Authorised by the Synod 1962* (Oxford/Madras: Oxford University Press, 1963).

[5] Ibid., xii.

[6] References to the Constitution on the Sacred Liturgy throughout this chapter are from *Vatican Council II: The Conciliar and Post Conciliar Documents*, ed.

produced a new *Missale Romanum* in 1969. The mandate of this Constitution included the following specific reforms to be made in the Missal that had been in use since 1570:

21. In this restoration, both texts and rites should be drawn up so that they express more clearly the holy things, which they signify; the Christian people, so far as possible, should be enabled to understand them with ease and to take part in them fully, actively, and as befits a community.

34. The rites should be distinguished by a noble simplicity; they should be short, clear, and unencumbered by useless repetitions; they should be within the people's powers of comprehension, and normally should not require much explanation.

50. The rite of the Mass is to be revised in such a way that the intrinsic nature and purpose of its several parts, as also the connection between them, may be more clearly manifested, and that devout and active participation by the faithful may be more easily achieved.

For this purpose the rites are to be simplified, due care being taken to preserve their substance; elements which, with the passage of time, came to be duplicated, or were added with but little advantage, are now to be discarded; other elements which have suffered injury through accidents of history are now to be restored to the vigor which they had in the days of the holy Fathers, as may seem useful or necessary.

51. The treasures of the bible are to be opened up more lavishly, so that richer fare may be provided for the faithful at the table of God's word. In this way a more representative portion of the holy Scriptures will be read to the people in the course of a prescribed number of years.

52. By means of the homily the mysteries of the faith and the guiding principles of the Christian life are expounded from the sacred text, during the course of the liturgical year; the homily, therefore, is to be highly esteemed as part of the liturgy itself; in fact, at those Masses which are celebrated with the assistance of the people on Sundays and feasts of obligation, it should not be omitted except for a serious reason.

53. Especially on Sundays and feasts of obligation there is to be restored, after the Gospel and the homily, "the common prayer" or "the prayer of the faithful."

Austin Flannery (Collegeville, MN: Liturgical Press, 1975/1984), 1–44. Whenever quoted, references to paragraph numbers will appear in the body of the text.

55. That more perfect form of participation in the Mass whereby the faithful, after the priest's communion, receive the Lord's body from the same sacrifice is strongly commended.

56. The two parts which, in a certain sense, go to make up the Mass, namely, the liturgy of the word and the eucharistic liturgy, are so closely connected with each other that they form but one single act of worship. Accordingly this sacred Synod strongly urges pastors of souls that, when instructing the faithful, they insistently teach them to take their part in the entire Mass, especially on Sundays and feasts of obligation.

Other churches prepared and adopted similar new eucharistic liturgies and worship books in the years following the publication of the current Roman rites. Beginning as early as 1950, The Episcopal Church in the United States (TEC), for example, produced a series of various *Prayer Book Studies*, including rites for trial use in the early 1970s; in 1976 it issued and in 1979 approved a new *Book of Common Prayer* (BCP).[7] The Church of England itself published an *Alternative Service Book 1980*[8] and, more recently, *Common Worship* in 2000[9] to be used in conjunction with its official BCP (1662).

In close relationship to and dependency on the Episcopal *Prayer Book Studies* and the then-proposed BCP of TEC, the major North American Lutheran bodies also, after a similar series of trial rites,[10] eventually produced the *Lutheran Book of Worship* (LBW).[11] Although the Lutheran Church–Missouri Synod (LC–MS) was the original catalyst in forming the Inter-Lutheran Commission on Worship, which was to produce LBW, and while a number of its congregations do, in fact, use it as their worship book, the LC–MS withdrew from this proj-

---

[7] *The Book of Common Prayer and Administration of the Sacraments and Other Rites and Ceremonies of the Church: Together with the Psalter or Psalms of David; According to the Use of the Episcopal Church* (New York: Church Hymnal Corporation, 1979).

[8] *The Alternative Service Book 1980: Services Authorized for Use in the Church of England in Conjunction with the Book of Common Prayer; Together with the Liturgical Psalter* (Cambridge: Cambridge University Press, 1980).

[9] *Common Worship: Services and Prayers for the Church of England* (London: Church House Publishing, 2000).

[10] See, e.g., *Contemporary Worship 2: The Holy Communion* (Minneapolis, MN: Augsburg 1970).

[11] *Lutheran Book of Worship* (Minneapolis, MN: Augsburg, 1978).

ect near to its completion date and produced its own worship book, *Lutheran Worship*, in 1982.[12] The LBW, however, was replaced by *Evangelical Lutheran Worship* (ELW) in 2006,[13] and in the same year the LC–MS also produced a new worship book, *Lutheran Service Book* (LSB).[14] This development of new liturgical books in American Lutheranism is paralleled as well in European and Scandinavian Lutheranism, and similar processes and new books have been produced by many other Protestant bodies as well.[15]

So common are the eucharistic liturgies in several churches today that the Faith and Order Commission of the World Council of Churches in its significant 1982 document, *Baptism, Eucharist, and Ministry*, could point to a widespread modern convergence both in eucharistic theology and in the overall shape of eucharistic rites. That shape, easily recognizable from the eucharistic liturgies in the modern liturgical books of several churches, contains the following agreed upon structural elements:

> The eucharistic liturgy is essentially a single whole, consisting historically of the following elements in varying sequence and of diverse importance:
>
> - hymns of praise;
> - act of repentance;
> - declaration of pardon;
> - proclamation of the Word of God, in various forms;
> - confession of faith (creed);
> - intercession for the whole Church and for the world;
> - preparation of the bread and wine;
> - thanksgiving to the Father for the marvels of creation, redemption and sanctification (deriving from the Jewish tradition of the *berakah*);
> - the words of Christ's institution of the sacrament according to the New Testament tradition;
> - the *anamnesis* or memorial of the great acts of redemption, passion, death, resurrection, ascension and Pentecost, which brought the Church into being;

---

[12] *Lutheran Worship* (St. Louis, MO: Concordia Publishing House, 1982).
[13] *Evangelical Lutheran Worship* (Minneapolis, MN: Augsburg Fortress, 2006).
[14] *Lutheran Service Book* (St. Louis, MO: Concordia Publishing House, 2006).
[15] See below, 331–36.

- the invocation of the Holy Spirit (*epiklesis*) on the community, and the elements of bread and wine (either before the words of institution or after the memorial, or both; or some other reference to the Holy Spirit which adequately expresses the "epikletic" character of the eucharist);

- consecration of the faithful to God;

- reference to the communion of saints;

- prayer for the return of the Lord and the definitive manifestation of his Kingdom;

- the Amen of the whole community;

- the Lord's prayer;

- sign of reconciliation and peace;

- the breaking of the bread;

- eating and drinking in communion with Christ and with each member of the Church;

- final act of praise;

- blessing and sending.[16]

Such convergence and commonality are due to a number of factors. The "return to the sources" of Scripture and early Christian tradition, initially brought about, as we noted in the previous chapter, by the Protestant and Catholic Reformations of the sixteenth century, was given further impetus by the rise of the historical-critical reading of biblical and other texts in the eighteenth-century Enlightenment, the period of Romanticism and restoration mentality of the nineteenth century, and not least by the development of patristic scholarship at the University of Tübingen and elsewhere. Such a patristic focus brought with it the increasing desire to move away from medieval scholasticism and a narrow institutional understanding of the Church toward the recovery of a richer sacramental worldview, an understanding of the church corporately as the Body of Christ and People of God, and the rediscovery of the theology and spirituality of the Christian East by the West. So also the various and related "movements" taking shape throughout the church (e.g., the Anglo-Catholic Oxford and High Church Cambridge Movements in England; the beginnings

---

[16] Faith and Order Commission, *Baptism, Eucharist and Ministry* (Geneva: World Council of Churches, 1982), section 3.27; hereafter, BEM.

of the Benedictine-based Liturgical Movement in the monasteries of Germany, France, and Belgium; the confessional revival among Lutherans in Germany and North America; and the Mercersburg Movement among some of the American Reformed churches); the coming to light of long-lost early Christian liturgical texts (e.g., the *Didache*, discovered in 1875 in Constantinople, and the so-called *Apostolic Tradition*, first published in a modern edition in 1891); and, not least, the devastating European experience of two world wars in the first half of the twentieth century—all this contributed to setting the stage for renewed attention to the liturgy and its role in Christian formation.

The "homogeneity" of Christian worship throughout the churches today stems from a number of different causes. The rise of modern liturgical scholarship was, of course, a major factor, particularly in its earlier—primarily historical—phase, which revealed the changing past that existed behind current forms of public worship. This not only demonstrated how very different were the liturgical practices of all churches today from those of the first few centuries of Christians but also appeared to point toward a unified way of worship among those early Christians that contrasted sharply with the diverse traditions of modern denominations. Historical scholarship both gave birth to and, in turn, was stimulated by the Liturgical Movement, which sought to bring renewal to Christian worship in large measure by a return to what was thought to be the pattern of worship in the early church. But the movement also provided a common theology of worship to undergird the changes and supply a rationale for them.

One other great movement of the twentieth century—ecumenism—must be counted as both cause and effect of the phenomenon that we are considering. The desire to overcome the barriers that had for centuries divided one denomination from another inevitably led to an examination of the differences in liturgical customs that existed between the churches and to the wish not to do separately what we could do together in the area of liturgical revision. Nor must we forget that—just as in the fourth century—the causes of liturgical reform were not located solely within the churches. At least in the developed nations of the Western world (which was where the agenda for official liturgical revision was primarily determined), the different denominations were strongly influenced by the same socio-cultural factors around them. They were subject to the same challenges and pressures from the so-called post-Christian society that was beginning to emerge from the 1960s onward, and so it is hardly surprising that from their embattled position they would look to one another for guidance or that they tended to come up with similar solutions to their common problems.[17] There is no question but that the dominant and most ecumenically influential of the modern liturgical reforms of the Eucharist have been those of the Roman Catholic Church, and it is clear that these reforms underlie a great deal of the modern liturgical revisions undertaken by other churches. Since this is the case, this chapter provides a descriptive overview of the current Roman Catholic rites and *some* of the rites in other modern churches, that is, the Anglican and Lutheran churches, whose current liturgical books provide the closest parallels to the Roman Catholic rites and whose rites have been decidedly influential throughout much of modern Protestantism. Thus, without intending to minimize the importance of modern liturgical development within other Protestant traditions or to gloss over any distinctive elements, the fact remains that if one knows the current Anglican and Lutheran eucharistic liturgies, one has at hand an appropriate model for studying several other Protestant rites as well (e.g., Methodist and Presbyterian). Such is one of the great gifts of ecumenical study and liturgical convergence today.

THE RITES

1. Roman Catholic: The Missale Romanum *of Pope Paul VI (1969)*

Leading up to the mandate of Vatican II for the restoration of the *Roman Missal*, in order that the liturgy might truly be "the summit toward which the activity of the Church is directed [and] the fountain from which all her power flows" (Constitution on the Sacred Liturgy 10), at least four relevant factors need to be mentioned.

First, in 1903 Pope Pius X, the "Pope of the Eucharist," issued a *motu proprio* ("on his own initiative"), *Tra la Sollecitudini* (Instruction on Sacred Music), in which he made the following reference to the church building:

> Filled as We are with a most ardent desire to see the true Christian spirit flourish in every respect and be preserved by all the faithful, We deem it necessary to provide before anything else for the sanctity and

---

[17] See Paul F. Bradshaw, "The Homogenization of Christian Liturgy—Ancient and Modern: Presidential Address," *Studia Liturgica* 26 (1996): 6–8. On the ecumenical liturgical movement see also Fenwick and Spinks, *Worship in Transition*; and James White, *Christian Worship in North America, A Retrospective: 1955–1995* (Collegeville, MN: Liturgical Press, Pueblo, 1997).

dignity of the temple, in which the faithful assemble for no other object than that of acquiring this spirit from its foremost and indispensable font, *which is the active participation in the most holy mysteries and in the public and solemn prayer of the Church.*[18]

Two years later he encouraged "frequent communion," including *daily* reception if possible, thus attempting to put an end to the centuries-long tradition of infrequent reception of communion among Roman Catholics. In *Quam Singulari* in 1910, Pius restored or reemphasized the traditional canonical age of seven for the reception of first communion.[19] In 1911 he revised the psalter of the Roman Breviary and, two years later in yet another *motu proprio* on this topic, *Abhinc duos annos*, indicated that a more thorough "purification" of the liturgy would take several years to accomplish.[20]

The language of "active participation in the most holy mysteries and in the public and solemn prayer of the Church," together with communion reception as one of the major ways in which such "active participation" is expressed, will become hallmarks of the more pastorally oriented phase of the Liturgical Movement among Roman Catholics in the first half of the twentieth century. And, while the first Latin-vernacular missal to assist the active participation of the faithful at Mass had been published at the Belgian Abbey of Maredsous in 1882, the early to mid-twentieth century saw a dramatic increase in these missals everywhere, so that people might pray the liturgical texts *of* the Mass rather than praying other devotions and prayers (e.g., the rosary) *at* the Mass.

Second, the restoration or reform of the Roman Missal actually began with Pope Pius XII, who in 1951 restored the Easter Vigil to Holy Saturday night[21] (it had migrated to Holy Saturday morning

---

[18] ET adapted from R. Kevin Seasoltz, *The New Liturgy: A Documentation, 1903–1965* (New York: Herder and Herder, 1966), 4, emphasis added.

[19] Sacred Congregation of Rites, *Quam Singulari* (August 8, 1910), AAS 2 (1910): 577–83; for ET see Seasoltz, *The New Liturgy*, 17–22. On this topic see Maxwell E. Johnson, *The Rites of Christian Initiation: Their Evolution and Interpretation*, rev. and exp. ed. (Collegeville, MN: Liturgical Press, Pueblo, 2007), 383.

[20] Pius X, *Abhinc Duos Annos* (October 23, 1913), AAS 5 (1913): 449–50; for ET see *Worship and Liturgy*, ed. James J. Megivern, Official Catholic Teaching (Wilmington, NC: McGrath Publishing, Consortium Books, 1978), 41–42.

[21] Sacred Congregation of Rites, *De Solemni Vigilia Paschali Instauranda* (February 9, 1951), AAS 43 (1951): 128–29; for ET (partial) see Megivern, *Worship and Liturgy*, 128.

due to pre-communion fasting regulations) and in 1955 restored all of the Holy Week liturgies, including the Mass of Jesus' Last Supper on the evening of Holy Thursday.[22] Similarly, Pius XII, shortly before his death in 1958, published *De Musica Sacra*, an Instruction of the Sacred Congregation of Rites[23] that legislated specific liturgical reforms beyond the restoration of those Holy Week liturgies. In particular, this instruction gave attention to various levels of active participation on the part of the faithful in both sung and recited ("High" and "Low") Masses and the ways in which such participation can be facilitated. It insisted that interior attention should be "joined to an outward participation manifested by external acts, such as the position of the body (kneeling, standing, sitting), ceremonial gestures, and, above all, by the responses, prayers, and singing" (22). It spoke of lectors and commentators at Low Masses (96) and indicated that "the priest celebrant, deacon or subdeacon, or [instituted] lector" may read the epistle and gospel in the vernacular at High Mass (16c). Popular vernacular hymns were to be permitted at both sung and recited Masses (14a-b; 33); this had already been going on for some time in Germany and France. And it was assumed that people would kneel during the *canon missae* only from after the *Sanctus* to the end of the narrative of institution, rather than through the Canon to the end of Mass.[24]

Third, what began with Pius X and Pius XII was continued by Pope John XXIII, who in 1960 issued his own *motu proprio* called *Rubricarum Instructum* (Instruction on Rubrics) in which he not only revised the rubrics of the Breviary and Missal but actually referred to the forthcoming liturgical work of Vatican II, which he had announced in 1959:

> Afterwards . . . through the inspiration of God, we decreed that an Ecumenical Council should be convened; we reflected—more than

---

[22] Sacred Congregation of Rites, *Maxima Redemptionis Nostrae Mysteria* or *Liturgicus Hebdomadae Sanctae Ordo Instauratur* (November 16, 1953), AAS 47 (1955): 838–47; for ET see Seasoltz, *The New Liturgy*, 209–18. On this topic, see also Annibale Bugnini, *The Reform of the Liturgy, 1948–1975* (Collegeville, MN: Liturgical Press, 1990), 10ff.

[23] Sacred Congregation of Rites, *De Musica Sacra* (September 3, 1958), AAS 50 (1958): 630–63; for ET see Seasoltz, *The New Liturgy*, 255–82. Our sincere thanks to our colleague Nathan D. Mitchell for directing us to this document of Pius XII and to the following one by John XXIII, and especially for sharing his translation of the 1960 *Rubricarum Instructum* with us.

[24] See Frederick McManus, "Responses," *Worship* 33 (1959): 600–603.

once—about what should be done concerning the kind of initiative undertaken by our Predecessor [Pius XII]. Having examined the matter long and maturely, we arrived at the conclusion that the deeper principles regarding a general liturgical renewal (*instaurationem*) should be proposed to the Fathers at the coming Ecumenical Council, but that the aforementioned correction of the rubrics of the Breviary and Missal should not be postponed any longer.[25]

With this *motu proprio* were published the revised rubrics; a new Roman Breviary was released in 1961 and during Vatican II in 1962, the new edition of the *Missale Romanum*, sometimes referred to as the "Missal of Blessed John XXIII" but which was actually but the latest edition of the Missal of Pius V. In addition to these rubrical changes and the addition of newer feasts, John XXIII took the radical step of inserting the name of St. Joseph after that of the Virgin Mary into the *Communicantes* of the Roman Canon, thus demonstrating that liturgical texts, even the venerable Roman Canon (!), can and could be changed.

Fourth and finally, the question of vernacular liturgy was discussed and addressed during Vatican II, with the following approach adopted in the Constitution on the Sacred Liturgy to guide episcopal conferences in the process:

> 36. 1. Particular law remaining in force, the use of the Latin language is to be preserved in the Latin rites. 2. But since the use of the mother tongue, whether in the Mass, the administration of the sacraments, or other parts of the liturgy, frequently may be of great advantage to the people, the limits of its employment may be extended. This will apply in the first place to the readings and directives, and to some of the prayers and chants. . . . 3. These norms being observed, it is for the competent territorial ecclesiastical authority . . . to decide whether, and to what extent, the vernacular language is to be used; their decrees are to be approved, that is, confirmed, by the Apostolic See. And, whenever it seems to be called for, this authority is to consult with bishops of neighboring regions which have the same language. 4. Translations from the Latin text into the mother tongue intended for use in the liturgy must be approved by the competent territorial ecclesiastical authority mentioned above.

---

[25] John XXIII, *Rubricarum Instructum* (July 25, 1960), AAS 52 (1960): 593–95, here at 593. ET by Nathan D. Mitchell.

While no one at Vatican II probably expected anything more than that "the readings . . . and some of the prayers and chants" would be in the vernacular—certainly *not* the Preface, *Sanctus*, or Roman *canon missae*—what was to become the cooperative venture among English-speaking bishops, the International Commission on English in the Liturgy (ICEL), was already being organized before the end of the council. And by the time the Roman Missal of Paul VI was promulgated in 1969, after various interim missals had been produced from 1964 on, official permission for the use of the vernacular for the entire liturgy had been granted and was already being used.[26]

Just as at the Council of Trent, so also the actual reform or restoration of the liturgical books at Vatican II was turned over to the pope and what came to be called the Consilium. In his apostolic constitution promulgating the new Missal on April 3, 1969, Pope Paul VI demonstrates the continuity of this latest version of the *Missale Romanum* with the previous Missal of Pius V, with the reforms of Pius XII, and with the mandate given at Vatican II:

> Since the beginning of this liturgical renewal, it has also become clear that the formularies of the Roman Missal had to be revised and enriched. A beginning was made by Pius XII in the restoration of the Easter Vigil and Holy Week services; he thus took the first step toward adapting the Roman Missal to the contemporary mentality.
>
> The Second Vatican Ecumenical Council, in the Constitution *Sacrosanctum Concilium*, laid down the basis for the general revision of the Roman Missal: "Both texts and rites should be drawn up so that they express more clearly the holy things they signify"; therefore, "the Order of Mass is to be revised in such a way that the intrinsic nature and purpose of its several parts, as also the connection between them, may be more clearly brought out, and devout, active participation by the faithful more easily achieved." The Council also decreed that "the treasures of the Bible are to be opened up more lavishly, so that a richer share in God's word may be provided for the faithful"; and finally that "a new rite for concelebration is to be drawn up and incorporated into the Roman Pontifical and Roman Missal."
>
> No one should think, however, that this revision of the Roman Missal has come out of nowhere. The progress in liturgical studies dur-

---

[26] On the use of the vernacular in Roman Catholic liturgy see Keith Pecklers, *Dynamic Equivalence: The Living Language of Christian Worship* (Collegeville, MN: Liturgical Press, Pueblo, 2002).

ing the last four centuries has certainly prepared the way. Just after the Council of Trent, the study "of ancient manuscripts in the Vatican library and elsewhere," as St. Pius V attests in the Apostolic Constitution *Quo primum*, helped greatly in the correction of the Roman Missal. Since then, however, other ancient sources have been discovered and published and liturgical formularies of the Eastern Church have been studied. Accordingly many have had the desire for these doctrinal and spiritual riches not to be stored away in the dark, but to be put into use for the enlightenment of the mind of Christians and for the nurture of their spirit. . . .

In the Order of Mass the rites have been "simplified, due care being taken to preserve their substance." "Elements that, with the passage of time, came to be duplicated or were added with but little advantage" have been eliminated, especially in the rites for the presentation of the bread and wine, the breaking of the bread, and communion.

Also, "other elements that have suffered injury through accident of history" are restored "to the tradition of the Fathers," for example, the homily, the general intercessions or prayer of the faithful, and the penitential rite or act of reconciliation with God and the community at the beginning of the Mass, which thus, as is right, regains its proper importance.[27]

And, in order that there would be no confusion about the canonical and binding status of this Missal for the celebration of the Roman Rite from this point on, Paul VI states clearly:

After what we have presented concerning the new Roman Missal [*novo Missali Romano*], we wish in conclusion to insist on one point in particular and to make it have its effect. When he promulgated the *editio princeps* of the Roman Missal, our predecessor St. Pius V offered it to the people of Christ as the instrument of liturgical unity and the expression of a pure and reverent worship in the Church. Even though, in virtue of the decree of the Second Vatican Council, we have accepted into the new Roman Missal lawful variations and adaptations, our own expectation in no way differs from that of our predecessor. It is that the faithful will receive the new Missal as a help toward witnessing and strengthening their unity with one another; that through the new Missal one and the same prayer in a great diversity of languages

[27] Paul VI, *Missale Romanum* (April 3, 1969); ET from International Commission on English in the Liturgy, *The Sacramentary of the Roman Missal* (Collegeville, MN: Liturgical Press, 1985), 10–11.

will ascend, more fragrant than any incense, to our heavenly Father, through our High Priest, Jesus Christ, in the Holy Spirit.

The effective date for what we have prescribed in this Constitution shall be the First Sunday of Advent of this year, 30 November. We decree that these laws and prescriptions be firm and effective now and in the future, notwithstanding, to the extent necessary, the apostolic constitutions and ordinances issued by our predecessors and other prescriptions, even those deserving particular mention and amendment.[28]

The henceforth normative legal status of this Missal was reinforced in 1974 by a notification of the Congregation for Divine Worship, *Conferentiarum Episcopalium*, which asserted the following:

> Both local and religious Ordinaries must . . . see to it—without prejudice to non-Roman liturgical rites lawfully recognized by the Church but *with no exception based on the claim of any, even immemorial custom*— that all priests and people of the Roman Rite, duly accept the Order of Mass in the Roman Missal; that through greater study and reverence they come to appreciate it for the treasures of both the word of God and of liturgical and pastoral teaching that it contains.[29]

Sometimes referred to inaccurately as the *Novus Ordo*, a term nowhere used officially to describe this version of the Roman Missal or its liturgy, it is clear that the Order of Mass in this new Missal parallels closely, with some important exceptions, the description of the papal Mass in the time of Pope Gregory the Great (590–604), as reflected in *Ordo Romanus Primus*, discussed above in chapter 6, and especially to the shape and contents of that rite as known in the eighth century.[30] Indeed, from a historical perspective, one could actually call the Mass of Pope Paul VI the "Gregorian Rite," or the "more ancient usage" (*usus antiquior*) of the Roman Rite. In the following chart, elements in brackets are additions or restorations to that older core.

---

[28] Ibid., 11, emphasis added.

[29] *Documents of the Liturgy 1963–1979: Conciliar, Papal, and Curial Texts* (Collegeville, MN: Liturgical Press, 1982), para. 1784, 549. On the development of this Missal see Bugnini, *The Reform of the Liturgy*; and, more recently, Piero Marini, *A Challenging Reform: Realizing the Vision of the Liturgical Renewal, 1963–1975* (Collegeville, MN: Liturgical Press, 2007).

[30] See above, 200–210.

Introductory Rites

Entrance Antiphon

[Greeting]

[Penitential Rite]

Kyrie

Gloria in excelsis (outside of Advent and Lent)

Collect (Opening Prayer)

Liturgy of the Word

[Old Testament Reading]

[Responsorial Psalm] (expands Gradual)

Epistle (New Testament Reading)

Gospel Acclamation (Alleluia or other verse during Lent)

Gospel

[Homily]

[Intercessions]

Liturgy of the Eucharist

Offertory Antiphon

[New prayers for the Preparation of the Gifts]

Prayer over the Gifts

Eucharistic Prayer [three new Canons along with the Roman Canon]

Lord's Prayer

Kiss of Peace

Fraction

Agnus Dei

Commixture

Communion

Communion Antiphon

Concluding Rites

Post-Communion Prayer

[Blessing]

Dismissal

While this Missal was mandated for use beginning on the First Sunday of Advent in 1969 in Latin, the fact that it would be used in the vernacular almost everywhere meant that its implementation would be delayed longer with the latest of the interim missals (1966) still used until translations could be completed. For English-speaking Roman Catholics, at least in the United States, the Order of Mass began to be used on Palm Sunday in 1970 (the new eucharistic prayers had appeared in their current form already in 1967 and, inserted into interim missals, were already widely used), with the full ICEL translation of the entire Missal completed for publication in 1973. And, thanks to the work of ICEL in union with two ecumenical bodies, the International Commission on English Texts (ICET, later renamed the English Language Liturgical Consultation, ELLC)[31] and the Consultation on Common Texts, since the early 1970s English-speaking Christians from a variety of liturgical traditions, including Anglicans, Lutherans, Methodists, and Presbyterians, have been using essentially the same texts for liturgical greetings and responses (e.g., "The Lord be with you." "And also with you."), as well as the *Kyrie, Gloria*, Nicene and Apostles' Creeds, *Sanctus*, and *Agnus Dei*.

The second edition of the Missal of Paul VI appeared in 1975 and the third in 2002, under Pope John Paul II. A document, significantly written not in Latin but in French, *Comme le prevoit*,[32] had guided the process of translating the Missal into the vernacular based not on the principle of literal translation but on what is called "dynamic equivalence," a process of translation focused more on equivalent "meanings" and interpretations rather than strict adherence to Latin terminology, grammar, and syntax.[33] Based still on that approach, ICEL produced in 1998 a completely new translation of the Missal, which was approved by over 75 percent of the world's English-speaking Catholic bishops. This version, however, was not approved by Rome, and in 2001 a new document governing translation, *Liturgiam Authen-*

---

[31] International Consultation on English Texts, *Prayers We Have in Common: Agreed Liturgical Texts* (London: Chapman; Philadelphia: Fortress Press, 1970, 1971; London: SPCK; Philadelphia: Fortress Press, 1975); English Language Liturgical Consultation, *Praying Together: Agreed Liturgical Texts* (Norwich: Canterbury Press, 1988, 1990).

[32] See *Documents of the Liturgy*, 284–91.

[33] On this see the work of Keith Pecklers, *Dynamic Equivalence*, as in note 26 above.

ticam, appeared from the Congregation for Divine Worship demanding a more literal word-for-word approach.[34] On the First Sunday of Advent 2011, English-speaking Roman Catholics in the United States began the liturgical use of a new translation of the third edition of the Missal of Paul VI (2002) based on the principles set out in *Liturgiam Authenticam*. Its use began somewhat earlier in Great Britain and South Africa.

It was not only the use of the vernacular that came to characterize the implementation of the Missal of Paul VI throughout the Catholic world. The principle of "full, active, and conscious participation," articulated initially by Pope Pius X and reaffirmed strongly by the Constitution on the Sacred Liturgy, led to the widespread participation of laypeople as lectors and leaders of the prayers of intercession as well as their functioning as extraordinary eucharistic ministers. Similarly, active participation was now encouraged by congregational song and chant,[35] whether that was the singing of the Ordinary of the Mass in Latin (still permitted and actually encouraged) or new vernacular Mass compositions or even hymns and other songs at the location of the introit, offertory chant, and communion antiphon, a practice permitted by the rubrics themselves. Perhaps nothing, however, came to symbolize this renewed sense of the assembled Christian community as celebrating the Eucharist corporately, of offering the eucharistic sacrifice together as the *totus Christus* of Head and members, more than the new placement of the altar as freestanding, with the priest now facing the congregation during the eucharistic prayer, and the resultant architectural renovations of existing churches and the construction of new churches.[36] The installation of freestanding altars was actually accomplished *before* the Missal of Paul VI appeared. Already

[34] For a critical review of this document see Peter Jeffrey, *Translating Tradition: A Chant Historian Reads* Liturgiam Authenticam (Collegeville, MN: Liturgical Press, Pueblo, 2005).

[35] See Congregation of Rites, *Musicam Sacram* (1967), nos. 7 and 16, in *Documents of the Liturgy*, 1295–96; and more recently, *Sing to the Lord: Music in Divine Worship* (Washington, DC: United States Conference of Catholic Bishops, 2007). See also Edward Foley, *A Lyrical Vision: The Music Documents of the US Bishops*, American Essays in Liturgy (Collegeville, MN: Liturgical Press, 2009).

[36] Cf. *Environment and Art in Catholic Worship* (Washington, DC: United States Conference of Catholic Bishops, 1978) and the more recent *Built of Living Stones: Art, Architecture, and Worship* (Washington, DC: United States Conference of Catholic Bishops, 2000).

in 1964 in the instruction from the Congregation of Rites, *Inter Oecumenici*, the following appeared: "In every church there should ordinarily be a fixed, dedicated altar, *which should be freestanding* to allow the ministers to walk around it easily and *Mass to be celebrated facing the people*. It should be so placed as to be a focal point on which the attention of the whole congregation centers naturally."[37] While this instruction did not mandate explicitly the celebration of Mass "facing the people," it does make the freestanding *altar*—not the tabernacle—the focal point of the Catholic church-building, and, very quickly, Mass facing the people became the norm throughout the Catholic world, as it remains today. Together with this renewed emphasis on the corporate celebration of the Mass came what might surely be called the "restoration" of the cup to the laity, hence, underscoring the overall sacrificial meal or banquet character of the Eucharist. As Pope Paul VI stated in 1967:

> Holy communion has a more complete form as a sign when it is received under both kinds. For in this manner of reception . . . a fuller light shines on the sign of the Eucharistic banquet. Moreover, there is a clearer expression of that will by which the new and everlasting covenant is ratified in the blood of the Lord and of the relationship of the Eucharistic banquet to the eschatological banquet in the Father's kingdom.[38]

There are three elements in this Missal in particular that need to be addressed briefly, namely, the lectionary employed for the Liturgy of the Word; the revision of the former "offertory rite," now the "preparation of the gifts"; and, most important, the new eucharistic prayers. First, the importance of the 1969 *Ordo Lectionum Missae* with its three-year cycle of Sunday readings for the eucharistic liturgy, including a first reading from the Old Testament outside the Easter Season, cannot be overestimated. Prior to its publication, a one-year cycle had been employed in the liturgies of the Roman Catholic Church (and of various Reformation churches as well) since the *Missale Romanum* of 1570, which, as we have seen, limited the Sunday readings to two, an

---

[37] *Inter Oecumenici* (1964), no. 91, in *Documents of the Liturgy*, 108, emphasis added.
[38] Paul VI, *Eucharisticum Mysterium* (1967), no. 32, in *Documents of the Liturgy*, 408.

epistle and gospel. With the exception of the Easter Vigil and the quarterly Ember Days, readings from the Old Testament tended to be excluded altogether. Indeed, as Martin Connell writes of the pre–Vatican II Lectionary, "only 1 percent of the Old Testament was proclaimed, less than 17 percent of the New Testament, and for the whole Bible—Old Testament and New Testament together—only 6 percent was proclaimed, 1,530 verses of the canon's 33,001."[39]

In light of the above, it is surely no exaggeration to say that the greatest ecumenical-liturgical gift of the twentieth century of the Roman Catholic Church to much of Protestantism in general has been this lectionary, which since its publication has been adapted and used in various versions, the most recent being the *Revised Common Lectionary* of 1992,[40] by "some 70 percent of Protestant churches in the English-speaking world."[41] With regard to the *Revised Common Lectionary*, Presbyterian liturgical scholar Horace Allen has said that "it . . . marks the first time since the Reformation that Catholics and Protestants find themselves reading the scriptures together Sunday by Sunday. . . . Who would have thought that 450 years after the Reformation, Catholics would be teaching Protestants how to read scripture in worship?"[42] In fact, it is precisely the use and preaching of the lectionary in these 70 percent of Protestant churches in the English-speaking world that has led as well to the recovery and introduction of the liturgical year itself, even, rather ironically, in those churches known historically for their rejection of calendars, feasts, and seasons.[43]

Second, instead of the former "offertory rite," sometimes referred to as the "little canon" since it tended to treat the bread and wine as already consecrated and focused strongly on offering language even in the first-person singular of the priest, the Missal of Paul VI has a rite of

[39] Martin Connell, *Eternity Today: On the Liturgical Year*, vol. 2: *Sunday, Lent, The Three Days, The Easter Season, Ordinary Time* (New York: Continuum, 2006), 207.

[40] Consultation on Common Texts, *The Revised Common Lectionary* (Norwich: Canterbury Press; Nashville, TN: Abingdon Press, 1992).

[41] Horace Allen, as quoted by John Allen, Jr., "Liturgist Says Ecumenical Dialogue Is 'Dead,'" *National Catholic Reporter* (May 24, 2002), http://www.encyclopedia.com/doc/1G1-87210384.html.

[42] Ibid.

[43] On this see James White, "Protestant Public Worship in America: 1935–1995," in *Christian Worship in North America*, 129.

"preparation" of the bread and wine pointing ahead logically to their being "offered" in the eucharistic prayer or anaphora (i.e., *the* prayer of offering). While the earlier intent for this rite called for restoring simply the action of placing the bread and wine on the altar during a chant with the "prayer over the gifts" as its conclusion, the following *berakah*-type prayers were added for the final edition:

> Blessed are you, Lord God of all creation,
> for through your goodness we have received
> the bread we offer you:
> fruit of the earth and work of human hands,
> it will become for us the bread of life.
> Blessed be God for ever.

> *The Deacon, or the Priest, pours wine and a little water into the chalice, saying quietly:*
> By the mystery of this water and wine
> may we come to share in the divinity of Christ
> who humbled himself to share in our humanity.

> Blessed are you, Lord God of all creation,
> for through your goodness we have received
> the wine we offer you:
> fruit of the vine and work of human hands,
> it will become our spiritual drink.
> Blessed be God for ever.

> *After this, the Priest, bowing profoundly, says quietly:*
> With humble spirit and contrite heart
> may we be accepted by you, O Lord,
> and may our sacrifice in your sight this day
> be pleasing to you, Lord God.

> *Then the Priest, standing at the side of the altar, washes his hands, saying quietly:*
> Wash me, O Lord, from my iniquity
> and cleanse me from my sin.

> Pray, brethren (brothers and sisters),
> that my sacrifice and yours
> may be acceptable to God,
> the almighty Father.

The people rise and reply:
May the Lord accept the sacrifice at your hands
for the praise and glory of his name,
for our good
and the good of all his holy Church.

Then the Priest, with hands extended, says the Prayer over the Offerings, at the end of which the people acclaim:
Amen.[44]

Unlike all previous editions of the Roman Missal since 1570, the Missal of Paul VI is unique in providing other eucharistic prayers or canons in addition to that of the traditional Roman *canon missae*, now known as Eucharistic Prayer I. In his apostolic constitution introducing the Missal, Paul VI addresses what he calls this "chief innovation":

> It must be acknowledged that the chief innovation in the reform concerns the eucharistic prayer. Although the Roman Rite over the centuries allowed for a multiplicity of different texts in the first part of the prayer (the preface), the second part, called the *Canon actionis*, took on a fixed form during the period of the fourth and fifth centuries. The Eastern liturgies, on the other hand, allowed a degree of variety into the anaphoras themselves. On this point, first of all, the eucharistic prayer has been enriched with a great number of prefaces—drawn from the early tradition of the Roman Church or recently composed—in order that the different facets of the mystery of salvation will stand out more clearly and that there will be more and richer themes of thanksgiving. But besides this, we have decided to add three new canons to the eucharistic prayer.[45]

The new eucharistic prayers are: Eucharistic Prayer II, based on the so-called *Apostolic Tradition*, ascribed to Hippolytus of Rome; Eucharistic Prayer III, an attempt at revising the Roman *canon missae* on the basis of various Gallican and Mozarabic sources; and Eucharistic Prayer IV,

---

[44] International Commission on English in the Liturgy, *The Roman Missal*, Third Edition (Collegeville, MN: Liturgical Press, 2011), 529–30.

[45] Paul VI, *Missale Romanum*, in *The Sacramentary of the Roman Missal*, 10. On the great number of new eucharistic prefaces and their sources see Nathaniel Marx, "The Revision of the Prefaces in the Missal of Paul VI," in *Issues in Eucharistic Praying in East and West*, ed. Maxwell E. Johnson (Collegeville: Liturgical Press/Pueblo, 2011), 349–82.

based on the Egyptian Anaphora of St. Basil (EgBAS).[46] Clearly, the attempt here has been to move beyond a rather narrow *Roman* view of the eucharistic liturgy to embrace the wider catholic liturgical traditions of both East and West.

In comparison with the Roman *canon missae* the most distinctive element in these new eucharistic prayers is the addition of an explicit consecratory epiclesis of the Holy Spirit *before* the narrative of institution and a communion epiclesis of the Holy Spirit for the fruits of communion *after* the anamnesis. All of these prayers, as well as several newer texts originally published not in Latin but in French or German and included in various language versions of the Missal (i.e., three Eucharistic Prayers for Masses with Children, the two Eucharistic Prayers for Reconciliation, and the more recent Eucharistic Prayer for Various Needs and Occasions with four thematic preface and intercession options), have the following structure:

> Preface (variable in Eucharistic Prayer III)
> *Sanctus*
> Post-*Sanctus* with Epiclesis I
> Narrative of Institution
> Mystery of Faith with Acclamation
> Anamnesis
> Epiclesis II
> Intercessions
> Concluding Doxology

While appeal has sometimes been made to the classic Alexandrian structure of the eucharistic prayer in order to justify and support this pattern for what is sometimes called a "split epiclesis,"[47] the fact is that it is the overall structure of the Roman Canon itself that had provided the model here. That is, these new eucharistic prayers provide epicleses corresponding to the Roman Canon's *Quam oblationem* and *Supplices te rogamus*. Nevertheless, the introduction of epicleses of the

---

[46] On the composition of these prayers, see Bugnini, *The Reform of the Liturgy*, 448–87; Cyprian Vagaggini, *The Canon of the Mass and Liturgical Reform* (New York: Alba House, 1967); and Enrico Mazza, *The Eucharistic Prayers of the Roman Rite* (Collegeville, MN: Liturgical Press, Pueblo, 1986).

[47] See the recent doctoral dissertation of our student, Annie Vorhes McGowan, *In Search of the Spirit: The Epiclesis in Early Eucharistic Praying and Contemporary Liturgical Reform* (PhD dissertation, University of Notre Dame, 2011).

Holy Spirit is theologically quite significant and has even led to some nuance in the official Catholic position about eucharistic consecration, since in the *Catechism of the Catholic Church* it is now stated explicitly that by the power of the Holy Spirit the gifts of bread and wine "become the body and blood of Jesus Christ." Even in describing the role of the narrative of institution, the *Catechism* goes on to say that Christ's presence is due to the "power of the words and the action of Christ, and the power of the Holy Spirit."[48] Here is clearly expressed that attention and openness to the doctrinal and spiritual riches of the Christian East referred to by Paul VI in his apostolic constitution. In fact, such reference to the agency of the Holy Spirit becomes particularly important for anaphoral texts like the Roman Canon, which does not contain an epiclesis of the Spirit and for now the liceity and validity of the Anaphora of Addai and Mari in the form used by the Ancient (Assyrian) Church of the East without the narrative of institution.[49]

At the time of the preparation of the Missal of Paul VI it was widely accepted by liturgical scholars that the so-called *Apostolic Tradition* was composed by Hippolytus of Rome in the early third century and that the eucharistic prayer in chapter 4 was thus the earliest representative of *Roman* eucharistic praying, a conclusion we have already seen can no longer be held uncritically today.[50] But rather than presenting for Eucharistic Prayer II the text of *Apostolic Tradition* as it appears in the fifth-century Verona Latin manuscript, perhaps as a simple alternative anaphora for daily Mass,[51] its structure was overhauled to incorporate elements originally foreign to it, namely, a *Sanctus*, pre–institution narrative epiclesis, as well as post-anamnesis intercessions. What is left of the original anaphora, as the following demonstrates, is confined to the preface (for which another seasonal, Sunday, or weekday preface may be and often is substituted) and some of the language introducing the narrative of institution and the anamnesis:

---

[48] *The Catechism of the Catholic Church* (Rome: Libreria Editrice Vaticana, 1994), par. 1353.

[49] See above, 170–71.

[50] See above, 40–41.

[51] Actually in 1983 ICEL did issue another version of this prayer for consultation purposes closely in line with the text of the Verona Latin. See ICEL, *Eucharistic Prayer of Hippolytus: Text for Consultation* (Washington, DC: United States Conference of Catholic Bishops, 1983).

It is truly right and just, our duty and our salvation,
always and everywhere to give you thanks, Father most holy,
through your beloved Son, Jesus Christ,
your Word through whom you made all things,
whom you sent as our Savior and Redeemer,
incarnate by the Holy Spirit and born of the Virgin.

Fulfilling your will and gaining for you a holy people,
he stretched out his hands as he endured his Passion,
so as to break the bonds of death and manifest the resurrection.

And so, with the Angels and all the Saints
we declare your glory,
as with one voice we acclaim:

Holy, Holy, Holy . . .

. . . At the time he was betrayed
and entered willingly into his Passion,
he took bread and, giving thanks. . . .

. . . Therefore, as we celebrate
the memorial of his Death and Resurrection,
we offer you, Lord,
the Bread of life and the Chalice of salvation,
giving thanks that you have held us worthy
to be [*adstare*, literally, "to stand"] in your presence and minister to
    you.[52]

And where the Roman Catholic liturgical reform went with this anaphora, liturgical reform followed suit elsewhere, with some version of the anaphora of "Hippolytus" (as it is still popularly known), or some other eucharistic prayer based on or inspired by it, making its way into the new liturgical books of many churches.

There is, of course, no question but that the Missal of Paul VI is *the* Roman Missal whose use is normative for Roman Catholic liturgy today. Nevertheless, it is important to note that some of the other traditional Catholic eucharistic liturgies have also undergone reform and

---

[52] *The Roman Missal*, 645–48. For an excellent study of the composition of this prayer, see Matthieu Smyth, "The Anaphora of the So-called 'Apostolic Tradition' and the Roman Eucharistic Prayer," in Johnson, *Issues in Eucharistic Praying in East and West*, 71–98.

renewal in recent years, namely, the Ambrosian Rite[53] for the diocese of Milan, Italy, and the Mozarabic Rite,[54] enjoying somewhat of a revival in Spain. And beginning in 1989, an officially approved African Rite was published for the dioceses of Zaïre, which is the fruit of several years of study, experimentation, and inculturation.[55]

At the same time, the Missal of Paul VI has been challenged over the years by various groups within Roman Catholicism, some calling today for a "reform of the reform" in terms of aesthetics (including music, architecture, and vesture), and others seeking a more thorough "reform" or return to preconciliar Roman Catholicism, including, of course, the use of the Missal of Pius V.[56] While Pope John Paul II had been sensitive to the request of some groups in 1984 by issuing an *Indult* to the world's bishops to allow the 1962 edition of the Missal of Pius V to be used when requested by certain groups attached to it, in 2007 Pope Benedict XVI, in his *motu proprio, Summorum Pontificum*, granted permission for any priest to be able to celebrate Mass from the 1962 Missal privately and, without episcopal permission, publically in response to groups attached to that Missal, a policy underscored by the document *Universae Ecclesiae* on May 13, 2011. From this point on a distinction is now to be made between two "uses" of the one Roman Rite: the "Ordinary Form," meaning the Missal of Paul VI, and the "Extraordinary Form," meaning the Missal of Pius V, in its 1962 version only, with "extraordinary" meaning not "superlative" but, rather, as an "exception" to the norm.[57] While this development was intended to bring about unity especially with the schismatic Society of St. Pius X, who, under the late Archbishop Marcel Lefebvre, had rejected all liturgical and most theological reforms of Vatican II, it is too soon to tell what the overall impact of this *motu proprio* will have throughout the

---

[53] *Missale Ambrosianum iuxta ritum Sanctae Ecclesiae Mediolanensis* (Milan: Centro Ambrosiano di Documentazione e Studi Religiosi, 1981). See also V. A. Lenti, "Liturgical Reform and the Ambrosian and Mozarabic Rites," *Worship* 68 (1994): 417–26.

[54] *Missale Hispano-Mozarabicum* (Madrid: Promocion Popular Christiana, 1991). See also Lenti as cited in the preceding note.

[55] *Missel Romain pour les Diocéses du Zaïre* (Kinshasa/Gambe, 1989).

[56] See the recent study of John Baldovin, *Reforming the Liturgy: A Response to the Critics* (Collegeville, MN: Liturgical Press, Pueblo, 2008).

[57] Cf. Mark Francis, "Beyond Language," *The Tablet* (November 29, 2008), http://www.the tablet.co.uk/article/10058.

Catholic world. Nevertheless, it is important to recall that on March 17, 1965, four years before he promulgated the new Missal, Paul VI said in a general audience:

> We should not think that after a while there can be a return to the for-mer, undisturbed devotion or apathy. No, the new way of doing things will have to be different; it will have to prevent and to shake up the passivity of the people present at Mass. Before, it was enough to assist; now it is necessary to take part. Before, being there was enough; now attention and activity are required.[58]

2. The Anglican Communion

A number of Anglican provinces had already engaged in some re-vision of their liturgies in the first half of the twentieth century, but it was the Lambeth Conference—a decennial meeting of the bishops from throughout the Communion—at its 1958 gathering that provided a blueprint for the way ahead in the report of the subcommittee on Prayer Book Revision. It proposed the following "suggested modifi-cations or additions for the further recovery of other elements of the worship of the Primitive Church":

1. Exhortations have a legitimate function in the liturgy but they should be shorter and fewer.
2. The present corporate expressions of penitence need to be modi-fied both in length and language.
3. More extensive provision of litanies, with shorter clauses, for corporate intercession, thanksgiving and adoration; with the dis-couragement of long strings of collects or other prayers for this purpose.
4. The recovery of the "People's Prayers" at the Eucharist by break-ing up the Prayer for the Church into sections, each followed by congregational response, or into a litany with short clauses.
5. The Offertory, with which the people should definitely be as-sociated, is to be more closely connected with the Prayer of Consecration.
6. The events for which thanksgiving is made in the Consecration Prayer are not to be confined to Calvary but include thanks-

---

[58] *L'Osservatore Romano* (March 18, 1965). Thanks to our colleague, Richard McBrien, for directing us to this reference.

giving for all the principal "mighty works of God", especially the resurrection and the ascension of our Lord, and his return in glory.[59]

The subcommittee went on to suggest the addition of a reading from the Old Testament as part of the Liturgy of the Word at the principal Eucharist on a Sunday, the resulting three readings being separated by psalms or portions of psalms, with the sermon following immediately afterward and before the Creed, together with the possibility of restoring the *Gloria in excelsis* to its original position near the beginning of the rite. It also believed, rather overoptimistically, that the time had come when "controversies about the Eucharistic Sacrifice can be laid aside" and "the tensions surrounding this doctrine transcended"; it gave a brief nod in the direction of the inclusion of an epiclesis of the Holy Spirit, and it drew attention to what it described as a "scriptural and primitive" concept of "consecration through thanksgiving"—that to give thanks over something was to consecrate it.[60]

Although underlying the report had been a desire for any revision to be quite conservative in character, this was not to be, and it was not long before new eucharistic rites in various parts of the Communion began not only to leave behind their Prayer Book heritage in terms of eucharistic theology and ritual shape in favor of a more patristic model but also to experiment with modern language rather than Tudor English.[61] While there was much borrowing of features between one province and another and a widespread adoption of the ecumenical common texts produced by ICET/ELLC and of the *Revised Common Lectionary*, a tradition of provincial autonomy together with a

[59] *The Lambeth Conference 1958: The Encyclical Letter from the Bishops Together with the Resolutions and Reports* (London: SPCK; Greenwich, CT: Seabury, 1958), 2:81.

[60] Ibid., 2:82–85.

[61] The texts of the various rites produced between 1958 and 1984 are conveniently collected in a series of volumes edited by Colin O. Buchanan, *Modern Anglican Liturgies 1958–1968* (London/New York: Oxford University Press, 1968); *Further Anglican Liturgies 1968–1975* (Nottingham: Grove Books, 1975); and *Latest Anglican Liturgies 1976–1984*, Alcuin Club Collections 66 (London: SPCK, 1985). Some account of more recent revisions can be found in *Our Thanks and Praise: The Eucharist in Anglicanism Today*, ed. David R. Holeton (Toronto: Anglican Book Centre, 1998).

fledgling sense of the importance of local inculturation in some parts of the world prevented a dull uniformity from emerging.

Some differences sprang from the absence of a definitive patristic precedent for the proper location of certain parts of the rite. This was particularly the case with regard to the act of penitence: should it come at the beginning of the service as part of the preparation for worship, or should it follow the prayers of intercession as part of the response to God's word in acknowledgment of the sinfulness of the human condition and not just of personal sin? The decision by the Roman Catholic Church to place the equivalent act near the beginning of its revised rite undoubtedly influenced many provinces to choose the same position. Other features of the Roman revision also exercised a strong influence throughout the Communion, in particular the decisions to make the intercessions flexible and open to local extemporization and the provision of more than a single eucharistic prayer. These eucharistic prayers not only tend to follow to a large extent the classic Syro-Byzantine model rather than that in the earlier Anglican Prayer Books but frequently offer a wider range of proper prefaces for seasons and occasions in the year than the older forms and usually incorporate one or more congregational acclamations or responses, besides the opening dialogue and *Sanctus*.

So, for example, the 1979 *Book of Common Prayer* of TEC has four prayers in its modern-language version of the Eucharist (known as Rite II): Prayer A is an adaptation of the prayer used in earlier American Prayer Books; Prayer B draws on patristic and biblical texts, including, in part, the early eucharistic prayer found in the so-called *Apostolic Tradition* attributed to Hippolytus; Prayer C is a modern composition that on the one hand adheres to the Eastern tradition of telling the story of salvation history expansively and not making use of proper prefaces to do so, but on the other hand places its epiclesis for consecration of the eucharistic elements before rather than after the institution narrative and also draws on much contemporary imagery (e.g., "the vast expanse of interstellar space, galaxies, suns, the planets in their courses, and this fragile earth, our island home");[62] and Prayer D is the so-called *Common Eucharistic Prayer*, an adaptation of the classic EgBAS that was produced in 1975 for ecumenical use in conjunction with the Consultation on Church Union and in parallel with the

---

[62] BCP, 370.

equivalent Roman Catholic prayer.[63] As can be seen, this too does not employ proper prefaces and it allows, rather unusually for an Anglican rite, for the possibility of including wider intercessions within it:

It is truly right to glorify you, Father, and to give you thanks; for you alone are God, living and true, dwelling in light inaccessible from before time and for ever. Fountain of life and source of all goodness, you made all things and fill them with your blessing; you created them to rejoice in the splendor of your radiance. Countless throngs of angels stand before you to serve you night and day; and, beholding the glory of your presence, they offer you unceasing praise. Joining with them, and giving voice to every creature under heaven, we acclaim you, and glorify your Name, as we sing (say),

Holy, holy, holy Lord, God of power and might, heaven and earth are full of your glory. Hosanna in the highest. Blessed is he who comes in the name of the Lord. Hosanna in the highest.

We acclaim you, holy Lord, glorious in power. Your mighty works reveal your wisdom and love. You formed us in your own image, giving the whole world into our care, so that, in obedience to you, our Creator, we might rule and serve all your creatures. When our disobedience took us far from you, you did not abandon us to the power of death. In your mercy you came to our help, so that in seeking you we might find you. Again and again you called us into covenant with you, and through the prophets you taught us to hope for salvation.

Father, you loved the world so much that in the fullness of time you sent your only Son to be our Savior. Incarnate by the Holy Spirit, born of the Virgin Mary, he lived as one of us, yet without sin. To the poor he proclaimed the good news of salvation; to prisoners, freedom; to the sorrowful, joy. To fulfill your purpose he gave himself up to death; and, rising from the grave, destroyed death, and made the whole creation new. And, that we might live no longer for ourselves, but for him who died and rose for us, he sent the Holy Spirit, his own first gift for those who believe, to complete his work in the world, and to bring to fulfillment the sanctification of all.

When the hour had come for him to be glorified by you, his heavenly Father, having loved his own who were in the world, he loved them to the end; at supper with them he took bread, and when he had given

---

[63] See Leonel E. Mitchell, "The Alexandrian Anaphora of St. Basil of Caesarea: Ancient Source of 'A Common Eucharistic Prayer,'" *Anglican Theological Review* 58 (1976): 194–206.

thanks to you, he broke it, and gave it to his disciples, and said, "Take, eat: This is my Body, which is given for you. Do this for the remembrance of me." After supper he took the cup of wine; and when he had given thanks, he gave it to them, and said, "Drink this, all of you: This is my Blood of the new Covenant, which is shed for you and for many for the forgiveness of sins. Whenever you drink it, do this for the remembrance of me."

Father, we now celebrate this memorial of our redemption. Recalling Christ's death and his descent among the dead, proclaiming his resurrection and ascension to your right hand, awaiting his coming in glory; and offering to you, from the gifts you have given us, this bread and this cup, we praise you and we bless you:

We praise you, we bless you, we give thanks to you, and we pray to you, Lord our God.

Lord, we pray that in your goodness and mercy your Holy Spirit may descend upon us, and upon these gifts, sanctifying them and showing them to be holy gifts for your holy people, the bread of life and the cup of salvation, the Body and Blood of your Son Jesus Christ. Grant that all who share this bread and cup may become one body and one spirit, a living sacrifice in Christ, to the praise of your Name. Remember, Lord, your one holy catholic and apostolic Church, redeemed by the blood of your Christ. Reveal its unity, guard its faith, and preserve it in peace.

> [Remember (NN. and) all who minister in your Church.]
> [Remember all your people, and those who seek your truth.]
> [Remember _____.]
> [Remember all who have died in the peace of Christ, and those whose faith is known to you alone; bring them into the place of eternal joy and light.]

And grant that we may find our inheritance with [the Blessed Virgin Mary, with patriarchs, prophets, apostles, and martyrs, (with _____) and] all the saints who have found favor with you in ages past. We praise you in union with them and give you glory through your Son Jesus Christ our Lord. Through Christ, and with Christ, and in Christ, all honor and glory are yours, Almighty God and Father, in the unity of the Holy Spirit, for ever and ever. **Amen.**[64]

The latest Church of England revision of the Eucharist, in its *Common Worship* series authorized in the year 2000, includes no fewer than eight eucharistic prayers in its modern rite (known as Order One). Prayer A is

---

[64] BCP, 372–75.

a conflation of two prayers from the earlier *Alternative Service Book 1980*; Prayer B is a revision of a third prayer from that book, itself based heavily on the one in the ancient *Apostolic Tradition*; Prayer C is a conservative revision of the fourth prayer in the *Alternative Service Book*, it having been developed from that in the 1662 Prayer Book; Prayers D and E are new compositions, employing vivid and concrete imagery; Prayer F is much influenced by the adaptation of EgBAS adopted in the 1979 American Rite; Prayer G derives from a eucharistic prayer composed by the Roman Catholic International Commission on English in the Liturgy in 1984 but never authorized for use; and Prayer H was produced in response to requests for a prayer with more congregational involvement. It is a dialogue between president and congregation, quite short and with the *Sanctus* placed as its conclusion. Four of these prayers (A, B, C, and E) are "Western" in shape, with the possibility of proper prefaces and with the invocation of the Holy Spirit on the bread and wine being placed before the institution narrative, while the other four (D, F, G, and H) adopt the "Eastern" model of an invariable preface and the epiclesis coming after the institution narrative and anamnesis.

Inevitably, the traditional Anglican—and Reformation—issues of eucharistic sacrifice and presence have played a significant part in the language adopted in rites throughout the Anglican Communion, especially in crucial parts of the eucharistic prayers. What can legitimately be said to be "offered" in the Eucharist? The formulation in some fourth-century prayers, "we offer you this bread and this cup," has proved too contentious to be acceptable in many provinces because of the suspicion by some that what others intend by this expression is really "we offer you this Body and Blood," and circumlocutions have had to be found. Similarly, "offertory prayers" over the bread and wine prior to the eucharistic prayer have been looked on with distrust in some quarters, and if they have been admitted into official texts, they are generally not described as such and have to be carefully worded, "bring before" or "set before" rather than "offer" often proving a workable compromise to their language.

With regard to eucharistic presence, petitions that ask that the bread and wine may "become" the body and blood of Christ have usually been judged too extreme in their implied theology to be adopted, even though the expression was used in the Anglican–Roman Catholic Agreed Statement on Eucharistic Doctrine,[65] and instead the more

[65] See below, 340–41.

traditional Anglican "be to us" or "be for us" has been preferred. Just as important as the words to be used has been the point in the eucharistic prayer where the petition for consecration should come. Under pressure from the Anglo-Catholic wing of the church, many provinces have retained the traditional Roman and Anglican position just prior to the institution narrative, so that the latter could be understood as that which effected the consecration. Others, following the lead set centuries earlier in the Scottish Episcopal Church and in TEC, have adopted more fully the West-Syrian or Syro-Byzantine pattern, locating an epiclesis of the Holy Spirit after the institution narrative and anamnesis, although often being ambiguous in wording about what exactly the Spirit is expected to do in relation to the bread and wine. As mentioned above, in its latest round of liturgical revision the Church of England itself has adopted this pattern for four of its eight eucharistic prayers but retained the more traditional "Western" shape for the other four. What has been broadly accepted throughout the provinces in their modern revisions, however, is that the words used for the administration of communion might often be reduced to simply, "The body/blood of Christ"; "The body of Christ, broken for you / The blood of Christ, shed for you"; "The body of Christ, the bread of heaven / The blood of Christ, the cup of salvation"; or a similar brief formula, without the need to retain the traditional qualifying conclusion: "Take and eat this / Drink this in remembrance. . . ."[66]

3. The Lutheran Communion

As noted at the beginning of this chapter, Lutheran liturgical renewal has been fostered by and accomplished in parallel with those in the Roman Catholic and Anglican communions. Unlike either the Roman Catholic Church or, for some time at least, the Anglican Churches, however, there is no typical edition of a normative book equivalent to a Missal or Book of Common Prayer to which Lutherans worldwide might subscribe as an expression of Lutheran unity. What this means is that it is next to impossible to survey the extent of modern liturgical renewal among the diversity of worship books employed by Lutherans in distinct geographical, linguistic, or cultural contexts. What unites Lutherans are common confessions in accepted confessional documents that have liturgical implications, not uniform liturgical-sacramental texts and uniform practices. In this section,

---

[66] See above, 276.

therefore, in order to give examples of modern Lutheran liturgical development, we are limiting ourselves to developments in the United States, where liturgical revision and renewal has been most dominant, together with some attention to Sweden and Germany.

What has characterized the Lutheran liturgical reforms in general, since the 1950s, has been the recovery of Luther's *Formula Missae*, rather than *Deutsche Messe*, pattern for worship, which, to a large extent, at least in the United States, was already the core of the 1888 *Common Service* of Henry Melchior Muhlenberg, a Lutheran missionary to the United States. While the worship books of some German or German-American churches continued to employ portions of the *Deutsche Messe* pattern for the consecration of the Eucharist (with the Lord's Prayer coming before the narrative of institution), the overall structure of the liturgy became and has continued to be that of the *Formula Missae*. The following outline, based on both the *Lutheran Book of Worship* (1978) and *Evangelical Lutheran Worship* (2006), demonstrates this structure easily:

- Confession/Forgiveness
- Entrance Hymn
- The grace . . .
- Kyrie (may be in litany form)
- Glory to God (or Worthy is Christ)
- Prayer of the Day
- First Lesson
- Psalm
- Second Lesson
- Verse
- Gospel
- Sermon
- Hymn of the Day
- Creed
- Prayers
- Peace
- Offertory
- Prayer
- Preface
- *Sanctus*
- Eucharistic Prayer
- Our Father
- Lamb of God

- Communion
- Canticle or Hymn
- Prayer
- Blessing
- Dismissal

Together with the recovery of this liturgical pattern, and in the light of ecumenical dialogues and participation in the Liturgical Movement in general in the early to mid-twentieth century, the story of Lutheran liturgical renewal has also been the story of the recovery of the classic Lutheran confessional norm of the centrality of the Eucharist for Sunday and festival worship (moving from quarterly, to monthly, to every Sunday celebrations) and, together with that, the recovery of a full eucharistic prayer. While the use of the narrative of institution alone, following the *Sanctus*, remains an option in the United States and Germany, ever since the sixteenth-century German Church Orders there have been occasional attempts, especially in German-speaking Lutheranism, to recover a full eucharistic prayer, and, of course, the use of a eucharistic prayer never really did disappear completely in Sweden. Influenced by these Orders, the *Kassel Agenda* of 1896 contained a prayer before the narrative of institution petitioning God for the consecration of the eucharistic gifts:

> Almighty God, heavenly Father, who hast delivered Thy Son, our Lord Jesus Christ, and hast ordained that His body and blood be our food unto eternal life, we bring these Thy gifts before Thy divine Majesty, Thy own from Thy own, and pray Thee to hallow and bless them through Thy divine mercy and power, that this bread and this cup may be the body and blood of our Lord Jesus Christ for all who eat and drink of the same, and that Thou wouldst let them be blessings unto eternal life for them.[67]

Even before this, in the 1879 *Agenda* of the Lutheran Church in Bavaria (used also by the former Joint Synod of Ohio), the rather full prayer in fact even contained a pre–institution and post–institution epiclesis of the Holy Spirit:

---

[67] Text cited in Peter Brunner, *Worship in the Name of Jesus*, trans. M. H. Bertram (St. Louis, MO: Concordia Publishing House, 1968), 301.

(*Before the Institution Narrative*): Sanctify us, therefore, we beseech Thee, in our bodies and souls, by Thy Holy Spirit, and thus fit and prepare us to come to Thy Supper, to the glory of Thy grace, and to our own eternal good.

(*After the Institution Narrative*): O Thou everlasting Son of the Father, sanctify us by Thy Holy Spirit, and make us worthy partakers of Thy sacred Body and Blood, that we may be cleansed from sin and made one with all the members of Thy Church in heaven and on earth.[68]

One of the most successful and lasting attempts at composing a Lutheran eucharistic prayer was made by Paul Zellar Strodach and Luther Reed,[69] a prayer ultimately included within the 1958 *Service Book and Hymnal* in the United States and, thanks to its inclusion as the first eucharistic prayer in *Evangelical Lutheran Worship*, is enjoying wide use among Lutherans again today. This eucharistic prayer, like all subsequent eucharistic prayers among North American Lutherans, is of the West Syrian or Syro-Byzantine type, an anaphoral pattern often considered by modern liturgical reformers as *the* classic anaphoral structure with parallels even to the usage of Jewish table prayer.[70] All four of the eucharistic prayers in *Lutheran Book of Worship* followed this model, as do all *eleven* in *Evangelical Lutheran Worship*. The Strodach-Reed anaphora, as the following demonstrates, is based ecumenically on a wide variety of ancient Eastern and Western sources, which are indicated in brackets:

You are indeed holy, almighty and merciful God; you are most holy, and great is the majesty of your glory [*JAS and CHR*]. You so loved the world that you gave your only Son, that whoever believes in him may not perish but have eternal life [*Twelve Apostles and CHR*]. Having come into the world, he fulfilled for us your holy will and accomplished our salvation [*CHR*]. [*Institution Narrative: In the night in which he was betrayed. . . . Do this for the remembrance of me.*] Remembering, therefore,

---

[68] Luther Reed, *The Lutheran Liturgy* (Philadelphia, PA: Fortress Press, 1959), 755–56.

[69] On the development of this prayer, which actually dates to the 1930s for use among Lutherans in India, see Paul Zellar Strodach, *A Manual on Worship*, rev. ed. (Philadelphia, PA: Muhlenberg Press, 1946), 253–54. See also Luther D. Reed, *The Lutheran Liturgy* (Philadelphia, PA: Fortress Press, 1959), 336–37.

[70] On this see the challenge of Bryan D. Spinks, "Berakah, Anaphoral Theory, and Luther," *Lutheran Quarterly* 3 (1989): 267–80.

his salutary command, his life-giving Passion and death, his glorious resurrection and ascension, and his promise to come again [*JAS, as amplified by the Scottish Presbyterian Book of Common Order, 1940*], we give thanks to you, Lord God Almighty, not as we ought, but as we are able [*Apostolic Constitutions VIII*]; and we implore you mercifully to accept our praise and thanksgiving, and, with your Word and Holy Spirit, to bless us, your servants, and these your own gifts of bread and wine [*Book of Common Prayer, 1549*]; that we and all who share in the body and blood of your Son may be filled with heavenly peace and joy [*Missale Romanum 1570*], and, receiving the forgiveness of sin, may be sanctified in soul and body [*JAS*], and have our portion with all your saints [*BAS*]. All honor and glory are yours, O God, Father, Son, and Holy Spirit, in your holy Church, now and forever. Amen.[71]

Of this prayer, Roman Catholic liturgical scholar Louis Bouyer once wrote:

It would be hard to be more ecumenical! But all of these elements, chosen with great discernment, have been molded into a composition that is as moderate as it is natural. In its brief simplicity this prayer has a concise fullness that we are not accustomed to seeing except in Christian antiquity. Here . . . its eschatological orientation gives it a very primitive sound. Once again, this liturgy must be judged Catholic and orthodox to the extent that the traditional formulas it uses, with hardly an echo of the polemics of the Reformation, are in fact taken in their full and primary sense by the Church that uses them.[72]

In the version of this prayer in *Evangelical Lutheran Worship*, however, the text following the epiclesis of the Word and Holy Spirit has been revised in such a way as to make the connection with its classic sources less clear: "so that we and all who share in the body and blood of Christ may be filled with *heavenly blessing and grace*, and receiving the forgiveness of sins, *may be formed to live as your holy people and be given our inheritance* with all your saints."[73]

---

[71] *Lutheran Book of Worship: Minister's Desk Edition* (Minneapolis, MN: Augsburg Publishing House, 1978), 225. See Frank Senn, *Christian Liturgy: Catholic and Evangelical* (Minneapolis, MN: Fortress Press, 1997), 627–78.

[72] Louis Bouyer, *Eucharist: The Theology and Spirituality of the Eucharistic Prayer* (Notre Dame, IN: University of Notre Dame Press, 1968), 441–42.

[73] ELW, 109.

As is the case with the current Roman Catholic and newer Anglican liturgical books, Lutherans have also adapted the famous eucharistic prayer of the so-called *Apostolic Tradition*. Unlike the versions in the Roman Missal or any of the Anglican books, however, Lutherans attempted in *Lutheran Book of Worship* to have this prayer used by itself, as it appears in the Verona Latin manuscript, without preface or *Sanctus*, as an alternative prayer for small group or weekday Eucharists. For some reason, while the prayer still appears as an integral whole in *Evangelical Lutheran Worship*, it now is used inexplicably as a prayer *after* a preface and *Sanctus*, although clearly the first part of the prayer now duplicates the focus of thanksgiving associated with the preface.

What is equally confusing with the version of this prayer in *Evangelical Lutheran Worship* is the way in which the anamnesis section now has been rendered. In *Lutheran Book of Worship*, the Latin phrase *offerimus tibi panem et calicem* ("we offer to you this bread and cup") was translated as "we *lift* this bread and cup before you." But in the *Evangelical Lutheran Worship* text this has become, "we *take* this bread and cup," thus reversing completely its direction. While no explanation has been offered for why a classic liturgical text should be changed in this way, this example demonstrates how, in parallel to many of the same concerns noted above for Anglican liturgical revision, Lutherans, especially in the United States, have been reticent to embrace either specific "offering" language or explicit consecratory epicleses of the Holy Spirit in eucharistic praying. Indeed, the recovery of eucharistic praying in modern Lutheranism has not been without great theological controversy,[74] and the texts of the eucharistic prayers included in Lutheran worship books are often the result of painstaking compromise and nuance.

Among Lutherans in Germany and Sweden the situation has been somewhat different. Recent German worship books, like their North American counterparts, have tended to embrace the West Syrian or Syro-Byzantine model of eucharistic praying, including an epiclesis of

---

[74] See Oliver K. Olson, "Contemporary Trends in Liturgy Viewed from the Perspective of Classic Lutheran Theology," *Lutheran Quarterly* 26 (1974): 110–57. But see also the various responses to Olson's position in this same volume. On the question of the epiclesis, see Maxwell E. Johnson, "The Holy Spirit and Lutheran Liturgical-Sacramental Worship," in *The Spirit in Worship—Worship in the Spirit*, ed. Teresa Berger and Bryan Spinks (Collegeville, MN: Liturgical Press, Pueblo, 2009), 155–78.

the Holy Spirit.[75] In Sweden, however, eucharistic revision, in a manner similar to the Church of England's *Common Worship*, has been able to employ alternate anaphoral models, and, together with that, a more open approach even to "offering" language, consistent with its own traditional theological stance. The following text is indicative of current Swedish Lutheran eucharistic praying and appears as Eucharistic Prayer A in the current Swedish worship book:

> Praise be to you, Lord of heaven and earth. You have revealed your mercy towards your people in giving your only begotten Son, that whoever believes in him should not perish, but have eternal life. We give thanks for the redemption you have prepared for us through Jesus Christ. Let Your Holy Spirit come into our hearts to enlighten us with a living faith. *Sanctify by your Spirit this bread and wine, which earth has given and human hands have made. Here we offer them to you, that through them we may partake of the true body and blood of our Lord Jesus Christ.* On the same night in which he was betrayed, he took bread, gave thanks, broke it, and gave it to his disciples, saying: "Take, eat. This is my body, which is given for you. Do this in remembrance of me." In the same way, he took the cup, gave thanks, and gave it to his disciples, saying: "Drink this, all of you. This is my blood of the new covenant, which is shed for you and for many for the forgiveness of sins. Do this, as often as you drink it, in remembrance of me." Therefore, heavenly Father, we celebrate this supper in remembrance of your Son's passion and death, his resurrection and ascension. We will eat the Bread of Life and drink the Cup of Blessing until the day when he comes again in glory. We ask you: remember the perfect and eternal sacrifice through which, in Christ, you have reconciled us with yourself. Grant that we may be united into one body, and be made a perfect living sacrifice in Christ. Through him, and with him, and in him, by the power of the Holy Spirit, all glory and honor is yours, almighty Father, forever and ever. Amen.[76]

Other Swedish Lutheran eucharistic prayers have the same or similar construction, including both an epiclesis and offering language before the narrative of institution, while two of the current seven prayers do follow the West Syrian or Syro-Byzantine model.

Almost more important than the various liturgical texts themselves has been a general agreement among Lutherans around the world as

---

[75] Cf. *Agende für Evangelisch-Lutherische Kirchen und Gemeinden*, vol. 3 (Hannover: Lutherisches Verlagshaus, 1988), 130.

[76] See http://www.svenskakyrkan.se/default.aspx?di=725797.

to the overall liturgical pattern to be employed in and for Lutheran worship. Clearly indebted to Gordon Lathrop's articulation of the *ordo* of Christian worship,[77] as well as to the convergence noted at the beginning of this chapter in the World Council of Churches' *Baptism, Eucharist, and Ministry*, local statements such as the Evangelical Lutheran Church in America's 1997 statement on liturgical and sacramental principles, *The Use of the Means of Grace*,[78] and international documents such as the 1996 Lutheran World Federation's *Nairobi Statement on Worship and Culture*,[79] give Lutherans a common way to speak about eucharistic liturgy. As the *Nairobi Statement* says, "The fundamental shape of the principal Sunday act of Christian worship, the Eucharist or Holy Communion, is shared across cultures: the people gather, the Word of God is proclaimed, the people intercede for the needs of the Church and the world, the eucharistic meal is shared, and the people are sent out into the world for mission."[80] What at least the majority of Lutherans in the world have, then, is not so much a common liturgy or worship book but authoritative statements, especially in the case of something like *The Use of the Means of Grace*, for ordering and even inculturating the Eucharist within different contexts around the world.[81]

4. Reformed and Methodist Traditions

Although we cannot provide the same detailed study of Reformed and Methodist eucharistic liturgies as we have for the Roman Catholic, Anglican, and Lutheran traditions, it is important to note that modern eucharistic revision has been a characteristic of some traditional "non-liturgical" churches as well. As we saw in the previous chapter, John Wesley had a deep eucharistic piety. The early Methodist movement in eighteenth-century England was a sort of liturgical movement in

[77] See above, 28–29.

[78] Evangelical Lutheran Church in America, *The Use of the Means of Grace; A Statement on the Practice of Word and Sacrament* (Minneapolis, MN: Augsburg, 1997). See also Evangelical Lutheran Church in America, *Renewing Worship: Principles for Worship* (Minneapolis, MN: Augsburg, 2002).

[79] Lutheran World Federation, *Nairobi Statement on Worship and Culture* (Geneva: Lutheran World Federation, 1996).

[80] Ibid., I, 2.1.

[81] On this, see Maxwell E. Johnson, "Is Anything Normative in Contemporary Lutheran Worship?" in *The Serious Business of Worship: Essays in Honour of Bryan D. Spinks*, ed. Melanie Ross and Simon Jones (London: T & T Clark, 2010), 171–84.

itself, centered on the frequent celebration of the Eucharist among the various "bands" or small groups of participants. But such an emphasis did not last long, and Wesley's own liturgical-sacramental focus did not make it across the Atlantic to the United States.[82]

Today, however, a recovery of Wesley's approach has led the United Methodist Church in the United States to a restoration of a more traditional liturgical shape for worship,[83] including, of course, the *Revised Common Lectionary* and the recovery of a more eucharistic emphasis. Thanks to the liturgical work of great Methodist liturgical scholars like James F. White, Don Saliers, Hoyt Hickman, and, not least, British Methodist theologian, Geoffrey Wainwright and his elucidation of the theology of the Eucharist in Charles Wesley's eucharistic hymns,[84] Methodism has been able to restore an emphasis on the liturgical year and, of great importance, an introduction of some *twenty-two* eucharistic prayers, all of the West Syrian or Syro-Byzantine type;[85] one of those eucharistic prayers has been the *Common Eucharistic Prayer*, based on EgBAS, noted above. A similar revision has taken place in Britain, but there the *Methodist Worship Book* of 1999 provides not just seasonal proper prefaces to its eucharistic prayers but entire orders of service for Advent, Christmas and Epiphany, Lent and Passiontide, Easter, and Pentecost.

The *Common Eucharistic Prayer* is also included among the twenty-six eucharistic prayers in the 1993 *Book of Common Worship*[86] of the Presbyterian Church USA, reflecting several years of liturgical renewal and scholarship among Reformed Christians, again in the United States particularly. This development is highly significant, given the fact that the Reformed tradition in general since the sixteenth century has been reluctant to embrace either a more traditional shape for its liturgy or a strong eucharistic emphasis, including the frequency of

---

[82] See James White, *Protestant Worship: Traditions in Transition* (Louisville, KY: Westminster John Knox Press, 1989), 152ff.

[83] See *The United Methodist Hymnal: Book of United Methodist Worship* (Nashville, TN: The United Methodist Publishing House, 1989), 2–31.

[84] See his *Doxology: The Praise of God in Worship and Life: A Systematic Theology* (New York: Oxford University Press, 1980).

[85] See *At the Lord's Table,* Supplemental Worship Resources 9 (Nashville, TN: Abingdon Press, 1976).

[86] *Book of Common Worship* (Louisville, KY: Westminster John Knox Press, 1993).

communion. Most intriguing about this is not only the use of the (
mon *Eucharistic Prayer*, with its reference to "*offering* to you, from *
gifts you have given us, this bread and this cup, we praise you and
we bless you" after the narrative of institution, but the fact that it is
the Presbyterians who, contrary to the current Lutheran version, more
closely translate the anamnesis of the prayer from *Apostolic Tradition* as
"we *set* before you this bread and cup."[87] What makes this so intriguing is that the Reformed tradition, along with the Lutheran tradition,
has been equally adamant in rejecting any kind of sacrificial or offering language with regard to the Eucharist, but unlike recent Lutheran
liturgical revision, with the exception of Sweden, the Presbyterians
have been willing to embrace the traditional language of classic eucharistic texts without seeing the need to change them according to a particular theological orientation.

We saw in the previous chapter that Calvin's strong pneumatological approach to the real presence of Christ in the Eucharist did not
become expressed liturgically in his own eucharistic revisions. How
significant, then, that by embracing a more classic approach to eucharistic praying, including anaphoras with epicleses of the Holy Spirit,
Calvin's own convictions about the activity of the Holy Spirit in uniting believers to Christ in the Eucharist are given clearer liturgical
emphasis.

While other forms of Protestantism, including those of a more Free
Church or Evangelical orientation, have also been involved in the
renewal of worship, including attention to the importance of the Eucharist or Lord's Supper,[88] it is important to note that many of the
churches discussed above have now entered into situations of full
communion with each other. Hence, The Episcopal Church and Evangelical Lutheran Church in America established full communion
through the document *Called to Common Mission* in 1999/2000, with
the Church of England and the various Scandinavian and Baltic
Lutheran Churches entering similar full communion relationships
through what is known as the *Porvoo Common Statement* and *Agreement*, beginning in 1989 and still continuing to be signed by various

[87] Ibid., 151.
[88] On this, see Melanie Ross' attempt to articulate a liturgical theology for
evangelical Christian worship in her recent Notre Dame doctoral dissertation,
Ecumenism after Charles Finney: A Free Church Liturgical Theology (PhD dissertation, University of Notre Dame, 2010).

Table 8.1

Some Contemporary Eucharistic Liturgies Compared (United States)[1]

ROMAN CATHOLIC	LUTHERAN	EPISCOPAL	PRESBYTERIAN	METHODIST
	Confession/Forgiveness			
Entrance Song	Entrance Hymn	Hymn, Psalm, Anthem	Call to Worship	Gathering
In the Name....				Greeting
The grace....	The grace....	Blessed be God...		
		Collect for purity	Prayer of the Day	
Penitential Rite				
Kyrie	Kyrie (litany)	Kryie/Trisagion		
Glory to God	Glory to God	Glory to God	Hymn of Praise	Hymn of Praise
	(or Worthy is Christ)		Confession/Pardon/	
			(Peace)	
			Canticle, Psalm, hymn	
Opening Prayer	Prayer of the Day	Collect	Prayer for Illumination	Opening Prayer/Prayer for Illumination
First Reading	First Lesson	First Lesson	First Reading	Lesson
Responsorial Psalm	Psalm	Psalm, hymn, anthem	Psalm	(Psalm)
Second Reading	Second Lesson	Second Lesson	Second Reading	Lesson
Alleluia or Tract	Verse	Psalm, hymn, anthem	Psalm, hymn....	Hymn/Song
Gospel	Gospel	Gospel	Gospel	Gospel
Homily	Sermon	Sermon	Sermon	Sermon
	Hymn of the Day			

Creed	Creed	Creed	Affirmation of Faith	Apostles' Creed
Intercessions	Prayers	Prayers of the People	Prayers of the People	Prayers
		Confession		Invitation
				Confession/Pardon
Preparation of Gifts	Peace	Peace	Peace	Peace
Prayer over the Gifts	Offertory	Verse, hymn, psalm . . .	Offering	Offering
	Prayer			
			Invitation	
Preface	Preface	Preface	Preface	Preface
Sanctus	Sanctus	Sanctus	Sanctus	Sanctus
Eucharistic Prayer	Eucharistic Prayer	Eucharistic Prayer	Eucharistic Prayer	Eucharistic Prayer
Our Father	Our Father	Our Father	Lord's Prayer	Lord's Prayer
Peace				
Lamb of God	Lamb of God	Lamb of God		
Communion	Communion	Communion	Communion	Communion
Communion verse	Canticle or hymn		Hymn, Spiritual . . .	
Prayer	Prayer	Prayer		Prayer
				Hymn/Song
Blessing	Blessing	Blessing	Charge and Blessing	Dismissal with blessing
Dismissal	Dismissal	Dismissal		

[1] This comparative table is adapted from Frank C. Senn, *Christian Worship: Evangelical and Catholic* (Minneapolis, MN: Fortress Press, 1997), 646–47.

urches. Similarly, the Evangelical Lutheran Church in America established full communion with the Presbyterian Church USA, the United Church of Christ, the Reformed Church in America (1997), and the United Methodist Church (2008/2009). And both The Episcopal Church (since 2011) and the Evangelical Lutheran Church in America (since 1999) are in full communion with the Moravian Church in America. These full communion agreements have been modeled on and related to a similar European agreement between Lutherans and various Reformed bodies, known as the *Leuenberg Agreement* of 1973.[89] Full communion means not only the ability to share and receive the Eucharist in each of these various churches by members of the other churches but also the full exchange of ordained ministers in preaching and presiding at the Eucharist. Indeed, the extent of *liturgical* agreement among these churches is clearly reflected in table 8.1. Although no such agreements have yet been reached with the Roman Catholic Church or any of the Eastern Churches, the establishment of full communion remains the ultimate goal of ecumenical dialogue and cooperation.[90]

EUCHARISTIC THEOLOGY

Closely related to the liturgical developments summarized above, one of the characteristics shaping modern Roman Catholicism specifically is what some have called a "Copernican Revolution" in theology,[91] a revolution both in sacramental theology and ecclesiology which led to, and in turn was fostered by, the Second Vatican Council. Central to this transformation has been a renewed emphasis on Christ as the "primordial," or primary and fundamental, "Sacrament" of God and the church itself as the "sacrament" of Christ. J. D. Crichton summarizes this emphasis:

> The ultimate subject of the liturgical celebration . . . is . . . Christ who acts in and through his Church. Obviously his action is invisible, but the people of God, his body, is a visible and structured community

[89] On the *Leuenberg Agreement*, see Senn, *Christian Liturgy*, 652–53.
[90] For a hopeful view on this see R. Kevin Seasoltz, "One House, Many Dwellings: Open and Closed Communion," *Worship* 79 (2005): 405–19.
[91] See Mark Searle, "Infant Baptism Reconsidered," in *Living Water, Sealing Spirit: Readings on Christian Initiation*, ed. Maxwell E. Johnson (Collegeville, MN: Liturgical Press, Pueblo, 1995), 365.

and over the whole range of its liturgical action, which . . . consists of both word and sacrament, manifests Christ's presence, shows forth the nature of his activity, which is redemptive, and by his power makes his redeeming work effectual and available to men and women today. It is for these reasons that the Church is called the "sacrament of Christ." Like him it is both visible and invisible, and its sole *raison d'étre* is to mediate his saving love to humankind. . . . From Christ, the sacrament of the Father and of his saving purpose, to the Church, which is the sacrament of Christ, and then to the liturgy, which exists to manifest and convey the redeeming love of God, the line is clear. The liturgy then is essentially and by its nature sacramental. . . . It addresses a word to us but it *embodies* this word in actions, gestures and symbols; . . . [and] the gesture or thing (water, bread, wine) forces us to attend to the word, enables us to grasp its import and to appropriate its content.[92]

Such a renewed emphasis in sacramental theology and ecclesiology within Roman Catholicism led to even greater attention to ritual action, gesture, and symbol as the liturgical self-expression and self-actualization of the sacramental nature and identity of the church itself. While medieval scholastic sacramental theology had always maintained that "sacraments cause grace by signifying [*significando causant*]," theological emphasis had customarily been placed on the sacramental "cause" and "effects" of grace for and in the recipient rather than on the signifying dimension of the sacramental signs themselves within the liturgical celebration of the church. With the recovery of the notion of Christ as the "primordial Sacrament" of God and the church as the "sacrament of Christ," however, the door was also opened to renewed attention to this phenomenon as well.

This modern Roman Catholic transformation of sacramental theology and ecclesiology, long associated with names like Henri du Lubac, Yves Congar, Otto Semmelroth, Odo Casel, Edward Schillebeeckx, and Karl Rahner, many of whom were themselves *periti* ("theological experts" or "consultants") at Vatican II, has been

[92] J. D. Crichton, "A Theology of Worship," in *The Study of Liturgy*, ed. Cheslyn Jones, Geoffrey Wainwright, Edward Yarnold, and Paul Bradshaw, rev. ed. (New York/London: Oxford University Press, 1992), 23. A very helpful and readable summary of modern Roman Catholic sacramental theology appears in Adolf Adam, *Foundations of Liturgy: An Introduction to Its History and Practice* (Collegeville, MN: Liturgical Press, 1992), 103–13.

ecumenically fruitful as well. If, for example, the determination of the concrete form and number of the sacraments themselves are seen increasingly in relationship to the self-expression and celebration of the church as it seeks to be faithful to the saving will of God in Christ within changing historical periods and circumstances, then the relationship of all the "sacraments" to an explicit dominical word becomes less of a theological issue. That is, together with the primary biblical-dominical sacraments of baptism and Eucharist, the existence of other "sacraments" in the church can be attributed to the sacramental nature of the church itself as it "addresses itself to the whole human being, whom it seeks to draw into union with God by means that are consonant with human nature."[93] In other words, it is the church itself as the "sacrament of Christ" in history that has developed various "sacraments" and rites for proclaiming the Gospel of Christ to human beings as through word, gesture, and ritual act it celebrates the ongoing presence of Christ. As such, while modern Protestant theology has yet to articulate a clear and precise ecclesiology, some Protestant sacramental theologians have drawn upon contemporary Roman Catholic insights in such a way that, along with baptism and Eucharist, the other traditional "Roman Catholic" sacraments are often included either as "apostolic" or "ecclesial" sacraments in their overall approaches.[94] Similarly, if the sacraments are increasingly understood as grace-filled "encounters" with Christ, which manifest the "graced character of all human life" and are designed to "promote growth in Christ,"[95] then an overly narrow, almost magical understanding of the scholastic phrase *ex opere operato* ("from the work worked" or "from the finished work"), coined originally to safeguard the objective role of Christ in the sacraments against a Donatist approach, is avoided in favor of underscoring the necessity of active faith in this "encounter" both on the part of the celebrating community and the individual "recipient." And, if the sacraments themselves are not abstracted theologically from the

---

[93] Mark Searle, "Infant Baptism Reconsidered," in Johnson, ed., *Living Water, Sealing Spirit*, 365.

[94] Cf. James F. White, *Sacraments as God's Self-Giving* (Nashville, TN: Abingdon, 1983); Carl Braaten, *Visible Words* (Philadelphia, PA: Fortress Press, 1978); and Gordon Lathrop, *Holy Things: A Liturgical Theology* (Minneapolis, MN: Augsburg Fortress, 1993), where Protestant sacramental theology or the number of the sacraments are not limited to baptism and Eucharist alone.

[95] Searle, "Infant Baptism Reconsidered," 365.

actual liturgical doing of them in the liturgical assembly, then atter tion to the overall shape, contents, and structure of the rites, and the "significance" of such words, gestures, actions, and signs in their liturgical performance, will be of paramount importance. Here as well, the modern Roman Catholic patristic-based recovery of the importance of sacramental signs *as signs* has been influential in the liturgical revision among modern Protestants, leading away from minimalism in sign toward greater use of real bread broken and abundant wine poured out and shared in eucharistic celebrations as well as attention to vesture, gesture, art, and architecture.

As we have done in previous chapters, our discussion of eucharistic theology will continue to be approached by dividing real presence and, hence, communion, from eucharistic sacrifice as a helpful organizing structure. Here, however, the distinction has become largely artificial once again. That is, recent theologies of presence and sacrifice, especially in light of ecumenical dialogue and *rapprochement*, have tended to place these together theologically, viewing them as but two sides of the same coin, as integrally connected. Or, as the 1982 document *Baptism, Eucharist, and Ministry* phrases it, "The eucharist is the *sacrament* of the unique *sacrifice* of Christ, who ever lives to make intercession for us."[96]

Real Presence

Whether perceived or real, perhaps nothing has divided Christianity on the Eucharist since the time of the Protestant and Catholic Reformations in the sixteenth century more than the question of the real presence of Christ, whether the bread and wine *are* or merely point to, or "signify," his body and blood. While all of the Protestant Reformation traditions had abandoned the doctrine of transubstantiation as the explanation for this presence, it is clear historically that Roman Catholics, Lutherans, and some Anglicans have been on one side of this divide with other Anglicans, Reformed, and other Protestants at various locations on the other side. How significant, then, that modern ecumenical convergence, together with Roman Catholic involvement in the World Council of Churches' Faith and Order Commission, on the real presence of Christ in the Eucharist, has led to the following assertion in *Baptism, Eucharist, and Ministry*:

[96] "Eucharist," II.B.8, in World Council of Churches, *Baptism, Eucharist, and Ministry*, emphasis added.

Christ's mode of presence in the eucharist is unique. Jesus said over the bread and wine of the eucharist: "This is my body . . . this is my blood." What Christ declared is true, and this truth is fulfilled every time the eucharist is celebrated. The Church confesses Christ's real, living, and active presence in the eucharist. While Christ's real presence in the eucharist does not depend on the faith of the individual, all agree that to discern the body and blood of Christ, faith is required.[97]

Although various traditions might interpret that assertion differently, especially with regard to the precise relationship of the bread and wine to the body and blood of Christ, to say that Christ's presence is "unique, real, living, active, and objective" would seem to go a long way beyond earlier divisions on this question.

Mention was made above of the *Agreed Statement on Eucharistic Doctrine* first produced by the Anglican–Roman Catholic International Commission (ARCIC) in 1971, which sought to overcome the traditional differences between the two churches on eucharistic sacrifice and presence. With regard to eucharistic presence, the statement affirmed that Christ was active and present in various ways in the whole eucharistic celebration and insisted on both the objective reality of his presence "in the eucharistic signs" and also the need for the subjective response of faith:

> The sacramental body and blood of the Saviour are present as an offering to the believer awaiting his welcome. When this offering is met by faith, a lifegiving encounter results. Through faith Christ's presence—which does not depend on the individual's faith in order to be the Lord's real gift of himself to his Church—becomes no longer just a presence *for* the believer, but also a presence *with* him. Thus, in considering the mystery of the eucharistic presence, we must recognize both the sacramental sign of Christ's presence and the personal relationship between Christ and the faithful which arises from that presence.[98]

Two somewhat surprising features of the statement were its willingness to affirm in one place that the bread and wine "become" the body and blood of Christ—though this language caused considerable

[97] Ibid., II.B.13.
[98] Anglican–Roman Catholic International Commission, "Eucharistic Doctrine" (The Windsor Statement, 1971), in *The Final Report* (Cincinnati, OH: Forward Movement Publications; Washington, DC: United States Catholic Conference, 1982), 15, par. 8.

disquiet among some Anglican readers of the statement and had to be defended as not implying a "material change" by the Commission in its 1979 "Elucidations"[99]—and to acknowledge in a footnote that "the word *transubstantiation* is commonly used in the Roman Catholic Church to indicate that God acting in the eucharist effects a change in the inner reality of the elements. The term should be seen as affirming the *fact* of Christ's presence and of the mysterious and radical change which takes place. In modern Roman Catholic theology it is not understood as explaining *how* the change takes place."[100] And, not surprisingly, given the historic Lutheran focus on the body and blood of Christ "in, with, and under" the bread and wine, the 1967 bilateral Lutheran-Catholic dialogue on the Eucharist in the United States issued the following joint statement on Christ's real presence: "We affirm that in the sacrament of the Lord's supper, Jesus Christ, true God and true man, is present wholly and entirely, in his body and blood, under the signs of bread and wine."[101]

Ever since Pope Paul VI's *Credo of the People of God* in 1968, Roman Catholic theologians have been required to adhere to the terminology of transubstantiation as the church's official position on the eucharistic transformation of the bread and wine.[102] Nevertheless, modern Roman Catholic theologians have sought alternative ways to express and explain transubstantiation, with words like "transignification," related to what the Eucharist celebrates and signifies, i.e., what receiving the bread and cup, after consecration, "means" for the celebrating community; or "transfinalization," in reference to the final end for which these eucharistic gifts are consecrated in the first place, i.e., their reception as Christ's body and blood in holy communion. While such terms have often been rejected as inadequate by Rome, one of those theologians most associated with articulating and defending this terminology was the late Dutch Dominican Edward Schillebeeckx, who wrote the following in the mid-1960s:

[99] Ibid., 17–25; here at 20, par. 6.
[100] Ibid., 14, n. 2.
[101] "The Eucharist as Sacrifice," in *Lutherans and Catholics in Dialogue III: The Eucharist as Sacrifice*, ed. Paul C. Empie and T. Austin Murphy (Minneapolis, MN: Augsburg Publishing House, 1967), 192.
[102] See Paul VI, *Solemnis Professio Fidei* (30 June 1968), AAS 60 (1968): 433–45, here at 442–43, par. 25.

The "real presence" must be viewed against the background of the saving act of Christ, who in this sacramental bread gives himself to us. Christ remains truly present in the sacred host before being received in communion, but always as an offer. . . . The presence becomes reciprocal—that is to say, presence in the full and completive human sense—only in the acceptance of this offered presence, and in that way it becomes the presence of Christ in our hearts, which is the very purpose of the eucharist. Only a eucharistic presence that is personally *offered and accepted* becomes an altogether complete presence. The presence of Christ in the tabernacle is therefore real, but as such it is only offered, and in this sense it is secondary in relation to the complete, reciprocal presence to which it is directed as to its end and perfection. . . .

. . . [I]n the eucharist we ought to be concerned with an interpersonal relationship between Christ and us, an interpersonal relationship in which Christ gives himself to [us] by means of bread and wine, which by this very gift, have undergone a transfinalization and an ontological and therefore radical transignification. The bread and wine have become this real presence offered by Christ, who gave his life for us on the cross; offered by Christ in order that we might participate in this sacrifice and in the new covenant which is life for us all. The chemical, physical, or botanical reality of bread and wine is not changed; otherwise, Christ would not be present under the sign of eatable bread and drinkable wine. Eucharistic sacramentality demands precisely that the physical reality does not change, otherwise there would no longer be a eucharistic sign.[103]

Even with regard to the reservation of the Eucharist in the tabernacle, referred to in the above quote, there has been significant ecumenical convergence in thought and practice. Again, it is *Baptism, Eucharist, and Ministry* which reminds all churches "that, on the one hand, it be remembered, especially in sermons and instruction, that the primary intention of reserving the elements is their distribution among the sick and those who are absent, and on the other hand, it be recognized that the best way of showing respect for the elements served in the eucharistic celebration is by their consumption, without excluding their use for communion of the sick."[104] In an article on

---

[103] Edward Schillebeeckx, "Transubstantiation, Transfinalization, Transignification," *Worship* 40 (1966): 336–38; and *idem, The Eucharist* (London: Sheed and Ward, 1968). See also Nathan Mitchell, *Real Presence: The Work of Eucharist* (Chicago, IL: Liturgy Training Publications, 1998).

[104] "Eucharist," III.32, in *Baptism, Eucharist, and Ministry.*

eucharistic reservation in modern Roman Catholicism, Jesuit liturgist Peter Fink echoes this approach:

> The food of the eucharist is reserved after the eucharistic celebration primarily to extend the nourishment and the grace of Christ's table to those unable to participate in the liturgy itself, particularly the sick and the dying. This is clearly stated in the 1967 instruction *Eucharisticum mysterium*: "the primary and original purpose of the reserving of the sacred species in church outside Mass is the administration of the Viaticum" (E.M. III, I, A.).[105]

Of course, even the Council of Trent had made essentially the same point:

> The custom of reserving the Holy Eucharist in a sacred place is so ancient that even the period of the Nicene Council recognized that usage. Moreover, the practice of carrying the Sacred Eucharist to the sick and of carefully reserving it for this purpose in churches, besides being exceedingly reasonable and appropriate, is also found enjoined in numerous councils and is a very ancient observance of the Catholic Church. Wherefore, this holy council decrees that this salutary and necessary custom be by all means retained (Session XIII, *Decree Concerning the Most Holy Sacrament of the Eucharist*, chap. 6).[106]

Closely related is the classic statement often attributed to the early liturgical movement pioneer and Belgian Benedictine Lambert Beauduin that "the Eucharist is adored *because* it is reserved; it is not reserved in order to be adored." And it is also significant that among Anglicans and Lutherans modern rites for bringing communion to the sick and others from the eucharistic liturgy itself—without a separate consecration—have been provided,[107] with some Anglican and even some Lutheran communities beginning to practice some form of

---

[105] Peter Fink, "Eucharist, Reservation of," in *The New Dictionary of Sacramental Worship*, ed. *idem* (Collegeville, MN: Liturgical Press, Michael Glazier, 1990), 428. See also R. Kevin Seasoltz, "Eucharistic Devotion and Reservation: Some Reflections," *Worship* 81 (2007): 426–47; and Nathan D. Mitchell, "The History of Eucharistic Reservation in the West," *Worship* 85 (2011): 155–66.

[106] ET from H. J. Schroeder, *The Canons and Decrees of the Council of Trent* (St. Louis, MO: B. Herder Book Co., 1941), 77.

[107] Cf. *Occasional Service Book* (Minneapolis, MN: Augsburg Fortress, 1982), 76–82; and BCP, 396–99.

eucharistic reservation, either in sacristy aumbries or on or near the main altar.

Integrally connected as well to the theology of real presence has been in the West the recovery of the role of the Holy Spirit in the Eucharist, especially with regard to the liturgical expression of that role in the restoration of epicleses in all contemporary liturgical traditions, Roman Catholic and Protestant. Ongoing attention to this significant sacramental theological approach in the Christian East, as we have seen, has assisted the West in embracing a more active trinitarian approach to the Eucharist as well as overcoming what might be called the rather narrow emphasis on eucharistic consecration by the institution narrative alone. In words remarkably similar to those of the current *Catechism of the Catholic Church*, it is *Baptism, Eucharist, and Ministry* again which underscores the eucharistic role of the Holy Spirit: "It is in virtue of the living word of Christ and by the power of the Holy Spirit that the bread and wine become the sacramental signs of Christ's body and blood. They remain so for the purpose of communion."[108]

Another related dimension of the Eucharist that was to some extent also recovered in the twentieth century is that of eschatology. Although the understanding of the Eucharist as looking forward to and foretaste of the heavenly banquet that believers would enjoy when the kingdom of God was finally fulfilled seems to have been a prominent feature of early eucharistic meals, that facet gradually subsided from view in Western eucharistic theology and spirituality, though it was better preserved in the East.[109] Even in the West, however, this was an emphasis in the eucharistic theology of St. Thomas Aquinas, who in his *Magnificat* antiphon *O Sacrum Convivium* for the feast of *Corpus Christi* described the Eucharist in the following way: "O holy banquet, in which Christ is received, in which the memory of his passion is renewed, in which the soul is filled with grace and *a pledge of future glory* is given to us, alleluia!"[110]

Thanks especially to the renewal of biblical theology in modern times, that deficiency has begun to be filled, and not simply in terms of an "other-worldly" experience but very much as pointing to the

---

[108] "Eucharist," II.C.15, in *Baptism, Eucharist, and Ministry*, emphasis added.

[109] See the now classic study by Geoffrey Wainwright, *Eucharist and Eschatology* (New York: Oxford University Press, 1981).

[110] ET from *Benedictine Daily Prayer: A Short Breviary*, ed. Maxwell E. Johnson, et al. (Collegeville, MN: Liturgical Press, 2005), 1657.

church's mission in this world, as it seeks to identify and bring into existence the values of God's kingdom here and now. This theological recovery was well summarized in a further section of *Baptism, Eucharist, and Ministry*, "The Eucharist as Meal of the Kingdom":

22. The eucharist opens up the vision of the divine rule which has been promised as the final renewal of creation, and is a foretaste of it. Signs of this renewal are present in the world wherever the grace of God is manifest and human beings work for justice, love and peace. The eucharist is the feast at which the Church gives thanks to God for these signs and joyfully celebrates and anticipates the coming of the Kingdom in Christ (1 Cor 11:26; Matt 26:29).

23. The world, to which renewal is promised, is present in the whole eucharistic celebration. The world is present in the thanksgiving to the Father, where the Church speaks on behalf of the whole creation; in the memorial of Christ, where the Church, united with its great High Priest and Intercessor, prays for the world; in the prayer for the gift of the Holy Spirit, where the Church asks for sanctification and new creation.

24. Reconciled in the eucharist, the members of the body of Christ are called to be servants of reconciliation among men and women and witnesses of the joy of resurrection. As Jesus went out to publicans and sinners and had table-fellowship with them during his earthly ministry, so Christians are called in the eucharist to be in solidarity with the outcast and to become signs of the love of Christ who lived and sacrificed himself for all and now gives himself in the eucharist.

25. The very celebration of the eucharist is an instance of the Church's participation in God's mission to the world. This participation takes everyday form in the proclamation of the Gospel, service of the neighbor, and faithful presence in the world.

26. As it is entirely the gift of God, the eucharist brings into the present age a new reality which trans-forms Christians into the image of Christ and therefore makes them his effective witnesses. The eucharist is precious food for missionaries, bread and wine for pilgrims on their apostolic journey. The eucharistic community is nourished and strengthened for confessing by word and action the Lord Jesus Christ who gave his life for the salvation of the world. As it becomes one people, sharing the meal of the one Lord, the eucharistic assembly must be concerned for gathering also those who are at present beyond its visible limits, because Christ invited to his feast all for whom he died. Insofar as Christians cannot unite in full fellowship around the

same table to eat the same loaf and drink from the same cup, their missionary witness is weakened at both the individual and the corporate levels.[111]

Liturgically, this renewed emphasis has been incorporated into recent eucharistic liturgies in various ways: (1) by acclamations within the eucharistic prayers (e.g., "We proclaim your Death, O Lord, and profess your Resurrection until you come again"; "Amen. Come Lord Jesus"; or the ecumenically popular "Christ has died, Christ is risen, Christ will come again"); (2) by invoking the coming of the kingdom in relationship to the anamnesis or epiclesis in the eucharistic prayer (e.g., "Therefore, O Lord, as we celebrate the memorial of the saving Passion of your Son . . . and as we look forward to his second coming, we offer you in thanksgiving this holy and living sacrifice," Eucharistic Prayer III, *Roman Missal*; or "Sanctify us also that we may faithfully receive this holy Sacrament, and serve you in unity, constancy, and peace; and at the last day bring us with all your saints into the joy of your eternal kingdom," Prayer A, BCP 1979); and (3) by means of other texts elsewhere in the eucharistic liturgy (e.g., the petition "Give us a foretaste of the feast to come," in one of the offertory chants in *Evangelical Lutheran Worship*, or the embolism to the Lord's Prayer in the *Roman Missal*, "Deliver us, Lord, we pray, from every evil, graciously grant peace in our days, that, by the help of your mercy, we may be always free from sin and safe from all distress, as we await the blessed hope and the coming of our Savior, Jesus Christ"). Indeed, as Episcopal liturgical scholar Marion J. Hatchett noted several years ago, "The content of good liturgy is remembrance (*anamnesis*, the opposite of amnesia) and *prolepsis* (anticipation, expectation, foretaste)."[112]

Attending to eschatology in eucharistic theology also has something to say about the identity of the eucharistic elements of bread and wine themselves. Geoffrey Wainwright says that "the bread and wine become the first-fruits of that renewed creation which will be so entirely submitted to the divine Lordship that it will enjoy total penetration by the divine glory while remaining distinct from the transcendent God it worships."[113] In the Eucharist, then, not only are the consecrated bread

---

[111] "Eucharist," II.C.22–26, in *Baptism, Eucharist, and Ministry.*

[112] Marion J. Hatchett, *Sanctifying Life, Time, and Space* (New York: The Seabury Press, 1976), 4.

[113] Wainwright, *Eucharist and Eschatology*, 110.

and wine the body and blood of Christ here and now, they are, at the same time, given new meaning and significance ("transignified") as signs of the *new* creation itself. Elements of *this* creation become in the Eucharist elements already of the new creation to come. They become already then part of the "not yet" of the fullness of salvation in addition to the "now" of salvation. As the 1971 *Agreed Statement on Eucharistic Doctrine* of the Anglican–Roman Catholic International Commission says: "in the Eucharistic celebration we anticipate the joys of the age to come. By the transforming action of the Spirit of God, earthly bread and wine become the heavenly manna and the new wine, the eschatological banquet for the new man: elements of the first creation become pledges and first fruits of the new heaven and the new earth."[114]

Finally, with regard to modern approaches to the question of real presence, it must be noted that even the age-old emphases on Word (Protestant) *or* Sacrament (Roman Catholic and Eastern Christian) rather than Word *and* Sacrament have been largely overcome by ecumenical liturgical and theological convergence. This is not simply to be located in the fact that both preaching the Word and celebrating the Eucharist are seen as necessarily connected in the Sunday liturgies of the various churches today. Rather, what has taken place is the recovery of the Word itself as the very content of the Eucharist! No one has expressed this more clearly in the West than the Roman Catholic liturgical theologian Louis-Marie Chauvet:

> [I]t is clear theologically that every sacrament is a sacrament of the word, or to say it differently, *the word itself mediated under the ritual mode, different from the mode of Scripture.* Although the distinction between word and sacrament is a legitimate one, their dichotomy has had disastrous results. Initiated by the Reformers of the sixteenth century in the context of excessive sacramentalism, against which a reaction in favor of returning to the word is easily understandable, this reaction, recently reconfigured by the ideological opposition between "faith" and "religion," ended by establishing a true competition between the two. The word, source of the "true" faith, would be endowed with all virtues of "authenticity," "responsibility," "commitment," Christian "adulthood" or "maturity" finally reached, whereas sacraments would be suspected of bordering on magic, of fostering the

---

[114] Anglican–Roman Catholic International Commission, "Eucharistic Doctrine," in *The Final Report*, 16, par. 11.

most dubious anthropological and social archaism, of encouraging dependency among believers, and so on. Such reasoning shows forgetfulness of two things; first, that the word also reaches us only through the mediation of a body of writings which is as liable to manipulation as anything else and which is subject to highly ritualized uses even in the most spare liturgies; second, that the sacraments, obviously exposed to pitfalls because of their ritual character . . . are nothing but a particular modality of the word. . . . It is always *as word* that Christ gives himself to be eaten in the Eucharist. It is impossible to receive communion fruitfully without having "eaten the book" (see Ezek 2–3; Rev 10:9-10), ruminated the word in the Spirit. Here again, nothing is more traditional. Thus Ambrose in the fourth century, speaking of the Scriptures: "Eat this food first, in order to be able to come afterward to the food of the body of Christ"; or Augustine: "Sisters and brothers, see that you eat the heavenly bread in a spiritual sense . . . so that all this may help us, beloved, not to eat the flesh and blood of Christ merely in the sacrament, as many of the wicked do, but to eat and drink in order to participate in the Spirit."[115]

And, as Karl Rahner and Heinrich Fries once wrote:

> *Pulpit fellowship* is already being practiced in many cases; and it no longer presents a disquieting exception, even to Catholic Christians. But one really should think about this more than ever, *since it is precisely a pulpit fellowship which presupposes a community of faith.* Consider the reality of salvation of the Word of God; consider Christ's presence in its various forms, including the form of proclamation; finally consider the theological conformity of Word *and* Sacrament—sacrament as visible Word (*verbum visibile*), the Word as audible sacrament (*sacramentum audibile*).[116]

Eucharistic Sacrifice

As has been the case with modern ecumenical convergence on real presence, so also have there been remarkable developments on the

---

[115] Louis-Marie Chauvet, *The Sacraments: The Word of God at the Mercy of the Body* (Collegeville, MN: Liturgical Press, Pueblo, 2001), 47–48. For an Eastern Christian approach to this same question, see M. Daniel Findikyan, "The Unfailing Word in Eastern Sacramental Prayers," in *Studia Liturgica Diversa: Essays in Honor of Paul F. Bradshaw*, ed. Maxwell E. Johnson and L. Edward Phillips (Portland, OR: Pastoral Press, 2004), 179–90.

[116] *Unity of the Churches: An Actual Possibility* (New York/Philadelphia: Paulist Press and Fortress Press, 1985), 125, emphasis added.

question of the Eucharist as sacrifice, *the* eucharistic issue dividing Roman Catholicism and Eastern Christianity from the churches of the Reformation over the past five centuries. For Roman Catholics in particular, the Protestant challenge has necessitated the need to articulate the theology of eucharistic sacrifice, including its interpretation as being "propitiatory," in such a way so as to affirm the uniqueness and unrepeatability of the historic sacrifice of Christ on the cross as the *ephapax* ("once-for-all") character of salvation in light of Hebrews 10:12ff. Beginning with the German Benedictine scholar at Maria Laach Abbey in the mid-1900s, Dom Odo Casel and his "Mystery Theology" (*Mysterienlehre*),[117] Roman Catholics began to speak of "re-presentation" (*Gegenwärtigzetsung*) with regard not simply to the sacrifice of the cross but to the presence of the whole "Paschal Mystery" of Christ's incarnation, life, death, resurrection, and ascension, being present salvifically in the church's liturgical celebrations. Hence, Casel's theology enabled Catholic theology to move beyond a narrow Anselmian understanding of what constituted Christ's sacrificial self-giving, as encompassing only his death as blood-payment to God for the debt of human sin, rather than his entire life of self-giving love for us. While Casel's own approach was criticized strongly for turning Christianity into essentially a Hellenistic Mystery Religion or "cult,"[118] the notion of "re-presentation" of the one sacrifice of Christ made present in the Eucharist has remained an important concept for Roman Catholic eucharistic theology and for ecumenical dialogue.

Real presence, communion, and the eucharistic sacrifice cannot be separated in modern Roman Catholic theology. For, what is at stake here is not the presence or "re-presentation" of a historical event but the presence of Christ himself in the totality of his paschal mystery. Thus, if Christ himself is present, then the fullness of who Christ is, including his "sacrifice on the cross," is also present. As Robert Taft has said: "Not only is his saving, self-offering eternal; he IS his eternal self-offering, and it is in his presence among us that this sacrifice is eternally present to us."[119] And if the once-for-all sacrifice of Christ

[117] Odo Casel, *The Mystery of Christian Worship* (Westminster: Newman Press, 1963).

[118] Cf. Alexander Schmemann, *Introduction to Liturgical Theology* (London: Faith Press, 1966), 81–86.

[119] Robert Taft, "What Does Liturgy Do? Toward a Soteriology of Liturgical Celebration: Some Theses," *Worship* 66 (1992): 194–211, here at 198.

was "propitiatory," historically, and if it is that one sacrifice of Christ which has now assumed real presence with Christ in the Eucharist, then the eucharistic sacrifice must also be "propitiatory." Thus, as Taft explains, the Eucharist "does not celebrate a past event, but *a present person*, who contains forever all he is and was, and all he has done for us."[120] And here we see the modern Catholic recovery of the mid-fifth-century theology of St. Leo I's classic phrase, *Quod itaque Redemptoris nostri conspicuum fuit, in sacramenta transivit* ("what was visible in our Redeemer has passed into sacraments").[121] What is different is but the "mode" in which the same salvation is present, not the historical or physical modes of being, but now the "sacramental."

But if it is the one, unrepeatable, sacrifice of Christ that is "re-presented" in the eucharistic celebration because it is the "present Person," the "Trans-historical Christ,"[122] who is present in a saving way, it is precisely through the faithful reception of holy communion, participation in the "sacrificial meal" itself, which becomes the primary way by which Christ the High Priest unites the faith community with his one saving sacrifice. As Edward Kilmartin has written, underscoring a trinitarian theology of sacrifice:

> [T]he New Testament concept of sacrifice is mirrored in Holy Communion. This is a reversal of the concept which comes from the history of religions. For sacrifice is not, in the first place, an activity of human beings directed to God and, in the second place, something that reaches its goal in the response of divine acceptance and bestowal of divine blessing on the cultic community. Rather, sacrifice in the New Testament understanding—and thus in its Christian understanding—is, in the first place, the self-offering of the Father in the gift of his Son, and in the second place the unique response of the Son in his humanity to the Father, and in the third place, the self-offering of believers in union with Christ by which they share in his covenant relationship with the Father. . . . The Holy Spirit brings about the presence of the historical sacrifice of Christ, and acts through it as the source of the transmission of the sacrificial attitudes of Christ that enable the liturgical assembly to participate in Christ's self-offering through the medium of the Eucharistic Prayer. The Holy Spirit effects the sancti-

---

[120] Ibid., 199.

[121] Leo I, Sermon 74.2, *De Ascensione II.*

[122] See Taft, "What Does Liturgy Do?," 200. The term "Trans-historical Christ" belongs to Thomas Talley.

350

fication of the bread and wine, symbols of the Church's self-offering, making them the sacraments of Christ's body and blood. Likewise the Spirit sanctifies the community so that the communicants communicate spiritually with the Lord whom they encounter sacramentally in the consecrated gifts. In a word the whole liturgy happens "through the power of the Spirit." . . . The Eucharistic sacrifice, just as the historical sacrifice of the cross, is ground on the initiative of the Father. The whole point of the Eucharist is the participation in Christ's Passover from suffering to glory. This is only possible because of the Father's self-gift in the sending of the Son and the response of the Son in his humanity, and the sanctifying work of the Spirit in the Incarnation and in the life of faith of Jesus.[123]

Such an approach to eucharistic sacrifice is also reflected in the current *Catechism of the Catholic Church*. After noting that the eucharistic sacrifice must be treated as thanksgiving and praise to the Father, the sacrificial memorial of Christ and his body, and the presence of Christ by the power of his word and of his Spirit, the *Catechism* goes on to state, "the Eucharist is the memorial of Christ's Passover, the making present and the sacramental offering of his unique sacrifice, in the liturgy of the Church which is his Body. In all the Eucharistic Prayers we find after the words of institution a prayer called the anamnesis or memorial" (par. 1362). Further:

> The sacrificial character of the Eucharist is manifested in the very words of institution: "This is my body which is given for you" and "This cup which is poured out for you is the New Covenant in my blood." In the Eucharist Christ gives us the very body which he gave up for us on the cross, the very blood which he "poured out for many for the forgiveness of sins." The Eucharist is thus a sacrifice because it *re-presents* (makes present) the sacrifice of the cross, because it is its *memorial* and because it *applies* its fruit. (1365–66)

And, the *Catechism* draws attention to the importance of the concept of intercession in the celebration of the Eucharist, which also becomes a rather key emphasis in modern Catholic and ecumenical theological thought on the topic of sacrifice:

---

[123] E. Kilmartin, *The Eucharist in the West*, ed. Robert Daly (Collegeville, MN: Liturgical Press, Pueblo, 1998), 381–82.

The Eucharist is also the sacrifice of the Church. The Church which is the Body of Christ participates in the offering of her Head. With him, she herself is offered whole and entire. She unites herself to his intercession with the Father for all. In the Eucharist the sacrifice of Christ becomes also the sacrifice of the members of his Body. The lives of the faithful, their praise, sufferings, prayer, and work, are united with those of Christ and with his total offering, and so acquire a new value. Christ's sacrifice present on the altar makes it possible for all generations of Christians to be united with his offering. In the catacombs the Church is often represented as a woman in prayer, arms outstretched in the praying position. Like Christ who stretched out his arms on the cross, through him, with him, and in him, she offers herself and intercedes for all. (1368)

As noted, the notion of "re-presentation" of the one sacrifice of Christ in the Eucharist has been ecumenically fruitful. *Baptism, Eucharist, and Ministry* places this under the category of "anamnesis" or "memorial":

5. The eucharist is the memorial of the crucified and risen Christ, i.e., the living and effective sign of his sacrifice, accomplished once and for all on the cross and still operative on behalf of all humankind. The biblical idea of memorial as applied to the eucharist refers to this present efficacy of God's work when it is celebrated by God's people in a liturgy.

6. Christ himself with all that he has accomplished for us and for all creation (in his incarnation, servant-hood, ministry, teaching, suffering, sacrifice, resurrection, ascension and sending of the Spirit) is present in this anamnesis, granting us communion with himself. The eucharist is also the foretaste of his parousia and of the final kingdom.

7. The anamnesis in which Christ acts through the joyful celebration of his Church is thus both representation and anticipation. It is not only a calling to mind of what is past and of its significance. It is the Church's effective proclamation of God's mighty acts and promises.

8. Representation and anticipation are expressed in thanksgiving and intercession. The Church, gratefully recalling God's mighty acts of redemption, beseeches God to give the benefits of these acts to every human being. In thanksgiving and intercession, the Church is united with the Son, its great High Priest and Intercessor (Rom. 8:34; Heb. 7:25). The eucharist is the sacrament of the unique sacrifice of Christ, who ever lives to make intercession for us. It is the memorial of all that God has done for the salvation of the world. What it was God's will to accomplish

in the incarnation, life, death, resurrection and ascension of Christ, God does not repeat. These events are unique and can neither be repeated nor prolonged. In the memorial of the eucharist, however, the Church offers its intercession in communion with Christ, our great High Priest.[124]

And in the commentary attached to this section, a correlation between re-presentation, intercession and propitiation is made: "It is in the light of the significance of the eucharist as intercession that references to the eucharist in Catholic theology as 'propitiatory sacrifice' may be understood. The understanding is that there is only one expiation, that of the unique sacrifice of the cross, made actual in the eucharist and presented before the Father in the intercession of Christ and of the Church for all humanity."[125] A similar approach was taken years before *Baptism, Eucharist, and Ministry* by the Anglican–Roman Catholic International Commission (1971), which emphasized the once-for-all nature of Christ's death on Calvary but saw what it claimed to be the biblical understanding of remembrance (*anamnesis*), "the making effective in the present of an event in the past," as offering a way of understanding the connection between that salvific act and the Eucharist:

> There can be no repetition of or addition to what was then accomplished once for all by Christ. . . . Yet God has given the eucharist to his Church as a means through which the atoning work of Christ on the cross is proclaimed and made effective in the life of the Church. . . . The eucharistic memorial is no mere calling to mind of a past event or of its significance, but the church's effectual proclamation of God's mighty acts. Christ instituted the eucharist as a memorial (*anamnesis*) of the totality of God's reconciling action in him. In the eucharistic prayer the church continues to make a perpetual memorial of Christ's death, and his members, united with God and one another, give thanks for all his mercies, entreat the benefits of his passion on behalf of the whole church, participate in these benefits and enter into the movement of his self-offering.[126]

And even earlier (1967) the Lutheran-Catholic dialogue on the Eucharist in the United States had employed the language of "re-presentation" in such a way as to foster a common theological understanding.

---

[124] "Eucharist," II.B.5–8.

[125] Ibid.

[126] Anglican–Roman Catholic International Commission, "Eucharistic Doctrine," in *The Final Report*, 13–14, par. 5.

Roman Catholics have called the Mass a sacrifice. They mean by this that the Eucharist is a gracious act in which God makes present this propitiatory sacrifice for man. This is not a new, or different sacrifice but the same sacrifice of Calvary. The Mass is properly, and necessarily, called sacrifice because the Christ who is the sacrifice is present in the Supper. . . . . Lutherans have often understood Roman Catholics to say that the Mass adds to Calvary, is a "re-doing" of Calvary and by this have implied that the one sacrifice of Christ is defective and incomplete. . . . Now we can agree that this is not what Roman Catholics intend to say. The sacrifice of Christ is complete and unalterable and cannot be supplemented or completed by any subsequent action. Rather, that sacrifice, complete in itself, is made present, made effective and its benefits communicated in the Eucharist. . . . Catholics have used the word "re-presentation," not in the sense of doing again, but in the sense of "presenting again." Lutherans can agree wholeheartedly. Lutherans have sometimes used the term "actualize" to communicate the same understanding. . . . It was agreed that the unrepeatable sacrifice which *was*, now *is* in the Eucharist. There is therefore a continuing work of Christ in the sense that he continues to plead before the Father and continues to communicate to man his work of redemption.[127]

Although the results of these dialogues have been important theologically both to Anglicans and those Lutherans now making up the Evangelical Lutheran Church in America, they have since then played little part in the formulation of liturgical texts for Anglican or Lutheran eucharistic rites. While Episcopalians in the United States use offering language in the anamnesis sections of the eucharistic prayers in the 1979 BCP, North American Lutherans and Anglicans in England, as we noted above, have been reluctant to embrace "offering" terminology at all. That is, if agreement has been reached on the eucharistic sacrifice theologically, that does not mean it has necessarily been reached at a liturgical-textual level.

Whether or not that must remain the case, however, is open to discussion. Geoffrey Wainwright, for example, has written that attention to the concept and liturgical expression of eucharistic sacrifice might well underscore an "Anti-Pelagian" affirmation of grace: "Could not the contentious notion 'we offer Christ' paradoxically be seen as an-

---

[127] Kent S. Knutson, "Eucharist as Sacrifice: Roman Catholic–Lutheran Dialogue," in *Lutherans and Catholics in Dialogue III*, ed. Empie and Murphy, 12–13.

tipelagian? It could be an acknowledgement that we have nothing else to offer. . . . To say 'we offer Christ' may then become a bold way of acknowledging the transforming presence and work of Christ within us. Again, paradoxically, it could thus be the very opposite of Pelagianism."[128] And, similarly to Wainwright, Regin Prenter from within, not surprisingly, the Swedish Lutheran tradition, argued that for Lutherans the liturgical recovery of the language of eucharistic sacrifice would actually affirm both salvation by "grace alone" and through "faith alone."

> [I]n the Holy Eucharist Christ is present as our High Priest in a peculiar manner. He is present . . . bodily, in his sacrificed body and blood, sacramentally present under bread and wine. Through the real sacramental presence . . . he unites us with himself as the Priest and victim. He takes us into his own sacrifice. Sitting at his table and receiving his body and blood we are, so to speak, not only behind him, when he enters the heavenly sanctuary with our prayers and thanksgivings, but we are with him, nay in him, because his is with us. Thus we offer Christ to God, imploring him, giving him occasion and moving him to offer himself for us and us with himself in the Eucharistic meal, while he through his body and blood under bread and wine communicates with us.[129]

And:

> Through this sacrifice of thanksgiving we plead His one perfect atoning sacrifice in order to assert our right to appear before God. In so doing we offer bread and wine to God in remembrance of Christ. If we thank God for the sacrifice, offered by Christ on Calvary for our sins, we thereby confess that we have no right whatsoever to appear before God in our own righteousness, but only in the righteousness of Jesus Christ, our only high priest and mediator. Thus our self-sacrifice in Jesus Christ implies that we abandon any righteousness of our own. . . . The Eucharistic sacrifice . . . is the liturgical expression of the "sola fide" corresponding to the Eucharistic sacrament as the liturgical expression of the "sola gratia."[130]

---

[128] *Doxology*, 272–73.

[129] Regin Prenter, "Eucharistic Sacrifice according to the Lutheran Tradition," *Theology* 67, 529 (1964): 286–95, here at 290.

[130] Regin Prenter, "A Lutheran Doctrine of Eucharistic Sacrifice?," *Studia Theologica* 19 (1965): 189–99, here at 195–97.

Nevertheless, to embrace the idea of eucharistic sacrifice theologically as the "re-presentation" or "actualization" of the one expiatory or propitiatory sacrifice of Christ, certainly may, but does not necessarily, lead to a precise liturgical expression of "offering" this sacrifice. As we saw earlier in this study, one ancient liturgical tradition, namely, that of the West Syrian East, especially in its eucharistic prayer known as the *Twelve Apostles*, which either formed the basis for CHR or is from a common source, did not employ offering language in the anamnesis at all but made *thanksgiving* itself the major focus of the eucharistic memorial:

> *Priest*: While therefore we remember, Lord, your saving command and all your dispensation which was for us, your cross, your resurrection from the dead on the third day, your ascension into heaven and your session at the right hand of the Father, and your glorious second coming, in which you will come in glory to judge the living and the dead, and to repay all men according to their works in your love for man— for your Church and your flock beseech you, saying through you and with you to the Father, "have mercy on me,"

> *People*: Have mercy [on us, O God, almighty Father, have mercy on us]—

> *Priest*: we also, Lord, give thanks and confess you on behalf of all men for all things

> *People*: We praise you, [we bless you, we give thanks to you, Lord, and we ask you, our God, "be gracious, for you are good, and have mercy on us"].

Indeed, as the anamnesis in the Strodach-Reed Eucharistic Prayer, reflecting this same tradition as it appears in *Apostolic Constitutions*, book 8, states: "we give thanks to you, Lord God Almighty, not as we ought, but as we are able." And it was this phrase, according to John R. K. Fenwick, that constituted the "ancient heart of the Antiochene anamnesis." [131] Basic agreement on theological interpretations, therefore, still leaves room for a variety of liturgical expressions not only in the ancient churches but in the churches today. A unity in faith does not necessitate a uniformity in eucharistic texts or eucharistic practice.

[131] J. R. K. Fenwick, *The Missing Oblation: The Contents of the Early Antiochene Anaphora*, Alcuin/GROW Liturgical Study 11 (Cambridge: Grove Books, 1989), 24–25.

SUMMARY

1. Twentieth-century liturgical revisions have witnessed a widespread convergence in all the mainstream churches in eucharistic theology, in the shape of eucharistic rites, and in the adoption of shared lectionaries and common liturgical texts.

2. The Roman Catholic revision was characterized by the adoption of the vernacular, by the use of a new three-year lectionary, by the provision of more than one eucharistic prayer, and above all by implementation of the principle of the "full, active, and conscious participation" of the faithful in the eucharistic celebration.

3. Revision in the Anglican Communion has been characterized by a return to a more classic ritual shape than that of the *Book of Common Prayer*, 1662, by the adoption of modern language in place of the traditional Tudor English, and by small steps toward local inculturation.

4. Revision in the Lutheran communion has been characterized by a recovery of the pattern of Luther's *Formula Missae*, of the centrality of the Eucharist for Sunday worship, and the use of a full eucharistic prayer.

5. Revision in the United Methodist Church and the Presbyterian Church (USA) has been characterized by the adoption of a more traditional liturgical shape for the Eucharist, by the use of the *Revised Common Lectionary*, and by a greater eucharistic prominence in the patterns of worship, resulting in a plethora of eucharistic prayer options.

6. Modern Roman Catholic theology has emphasized Christ as the primordial sacrament and the church as the sacrament of Christ, thus setting the individual sacramental celebrations within this broader context. Ecumenical dialogue on eucharistic presence and sacrifice has often taken this understanding as a fertile starting point for consideration of questions and issues that long have been considered divisive.

Index

Augustine of Hippo, xiv, 73–74, 132–35, 209, 222, 240, 265, 348.

B

Babylonian Captivity of the Church, The, 235–40, 245 n. 25.
Badarak, 141–42.
Baldovin, John, 29 n. 6, 61–62, 70, 74 n. 45, 181 n. 85, 202 n. 11, 204 n. 15, 222 n. 50, 317 n. 56.
Baptism(-al), 26, 29, 116–17, 128, 134, 139, 148, 169, 235–37, 241, 264, 291, 338;
of Jesus, *see* Jesus, baptism of.
Baptism, Eucharist, and Ministry (BEM), 297–98, 331, 339–46 *passim*, 352–53.
Barberini Euchologion, 336, 137–38, 157, 173, 178.
Barcelona Papyrus, 42, 75, 121.
Basil of Caesarea, xiv, 85, 89, 123; Anaphora(s) of St. (BAS), 64, 75–77, 85–93, 95 n. 76, 105, 130, 153, 157, 162, 171, 181, 192, 328.
Baumstark, Anton, 149, 157.
Bell(s), 229, 256;
Sacring, 229.
Bellarmine, Robert, 290.
Benedict VIII, pope, 204.
Benedict XVI, pope, 317
Benedictus, 76, 111–18 *passim*, 120, 159, 197, 248, 250.
Berakah, 6, 297, 312.
Berengarius of Tours, 224–25, 240.
Berger, Teresa, xiii, 186 n. 94, 329 n. 74.
Biel, Gabriel, 244.
Birkat ha-mazon, 6–7, 16.
Black Rubric, 276–77, 281.
Bonaventure, 227.
Book of Common Order, 278, 280, 328.
Book of Common Prayer, 324;
American, 296, 320–22;
English, xiv, 272–78, 322, 328, 357.

Book of Common Worship (Church of South India), 294.
Book of Common Worship (Presbyterian Church USA), 332.
Botte, Bernard, 106 n. 89.
Bouley, Allan, 70 n. 26, 101 n. 80, 109 n. 95.
Bouyer, Louis, 253, 328.
Bradshaw, Paul F., xvi, 2 n. 2, 11 n. 28, 16 nn. 37–38, 19 n. 43, 35 n. 13, 40 n. 19, 41 n. 21, 43 n. 22, 46 n. 26, 46 n. 27, 54 n. 43, 61 nn. 1–2, 64 n. 11, 68 n. 22, 72 n. 33, 75 n. 47, 78 n. 58, 81 n. 68, 93 n. 72, 95 n. 76, 98 n. 78, 101 n. 82, 102 n. 84, 120 n. 25, 140 n. 9, 141 n. 13, 162 n. 53, 180 n. 84, 204 n. 13, 300 n. 17, 337 n. 92, 348 n. 115.
Brightman, F. E., 73 n. 34, 75 n. 49, 84 n. 63, 106 n. 91, 144 n. 24, 145 n. 27, 149 n. 33.
Brock, Sebastian, 50 n. 35, 57 n. 50, 119 n. 23, 179 n. 81, 185 n. 94, 226 n. 57.
Bucer, Martin, 259–60, 270–71.
Byzantine, xiv, 76, 85, 89–93, 137–53 *passim*, 157, 159, 171–91 *passim*, 294, 320, 324, 327–32 *passim*.

C

Cabasilas, Nicholas, 181–83, 187–88, 190–91.
Calvin, John, 237, 257, 264–71, 283, 299, 333.
Canon missae, 76, 104, 107, 109, 132, 182, 201, 205, 246, 249–50, 288, 302, 304, 313–14; *see also* Roman Canon.
Cappadocia(n), 85, 116–17, 123, 125, 141.
Carr, Ephrem, 137 n. 1, 139.
Carthage, 14, 33–34;
Third Council of, *see* Councils and Synods, Carthage.

359

Casel, Odo, 337, 349.

Chalcedon, Council of. *See* Councils and Synods, Chalcedon.

Chaldean Catholic Church, 138, 170, 180.

Chantry(-ies), 215, 220, 221 n. 48.

Charlemagne, emperor, 193–95.

Chemnitz, Martin, 290 n. 114.

Christology, christological, 45, 70, 98, 106, 118, 123, 139–40, 148, 170, 173 n. 66, 179–80, 222, 240, 251, 258, 268–69.

Chrysostom, John, xiv, 62–66 *passim*, 73–74, 78, 94, 97–98, 130, 139, 174, 185, 268;
    Anaphora of St. (CHR), 74, 76, 77, 89, 93–94, 98–101, 153, 157, 171, 181, 250, 327, 356.

Church of England, 277–81 *passim*, 296, 322, 324, 330, 333.

Church of South India, 293–94.

Church of Sweden. *See* Swedish Lutheran.

Church of the East. *See* Ancient (Assyrian) Church of the East.

Clark, Francis, 285.

Clement of Alexandria, 114.

Commentaries, 79–80, 82, 130;
    Medieval Latin, 215–18;
    Eastern Christian, 79–80, 82, 185–89, 192.

Commingling, 172, 178, 210.

Commixture, 78, 172–73, 202, 210, 307.

Common Eucharistic Prayer, 320–22, 332–33.

Common Worship, 296, 322, 330.

Concord, Formula of, 241–42, 255.

Congregation for Divine Worship, 288, 306, 309.

Congregation of Rites, 288, 301 nn. 19 & 21, 302, 309 n. 35, 310.

Congregationalist, 293.

Consecration, xv, 47–50 *passim*, 57, 103–17 *passim*, 122, 124, 170,

171 n. 60, 180–84, 187, 192, 206, 210, 221–28 *passim*, 242–44, 256, 274, 280–90 *passim*, 298, 315–26 *passim*, 341–44 *passim*.

Consilium, 304.

Constantine, emperor, 62, 193.

Constantinople, 36, 68, 71, 74, 89, 93, 97, 138, 143–52 *passim*, 157, 174–75, 182–94 *passim*, 299;
    Council of. *See* Councils and Synods, Constantinople.

Constitution on the Sacred Liturgy, 294–96, 300, 303–4, 309.

Consubstantiation, 240.

Coptic, xiv, 18, 74–77, 82, 85–86, 106, 137, 140, 142, 146–50, 157, 173, 176–77, 179, 182.

Councils and Synods, 233, 343;
    Carthage, 70;
    Chalcedon, 139–40;
    Constantinople, 123;
    Ephesus, 139, 171;
    Florence, 182;
    Lateran IV, 211, 225;
    Milevis, 70;
    Seleucia-Ctesiphon, 139;
    Trent, 235, 282–92 *passim*, 304–5, 343;
    Vatican II, xv, 104, 152, 294, 300–318 *passim*, 336–37.

Cranmer, Thomas, 195, 230, 237, 271–73, 277.

Creed(s), 98, 123, 147–52 *passim*, 182, 198, 201, 204, 246, 251–52, 256, 262, 274, 282, 297, 319, 325, 334–35.

Cuming, Geoffrey J., 82 n. 62, 94 n. 74, 162, 250 n. 32, 271 n. 78, 281 n. 90.

Cyprian of Carthage, 14, 33–35, 39 n. 18, 54 n. 41, 57–59, 130, 136, 218.

Cyril, Anaphora of St., 75, 82, 106 n. 91, 157.

Cyril of Alexandria, 75, 172.

Cyril of Jerusalem, 76–77, 79, 117, 120, 129, 162, 171, 185.

D

Damasus, pope, 109.

De Canone Missae Epicheiresis, 261.

De sacramentis, 77–78, 102–4, 107–9, 133.

De Virginitate, 125–27.

Deir Balizeh Papyrus, 75, 77.

Deutsche Messe, 251, 253–54, 325.

Didache, 11 n. 28, 14–16, 18–21, 36–40 *passim*, 51, 124–25, 299.

Didascalia Apostolorum, 30 n. 7, 35, 50, 54–58 *passim*, 139.

Didymus the Blind, 172.

Dismissal(s), 66, 75, 147–48, 171–77, 191, 197–98, 201–2, 210, 221, 243, 307, 326, 335.

Distribution formula(s), 78, 248, 261–62, 276–78, 280, 324.

Divine Liturgy, 141–42, 144–45, 149, 157, 175, 181–89 *passim*.

Dix, Gregory, 12 n. 29, 20–21, 50 n. 34, 111–15.

Dominican, 141, 175, 226, 288, 341.

Doresse, J., 85 n. 64.

Duffy, Eamon, 212 n. 29, 214, 220 n. 48, 229 n. 67, 230 n. 69.

Duns Scotus, John, 227.

E

East Syria(n), xiv, 35, 39, 76–77, 116, 124, 137–47 *passim*, 150, 152, 166, 170–71, 173, 176–79 *passim*, 185 n. 94, 294.

Easter Vigil, 116, 157, 301, 304, 311.

Ecumenical, xv, 28, 170, 180, 183, 291, 293, 300, 302–4, 308, 311, 319–20, 326–28, 336, 338–39, 342, 346–52 *passim*, 357.

Edward VI, king, 272, 277.

Egeria, 69 n. 25, 74.

Egypt, Egyptian, 4, 8, 42–43, 64, 68, 75, 82, 85–86, 89, 105, 107, 111–12, 114, 120–21, 137 n. 1, 140, 172, 314.

Elevation, 171, 176, 183, 191, 214, 228–29, 242, 248, 250–53, 272.

Elizabeth I, queen, 277, 279–80.

Enarxis, 143, 146, 190.

Engberding, H., 94 n. 74.

Enoch, book of, 120, 159.

Entrance, 72, 142–43, 192, 264, 307, 325, 334;
    Great, 72, 143, 149, 151–52, 172, 186, 191;
    Little, 144–46, 190.

Ephesus, 45;
    Council of. *See* Councils and Synods, Ephesus.

Ephrem the Syrian, St., 119, 139

Epiclesis, *epiklesis*, 47, 77, 58, 80–89 *passim*, 94, 102–15 *passim*, 121–23, 129, 136, 153, 159, 161, 166, 171–72, 181–85 *passim*, 192, 281, 298, 314–30 *passim*, 346.

Episcopal Church, 324;
    Scotland, 281, 324;
    United States, 296, 324, 333, 336, 354.

Erigena, Johannes Scotus, 224.

Eschatology, eschatological, 18, 22, 39, 310, 328, 344, 346–47.

Essenes, 51; *see also* Qumran.

Ethiopia(n), 102, 124, 140, 142, 148–49, 157–59, 161, 174, 179, 185.

Eucharistic Prayer D (Episcopal Church). See *Common Eucharistic Prayer*.

Eucharistic Prayer I, 313; *see also* Roman Canon.

Eucharistic Prayer II (Roman Catholic), 313, 315.

Eucharistic Prayer III (Roman Catholic), 313–14, 346.

Eucharistic Prayer IV (Roman Catholic), 313.

Eugenikos, Mark, 182–83,

Evangelical Lutheran Church in America, 331, 333, 336, 354.

Intercession(s), 43, 56, 74–75, 77, 80,
83, 86, 93, 95, 106, 131, 150, 156,
159–60, 165–66, 197, 201, 204, 206,
209, 215, 275, 294, 297, 305, 307,
309, 314–15, 318, 320–21, 335,
351–53.
Inter-Lutheran Commission on
Worship, 296–97.
Irenaeus of Lyons, 18, 37, 46–49,
53–54, 57.
Isho'yabh III, patriarch, 139.

J

James, Anaphora of St. (JAS), 76–77,
94, 157, 161–66, 294, 327–28.
Jansenist Movement, 289.
Jasper, R. C. D., 162, 281 n. 90.
Jerome, 14 n. 32, 68.
Jerusalem, 7–8, 12–13, 69–79
passim, 94, 117, 120, 129, 138–41,
152, 162–63, 171, 175, 178, 185, 189,
191, 215, 217.
Jesus, 1–28 *passim*, 36, 38, 41–46,
49–57 *passim*, 64, 67, 77, 131, 133,
171, 212, 216–17, 225, 228, 240, 244,
247, 265–66, 281, 340, 345, 355;
and institution of the Eucharist,
1, 8, 19–24;
baptism of, 116, 190;
table companionship with, 1, 8–11.
John, Acts of, 36, 115–18, 120.
John, Gospel of, 8, 9, 15, 21, 44, 54,
134, 175, 177, 202, 210, 229, 266–67.
John the Baptist, St., 92, 100, 190.
John XXIII, pope, 302 n. 23, 303.
John Paul II, pope, 308, 317.
Johnson, Maxwell E., xiv n. 3, xvi,
11 n. 28, 19 n. 43, 41 nn. 20–21,
43 n. 22, 44 n. 24, 54 n. 43, 55 n. 46,
64 n. 11, 68 n. 22, 72 n. 32, 75 nn.
47–48, 78 n. 58, 79 n. 59, 80 n. 60,
85 n. 65, 101 n. 82, 101 n. 83, 105 n.
88, 111 n. 2, 113 n. 9, 115 n. 16,

116 n. 18, 120 n. 25, 121 n. 28,
125 n. 39, 129 nn. 43 & 45, 137 n. 1,
143 n. 19, 149 n. 32, 159 n. 49,
171 n. 60, 183 n. 87, 301 n. 19,
316 n. 52, 329 n. 74, 331 n. 81,
336 n. 91, 338 n. 93, 344 n. 110,
348 n. 115.
Jungmann, Josef A., 64 n. 12, 174 n.
71, 203 n. 12, 205 n. 16, 206 nn.
19–20, 209 n. 21, 212 n. 30, 213 nn.
32 & 34, 219, 221 n. 50, 289 n. 110.
Justin Martyr, 11 n. 28, 26–30, 45–47,
49, 51–53, 57, 70, 72, 124.
Justinian, 138, 145.

K

Keddase, 142.
Kilmartin, Edward, 219 n. 44, 223 n.
52, 224 n. 54, 226 n. 57, 286 n. 101,
290 n. 113, 350–51.
Kiss, 26, 29, 65, 72, 75, 149, 151–52,
201–2, 204, 215, 229, 307.
Knox, John, 278.
Kretschmar, Georg, 112, 114–15.

L

Laetetus Coeli, 182.
Laku Mara, 145.
Last Supper, 1–2, 8, 16–24 *passim*, 33,
45–46, 49, 98, 111, 133, 136, 143,
181, 191, 212, 239, 253.
Lateran IV, Council of. *See* Councils
and Synods, Lateran IV.
Lathrop, Gordon, 28–29, 71, 233 n. 1,
331, 338 n. 94.
Latin Rite, 303; *see also* Roman
Catholic.
Leaven(-ed), 5, 142–43.
Lectionary(-ies), 74, 148, 246, 310–11,
357;
Armenian, 73, 141;
Georgian, 73;
Revised Common, 311, 319, 332, 357.

363

Leo I (the Great), pope, 74, 195, 350.
Leo IX, pope, 224.
Leonine Sacramentary. *See* Sacramentary, Verona (Leonine).
Litany, 143–51 *passim*, 176–77, 202, 256, 272, 278, 294, 318, 325, 334.
Liturgiam Authenticam, 308–9.
Liturgical Year, 157, 195–96, 198, 295, 311, 332.
Louvain Coptic Papyrus, 75, 77.
Luke, Gospel of, 1, 5, 8, 9, 12, 22, 23, 28, 48, 216, 249.
Luther, Martin, 235–61, 266–69, 271, 285, 291
Lutheran, xv, 234, 237–61 *passim*, 268–69, 290, 296–97, 299, 308, 324–46 *passim*, 353–55, 357.
Lutheran Book of Worship (LBW), 296.
Lutheran Church–Missouri Synod (LC–MS), 296–97.
Lutheran World Federation, 331.

M

Macomber, William F., 140, 166.
Macy, Gary, 135 n. 53, 193–94, 211 n. 27, 215 n. 39, 219 n. 44, 223 n. 52, 224 n. 54, 226, n. 57, 227 nn. 58–59, 234, 258–59.
Malabar, 147, 151; *see also* Syro-Malabar.
Malka, 143, 179.
Marburg Colloquy, 259–60.
Mark, Anaphora of St., 43, 75, 77, 82, 106, 112, 157.
Mark, Gospel of, 1, 8–9, 22, 257.
Maronite, xiv, 76, 116, 137, 140, 142–43, 152, 166, 174, 178.
Mary, queen, 277.
Mass, 70, 75, 101, 175, 194, 205, 211–21 *passim*, 228–229, 231, 239, 244–55 *passim*, 260–61, 272–73, 277, 285–92 *passim*, 295–96, 301–10 *passim*, 315, 317–18, 343, 354.

Mateos, Juan, 143 n. 21, 144–45, 148.
Matthew, Gospel of, 1, 22–23, 50–51.
Maximus the Confessor, 149, 187–91 *passim*.
Mazza, Enrico, 18, 78 n. 58, 105 n. 87, 106–7, 109 n. 95, 111, 125, 198 n. 8, 205 n. 18, 206 n. 20, 219 n. 44, 223 n. 52, 224 n. 54, 227 n. 58, 314 n. 46.
McGowan, Andrew B., 3 n. 8, 11 nn. 27–28, 13, 17 n. 39, 18 n. 42, 25 n. 1, 28 n. 3, 32–34.
McGowan, Anne Vorhes, 85 n. 65, 314 n. 47.
Meal(s), 1–3, 56, 245–46, 310, 331, 345, 350, 355;
    Early Christian, 8–36, 50, 56, 58, 174;
    Jewish, 4–8, 212.
Melanchthon, Phillip, 242, 250.
Melismos, 173; *see also* Fraction.
Memorialism, 261.
Merkavah, 119.
Methodist, xv, 282, 292–93, 300, 308, 331, 332–36 *passim*, 357.
Miaphysite, 140, 179; *see also* Monophysite.
Miracles, Eucharistic, 259.
Missal, *Missale*, 220, 324;
    Missale Aboense, 288.
    Missale Benentanum, 288.
    Missale Romanum (Roman Missal), 253, 300–301, 306, 329, 346;
    edition of 1474, 288;
    edition of Pius V (1570–1962), xiv, 234, 237, 282, 287, 303, 310, 313, 317, 328;
    edition of Paul VI (1969), xv, 295, 300, 304–8, 313, 316;
    third edition (2002), 308–9.
Mitchell, Nathan, xiii n. 1, 9, 180, 181 n. 85, 212 nn. 29 & 31, 213 nn. 32 & 33, 222 n. 50, 223 n. 52, 224 n. 54,

228 nn. 61–63, 273 n. 80, 289, 302 n. 23, 303 n. 25, 342 n. 103, 343 n. 105.

Monogenes. See *Hō Monogenēs.*

Monophysite, 148, 179, 269; *see also* Miaphysite.

Moravian, 336.

Moss, Candida, 55–56.

Motu proprio, 300–303, 317.

Mozarabic, xiv, 107, 109, 193, 195–98, 313, 317.

Muhlenberg, Henry Melchior, 325.

Mystagogical Catecheses, 65, 76–80, 82, 117, 122, 129 n. 44, 130–31, 133, 162, 171–72.

Mystagogy, mystagogues, 102, 185, 187, 189, 192.

Mysterium tremendum et fascinans, 118–19.

Mystery Religion, 67, 189, 349.

Mystery Theology (*Mysterienlehre*), 349.

N

Narrative of Institution. *See* Institution Narrative.

Narsai, 139.

Nestorius, 139, 171; Anaphora of, 171.

Nicholas of Andida, 190–91.

North Africa(n), 14, 30, 32–33, 68–70, 74, 101, 196.

Nubian, 178.

O

O Sacrum Convivium, 344.

Oblation, 41, 54–57, 94, 98, 119, 151, 180, 182, 274–75, 280–81, 90.

Offering, 7, 37, 41, 43, 47, 51–59 *passim,* 67, 72, 77, 80–83, 85, 89, 94, 98–113 *passim,* 121, 129–32, 142, 147, 151–52, 154, 165–67, 170, 174, 180–82, 186, 188, 204–7, 213, 218–19, 225, 230, 239, 243–44, 250, 272,

284–86, 290, 309–13 *passim,* 322, 329–30, 333, 335, 340, 349–54, 356.

Old Gelasian Sacramentary. *See* Sacramentary, Gelasian (old).

Opisthambonos, 175.

Ordo, 28, 29, 71–72, 196, 287, 306–7, 310, 331.

Ordo Romanus Primus, 201, 306

Ordo Romanus 11, 203.

Ornaments, 278.

Origen, 35, 50, 58 n. 52, 63 n. 8, 112–14, 120.

Orthodox, 14, 44, 70, 88, 97, 100, 123, 137–41, 156, 165, 173, 179–85 *passim,* 191, 242, 328.

P

Parenti, Stefano, 138 n. 2, 142, 152 n. 36, 157 n. 45, 189.

Paul, St., 8, 10, 11, 12–13, 17–18, 21, 23–24, 50, 147, 222, 258, 262, 269.

Paul VI, pope, xv, 304–18 *passim,* 341.

Paverd, F. van de, 73 n. 34, 74 n. 44, 78 n. 57, 173.

Pax/Pax-brede, 215, 252.

Penance, 174, 211, 235, 237, 270, 291.

Peregrinatio Egeriae, 69 n. 25, 74.

Petri, Laurnetius, 251.

Petri, Olavus, 251.

Philo of Alexandria, 4–5.

Pius X, pope, 300–302, 309; Society of St., 317.

Pius XII, pope, 301–4.

Pneumatological, 268, 333.

Pneumatomachian(s), 89, 123.

Polycarp, 54–56, 124.

Porvoo Common Statement and *Agreement,* 333.

Post-*Sanctus,* 77, 86, 102, 105, 113, 158–60, 199–200, 250, 314.

Preface(s), 70, 77, 82–83, 102, 106, 107, 159, 198–99, 205–6, 217, 248–56

365

Verona Sacramentary. *See*
Sacramentary, Verona (Leonine).
Vigilius, pope, 109.
Visigothic, 193; *see also* Mozarabic.

W

Wainwright, Geoffrey, 137 n. 1, 194 n.
2, 273 n. 80, 293 n. 1, 332, 337 n. 92,
344 n. 109, 346, 354–55.
Wawrykow, Joseph, 134–35, 226 n. 57.
Wesley, Charles, 332.
Wesley, John, 282, 331–32.
West Syria(n), xiv, 41, 76–77, 86, 101,
116, 124, 137–53 *passim*, 157, 161,
166, 172–78 *passim*, 182, 294, 324,
327–32 *passim*, 356.
Westminster Directory of Public
Worship, 280.
White, James F., xiv, 61–62, 71,
194–95, 236, 254, 264 n. 65, 265 nn.

67–68, 269–70, 282 n. 93, 300 n. 17,
311 n. 43, 332, 338 n. 94.
Willis, G.W., 74 n. 41.
Winkler, Gabriele, 85, 111 n. 2, 115–
18, 120, 121 n. 28, 124, 140 n. 9,
141, 142 n. 15, 144 n. 23, 152 n. 36,
153, 157 n. 45, 159 n. 49, 162.
World Council of Churches, 297–98,
331, 339.

Y

Yarnold, Edward, 337 n. 92.
Young, Robin Darling, 54.

Z

Zeon, 172–73, 176, 191.
Zheltov, Michael, 42 n. 22, 75 n. 47,
121, 183.
Zwingli, Ulrich, 237, 257–66, 268–69,
271, 283, 291.